# Workshop manual
# DEFENDER 300Tdi

## This manual covers vehicles from 1996 model year

GW00771264

Publication Part No. LRL 0097 ENG (3rd Edition)
Published by Rover Technical Communication
© 1999 Rover Group Limited

 01 04 05 07 09

 10

 12

 19

 26

 30

 33

 37 41

 47 51 54

 57

 60 64 74

 70

 76

 80 82

84 86 88

This Workshop Manual covers diesel powered Defender models from
1996 up to the end of the 1998 model year.

A separate Workshop Manual Supplement is available covering
the 4.0 V8i petrol engined model and can be used in
conjuction with this manual.

Defender V8i - LRL 0185

Separate Overhaul manuals are available to
compliment this workshop manual:

3.5, 3.9 & 4.2 V8 petrol engines - LRL 0164
4.0 and 4.6 petrol engines - LRL 0004
300 Tdi diesel engine - LRL 0070
R380 Manual gearbox - LRL 0003
LT230T Transfer gearbox - LRL 0081
LT230Q Transfer gearbox - LRL 0082

# 01 - INTRODUCTION

## CONTENTS

Page

**INTRODUCTION**

# Notes

## INTRODUCTION

This workshop manual covers vehicles from 1996 model year onwards. Amendments and additional pages will be issued to ensure that the manual covers latest models. Amendments and additions will be identified by the addition of a dated footer at the bottom of the page.

This Workshop Manual is designed to assist skilled technicians in the efficient repair and maintenance of Land Rover Defender 300Tdi, Td5, and V8i vehicles.

Individuals who undertake their own repairs should have some skill and training, and limit repairs to components which could not affect the safety of the vehicle or its passengers. Any repairs required to safety critical items such as steering, brakes, suspension or supplementary restraint system should be carried out by a Land Rover Dealer. Repairs to such items should NEVER be attempted by untrained individuals.

**WARNINGS, CAUTIONS** and **NOTES** are given throughout this Manual in the following form:

 **WARNING: Procedures which must be followed precisely to avoid the possibility of personal injury.**

 **CAUTION: This calls attention to procedures which must be followed to avoid damage to components.**

 **NOTE: This calls attention to methods which make a job easier or gives helpful information.**

## DIMENSIONS

The dimensions quoted are to design engineering specification. Alternative unit equivalents, shown in brackets following the dimensions, have been converted from the original specification.

## REFERENCES

References to the left or right hand side in the manual are made when viewing the vehicle from the rear. With the engine and gearbox assembly removed, the crankshaft end of the engine is referred to as the front.

To reduce repetition, some operations covered in this Manual do not include reference to testing the vehicle after repair.

It is essential that work is inspected and tested after completion and if necessary a road test of the vehicle is carried out, particularly where safety related items are concerned.

## REPAIRS AND REPLACEMENTS

When replacement parts are required it is essential that Land Rover parts are used.
Attention is particularly drawn to the following points concerning repairs and the fitting of replacement parts and accessories: Safety features embodied in the vehicle may be impaired if other than Land Rover parts are fitted. In certain territories, legislation prohibits the fitting of parts not to the vehicle manufacturer's specification. Torque spanner values given in the Workshop Manual must be strictly adhered to. Locking devices, where specified, must be fitted. If the efficiency of a locking device is impaired during removal it must be replaced with a new one. Certain fasteners must not be re-used. These fasteners are specified in the Workshop Manual.

## POISONOUS SUBSTANCES

Many liquids and other substances used are poisonous and therefore must not be consumed. It is also advisable to keep all substances away from open wounds. These substances among others include anti-freeze, brake fluid, fuel, windscreen washer additives, air conditioning refrigerant, lubricants and various adhesives.

## FUEL HANDLING PRECAUTIONS

The following information provides basic precautions which must be observed if fuel is to be handled safely. It also outlines the other areas of risk which must not be ignored.

This information is issued for basic guidance only, and in any case of doubt, appropriate inquiries should be made of your local Fire Officer or Fire Department.

Fuel vapour is highly flammable and in confined spaces is also very explosive and toxic and when diluted with air becomes a readily ignitable mixture. The vapour is heavier than air and will always fall to the lowest level. It can readily be distributed throughout a workshop by air current, consequently, even a small spillage of fuel is very dangerous.

Always have a fire extinguisher containing **FOAM CO₂ GAS,** or **POWDER** close at hand when handling fuel, or when dismantling fuel systems and in areas where fuel containers are stored.

 **WARNING: It is imperative that the battery is not disconnected during fuel system repairs as arcing at the battery terminal could ignite fuel vapour in the atmosphere. Always disconnect the vehicle battery BEFORE carrying out work on the fuel system. Whenever fuel is being handled, transferred or stored, or when fuel systems are being dismantled all forms of ignition must be extinguished or removed, any lead lamps used must be flame proof and kept clear of spillage. No one should be permitted to repair components associated with fuel without first having had fuel system training.**

### Hot fuel handling precautions

 **WARNING: Before commencing any operation requiring fuel to be drained from the fuel tank, the following procedure must be adhered to:**

1. Allow sufficient time for the fuel to cool, thus avoiding contact with hot fuels.
2. Vent the system by removing the fuel filler cap in a well ventilated area. Refit the filler cap until the commencement of fuel drainage.

### Fuel transfer

 **WARNING: Fuel must not be extracted or drained from any vehicle while it is standing over a pit.**

The transfer of fuel from the vehicle fuel tank must be carried out in a well ventilated area. An approved transfer tank must be used according to the transfer tank manufacturer's instructions and local regulations, including attention to grounding of tanks.

### Fuel tank removal

A **FUEL VAPOUR** warning label must be attached to the fuel tank upon removal from the vehicle.

### Fuel tank repair

Under no circumstances should a repair to any tank be attempted.

## SYNTHETIC RUBBER

Many 'O' ring seals, flexible pipes and other similar items which appear to be natural rubber are made of synthetic materials called Fluoroelastomers. Under normal operating conditions this material is safe, and does not present a health hazard. However, if the material is damaged by fire or excessive heat, it can break down and produce highly corrosive Hydrofluoric acid which can cause serious burns on contact with skin. Should the material be in a burnt or overheated condition handle only with seamless industrial gloves. Decontaminate and dispose of the gloves immediately after use.

If skin contact does occur, remove any contaminated clothing immediately and obtain medical assistance without delay. In the meantime, wash the affected area with copious amounts of cold water or limewater for fifteen to sixty minutes.

## RECOMMENDED SEALANTS

A number of branded products are recommended in this manual for use during maintenance and repair work.
These items include:
**HYLOMAR GASKET AND JOINTING COMPOUND**
and
**HYLOSIL RTV SILICONE COMPOUND.**

They should be available locally from garage equipment suppliers. If there is any problem obtaining supplies, contact the following company for advice and the address of the nearest supplier.

**MARSTON LUBRICANTS LTD.**
**Hylo House,**
**Cale Lane,**
**New Springs,**
**Wigan WN2 1JR**

**Tel 01942 824242**

## USED ENGINE OIL

 **WARNING: Prolonged and repeated contact with engine or motor oil will result in the removal of natural fats from the skin, leading to dryness, irritation and dermatitis. Used engine oil contains potentially harmful contaminants which may cause skin cancer. Adequate means of skin protection and washing facilities should be provided.**

### Handling precautions

1. Avoid prolonged and repeated contact with oils, particularly used engine oils.
2. Wear protective clothing, including impervious gloves where applicable.
3. Do not put oily rags in pockets.
4. Avoid contaminating clothes, particularly underwear, with oil.
5. Overalls must be cleaned regularly. Discard unwashable clothing and oil impregnated footwear.
6. First aid treatment must be obtained immediately for open cuts and wounds.
7. Use barrier creams, before each work period, to help the removal of oil from the skin.
8. Wash with soap and water to ensure all oil is removed (skin cleansers and nail brushes will help). Preparations containing lanolin replace the natural skin oils which have been removed.
9. Do not use gasoline, kerosene, diesel fuel, petrol, thinners or solvents for washing the skin.
10. If skin disorders develop, obtain medical advice.
11. Where practicable, degrease components prior to handling.
12. Where there is a risk of eye contact, eye protection should be worn, for example, goggles or face shields; in addition an eye wash facility should be provided.

### Disposing of used oils

### Environmental protection precaution

It is illegal to pour used oil onto the ground, down sewers or drains, or into waterways.

Dispose of used oil through authorised waste disposal contractors. If in doubt contact your Local Authority for advice on disposal facilities.

## ACCESSORIES AND CONVERSIONS

**DO NOT FIT** unapproved accessories or conversions, as they could affect the safety of the vehicle.
Land Rover will not accept liability for death, personal injury, or damage to property which may occur as a direct result of the fitting of non-approved conversions to the vehicle.

## WHEELS AND TYRES

⚠ **WARNING: DO NOT replace the road wheels with any type other than genuine Land Rover wheels which are designed for multi-purpose on and off road use and have very important relationships with the proper operation of the suspension system and vehicle handling. Replacement tyres must be of the make and sizes recommended for the vehicle, and all tyres must be the same make, ply rating and tread pattern.**

## STEAM CLEANING

To prevent consequential rusting, any steam cleaning within the engine bay **MUST** be followed by careful re-waxing of the metallic components affected. Particular attention must be given to the steering column, engine coolant pipes and hose clips.

## SPECIFICATION

The specification details and instructions set out in this Manual apply only to a range of vehicles and not to any one. For the specification of a particular vehicle purchasers should consult their Dealer.
The Manufacturer reserves the right to vary specifications with or without notice, and at such times and in such manner as it thinks fit. Major as well as minor changes may be involved in accordance with the Manufacturer's policy of constant product improvement.

Whilst every effort is made to ensure the accuracy of the particulars contained in this Manual, neither the Manufacturer or Dealer, by whom this Manual is supplied, shall in any circumstances be held liable for any inaccuracy or the consequences thereof.

## SPECIAL SERVICE TOOLS

The use of approved special service tools is important. They are essential if service operations are to be carried out efficiently, and safely. Where special tools are specified, **only these tools should be used to avoid the possibility of personal injury or damage to the components.** Also, the amount of time which they save can be considerable.

Special tools bulletins will be issued periodically giving details of new tools as they are introduced.

All orders and enquiries from the United Kingdom should be sent direct to Cartool (UK) Ltd. Overseas orders should be placed with the local Cartool distributor, where one exists. Countries where there is no distributor may order direct from:
Cartool (UK) Ltd.
Unit 3,
Sterling Business Park,
Brackmills,
Northampton,
England, NN4 7EX.

The tools recommended in this Workshop Manual are listed in an illustrated catalogue, obtainable from:
Land Rover Publications,
Character Mailing,
Heysham Road,
Bootle,
Merseyside, L70 1JL

## COPYRIGHT

## JACKING

The following instructions must be carried out before raising the vehicle off the ground.

1. Use a solid level ground surface.
2. Apply parking brake.
3. Select 1st gear in main gearbox.
4. Select Low range in transfer gearbox.

⚠ **CAUTION: To avoid damage occurring to the under body components of the vehicle the following jacking procedures must be adhered to.**

**DO NOT POSITION JACKS OR AXLE STANDS UNDER THE FOLLOWING COMPONENTS.**

**Body structure
Bumpers
Fuel lines
Brake lines
Front radius arms
Panhard rod
Steering linkage
Rear Trailing links
Fuel tank
Engine sump
Gearbox bell housing**

**Jack or support vehicle by axles only.**

**Vehicle jack**

The jack provided with the vehicle is only intended to be used in an emergency, for changing a tyre. Do **NOT** use the jack for any other purpose. Refer to Owner's Manual for vehicle jack location points and procedure. Never work under a vehicle supported by the vehicle jack.

**Hydraulic jack**

A hydraulic jack with a minimum 1500 kg, 3,300 lbs load capacity must be used, see J6083.

⚠ **CAUTION: Do not commence work on the underside of the vehicle until suitable axle stands have been positioned under the axle, see J6084.**

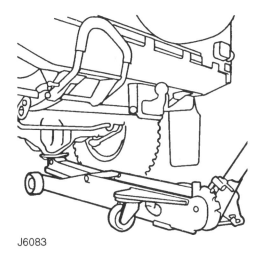

J6083

J6084

**Raise the front of the vehicle**

1. Position cup of hydraulic arm under differential casing.

⚠ **NOTE: The differential casing is not central to the axle. Care should be taken when raising the front road wheels off the ground as the rear axle has less sway stiffness.**

2. Raise front road wheels to enable an axle stand to be installed under left hand axle tube.

3. Position an axle stand under right hand axle tube, carefully lower jack until axle sits securely on both axle stands, remove trolley jack.
4. Before commencing work on underside of vehicle re-check security of vehicle on stands.
5. Reverse procedure when removing vehicle from stands.

**Raise rear of vehicle**

1. Position cup of hydraulic arm under differential casing.
2. Raise vehicle to enable axle stands to be installed under left and right hand axle tubes.
3. Lower jack until axle sits securely on axle stands, remove trolley jack.
4. Before commencing work on underside of vehicle re-check security of vehicle on stands.
5. Reverse procedure when removing vehicle from stands.

## HYDRAULIC VEHICLE RAMP (FOUR POST)

Use only a 'drive on' type ramp which supports vehicle on its road wheels. If a 'wheel-free' condition is required, use a 'drive on' ramp incorporating a 'wheel-free' system providing support beneath axle casings. Alternatively, place vehicle on a firm, flat floor and support on axle stands.

## TWO POST VEHICLE RAMPS

**The manufacturer of LAND ROVER VEHICLES DOES NOT recommend using 'Two Post' ramps that employ four adjustable support arms. These are NOT considered safe for Land Rover vehicles. If vehicle is installed on a Two Post ramp responsibility for safety of vehicle and personnel performing service operations is in the hands of the Service Provider.**

## DYNAMOMETER TESTING

The front and rear axles cannot be driven independently.

 **WARNING: DO NOT attempt to drive individual wheels with vehicle supported on floor jacks or stands.**

**Four wheel dynamometers**

Provided that front and rear dynamometer rollers are rotating at identical speeds and that normal workshop safety standards are applied, there is no speed restriction during testing except any that may apply to the tyres.

**Two wheel dynamometers**

**IMPORTANT: Use a four wheel dynamometer for brake testing if possible.**

If brake testing on a single axle rig is necessary it must be carried out with propeller shaft to rear axle removed, AND neutral selected in BOTH main gearbox and transfer gearbox. When checking brakes, run engine at idle speed to maintain servo vacuum. If checking engine performance, the transfer box must be in high range and propeller shaft to stationary axle must be removed.

## TOWING

 CAUTION: The vehicle has permanent four-wheel drive. The following towing instructions must be adhered to:

**Towing the vehicle on all four wheels with driver operating steering and brakes.**

1. Turn ignition key to position '1' to release steering lock.
2. Select neutral in main gearbox and transfer gearbox.

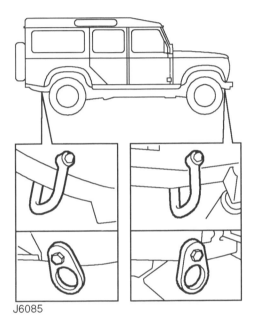

J6085

3. Secure tow rope, chain or cable to front towing eyes (alternative types shown).
4. Release the parking brake.

 CAUTION: The brake servo and power assisted steering system will not be functional without the engine running. Greater pedal pressure will be required to apply the brakes, the steering system will require greater effort to turn the front road wheels. The vehicle tow connection should be used only in normal road conditions, 'snatch' recovery should be avoided.

**Rear suspended tow by breakdown vehicle**

1. If the front axle is to be trailed turn ignition key to position '1' to release steering lock.
2. Select neutral in main gearbox and transfer box.

 CAUTION: The steering wheel and/or linkage must be secured in a straight ahead position. DO NOT use the steering lock mechanism for this purpose.

## TRANSPORTING THE VEHICLE BY TRAILER

Lashing/towing eyes are provided on front and rear of the chassis side members, see J6085, to facilitate the securing of the vehicle to a trailer or other means of transportation.

 CAUTION: Underbody components must not be used as lashing points.

Install vehicle on trailer and apply park brake. Select neutral in main gearbox.

## JUMP STARTING

 **WARNING: Hydrogen and oxygen gases are produced during normal battery operation. This gas mixture can explode if flames, sparks or lighted tobacco are brought near battery. When charging or using a battery in an enclosed space, always provide ventilation and shield your eyes.**

**Keep out of reach of children. Batteries contain sulphuric acid. Avoid contact with skin, eyes, or clothing. Also, shield eyes when working near battery to protect against possible splashing of acid solution. In case of acid contact with skin, eyes, or clothing, flush immediately with water for a minimum of fifteen minutes. If acid is swallowed, drink large quantities of milk or water, followed by milk of magnesia, a beaten egg, or vegetable oil.**

**SEEK MEDICAL AID IMMEDIATELY.**

**To Jump Start - Negative Ground Battery**

 **WARNING: To avoid any possibility of injury use particular care when connecting a booster battery to a discharged battery.**

1. Position vehicles so that jump leads will reach, ensuring that vehicles **DO NOT TOUCH,** alternatively a fully charged slave battery may be positioned on floor adjacent to vehicle.
2. Ensuring that ignition and all electrical accessories are switched off, that parking brake is applied and neutral is selected, connect the jump leads as follows;

**A.** Connect one end of first jumper cable to positive (+) terminal of booster battery.
**B.** Connect other end of first jumper cable to positive (+) terminal of discharged battery.
**C.** Connect one end of second jumper cable to negative terminal of booster battery.
**D.** Connect other end of second jumper cable to a good earth point on the disabled vehicle (eg. engine front lifting eye, as shown in J6086), **NOT TO NEGATIVE TERMINAL OF DISCHARGED BATTERY.** Keep jumper lead away from moving parts, pulleys, drive belts and fan blade assembly.

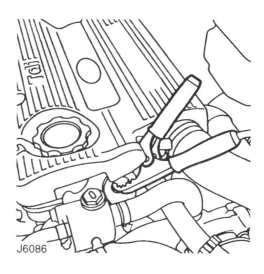

J6086

 **WARNING: Making final cable connection could cause an electrical arc which if made near battery could cause an explosion.**

3. If booster battery is installed in another vehicle, start engine and allow to idle.
4. Start engine of vehicle with discharged battery, following starting procedure in Owners' Manual.

 **CAUTION: If vehicle fails to start within a maximum time of 12 seconds, switch ignition off and investigate cause. Failing to follow this instruction could result in irrepairable damage to catalyst, if fitted.**

5. Remove negative (-) jumper cable from the engine and then terminal of booster battery.
6. Remove positive (+) jumper cable from positive terminals of booster battery and discharged battery.

## ABBREVIATIONS AND SYMBOLS USED IN THIS MANUAL

| | |
|---|---|
| Across flats (bolt size) | AF |
| After bottom dead centre | ABDC |
| After top dead centre | ATDC |
| Alternating current | a.c. |
| Ampere | amp |
| Ampere hour | amp hr |
| Before bottom dead centre | BBDC |
| Before top dead centre | BTDC |
| Bottom dead centre | BDC |
| Brake horse power | bhp |
| British Standards | BS |
| Carbon monoxide | CO |
| Centimetre | cm |
| Centigrade (Celsius) | C |
| Cubic centimetre | $cm^3$ |
| Cubic inch | $in^3$ |
| Degree (angle) | deg or ° |
| Degree (temperature) | deg or ° |
| Diameter | dia. |
| Direct current | d.c. |
| Electronic Control Unit | ECU |
| Fahrenheit | F |
| Feet | ft |
| Feet per minute | ft/min |
| Fifth | 5th |
| First | 1st |
| Fluid ounce | fl oz |
| Foot pounds (torque) | lbf ft |
| Fourth | 4th |
| Gramme (force) | gf |
| Gramme (mass) | g |
| Gallons | gal |
| High tension (electrical) | H.T. |
| Internal diameter | I.D. |
| Inches of mercury | in. Hg |
| Inches | in |
| Kilogramme (force) | kgf |
| Kilogramme (mass.) | kg |
| Kilogramme centimetre (torque) | kgf.cm |
| Kilogramme per square millimetre | $kgf/mm^2$ |
| Kilogramme per square centimetre | $kgf/cm^2$ |
| Kilogramme metres (torque) | kgf.m |
| Kilometres | km |
| Kilometres per hour | km/h |
| Kilovolts | kV |
| Left-hand | LH |
| Left-hand steering | LHStg |
| Left-hand thread | LHThd |
| Litres | litre |

| | |
|---|---|
| Low tension | l.t. |
| Maximum | max. |
| Metre | m |
| Millilitre | ml |
| Millimetre | mm |
| Miles per gallon | mpg |
| Miles per hour | mph |
| Minute (angle) | ' |
| Minus (of tolerance) | - |
| Negative (electrical) | - |
| Newton metres (torque) | Nm |
| Number | No. |
| Ohms | ohm |
| Ounces (force) | ozf |
| Ounces (mass) | oz |
| Ounce inch (torque) | ozf.in. |
| Outside diameter | O.D. |
| Part number | Part No. |
| Percentage | % |
| Pints | pt |
| Plus (tolerance) | + |
| Positive (electrical) | + |
| Pound (force) | lbf |
| Pounds inch (torque) | in.lbf |
| Pound (mass) | lb |
| Pounds per square inch | P.S.I. |
| Ratio | : |
| Reference | ref. |
| Revolution per minute | rev/min |
| Right-hand | RH |
| Second (angle) | " |
| Second (numerical order) | 2nd |
| Specific gravity | sp.gr. |
| Square centimetres | $cm^2$ |
| Square inches | $in^2$ |
| Standard wire gauge | s.w.g. |
| Synchroniser/Synchromesh | synchro. |
| Third | 3rd |
| Top dead centre | TDC |
| United Kingdom | UK |
| Vehicle Identification Number | VIN |
| Volts | V |
| Watts | W |

### SCREW THREADS

| | |
|---|---|
| British Standard Pipe | BSP |
| Unified Coarse | UNC |
| Unified Fine | UNF |

## CROSS REFERENCE OF EMISSION SYSTEM TERMINOLOGY

| NEW TERM | (ACRONYM) | OLD TERM | (ACRONYM) |
|---|---|---|---|
| Accelerator pedal | (AP) | Throttle pedal | (-) |
| Air cleaner | (ACL) | Air cleaner | (-) |
| Air conditioning | (AC) | Air conditioning | (AC) |
| Battery positive voltage | (B+) | Battery plus, bat +, bat feed | (B+) |
| Closed loop | (CL) | Closed loop | (-) |
| Closed throttle position | (CTP) | Closed throttle, idle position | (-) |
| Canister purge valve | (CANPV) | Charcoal canister purge valve | (-) |
| Data link connector | (DLC) | Serial link | (-) |
| Diagnostic trouble code | (DTC) | Fault code | (-) |
| Distributor ignition | (DI) | Electronic ignition | (-) |
| Engine control module | (ECM) | Electronic control unit | (ECU) |
| Engine coolant level | (ECL) | Coolant level | (-) |
| Engine coolant temperature | (ECT) | Coolant temperature | (temp) |
| Engine coolant temperature sensor | (ECTS) | Coolant temperature thermistor | (-) |
| Engine speed | (RPM) | Engine speed | (rev/min) |
| Evaporative emission system | (EVAP) | Evaporative loss system | (ELC) |
| Engine fuel temperature sensor | (EFTS) | Fuel temperature thermistor | (-) |
| 4th gear, 3rd gear etc. | (4GR, 3GR) | Fourth gear, 3rd gear | (-) |
| Fuel pump | (FP) | Fuel pump | (-) |
| Fan control module | (FCM) | Condenser fan timer | (-) |
| Generator | (GEN) | Alternator | (-) |
| Ground | (GND) | Ground, earth | (B-) |
| Heated oxygen sensor | (H02S) | Lambda (02) sensor | (-) |
| Idle air control | (IAC) | Idle speed control | (ISC) |
| Idle air control valve | (IACV) | Stepper motor | (-) |
| Ignition control module | (ICM) | Ignition module | (-) |
| Intake air temperature | (IAT) | Intake temperature/ambient temperature | (-) |
| Manifold vacuum zone | (MVZ) | Manifold depression, vacuum | (-) |
| Mass air flow sensor | (MAFS) | Air flow meter | (-) |
| Open loop | (OL) | Fault code display unit | (-) |
| Relay module | (RM) | Open loop | (-) |
| Solid state relay module | (SSRM) | Relay | (-) |
| Three way catalytic converter | (TWC) | Control unit | (-) |
| Throttle body | (TB) | Catalyst, catalytic converter | (CAT) |
| Throttle position sensor | (TPS) | Throttle housing | (-) |
| Transmission range | (TR) | Transmission gear | (-) |
| Wide open throttle | (WOT) | Full throttle, wide open throttle | (WOT) |

## VEHICLE IDENTIFICATION NUMBER (VIN)

The Vehicle Identification Number and the recommended maximum vehicle weights are stamped on a plate riveted to the brake pedal box in the engine compartment. The VIN is also stamped on a plate visible through the LH side of the windscreen, see J6088.

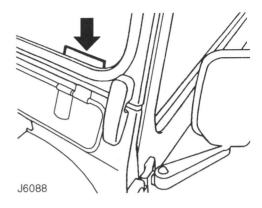

J6088

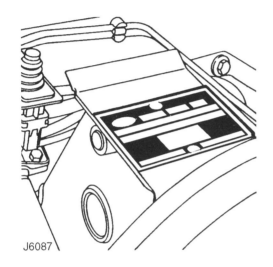

J6087

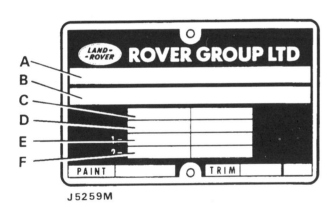

J5259M

**A.** Type approval
**B.** Identification
**C.** Maximum permitted laden weight for vehicle
**D.** Maximum vehicle and trailer weight
**E.** Maximum road weight-front axle
**F.** Maximum road weight-rear axle

The number is also stamped on the RH side of the chassis to the rear of the front lashing eye, see J6089.

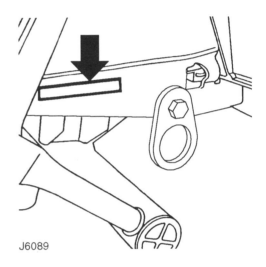

J6089

The Vehicle Identification Number identifies the manufacturer, model range, wheel base, body type, engine, steering, transmission, model year and place of manufacture. The following example shows the coding process.

**SAL LD H M F 7 T A**

**SAL** = World manufacturer identifier
**LD** = Land Rover Defender
**H** = 110 inch, **V**= 90inch, **K**= 130 inch
**M** = 4 door Station Wagon, **A**= 90 Soft Top, Hard Top, Pick-up, **B**= 2 door Station Wagon, **E**= 2 door 130 Crew cab, **F**= 4 door 130 Crew cab, **H**= 130 High Capacity Pick-up
**F**= 2.5L (300Tdi)
**7**= RH drive, 5 speed manaul, **8**= LH drive, 5 speed manual
**T**= 1996 MY, volume build, **N**= 1996 MY, non-volume build
**A**= Solihull build, **F**= CKD, assembled locally from kit

## LOCATION OF IDENTIFICATION NUMBERS

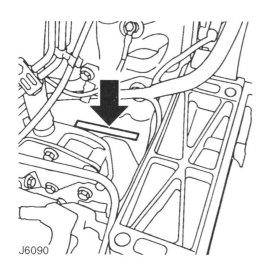

J6090

**Engine serial number - 300Tdi Engine**

The 300Tdi engine number is stamped on the cylinder block on the RH side of the engine above the camshaft front cover plate.

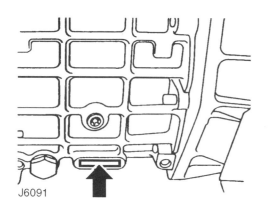

J6091

**Main gearbox R380 serial number**

Stamped on a cast pad on the bottom RH side of the gearbox.

**Transfer gearbox LT230 serial number**

The serial number is stamped on the LH side of the gearbox casing below the mainshaft rear bearing housing adjacent to the bottom cover, see J6092.

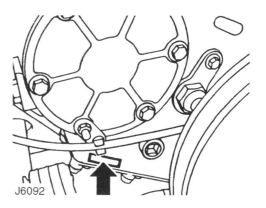

J6092

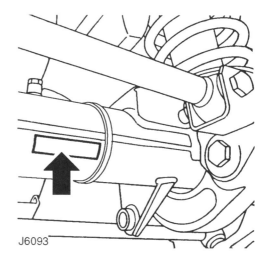

J6093

**Front axle serial number**

Stamped on the front of LH axle tube, inboard of radius arm mounting bracket.

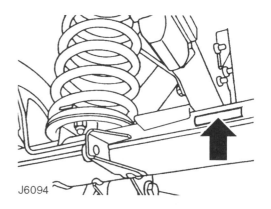

J6094

**Rear axle serial number**

Stamped on the rear of LH axle tube, inboard of spring mounting.

## FAULT DIAGNOSTIC EQUIPMENT

### TESTBOOK

For Defender models fitted with the vehicle Anti-theft Immobilisation and Alarm System, diagnostic equipment, named TestBook, is available to assist in the diagnostic and fault finding abilities of the Dealer workshop. A diagnostic connector, located under the front centre seat, or cubby box, as shown below, is provided to facilitate the procedures.

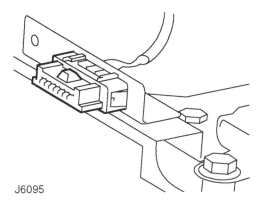

J6095

If an exhaust gas recirculation (EGR) system is fitted, this too can be checked using TestBook. A diagnostic connector, also located under the front centre seat or cubby box, is provided.

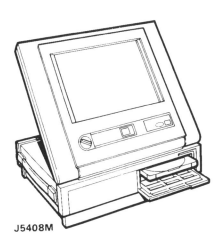

J5408M

Features of Testbook include :-

Fully upgradable support for the technician.
Structured diagnostics to accommodate all skill levels.
Touch screen operation.
Direct print out of screen information and test results.

## READING THIS MANUAL

This manual is divided into sections shown on the contents page, alongside a range of icons, familiar to service technicians.

Relevant information is contained within each of these sections. These are further divided into the following sub-sections which appear at the foot of each page :-

**Description and operation.**
**Fault diagnosis.**
**Adjustment.**
**Repair.**
**Overhaul.**
**Specifications, Torque.**

To avoid repeating information through the sections, where part of the repair operation impacts on another section, a cross reference is given to direct the reader to where the information is sited.

For example:
The maintenance section states the need to renew drive belt. A cross reference sites this information in:
Section 12 Engine
- Sub-section: Repairs
- Heading: Drive belt renew.

# Notes

# 04 - GENERAL SPECIFICATION DATA

## CONTENTS

Page

**INFORMATION**

# Notes

## 300Tdi ENGINE

Type .................................................................... Direct injection, turbocharged, intercooled
Number of cylinders .......................................... 4
Bore ................................................................... 90,47 mm
Stroke ................................................................ 97,00 mm
Capacity ............................................................ 2495 cc
Compression ratio ............................................ 19.5:1 ± 0.5:1
Valve operation ................................................ O.H.V. pushrod operated

### Crankshaft

Main bearing journal diameter ......................... 63,475 - 63,487 mm
Regrind dimensions ......................................... 63,233 - 63,246 mm
Crankpin journal diameter ............................... 58,725 - 58,744 mm
Regrind dimensions ......................................... 58,471 - 58,490 mm
Crankshaft end thrust ...................................... Taken on thrust washers at centre main bearing
Crankshaft end float ........................................ 0,05 - 0,15 mm

### Main bearings

Number and type ............................................. 5 halved shells with oil grooves
Diametrical clearance ...................................... 0,0792 - 0,0307 mm

### Connecting rods

Length between centres .................................... 175,38 - 175,43 mm
Diametrical clearance (big-end bearings) ........ 0,025 - 0,075 mm
End float on crankpin ....................................... 0,15 - 0,356 mm

### Pistons

Type .................................................................... Aluminium alloy, combustion chamber in crown.
                                                                               Graphite coating on sidewalls.
Skirt diametrical clearance (at r/angle to gudgeon pin) .... 0,025 - 0,05 mm
Maximum height above combustion face ......................... 0,8 mm

### Gudgeon pins

Type ................................................................... Fully floating
Fit in piston ...................................................... Hand push fit
Diameter ........................................................... 30,156 - 30,163 mm
Clearance in connecting rod ............................ 0,003 - 0,016 mm

### Piston rings

Type:
    - Top ................................................................ Barrel edge, chrome plated
    - Second .......................................................... Taper faced
    - Oil control ..................................................... Expander and rails
Gap in bore:
    - Top ................................................................ 0,40 - 0,60 mm
    - Second .......................................................... 0,30 - 0,50 mm
    - Oil control ..................................................... 0,30 - 0,60 mm
Clearance in piston grooves:
    - Second .......................................................... 0,050 - 0,085 mm
    - Oil control ..................................................... 0,050 - 0,085 mm

## Camshaft

Drive ................................................................................ 30 mm wide dry toothed belt
Location .......................................................................... Right hand side (thrust side)
End float ......................................................................... 0,1 - 0,2 mm
Number of bearings ....................................................... 4
Material .......................................................................... Steel shell, white metal lined

## Valves

Tappet clearance:
    - Inlet and exhaust ................................................. 0,20 mm
Seat angle:
    - Inlet .................................................................... 30°
    - Exhaust ............................................................... 45°
Head diameter:
    - Inlet .................................................................... 38,75 - 39,05 mm
    - Exhaust ............................................................... 36,35 - 36,65 mm
Stem diameter:
    - Inlet .................................................................... 7,960 - 7,975 mm
    - Exhaust ............................................................... 7,940 - 7,960 mm
Valve lift:
    - Inlet .................................................................... 9,67 mm
    - Exhaust ............................................................... 9,97 mm
Cam lift:
    - Inlet .................................................................... 6,81 mm
    - Exhaust ............................................................... 7,06 mm
Valve head stand down:
    - Inlet .................................................................... 0,81 - 1,09 mm
    - Exhaust ............................................................... 0,86 - 1,14 mm

## Valve springs

Type ................................................................................ Single coil
Length, free .................................................................... 46,28 mm
Length, under 21 kg load ............................................... 40,30 mm

## Lubrication

System ............................................................................ Wet sump, pressure fed
Pressure, engine warm at normal operating speeds ........ 1,76 - 3,87Kgf/cm$^2$ (25 - 55 lbf/in$^2$)
Oil pump:
    - Type .................................................................... G-rotor integral with front cover.
    - Drive .................................................................... off crankshaft nose
Oil pressure relief valve ................................................. Non-adjustable
Relief valve spring:
- Full length .................................................................... 51,6mm
- Compressed length at 7.71Kg load .............................. 31mm
Oil filter .......................................................................... Screw-on disposable canister
Engine oil cooler ............................................................ Combined with coolant radiator and intercooler

## FUEL SYSTEM

Fuel lift pump type ............................................................. Mechanical with hand primer
Fuel lift pump pressure ..................................................... 42 - 55 Kgf/cm² (3 - 4 lbf/in²) at 1800 rpm
Fuel filter ....................................................................... Paper element in disposable canister
Air cleaner .................................................................... Paper element type

## COOLING SYSTEM

System type .................................................................. Pressurised, spill return, thermostatically controlled
water and anti freeze mixture. Pump assisted thermo
syphon. Coolant radiator combined with oil cooler and
turbo intercooler.
Cooling fan ................................................................... 11 blade axial flow 433 mm diameter, 1.29:1 drive
ratio, with viscous coupling.
Pump type ..................................................................... Centrifugal, impellor, belt driven
Thermostat opening ...................................................... 88° C
Expansion tank cap pressure .......................................... 1,06 Kgf/cm² (15 lbf/in²) (system pressure)

## CLUTCH

Type .............................................................................. Valeo diaphragm spring
Centre plate diameter..................................................... 235 mm
Facing material.............................................................. Verto F202 grooved
Release bearing ............................................................. Ball journal

## TRANSMISSION

### Main gearbox

Type R380 ..................................................................... Single helical constant mesh
Speeds .......................................................................... 5 forward, 1 reverse, all synchromesh

### Transfer box

Type LT230 .................................................................... Two speed reduction on main gearbox output. Front
and rear drive permanently engaged via a lockable
differential

### Rear axle

Type .............................................................................. Spiral bevel, fully floating shafts
Ratio .............................................................................. 3.54:1

## Front axle

Type ........................................................................ Spiral bevel, enclosed constant velocity joints, fully floating shafts, 32° angularity of universal joint on full lock

Ratio ....................................................................... 3.54:1

## Propeller shafts

Type, front and rear ........................................... Tubular 51 mm dia.

Universal joints .................................................. Open type Hookes O3EHD

## STEERING

### Power steering box

Make/type ........................................................ Adwest Varamatic - worm and roller box

Ratio ................................................................. Variable: straight ahead 19.3:1 on lock 14.3:1

Steering wheel turns, lock-to-lock ..................... 3.375

### Steering pump

Make/type ........................................................ Hobourn-Eaton series 500

### Steering geometry

Steering wheel diameter .................................. 412 mm (16.22 in)

Toe-out measurement ...................................... 0 to 2 mm toe out

Toe-out included angle .................................... 0° to 0° 20'

Camber angle .................................................. 0° *

Castor angle .................................................... 3° *

Swivel pin inclination static .............................. 7° *

* Check with vehicle on level ground, in unladen condition and five gallons of fuel. Rock the front of the vehicle up and down to allow it to take up a normal static position.

### Turning circle between kerbs

**90 models:**

265/75 x 16 tyres ............................................. 12,65 m (41.5 ft)

All other tyres .................................................. 11,70 m (38.4 ft)

**110 models:**

750 x 16 tyres ................................................. 13,41 m (44 ft)

**130 models:**

750 x 16 tyres ................................................. 15,24 m (50 ft)

## SUSPENSION

| | |
|---|---|
| Type .............................................................................. | Coil springs controlled by telescopic dampers front and rear. |
| Front .............................................................................. | Transverse location of axle by Panhard rod, and fore and aft location by two radius arms. Anti-roll bar fitted as standard on 90 models with 265/75 tyres and 130 models. |
| Rear .............................................................................. | Fore and aft movement inhibited by two tubular trailing links. Lateral location of axle by a centrally positioned 'A' frame, upperlink assembly, bolted at the apex to a ball joint mounting. Anti-roll bar fitted as standard on 90 models with 265/75 tyres, 110 models with self levelling unit, and 130 models. |

## ROAD SPRING DATA

| | Part No. | Colour Code |
|---|---|---|
| **90 (2400 Kg)** | | |
| Front - Driver's side | NRC 9446 | Blue/green |
| Front - Passenger side | NRC 9447 | Blue/yellow |
| Rear - Driver's side | NRC 9448 | Blue/red |
| Rear - Passenger side | NRC 9449 | Yellow/white |
| | | |
| **90 (2550 Kg)** | | |
| Front - Driver's side | NRC 9446 | Blue/green |
| Front - passenger side | NRC 9447 | Blue/yellow |
| Rear - Driver's side | NRC 9462 | Green/yellow/red |
| Rear - Passenger side | NRC 9463 | Green/yellow/white |
| | | |
| **110 (3050 Kg)** | | |
| Front - both sides | NRC 8045 | Yellow/yellow |
| Rear - both sides | NRC 6904 | Red/green |
| | | |
| **110 Levelled (2950 Kg)** | | |
| Front - both sides | NRC 8045 | Yellow/yellow |
| Rear - both sides | NRC 7000 | Green/white |
| | | |
| **110 (3400 Kg)** | | |
| Front - both sides | NRC 8045 | Yellow/yellow |
| Rear - both sides | NRC 6904 | Red/green |
| Rear helper springs - both sides | RRC 3266 | No colour code |
| | | |
| **110 (3600 Kg)** | | |
| Front - Driver's side | NRC 9448 | Blue/red |
| Front - passenger side | NRC 9449 | Yellow/white |
| Rear - both sides | NRC 6904 | Red/green |
| Rear helper springs - both sides | RRC 3226 | No colour code |
| | | |
| **130 (3500 Kg)** | | |
| Front - driver's side | NRC 9448 | Blue/red |
| Front - passenger side | NRC 9449 | Yellow/white |
| Rear - driver's side | NRC 6389 | Red/red |
| Rear - passenger side | NRC 6904 | Red/green |
| Front/rear helper springs - both sides | RRC 3266 | No colour code |

## SHOCK ABSORBERS

| | |
|---|---|
| Type | Telescopic, double-acting non-adjustable |
| Bore diameter | 35.47mm |

## BRAKES

### Front service brake

| | |
|---|---|
| Caliper | AP Lockheed, four opposed pistons |
| Operation | Hydraulic, self adjusting |
| Disc | 90 - Solid, outboard, 110/130 - Ventilated, outboard |
| Disc diameter | 298 mm (11.73 in.) |
| Disc thickness | 90 - 14,1 mm (0.56in.), 110/130 - 24mm (0.95 in.) |
| Wear limit | 1 mm (0.04in.) per side of disc |
| Disc run-out maximum | 0,15mm (0.006 in.) |
| Pad area | 58 cm$^2$ (9.0 in$^2$.) |
| Total swept area | 801,3 cm$^2$ (124.2 in$^2$.) |
| Pad material | Ferodo 3440 non asbestos |
| Pad minimum thickness | 3 mm (0.12in.) |

### Rear service brake

| | |
|---|---|
| Caliper | AP Lockheed opposed piston |
| Operation | Hydraulic, self adjusting |
| Disc | Solid, outboard |
| Disc diameter | 90 - 290 mm (11.42 in.), 110/130 - 298 mm (11.73) |
| Disc thickness | 90 - 12,5 mm (0.49 in.), 110/130 - 14,1 mm (0.56 in.) |
| Wear limit | 90 - 0,38 mm (0.015 in.), 110/130 - 1,0 mm (0.04 in.) per side of disc |
| Disc run-out maximum | 0,15 mm (0.006 in.) |
| Pad area | 90 - 30,5 cm$^2$ (4.37 in$^2$.), 110/130 - 36,2 cm$^2$ (5.61 in$^2$.) |
| Total swept area | 90 - 694 cm$^2$ (106.98 in$^2$.) |
| Pad material | Ferodo 3440 non asbestos |
| Pad minimum thickness | 3 mm (0.12 in.) |

### Parking brake

| | |
|---|---|
| Type | Mechanical, cable operated drum brake on the rear of the transfer gearbox output shaft |
| Drum internal diameter | 254 mm (10.0 in.) |
| Width | 70 mm (2.75 in.) |
| Pad material | Ferodo 3611 non asbestos |

### Servo/master cylinder

| | |
|---|---|
| Manufacturer | Lucas |
| Servo type | LSC 80 |
| Master cylinder type | 25,4 mm (1.0 in.) diameter, tandem |
| Pressure reducing valve, failure conscious | Cut-in pressure, 90 - 24 bar (360 lbf/in$^2$) ratio 4.0:1, 110 - 43 bar (645 lbf/in$^2$) ratio 2.9:1* |

 **NOTE: * Pressure reducing valves are not fitted to all 110 specifications.**

## AIR CONDITIONING

System ............................................................... CFC free expansion valve system
Compressor ....................................................... Sanden TRS105N
Refrigerant ....................................................... R134a CFC free
Charge quantity ............................................... 1.1 Kg

## WIPER MOTORS

### Tailgate wiper motor

Make/type ......................................................... IMOS (non-serviceable)
Running current, wet screen at 20°C ambient ................. 1.0 to 2.8 amps
Wiper speed, wet screen at 20°C ambient ....................... 37 to 43 cycles per minute

### Windscreen wiper motor

Make/type ......................................................... Lucas 14W uprated two speed
Armature end float .............................................. 0,1 to 0,2 mm
Brush length, minimum ........................................ 4,8 mm
Brush spring tension .......................................... 140 to 200 g
Resistance of armature winding
at 16°C (69°F) measured between adjacent
commutatator segments ....................................... 0.23 to 0.35 ohms
Light running, rack disconnected: current at 13.5 V ......... 2.0 amps
Wiper speed, wet screen, 60 seconds from cold ............. Low speed - 45 ± 3 rev/min, High speed - 65 ± 5 rev/min

## ELECTRICAL

System ............................................................. 12 volt, negative ground

### Battery

Make/type - standard ........................................ Land Rover Parts and Equipment/Lucas maintenance free 9-plate 072
Make/type - heavy duty ..................................... Land Rover Parts and Equipment/Lucas maintenance free 14-plate 663

### Generator

Manufacturer .................................................... Magnetti Marelli
Type ................................................................. A127 - 100amp
Polarity ........................................................... Negative ground
Brush length:
    New .............................................................. 17 mm
    Worn, minimum free protrusion from moulding ........ 5 mm
Brush spring pressure flush with moulding ..................... 1.3N to 2.7N
Regulator voltage .............................................. 13.6 to 14.4 volts
Nominal output
    Generator speed ............................................. 6000 rev/min
    Control voltage ............................................. 14 volt
    Amp ............................................................. 65 amp

**Fuses**

Type ........................................................................ Autofuse (blade type) blow ratings to suit individual circuits

**Horns**

Make/type ................................................................ Mixo TR99

**Starter motor**

Make and type ......................................................... Bosch 12v

## BULBS

| REPLACEMENT BULBS | TYPE | | |
|---|---|---|---|
| Headlamps | 12V | 60/55W | Halogen |
| Front side lamps | 12V | 5W | bayonet |
| Side repeater lamps | 12V | 5W | capless |
| Tail lamps | 12V | 5/21W | bayonet |
| Direction indicator lamps | 12V | 21W | bayonet |
| Number plate lamp | 12V | 5W | capless |
| Reverse lamp | 12V | 21W | bayonet |
| Rear fog guard lamp | 12V | 21W | bayonet |
| Interior roof lamps | 12V | 10W | festoon |
| Instrument illumination | 12V | 1.2W | capless |
| Warning light panel | 12V | 1.2W | bulb/holder unit |
| Hazard warning switch | 12V | 1.2W | capless |

 **CAUTION: The fitting of new bulbs with wattages in excess of those specified will result in damage to vehicle wiring and switches.**

## VEHICLE WEIGHTS AND PAYLOAD

When loading a vehicle to its maximum (Gross Vehicle Weight), consideration must be taken of the unladen vehicle weight and the distribution of the payload to ensure that axle loadings do not exceed the permitted maximum values.

It is the customer's responsibility to limit the vehicle's payload in an appropriate manner such that neither maximum axle loads nor Gross Vehicle Weight are exceeded.

**Maximum EEC kerb weight and distribution - all optional equipment**

### VEHICLE AXLE WEIGHTS

| **90 models** | **Standard** | **High load** |
|---|---|---|
| Front axle | 1200 Kg (2645 lb) | 1200 Kg (2645 lb) |
| Rear axle | 1380 kg (3042 lb) | 1500 Kg (3307 lb) |
| Gross vehicle weight | 2400 Kg (5291 lb) | 2550 Kg (5622 lb) |

| **110 models** | **Levelled** | **Unlevelled** |
|---|---|---|
| Front axle | 1200 Kg (2645 lb) | 1200 Kg (2645 lb) |
| Rear axle | 1750 Kg (3858 lb) | 1850 Kg (4078 lb) |
| Gross vehicle weight | 2950 Kg (6503 lb) | 3050 Kg (6724 lb) |

| **130 models** | |
|---|---|
| Front axle | 1580 Kg (3483 lb) |
| Rear axle | 2200 Kg (4850 lb) |
| Gross vehicle weight | 3500 Kg (7716 lb) |

 **NOTE: Axle weights are not accumulative. The individual maximum axle weights and gross vehicle weight must not be exceeded.**

### EEC VEHICLE KERB WEIGHTS

| **90 models** | **Standard** | **High load** |
|---|---|---|
| Soft top: | 1695 Kg (3736 lb) | 1699 Kg (3745 lb) |
| Pick-up: | 1694 Kg (3734 lb) | 1698 Kg (3743 lb) |
| Hard top: | 1746 Kg (3849 lb) | 1750 Kg (3858 lb) |
| Station wagon: | 1793 Kg (3952 lb) | 1797 Kg (3961 lb) |

| **110 models** | | |
|---|---|---|
| Soft top: | 1872 Kg (4127 lb) | 1882 Kg (4149 lb) |
| Pick-up: | 1880 Kg (4144 lb) | 1890 Kg (4166 lb) |
| High capacity pick-up: | 1917 Kg (4226 lb) | 1927 Kg (4248 lb) |
| Hard top: | 1913 Kg (4217 lb) | 1923 Kg (4239 lb) |
| Station wagon: | 2018 Kg (4448 lb) | 2028 Kg (4470 lb) |
| County station wagon: | 2054 Kg (4528 lb) | 2064 Kg (4550 lb) |

| **130 models** | |
|---|---|
| Crew cab and High capacity pick-up: | 2086 Kg (4598 lb) |

EEC kerb weight = Unladen weight + Full fuel tank + 75 Kg (165 lb).

## TOWING WEIGHTS

| | On-road | Off-road |
|---|---|---|
| Unbraked trailers | 750 Kg (1653 lb) | 500 Kg (1102 lb) |
| Trailers with overrun brakes | 3500 Kg (7716 lb) | 1000 Kg (2204 lb) |
| 4 wheel trailers with coupled brakes * | 4000 Kg (8818 lb) | 1000 Kg (2204 lb) |

NOTE: * Only applies to vehicles modified to accept coupled brakes.

NOTE: All weight figures are subject to local restrictions.

## OFF-ROAD PERFORMANCE

**90 models**

Max. gradient (EEC kerb weight) ..................................... 45°

Approach angle:
        Soft top and Pick-up (EEC kerb weight) ................. 48°
        Hard top and station wagon (EEC kerb weight) ...... 51.5°

Departure angle
        Soft top and Pick-up (EEC kerb weight) ................. 49°
Hard top and Station wagon (EEC kerb weight) .............. 53°

Wading depth .............................................................. 500 mm (20 in)

Min. ground clearance (unladen):
        Soft top and pick-up ................................................ 191 mm (7.5 in)
        Hard top and station wagon ................................... 229 mm (9.0 in)

NOTE: Departure angles do not account for the addition of a tow hitch.

**110 and 130 models**

Max. gradient (EEC kerb weight) ..................................... 45°

Approach angle (EEC kerb weight) ................................. 50°

Departure angle (EEC kerb weight)
110 models ................................................................. 35°
130 models ................................................................. 34°

Wading depth .............................................................. 500 mm (20 in)
Min. ground clearance (unladen ...................................... 215 mm (8.5 in)

NOTE: Departure angles do not account for the addition of a tow hitch.

## TYRE SIZE AND PRESSURES

| | Front | Rear |
|---|---|---|
| **90 models** | | |
| Normal - all load conditions | | |
| **205 R16 radial** | | |
| **& 265/75 R16 (multi-terrain)** | 1,9 bar | 2,4 bar |
| | 28 lbf/in$^2$ | 35 lbf/in$^2$ |
| | 2,0 kgf/cm$^2$ | 2,5 kgf/cm$^2$ |
| **750 R16 radial** | 1,9 bar | 2,75 bar |
| | 28 lbf/in$^2$ | 40 lbf/in$^2$ |
| | 2,0 kgf/cm$^2$ | 2,8 kgf/cm$^2$ |
| **110 models** | | |
| Normal - all load conditions | | |
| **750 R16 Radial** | 1,9 bar | 3,3 bar |
| | 28 lbf/in$^2$ | 48 lbf/in$^2$ |
| | 2,0 kgf/cm$^2$ | 3,4 kgf/cm$^2$ |
| **130 models** | | |
| Normal - all load conditions | | |
| **750 R16 Radial** | 3,0 bar | 4,5 bar |
| | 44 lbf/in$^2$ | 65 lbf/in$^2$ |
| | 3,1 kgf/cm$^2$ | 4,6 kgf/cm$^2$ |

 **WARNING: Tyre pressures must be checked with the tyres cold, as the pressure is about 0,21 bar (3 lbf/in$^2$, 0,2 kgf/cm$^2$) higher at running temperature. If the vehicle has been parked in the sun or high ambient temperatures, DO NOT reduce the tyre pressures, move the vehicle into the shade and wait for the tyres to cool before checking the pressures.**

**WARNING: Always use the same make and type of radial-ply tyres, front and rear. DO NOT use cross-ply tyres, or interchange tyres from front to rear.**
- **If the the wheel is marked 'TUBED', an inner tube MUST be fitted, even with a tubeless tyre.**
- **If the wheel is marked 'TUBELESS', an inner tube must NOT be fitted.**

## WHEELS

**90 models**
Steel wheel size:
Heavy duty - UK and Western Europe ............................. 6.5F X 16
Other markets ................................................................. 5.5F X 16
Alloy wheel size .............................................................. 7J X 16

**110 models**
Steel wheel size:
Heavy duty - UK and Western Europe ............................. 6.5F X 16
Other markets ................................................................. 5.5F X 16

**130 models**
Steel wheel size:
Heavy duty - UK and Western Europe ............................. 6.5F X 16
Other markets ................................................................. 5.5F X 16

## VEHICLE DIMENSIONS

### 90 models
Overall length:
- Soft top and Pick-up ............................................. 3722 mm (146.5 in)
- Hard top and Station wagon .................................... 3883 mm (152.9 in)

Overall width: ................................................................ 1790 mm (70.5 in)

Overall height:
- Soft top ................................................................ 1965 mm (77.4 in)
- Pick-up and Station wagon .................................... 1963 mm (77.3 in)
- Hard top ............................................................... 1972 mm (77.6 in)

Wheelbase ................................................................. 2360 mm (92.9 in)
Track front/rear ......................................................... 1486 mm (58.5 in)
Width between wheel boxes ......................................... 925 mm (36.4 in)

### 110 models
Overall length:
- Soft top and Pick-up ............................................. 4438 mm (175 in)
- High capacity pick-up ............................................ 4631 mm (182 in)
- Hard top/Station and County .................................. 4599 mm (181 in)

Overall width: ................................................................ 1790 mm (70.5 in)
Overall height: .............................................................. 2035 mm (80.1 in)
Wheelbase ................................................................. 2794 mm (110 in)
Track front/rear ......................................................... 1486 mm (58.5 in)

Width between wheel boxes:
- High capacity pick-up ............................................ 1090 mm (43 in)
- all other models .................................................... 925 mm (36.4 in)

### 130 models
Overall length ............................................................. 5132 mm (202 in)
Overall width .............................................................. 1790 mm (70.5 in)
Overall height ............................................................. 2035 mm (80.1 in)
Wheelbase ................................................................. 3226 mm (127 in)
Track front/rear ......................................................... 1486 mm (58.5 in)
Width between wheel boxes ......................................... 1090 mm (43 in)

# 05 - ENGINE TUNING DATA

## CONTENTS

Page

**INFORMATION**

# Notes

## 300Tdi ENGINE

**Type** ................................................................. 2.5 Litre Turbo diesel intercooled

**Firing order** ...................................................... 1-3-4-2

**Injection timing** ............................................... 1,54 mm lift at T.D.C.

**Injection timing with electronic EGR** ............. 1,40 mm lift at T.D.C.

**Timing marks:**
Valve timing - manual ....................................... Slot for pin in flywheel and TDC mark on front pulley.
Injection timing ................................................. Timing pin (service tool)
Tappet clearances inlet and exhaust ............... 0,20 mm cold

**Valve timing:**

| | Inlet | Exhaust |
|---|---|---|
| - Opens | 16° B.T.D.C. | 51° B.B.D.C. |
| - Closes | 42° A.B.D.C. | 13° A.T.D.C. |
| - Peak | 103° A.T.D.C. | 109° B.T.D.C. |
| - Lift | 9,67 mm | 9,97 mm |

**Maximum governed speeds:**
- No load (neutral/full throttle) ........................ 4600 + 40 - 120 rev/min
- Idle speed at running temperature ................ 720 ± 20 rev/min
- Die-down time ............................................... 4 seconds

## INJECTION PUMP

Make & type - standard .................................... Bosch rotary R509 type with boost control and two speed mechanical governor with auto advance and solenoid electrical shut-off. Tamper proof sealing on, no load governed speed and fuel adjustment screws. Constant volume delivery valves

Make & type - Electronic EGR ......................... Bosch rotary R509/1 type with boost control and two speed mechanical governor with auto advance and solenoid electrical shut-off. Tamper proof sealing on flight speed and fuel adjustment screws. Constant volume delivery valves. Throttle position sensor for EGR control.

## HEATER PLUGS

Make & type ...................................................... Probe type, No.0100226129A Beru 12 volts
Time to reach operating temperature of 850° C .............. 8 seconds

## INJECTORS

Make & type - standard .................................................. Bosch KBAL 90 P37
Nozzle type ................................................................. DSLA 145P366
Opening pressure (working pressure) ........................... Initial pressure 200 atmospheres, Secondary 280
atmospheres

## TURBOCHARGER

Make & type ................................................................ Garrett T250 - 04
Maximum boost pressure .............................................. 0,93 - 1,07 bar (13.5 - 15.5 lbf/in$^2$) measured at
wastegate actuator 'T' piece

# 07 - GENERAL FITTING REMINDERS

## CONTENTS

Page

**INFORMATION**

# Notes

## GENERAL FITTING REMINDERS

### WORKSHOP SAFETY IS YOUR RESPONSIBILITY!

**The suggestions, cautions and warnings in the section are intended to serve as reminders for trained and experienced mechanics. This manual is not a definitive guide to automotive mechanics or workshop safety.**

**Shop equipment, shop environment, and the use and disposal of solvents, fluids, and chemicals are subject to government regulations which are intended to provide a level of safety. It is your responsibility to know and comply with such regulations.**

## PRECAUTIONS AGAINST DAMAGE

1. Always fit covers to protect fenders before commencing work in engine compartment.
2. Cover seats and carpets, wear clean overalls and wash hands or wear gloves before working inside vehicle.
3. Avoid spilling hydraulic fluid or battery acid on paint work. Wash off with water immediately if this occurs. Use Polythene sheets to protect carpets and seats.
4. Always use a recommended Service Tool where specified.
5. Protect temporarily exposed screw threads by replacing nuts or fitting plastic caps.

## SAFETY PRECAUTIONS

1. Whenever possible, use a lift when working beneath vehicle, in preference to jacking. Chock wheels as well as applying parking brake.

 **WARNING: Do not use a pit when removing fuel system components.**

2. Never rely on a jack alone to support vehicle. Use axle stands carefully placed at jacking points to provide rigid support.
3. Ensure that a suitable form of fire extinguisher is conveniently located.
4. Check that any lifting equipment used has adequate capacity and is fully serviceable.
5. Disconnect battery.

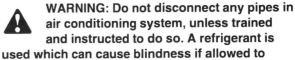 **WARNING: Do not disconnect any pipes in air conditioning system, unless trained and instructed to do so. A refrigerant is used which can cause blindness if allowed to contact eyes.**

6. Ensure that adequate ventilation is provided when volatile degreasing agents are being used.
7. Do not apply heat in an attempt to free stiff fixings; as well as causing damage to protective coatings, there is a risk of damage to electronic equipment and brake linings from stray heat.

## PREPARATION

1. Clean components and surrounding area prior to removal.
2. Blank off any openings exposed by component removal using greaseproof paper and masking tape.
3. Immediately seal fuel, oil or hydraulic lines when separated, using plastic caps or plugs, to prevent loss of fluid and entry of dirt.
4. Close open ends of oilways, exposed by component removal, with tapered hardwood plugs or readily visible plastic plugs.
5. Immediately a component is removed, place it in a suitable container; use a separate container for each component and its associated parts.
6. Before dismantling a component, clean it thoroughly with a recommended cleaning agent; check that agent is suitable for all materials of component.
7. Clean bench and provide marking materials, labels, containers and locking wire before dismantling a component.

## DISMANTLING

1. Observe scrupulous cleanliness when dismantling components, particularly when brake, fuel or hydraulic system parts are being worked on. A particle of dirt or a cloth fragment could cause a dangerous malfunction if trapped in these systems.
2. Blow out all tapped holes, crevices, oilways and fluid passages with an air line. Ensure that any O-rings used for sealing are correctly replaced or renewed, if disturbed.
3. Use marking ink to identify mating parts, to ensure correct reassembly. If a centre punch or scriber is used they may initiate cracks or distortion of components.
4. Wire together mating parts where necessary to prevent accidental interchange (e.g. roller bearing components).
5. Wire labels on to all parts which are to be renewed, and to parts requiring further inspection before being passed for reassembly; place these parts in separate containers from those containing parts for rebuild.
6. Do not discard a part due for renewal until it has been compared with the new part, to ensure that its correct replacement has been obtained.

## INSPECTION-GENERAL

1. Never inspect a component for wear or dimensional check unless it is absolutely clean; a slight smear of grease can conceal an incipient failure.
2. When a component is to be checked dimensionally against figures quoted for it, use correct equipment (surface plates, micrometers, dial gauges, etc.) in serviceable condition. Makeshift checking equipment can be dangerous.
3. Reject a component if its dimensions are outside limits quoted, or if damage is apparent. A part may, however, be refitted if its critical dimension is exactly limit size, and is otherwise satisfactory.
4. Use 'Plastigauge' 12 Type PG-1 for checking bearing surface clearances. Directions for its use, and a scale giving bearing clearances in 0,0025 mm steps are provided with it.

## BALL AND ROLLER BEARINGS

 **CAUTION: Never refit a ball or roller bearing without first ensuring that it is in a fully serviceable condition.**

1. Remove all traces of lubricant from bearing under inspection by washing in a suitable degreaser; maintain absolute cleanliness throughout operations.
2. Inspect visually for markings of any form on rolling elements, raceways, outer surface of outer rings or inner surface of inner rings. Reject any bearings found to be marked, since any marking in these areas indicates onset of wear.
3. Holding inner race between finger and thumb of one hand, spin outer race and check that it revolves absolutely smoothly. Repeat, holding outer race and spinning inner race.
4. Rotate outer ring gently with a reciprocating motion, while holding inner ring; feel for any check or obstruction to rotation, and reject bearing if action is not perfectly smooth.
5. Lubricate bearing generously with lubricant appropriate to installation.
6. Inspect shaft and bearing housing for discolouration or other marking suggesting that movement has taken place between bearing and seatings. (This is particularly to be expected if related markings were found in operation 2).
7. Ensure that shaft and housing are clean and free from burrs before fitting bearing.

8. If one bearing assembly of a pair shows an imperfection it is generally advisable to replace both with new bearings; an exception could be made if the faulty bearing had covered a low mileage, and it could be established that damage was confined to it only.

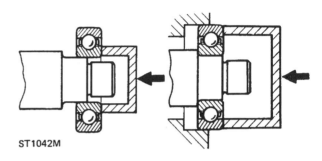

ST1042M

9. When fitting bearing to shaft, apply force only to inner ring of bearing, and only to outer ring when fitting into housing, as shown above.
10. In the case of grease lubricated bearings (e.g. hub bearings) fill space between bearing and outer seal with recommended grade of grease before fitting seal.
11. Always mark components of separable bearings (e.g. taper roller bearings) in dismantling, to ensure correct reassembly. Never fit new rollers in a used outer ring, always fit a complete new bearing assembly.

## OIL SEALS

⚠ **NOTE: Ensure that the seal running track is free from pits, scores, corrosion and general damage prior to fitting replacement seal.**

1. Always fit new oil seals when rebuilding an assembly.
2. Carefully examine seal before fitting to ensure that it is clean and undamaged.
3. Coat the sealing lips with clean grease; pack dust excluder seals with grease, and heavily grease duplex seals in cavity between sealing lips.
4. Ensure that seal spring, if provided, is correctly fitted.

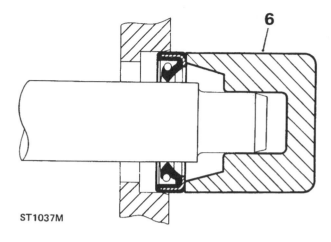

ST1037M

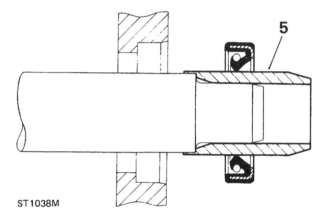

ST1038M

5. Place lip of seal towards fluid to be sealed and slide into position on shaft, using fitting sleeve when possible to protect sealing lip from damage by sharp corners, threads or splines. If fitting sleeve is not available, use plastic tube or tape to prevent damage to sealing lip.
6. Grease outside diameter of seal, place square to housing recess and press into position, using great care and if possible a 'bell piece' to ensure that seal is not tilted. In some cases it may be preferable to fit seal to housing before fitting to shaft. Never let weight of unsupported shaft rest in seal.

7. If correct service tool is not available, use a suitable drift approximately 0,4 mm (0.015 in) smaller than outside diameter of seal. Use a hammer **VERY GENTLY** on drift if a press is not suitable.
8. Press or drift seal in to depth of housing if housing is shouldered, or flush with face of housing where no shoulder is provided. Ensure that the seal does not enter the housing in a tilted position.

⚠ **NOTE: Most cases of failure or leakage of oil seals are due to careless fitting, and resulting damage to both seals and sealing surfaces. Care in fitting is essential if good results are to be obtained. NEVER use a seal which has been improperly stored or handled, such as hung on a hook or nail.**

## JOINTS AND JOINT FACES

1. Always use correct gaskets where they are specified.
2. Use jointing compound only when recommended. Otherwise fit joints dry.
3. When jointing compound is used, apply in a thin uniform film to metal surfaces; take great care to prevent it from entering oilways, pipes or blind tapped holes.
4. Remove all traces of old jointing materials prior to reassembly. Do not use a tool which could damage joint faces.
5. Inspect joint faces for scratches or burrs and remove with a fine file or oil stone; do not allow removed material or dirt to enter tapped holes or enclosed parts.
6. Blow out any pipes, channels or crevices with compressed air, fit new 'O' rings or seals displaced by air blast.

## FLEXIBLE HYDRAULIC PIPES, HOSES

1. Before removing any brake or power steering hose, clean end fittings and area surrounding them as thoroughly as possible.
2. Obtain appropriate plugs or caps before detaching hose end fittings, so that ports can be immediately covered to exclude dirt.
3. Clean hose externally and blow through with airline. Examine carefully for cracks, separation of plies, security of end fittings and external damage. Reject any hose found faulty.
4. When refitting hose, ensure that no unnecessary bends are introduced, and that hose is not twisted before or during tightening of union nuts.
5. Containers for hydraulic fluid must be kept absolutely clean.
6. Do not store brake fluid in an unsealed container. It will absorb water, and fluid in this condition would be dangerous to use due to a lowering of its boiling point.
7. Do not allow brake fluid to be contaminated with mineral oil, or use a container which has previously contained mineral oil.
8. Do not re-use brake fluid bled from system.
9. Always use clean brake fluid to clean hydraulic components.
10. Fit a cap to seal a hydraulic union and a plug to its socket after removal to prevent ingress of dirt.
11. Absolute cleanliness must be observed with hydraulic components at all times.
12. After any work on hydraulic systems, inspect carefully for leaks underneath the vehicle while a second operator applies maximum pressure to the brakes (engine running) and operates the steering.

## FUEL SYSTEM HOSES

⚠️ CAUTION: All fuel hoses are made up of two laminations, an armoured rubber outer sleeve and an inner viton core. If any of the fuel system hoses have been disconnected, it is imperative that the internal bore is inspected to ensure that the viton lining has not become separated from the amoured outer sleeve. A new hose must be fitted if separation is evident.

RR2302M

## METRIC BOLT IDENTIFICATION

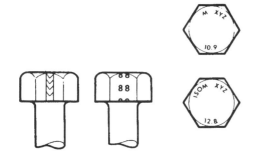

ST1035M

1. An ISO metric bolt or screw, made of steel and larger than 6 mm in diameter can be identified by either of the symbols ISO M or M embossed or indented on top of the head.
2. In addition to marks to identify the manufacture, the head is also marked with symbols to indicate the strength grade, e.g. 8.8, 12.9 or 14.9, where the first figure gives the minimum tensile strength of the bolt material in tens of kgf/mm$^2$.
3. Zinc plated ISO metric bolts and nuts are chromate passivated, a gold-bronze colour.

## METRIC NUT IDENTIFICATION

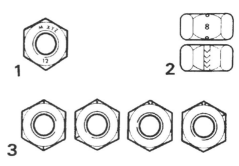

ST1036M

1. A nut with an ISO metric thread is marked on one face or on one of the flats of the hexagon with the strength grade symbol 8, 12 or 14. Some nuts with a strength 4, 5 or 6 are also marked and some have the metric symbol M on the flat opposite the strength grade marking.
2. A clock face system is used as an alternative method of indicating the strength grade. The external chamfers or a face of the nut is marked in a position relative to the appropriate hour mark on a clock face to indicate the strength grade.
3. A dot is used to locate the 12 O'clock position and a dash to indicate the strength grade. If the grade is above 12, two dots identify the 12 O'clock position.

## KEYS AND KEYWAYS

1. Remove burrs from edges of keyways with a fine file and clean thoroughly before attempting to refit key.
2. Clean and inspect key closely; keys are suitable for refitting only if indistinguishable from new, as any indentation may indicate the onset of wear.

## TAB WASHERS

1. Fit new washers in all places where they are used. Always fit a new tab washer.
2. Ensure that the new tab washer is of the same design as that replaced.

---

## COTTER PINS

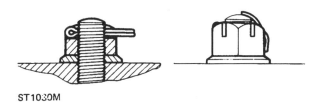

ST1030M

1. Fit new cotter pins throughout when replacing any unit.
2. Always fit cotter pins where cotter pins were originally used. Do not substitute spring washers: there is always a good reason for the use of a cotter pin.
3. All cotter pins should be fitted as shown unless otherwise stated.

## NUTS

1. When tightening a slotted or castellated nut never loosen it to insert cotter pin or locking wire except in those recommended cases where this forms part of an adjustment. If difficulty is experienced, alternative washers or nuts should be selected, or washer thickness reduced.
2. Where self-locking nuts have been removed it is advisable to replace them with new ones of the same type.

 **NOTE: Where bearing pre-load is involved nuts should be tightened in accordance with special instructions.**

## LOCKING WIRE

1. Fit new locking wire of the correct type for all assemblies incorporating it.
2. Arrange wire so that its tension tends to tighten the bolt heads, or nuts, to which it is fitted.

## SCREW THREADS

1. Both UNF and Metric threads to ISO standards are used. See below for thread identification.
2. Damaged threads must always be discarded. Cleaning up threads with a die or tap impairs the strength and closeness of fit of the threads and is not recommended.
3. Always ensure that replacement bolts are at least equal in strength to those replaced.
4. Do not allow oil, grease or jointing compound to enter blind threaded holes. The hydraulic action on screwing in the bolt or stud could split the housing.
5. Always tighten a nut or bolt to the recommended torque value. Damaged or corroded threads can affect the torque reading.
6. To check or re-tighten a bolt or screw to a specified torque value first loosen a quarter of a turn, then re-tighten to the correct value.
7. Oil thread lightly before tightening to ensure a free running thread, except in the case of threads treated with sealant/lubricant, and self-locking nuts.

## UNIFIED THREAD IDENTIFICATION

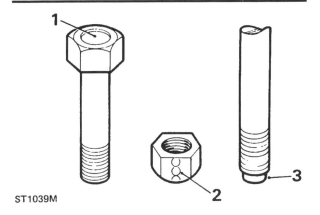

ST1039M

1. **Bolts**
   A circular recess is stamped in the upper surface of the bolt head.
2. **Nuts**
   A continuous line of circles is indented on one of the flats of the hexagon, parallel to the axis of the nut.
3. **Studs, Brake Rods, etc.**
   The component is reduced to the core diameter for a short length at its extremity.

# Notes

# 09 - LUBRICANTS, FLUIDS AND CAPACITIES

## CONTENTS

Page

**INFORMATION**

# Notes

## RECOMMENDED LUBRICANTS AND FLUIDS

**All climates and conditions**

| COMPONENT | SPECIFICATION | VISCOSITY | AMBIENT TEMPERATURE °C -30 to 50 |
|---|---|---|---|
| **Diesel** Engine sump | RES.22.OL.PD-2 or CCMC PD-2 or API CD | 15W/40 | (bar: approx -10 to 50) |
| Main Gearbox manual | ATF Dexron IID | | (bar: approx -30 to 50) |
| Final drive units Swivel pin housings | API or GL5 MIL - L - 2105 or MIL - L - 2105B C or D | 90 EP  80 EP * | (90 EP bar: approx -10 to 50) (80 EP bar: approx -30 to 30) |
| Power steering | ATF Dexron IID or Dexron III | | (bar: approx -30 to 50) |
| Transfer box LT230T | API GL4 or GL5 MIL - L - 2105 or MIL - L - 2105B C or D | 90 EP  80 EP | (90 EP bar: approx -10 to 50) (80 EP bar: approx -30 to 30) |

 **NOTE:** * Molytex EP 00 grease on later vehicles with filler plug only in swivel pin housing.

| Propeller shaft Front and Rear Lubrication nipples (hubs, ball joints etc.) Seat slides Door lock striker | NLGI - 2 Multi-purpose Lithium based GREASE |
|---|---|
| Brake and clutch reservoirs | Brake fluids having a minimum boiling point of 260° C (500° F) and complying with FMVSS 116 DOT4 |
| Engine coolant (Pre-99MY) | Use an ethylene glycol based anti-freeze (containing no methanol) with non-phosphate corrosion inhibitors suitable for use in aluminium engines to ensure the protection of the cooling system against frost and corrosion in all seasons. Use one part anti-freeze to one part water for protection down to -36° C (-33° F). **IMPORTANT: Coolant solution must not fall below proportions one part anti-freeze to three parts water, i.e. minimum 25% anti-freeze in coolant otherwise damage to engine is liable to occur. Maximum concentration is 60%.** |
| Engine coolant (99MY on) | Use Texaco XLC long life coolant. Use one part anti-freeze to one part water for protection down to -36° C (-33° F). **IMPORTANT: Coolant solution must not fall below 50% anti-freeze otherwise damage to the engine is liable to occur. Maximum concentration is 60%.** |
| Battery lugs, earthing surfaces where paint has been removed. | Petroleum jelly. **NOTE: Do not use Silicone Grease** |
| Air Conditioning System Refrigerant | Use only refrigerant R134a |
| Compressor Oil | Sanden oil |

## LUBRICATION PRACTICE

Use a high quality oil of the correct viscosity range and service classification in the engine during maintenance and when topping up. The use of oil not to the correct specification can lead to high oil and fuel consumption and ultimately to damaged components.

Oil to the correct specification contains additives which disperse the corrosive acids formed by combustion and prevent the formation of sludge which can block the oilways. Additional oil additives should not be used. Always adhere to the recommended servicing intervals.

 **WARNING: Many liquids and other substances used in motor vehicles are poisonous. They must not be consumed and must be kept away from open wounds. These substances, among others, include anti-freeze, windscreen washer additives, lubricants and various adhesives.**

## CAPACITIES

The following capacity figures are approximate and are provided as a guide only.

| Capacities (approx.)* | Litres | Pints |
|---|---|---|
| Engine sump oil | 5,8 | 10.20 |
| Extra when refilling after fitting new filter | 0,85 | 1.50 |
| Manual gearbox | 2,67 | 4.70 |
| Transfer gearbox oil | 2,30 | 4.00 |
| Front differential | 1,70 | 3.00 |
| Rear differential | 1,70 | 3.00 |
| Power steering box and reservoir LHD | 2,90 | 5.00 |
| Power steering box and reservoir RHD | 3,40 | 6.00 |
| Swivel pin housing oil/grease (each) | 0,35 | 0.60 |
| Fuel tank usable fuel | 79,5 | 17.5 gall |
| Cooling system | 11,50 | 20.20 |
| Washer bottle | 3,0 | 5.28 |

 **NOTE: * All levels must be checked by dipstick or level plugs as applicable.**

## ANTI-FREEZE

**PERCENTAGE CONCENTRATION - 50%**

**PROTECTION - LOWER TEMPERATURE LIMIT**

**Complete protection**
Vehicle may be driven away immediately from cold, -33° C (-36° F).

**Safe limit protection**
Coolant in semi-frozen state. Engine may be started and driven away after warm-up period, -41° C (-42° F).

**Lower protection**
Prevents frost damage to cylinder head, block and radiator. Thaw out before starting engine, -47° C (-53° F).

 **CAUTION: Anti-freeze content must never be allowed to fall below 25% (pre 99MY) or 50% (99MY on) otherwise damage to the engine is liable to occur. Anti-freeze content should not exceed 60% (all models) as this will greatly reduce cooling efficiency.**

## RECOMMENDED FUEL

### 300 Tdi Vehicles

Diesel fuel oil, distillate, diesel fuel, automotive gas or Derv to British standard 2869, Class A1 or A2. Using diesel fuel with a lower class rating could seriously impair vehicle performance.

### Td5 Vehicles

Refer to Defender Workshop Manual VDR 100350.

### V8i Vehicles

Refer to Defender Workshop Manual LRL 0185.

## FUEL TANK CAPACITY

**Side tank:**
90 models ...................................................................... 54,6 litres (12 gallons)
110 models * ................................................................. 68,2 litres (15 gallons)
110 Station wagon ....................................................... 45,5 litres (10 gallons)

* Except Station wagon

**Rear tank:**
110 and 130 models ...................................................... 79,5 litres (17,5 gallons)

# 10 - MAINTENANCE

## CONTENTS

Page

**MAINTENANCE**

# Notes

## SERVICE SCHEDULE

The following section describes the items detailed in the vehicle Service Schedule. Where required instructions are given for carrying out the service procedure, or a cross reference is given to the section in the manual where the procedure may be found.

Service Maintenance Schedules are published separately to reflect the needs and intervals for each vehicle variant. Procedures in the Workshop Manual must be used in conjunction with the Service Schedule sheets.

Service Maintenance Schedules are available from:
Land Rover Publications,
Character Mailing,
Heysham Road,
Bootle,
Merseyside, L70 1JL

## VEHICLE INTERIOR

### CHECK SEATS & BELTS

Check condition and security of seat belts, seat belt mountings, seat belt buckles and operation of inertia seat belts.

### CHECK OPERATION OF LAMPS

Check operation of all lamps, horns and warning indicators.

### CHECK OPERATION OF WIPERS

Check operation of front/rear wipers and washers and condition of wiper blades.

## CHECK OPERATION OF HANDBRAKE

**Handbrake check/adjust**

1. Chock road wheels.
2. Raise one rear wheel clear of ground and support securely with axle stand.
3. Release handbrake lever.

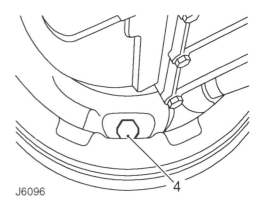

J6096

4. Underneath vehicle, tighten adjuster bolt clockwise to **25 Nm (18 lbf/ft)** to fully lock brake drum.
5. Slacken adjusting bolt by 1.5 turns to give brake shoes running clearance. Check that the drum is free to rotate.
6. Adjust handbrake cable locknuts to give pawl two notches free movement on the rachet before being fully operational on third notch of rachet.

△ NOTE: Cable adjustment must ONLY be used for initial setting and to compensate for cable stretch. It MUST NOT be used to take up brake shoe wear, which MUST be adjusted at brake drum.

7. Operate handbrake to settle brake shoes. Recheck handbrake is fully operational on third notch of rachet pawl. Readjust if necessary.
8. Remove axle stand and wheel chocks.

## BATTERY CONNECTIONS

⚠ NOTE: The vehicle may be fitted with an alarm and immobilisation system using a battery backed-up alarm sounder *See ELECTRICAL, Repair, Battery*

Disconnect battery leads, clean and grease with petroleum jelly, including battery terminals.

## CHECK OPERATION OF DOOR SWITCHES

When a Vehicle Immobilisation and Alarm System is fitted it is important that all door and bonnet switches operate correctly, otherwise perimeter and interior protection may not function if a door or the bonnet is opened.

## VEHICLE EXTERIOR

### CHECK/ADJUST HEADLAMP ALIGNMENT

Check/adjust headlamp alignment.

### CHECK ROAD WHEELS AND TYRES

Check road wheels for damage.

Check tyres, including spare, for compliance with manufacture's specificaton.

Check visually for cuts, lumps, bulges, uneven tread wear and tread depth. *See WHEELS AND TYRES, Repair, wheels and tyres*

Check/adjust tyre pressures. *See GENERAL SPECIFICATION DATA, Information, Tyres and pressures*

### INSPECT BRAKE PADS FOR WEAR, CALIPERS FOR LEAKS AND CONDITION OF DISCS

Check thickness of brake pads, and renew if thickness is less than 3,00 mm (0.12 in.). Check brake pads for oil contamination and fit a new set, if necessary, *See BRAKES, Repair, front brake pads* or *See BRAKES, Repair, rear brake pads*

 WARNING: When renewing brake pads, it is essential that only genuine components with correct grade of lining are used. Always fit new pads as complete axle sets, NEVER individually or as a single wheel set. Serious consequences could result from out of balance braking due to mixing of linings.

### CHECK FRONT WHEEL ALIGNMENT

Use recognised wheel alignment equipment to carry out this operation. *See STEERING, Adjustment, front wheel alignment*

### CHECK OPERATION OF ALL DOORS/TAILGATE, BONNET AND LOCKS

### LUBRICATE ALL DOOR/TAILGATE HINGES, AND DOOR CHECK/LOCK MECHANISMS

## UNDER BONNET MAINTENANCE

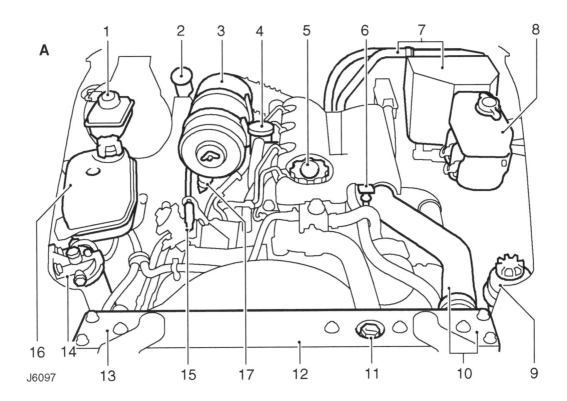

J6097

### UNDER BONNET COMPONENTS

**A - RH drive**

1. Brake fluid reservoir
2. Clutch fluid reservoir
3. Air cleaner element
4. Engine breather filter
5. Oil filler cap
6. Oil level dipstick
7. Heater/air conditioning unit
8. Windscreen washer reservoir
9. Power steering pump reservoir

10. Intercooler and hoses
11. Radiator filler plug
12. Radiator
13. Oil cooler
14. Fuel filter
15. Accelerator linkage
16. Expansion tank
17. Air cleaner dump valve

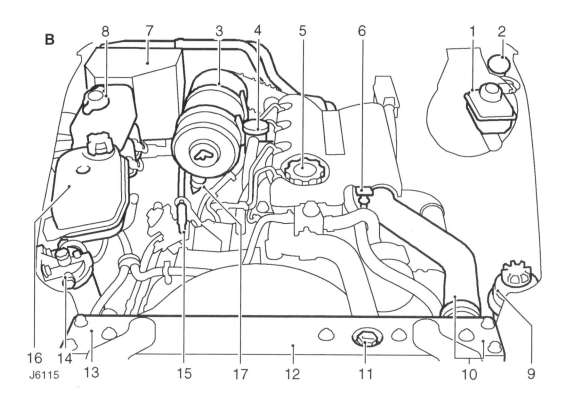

J6115

## UNDER BONNET COMPONENTS

**B - LH drive**

1. Brake fluid reservoir
2. Clutch fluid reservoir
3. Air cleaner element
4. Engine breather filter
5. Oil filler cap
6. Oil level dipstick
7. Heater/air conditioning unit
8. Windscreen washer reservoir
9. Power steering pump reservoir

10. Intercooler and hoses
11. Radiator filler plug
12. Radiator
13. Oil cooler
14. Fuel filter
15. Accelerator linkage
16. Expansion tank
17. Air cleaner dump valve

## CHECK COOLING, INTERCOOLING AND HEATING SYSTEMS

Check cooling, and heater systems for leaks and pipes/hoses for security and condition. Refill or top up as necessary.

⚠ **CAUTION: It is important that the correct procedure is followed when refilling or topping up the cooling system to avoid trapping air in the system.**

⚠ **WARNING: Do not remove caps and plugs when engine is hot because cooling system is pressurised and personal scalding could result.**

1. Remove plastic plugs from thermostat housing and radiator.
2. Fill cooling system with correct concentration and specification of anti-freeze. *See LUBRICANTS, FLUIDS AND CAPACITIES, Information, Recommended lubricants and fluids*
3. Fill from expansion tank until radiator is full, with level in expansion tank the same as in radiator.

△ **NOTE: Care should be taken to avoid excess coolant spillage from radiator.**

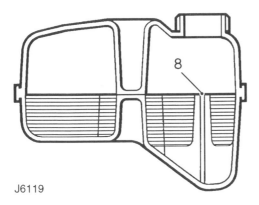

J6119

4. Fit plastic plug in radiator.
5. Add a further 1 litre (1.76 pints) of coolant to expansion tank and allow to settle.
6. Refit expansion tank cap and thermostat housing plug.
7. Run engine at idle speed for five minutes.
8. Switch off engine, check that expansion tank coolant is level with top of indicator post and top up as necessary.

Check intercooler and turbo-charger system for air leaks and pipes/hoses for security and condition.

All system hoses should be renewed at first signs of deterioration.

## VALVE CLEARANCES - CHECK/ADJUST

Check/adjust valve clearances. *See ENGINE , Adjustment, Valve clearances - check and adjust*

## RENEW FUEL FILTER ELEMENT

### Remove

1. Clean area around filter head and position a container beneath.
2. Unscrew and remove filter, catch fuel released.

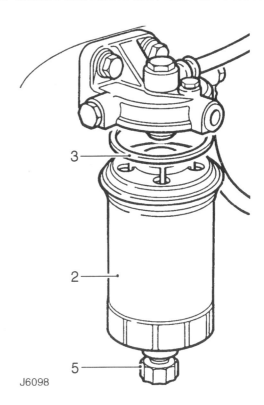

J6098

### Refit

3. Wet seal of new filter with fuel.
4. Screw new filter into position.
5. Ensure drain tap is fully closed.

## RENEW AIR CLEANER ELEMENT AND CLEAN DUMP VALVE

### Remove

1. Release 2 retaining clips and lift air cleaner from its cradle sufficiently to gain access to element.

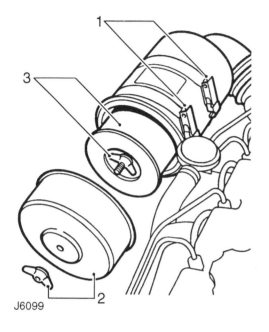

J6099

2. Unscrew wing nut and remove end cover.
3. Unscrew second wing nut and withdraw element from air cleaner casing.

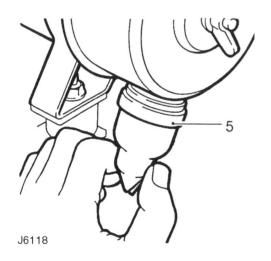

J6118

4. Clean interior and exterior of casing and cover.
5. Squeeze open dump valve and check that interior is clean. Renew valve, if perished.

### Refit

6. Fit new element, seal first, into casing and secure with wing nut.
7. Fit end cover, align mating arrows, and secure with wing nut.
8. Position air cleaner in mounting cradle and secure with retaining clips.

## CLEAN ENGINE BREATHER FILTER

### Remove

1. Disconnect breather top hose.
2. Remove single bolt and ease breather from rocker cover.

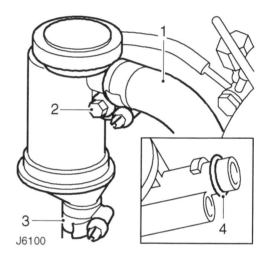

J6100

3. Disconnect bottom hose and remove engine breather.
4. Using suitable flushing solvent, thoroughly clean breather filter. Remove and discard rubber 'O' ring from breather pipe.

### Refit

5. Fit new rubber 'O' ring to engine breather.
6. Connect breather bottom hose.
7. Locate breather into rocker cover and secure with retaining bolt, tightening to *9 Nm (7 lbf/ft)*.
8. Connect breather top hose.

## RENEW AUXILIARY DRIVE BELT

Renew drive belt. *See ELECTRICAL, Repair, Auxiliary drive belt*

## RENEW COMPRESSOR DRIVE BELT

Renew compressor drive belt. *See AIR CONDITIONING, Repair, Compressor drive belt*

## CHECK/TOP UP POWER STEERING RESERVOIR

⚠ **WARNING: DO NOT start engine if fluid level in reservoir has dropped below dipstick - severe damage to the power steering system could result.**

⚠ **NOTE: Check fluid level with engine switched off and system cold. Ensure that steering wheel is not turned after stopping engine.**

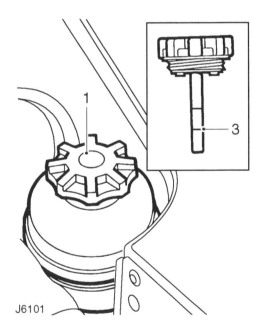

J6101

1. Clean and remove reservoir cap.
2. Wipe distick clean and fully refit cap.
3. Remove cap and check fluid level. Ensure fluid level is between UPPER mark and end of dipstick.
4. Top up, if necessary, with recommended fluid. *See LUBRICANTS, FLUIDS AND CAPACITIES, Information, Recommended lubricants and fluids* DO NOT fill above UPPER mark on dipstick.

## CHECK/TOP UP CLUTCH FLUID RESERVOIR

⚠ **WARNING: Clutch fluid will damage painted surfaces; clean up any spillage immediately and rinse with plenty of water. If clutch fluid should come into contact with the skin or eyes, rinse immediately with plenty of water.**

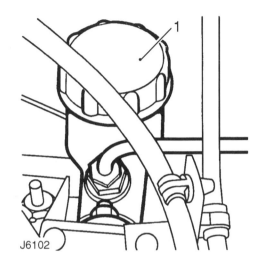

J6102

1. Clean and remove reservoir cap.
2. Check fluid level and top up if necessary, maintaining the level approximately 10 mm (0.39 in.) below top of reservoir, using recommended fluid. *See LUBRICANTS, FLUIDS AND CAPACITIES, Information, Recommended lubricants and fluids*

## CHECK/TOP UP BRAKE FLUID RESERVOIR

⚠ **WARNING: DO NOT drive the vehicle with the fluid level below 'MIN' mark.**
**Brake fluid will damage painted surfaces; clean up any spillage immediately and rinse with plenty of water.**
**If brake fluid should come into contact with skin or eyes, rinse immediately with plenty of water.**

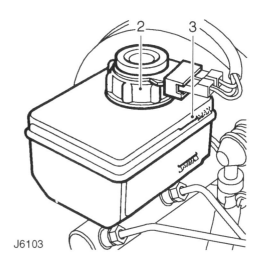

J6103

1. Check the fluid level visually through transparent side of reservoir without removing cap.
2. If level is below 'MAX' mark clean and remove reservoir cap.
3. Top up to 'MAX' mark with recommended brake fluid *See LUBRICANTS, FLUIDS AND CAPACITIES, Information, Recommended lubricants and fluids*

## CHECK/TOP UP WASHER RESERVOIR

Top up washer reservoir to within 25 mm (1.0 in.) of filler neck. Use a screen washer solvent/anti-freeze solution to assist removing mud, flies, and road film and protect against freezing.

## LUBRICATE ACCELERATOR LINKAGES

Lubricate accelerator cable at adjustment ferrule and linkage with injector pump and at pedal clevis pin.

## CHECK/ADJUST ENGINE IDLE SPEED

Check/adjust low and high engine idle speed with engine at normal running temperature. *See FUEL SYSTEM, Adjustment, low and high speed adjustment*

## CHECK/ADJUST STEERING BOX

Check steering box and pipes/hoses for fluid leaks.

Check that there is no backlash in steering box when in straight ahead position. Adjust steering box if necessary. *See STEERING, Adjustment, Power steering box*

## VISUALLY CHECK INTERCOOLER/RADIATOR FOR EXTERNAL OBSTRUCTIONS

Check intercooler/radiator for external obstructions. If necessary, apply air pressure to engine side of matrix to clear obstruction. If mud or dirt is evident, carefully use a hose to wash away obstruction.

## FLUSH DIESEL INTERCOOLER

### Remove

1. Remove intercooler matrix. *See FUEL SYSTEM, Repair, Intercooler*
2. Flush matrix with ICI 'GENKLENE' proprietary cleaner, following manufacturers instructions.
3. Dry intercooler completely ensuring that no liquid remains in matrix.

### Refit

4. Refit intercooler matrix. *See FUEL SYSTEM, Repair, Intercooler*

## UNDER VEHICLE MAINTENANCE

NOTE: A chassis undertray may be fitted on some vehicle derivatives to conform to legal requirements. When under chassis maintenance, or remove and refit procedures are required, it may be necessary to remove the undertray and/or integral access panels *See CHASSIS AND BODY, Repair, Front undertray* or *See CHASSIS AND BODY, Repair, Rear undertray*

### RENEW ENGINE OIL AND FILTER

1. Ensure vehicle is level.
2. Run engine to warm oil, switch off ignition.
3. Disconnect battery.
4. Place suitable drain tray under sump drain plug.

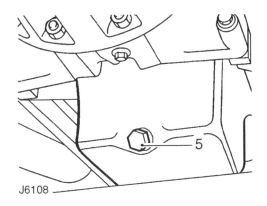

J6108

5. Remove drain plug from sump and allow oil to drain completely.
6. Fit new sealing washer, replace plug and tighten to **35 Nm (26 lbf/ft).**
7. Place drain tray under oil filter.
8. Unscrew filter anti-clockwise, using a strap wrench if necessary.
9. Clean mating face of oil filter adaptor.
10. Coat rubber sealing washer of new filter with clean engine oil.
11. Screw filter on clockwise until sealing washer touches adaptor mating face, tighten a further half turn by hand only. DO NOT overtighten.
12. Clean and remove filler cap from rocker cover.
13. Pour in correct quantity and grade of new oil from a sealed container. *See LUBRICANTS, FLUIDS AND CAPACITIES, Information, Recommended lubricants and fluids*

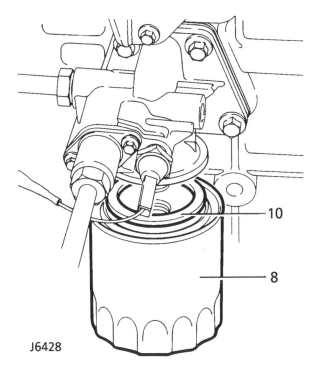

J6428

14. Check that oil level is between upper and lower marks on dipstick. DO NOT fill above upper mark.
15. Firmly replace filler cap.
16. Reconnect battery, run engine and check oil filter for leaks.
17. Stop engine, allow oil to run back into sump for a few minutes and check oil level again. Top up if necessary.

## RENEW GEARBOX OIL

1. Ensure vehicle is level.
2. Place suitable tray under gearbox.
3. Disconnect battery.

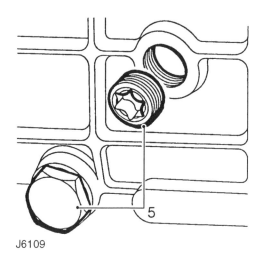

J6109

4. Clean area around filler/level plugs.
5. Remove both plugs and allow oil to drain completely.

 **WARNING: When draining gearbox, care should be taken to ensure that oil is not hot as personal scalding could result.**

6. Refit drain plug and tighten to **30 Nm (22 lbf/ft)**.
7. Inject new oil into gearbox until it runs out of filler hole. Allow excess oil to drain and wipe clean. **See LUBRICANTS, FLUIDS AND CAPACITIES, Information, Recommended lubricants and fluids**
8. Refit filler/level plug and tighten to **30 Nm (22 lbf/ft)**.
9. Reconnect battery.

## RENEW TRANSFER GEARBOX OIL

1. Ensure vehicle is level.
2. Disconnect battery.
3. Clean area around filler/level and drain plugs.

 **WARNING: When draining gearbox care should be taken to ensure that oil is not hot as personal scalding could result.**

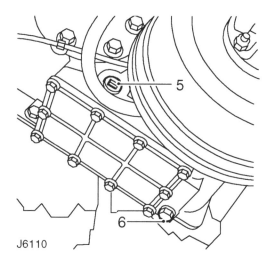

J6110

4. Place suitable tray under transfer gearbox.
5. Remove filler/level plug to vent gearbox and assist draining.
6. Remove drain plug and allow oil to drain.
7. Thoroughly clean drain plug threads and apply fresh 'Hylomar' sealant.
8. Refit drain plug and tighten to **30 Nm (22lbf/ft)**.
9. Inject new oil of correct quantity and grade into gearbox until oil runs out from filler/level hole. Allow excess oil to drain and wipe clean. **See LUBRICANTS, FLUIDS AND CAPACITIES, Information, Recommended lubricants and fluids**
10. Thoroughly clean filler/level plug and apply fresh 'Hylomar' sealant.
11. Refit plug and tighten to **30 Nm (22 lbf/ft)**.
12. Reconnect battery.

## CHECK/TOP UP TRANSFER GEARBOX OIL

1. Ensure vehicle is level.
2. Disconnect battery.
3. Clean area around filler/level plug.
4. Remove plug, check oil level and top up if necessary with correct grade of oil, **See LUBRICANTS, FLUIDS AND CAPACITIES, Information, Recommended lubricants and fluids** until oil runs out from filler/level hole. Allow excess oil to drain and wipe clean.
5. Thoroughly clean filler/level plug threads and apply fresh 'Hylomar' sealant.
6. Refit plug and tighten to **30 Nm (22 lbf/ft)**.
7. Reconnect battery.

## RENEW FRONT AND REAR AXLE OIL

1. Ensure vehicle is level and place suitable tray under axle to be drained.
2. Using 13mm square drive wrench, remove drain and filler/level plugs from axle and allow oil to drain completely.
3. Clean and refit drain plug.

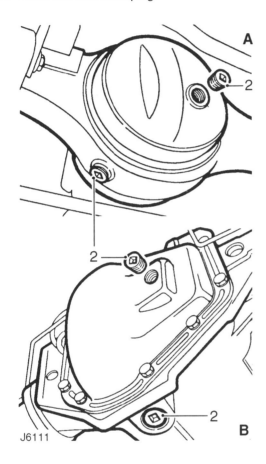

**A** - Front and rear axle, 90 models, front, 110/130 models. **B** - Rear axle, 110/130 models.

4. Inject new oil, *See LUBRICANTS, FLUIDS AND CAPACITIES, Information, Recommended lubricants and fluids* until it runs out from filler/level hole. Allow excess oil to drain and wipe clean.
5. Clean and refit filler/level plug.

## CHECK/TOP UP FRONT AND REAR AXLE

1. Ensure vehicle is level.
2. Using 13 mm square drive wrench, remove filler/level plug.

3. If necessary inject new oil until oil runs out from filler/level hole. Allow excess oil to drain and wipe clean. *See LUBRICANTS, FLUIDS AND CAPACITIES, Information, Recommended lubricants and fluids*
4. Clean and refit filler/level plug.

## RENEW SWIVEL PIN HOUSING OIL

1. Ensure vehicle is level and place suitable tray under swivel to be drained.
2. Remove drain and level plugs, allow oil to drain completely. Clean and refit drain plug.

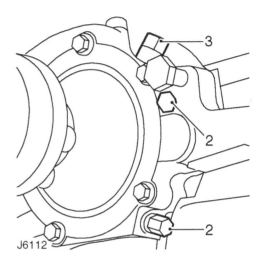

3. Remove filler plug and inject new oil until oil runs out from level hole. *See LUBRICANTS, FLUIDS AND CAPACITIES, Information, Recommended lubricants and fluids* Allow excess oil to drain and wipe clean.
4. Clean and refit filler and level plugs.

⚠ **NOTE: On later vehicles, the level and drain plugs have been deleted. The swivel pin housing is filled with grease on manufacture, for life service, and maintenance is not required.**

## CHECK/TOP UP SWIVEL PIN HOUSING OIL

1. Ensure vehicle is level.
2. Remove level and filler plug, check oil level and top up if necessary with new oil until oil runs out from level hole. Allow excess oil to drain and wipe clean. *See LUBRICANTS, FLUIDS AND CAPACITIES, Information, Recommended lubricants and fluids*
3. Clean and refit filler and level plugs.

## LUBRICATE PROPELLER SHAFT UNIVERSAL AND SLIDING JOINTS

1. Clean all grease nipples on front and rear propeller shafts.

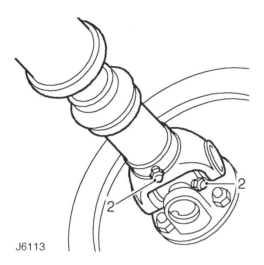

J6113

2. Using a low pressure hand grease gun, apply recommended grease *See LUBRICANTS, FLUIDS AND CAPACITIES, Information, Recommended lubricants and fluids* to grease nipples at front and rear propeller shaft universal and sliding joints.

## VISUALLY CHECK BRAKE, FUEL, CLUTCH HOSES/PIPES/UNIONS FOR CHAFING, LEAKS AND CORROSION

## CHECK EXHAUST SYSTEM FOR LEAKS, SECURITY AND DAMAGE

## RENEW CATALYTIC CONVERTERS *See MANIFOLD AND EXHAUST SYSTEM, Repair, manifolds and exhaust system*

## CHECK FOR FLUID LEAKS FROM POWER STEERING AND SUSPENSION SYSTEMS, HYDRAULIC PIPES AND UNIONS FOR CHAFING AND CORROSION

## CHECK/TIGHTEN STEERING UNIT AND STEERING ROD BALL JOINT FIXINGS, CHECK CONDITION OF BALL JOINTS AND DUST COVERS

Ball joints are lubricated for life during manufacture and require no further lubrication unless the rubber boot has been dislodged or damaged. All joints should be checked at specified service intervals, but more frequently if vehicle is used under arduous conditions.

1. Check for wear in joints by moving ball joint up and down vigorously. If free movement is apparent, fit a new joint assembly. *See STEERING, Repair, Drop arm ball See STEERING, Repair, Track rod and See STEERING, Repair, Drag link and drag link ends*

## CHECK/TIGHTEN FRONT AND REAR AXLE SUSPENSION LINK FIXINGS, CHECK CONDITION OF MOUNTING RUBBERS

## DRAIN AND CLEAN FUEL SEDIMENTER, IF FITTED

The fuel sedimenter is located on a chassis side member on the RH side of vehicle near rear wheel. It increases the working life of the fuel filter by removing larger droplets of water and other matter from fuel.

⚠ **NOTE: On 110/130 models with a twin tank fuel system, two sedimenters may be fitted, one on each side of the vehicle chassis.**

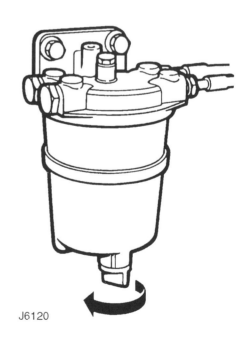

J6120

1. Slacken drain plug and allow any water to drain off.

2. When pure diesel is emitted, retighten drain plug.
3. Disconnect fuel inlet pipe at sedimenter. Raise and support pipe above level of fuel tank to prevent fuel draining from tank.

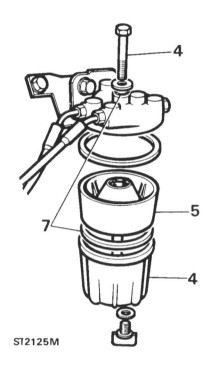

ST2125M

4. Support sedimenter bowl, unscrew bolt and remove bowl.
5. Remove sedimenter element.
6. Clean all components in kerosene.
7. Fit new seals.
8. Fit element into sedimenter bowl.
9. Secure bowl to sedimenter head.
10. Fit fuel inlet pipe to sedimenter.
11. Slacken drain plug and when pure diesel is emitted, retighten plug.
12. If necessary, prime the system.
   *See FUEL SYSTEM, Adjustment, Priming the fuel system*

## CHECK CONDITION OF ENGINE MOUNTING RUBBERS

## CHECK SECURITY OF TOWING BRACKET FITTINGS

## CARRY OUT ROAD OR ROLLER TEST

**WARNING: Two wheel roller tests MUST NOT be carried out.**

For details of dynamometer testing. *See INTRODUCTION, Information, Dynamometer testing*
Check the following components:

1. Engine for excessive noise.
2. Clutch for slip, judder or spin/drag.
3. Gear selection/noise - high/low range.
4. Steering for abnormal noise/effort.
5. Steering for free play.
6. All instruments, gauges and warning indicators.
7. Heater and air conditioning systems.
8. Heated rear screen.
9. Shock absorbers - ride irregularities.
10. Foot brake, on emergency stop, pulling to one side, binding and pedal effort.
11. Handbrake operation.
12. Seat reclining and latching.
13. Fully extend seat belt, check operation of retraction and latching. Inertia belts lock when snatched or vehicle on slope.
14. Road wheel balance.
15. Transmissions for vibrations.
16. Body noises, squeaks and rattles.
17. Excessive exhaust smoke.
18. Engine idle speed.
19. Endorse service record.
20. Report any unusual features of vehicle condition and additional work required.

## ENDORSE SERVICE RECORD

## ADDITIONAL MAINTENANCE SCHEDULES

### Camshaft drive belt

The engine timing gears are driven by a toothed rubber belt which must be renewed at intervals determined by the severity of operating conditions. In reasonable, temperate climate operation, the belt should be renewed every 120,000 km (72,000 miles) or every six years whichever occurs earlier.

In adverse operating conditions, such as work in dusty atmospheres, high ambient temperatures, desert and tropical zones, renew the belt every 60,000 km (36,000 miles) or every three years, whichever occurs earlier.

 **CAUTION: If the drive belt is not renewed at the correct interval, it could fail, resulting in serious engine damage.**

### Oil change diesel engines

If the vehicle is operated on fuel with a high sulphur content (over 1%) the oil change intervals must not exceed 5000 km (3000 miles).

### Anti-freeze

At two yearly intervals or at the onset of the second winter, the cooling system should be drained, flushed and refilled with the required water and anti-freeze solution.

### Hydraulic brake fluid.

It is recommended that at 40,000 km (24,000 miles) intervals or every two years, whichever is the earlier, the hydraulic brake fluid should be completely renewed.
At 80,000 km (48,000 miles) intervals or every four years, whichever is the earlier, all hydraulic brake fluid seals and flexible hoses should be renewed. All working surfaces of the master cylinder and caliper cylinders should be examined and renewed where necessary.

### Air cleaner

When the vehicle is used in dusty or field conditions or deep wading, frequent attention to the air cleaner may be required.

### Dampers

At 60,000 km (36,000 miles) intervals remove all suspension dampers, test for correct operation, refit or renew as necessary.

## SPECIAL OPERATING CONDITIONS

When the vehicle is operated in extremely arduous conditions or on dusty, wet or muddy terrain, more frequent attention should be paid to all servicing requirements.

### Additional daily or weekly attention depending on operating conditions:

Check/top-up transfer box oil.
Check steering rubber boots for security and condition. Renew if damaged.
Check brake fluid level: Investigate cause if any fluid loss is suspected.
Clean brake discs and calipers.
Lubricate front and rear propeller shaft universal/sliding joints. Under tropical or severe conditions, particularly where sand is encountered, the sliding joints must be lubricated very frequently to prevent ingress of abrasive material.
Every week and every maintenance inspection check tyre pressures and inspect tyre treads and side walls. Under arduous cross-country conditions the tyre pressures should be checked much more frequently, even to the extent of a daily check.

### Monthly

Renew gearbox oil.
Renew transfer box oil.
Check air cleaner element and renew every 6 months or as necessary.

# 12 - ENGINE

## CONTENTS

Page

# Notes

## VALVE CLEARANCES - CHECK AND ADJUST

**Service repair no - 12.29.48**

**Adjust**

⚠️ **CAUTION: If the crankshaft is rotated with excessive valve clearace, it is possible that the push rods could be dislodged from the cam follower seating and fracture the cam follower slide. To prevent damage, eliminate all clearance from any loose rockers before turning the crankshaft to adjust clearances.**

1. Rotate crankshaft until No.8 valve (counting from front of engine) is fully open.

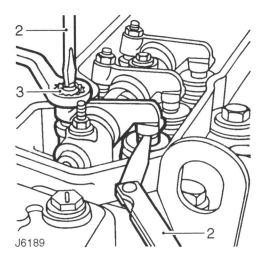

J6189

2. Using a 0,20 mm (0.008 in) feeler gauge adjust clearance of No.1 valve.
3. Slacken locknut and turn adjusting screw clockwise to reduce clearance and anti-clockwise to increase clearance. Tighten locknut to *16 Nm.*
4. Repeat operation for remaining tappets in the following sequence:

   No.3 tappet with No.6 valve fully open.
   No.5 tappet with No.4 valve fully open.
   No.2 tappet with No.7 valve fully open.
   No.8 tappet with No.1 valve fully open.
   No.6 tappet with No.3 valve fully open.
   No.4 tappet with No.5 valve fully open.
   No.7 tappet with No.2 valve fully open.

5. On completion, recheck clearances and adjust as necessary.

# Notes

## CYLINDER COMPRESSION TEST

**Service repair no - 12.25.01**

1. Start and run engine to normal operating temperature.
2. Switch off engine.
3. Disconnect spill return hose and fuel pipe from No.1 injector.
4. Remove retaining nut, release clamp and withdraw injector from cylinder head. *See FUEL SYSTEM, Repair, injector*
5. Disconnect electrical lead from fuel cut-off solenoid at injection pump to prevent delivery of fuel to injectors. On vehicles fitted with a digital diesel shut-off valve (DDS) immobilisation system, disconnect DDS multi-plug.
6. Ensure injector port is clean, If necessary, crank the engine a few revolutions to remove any loose carbon.

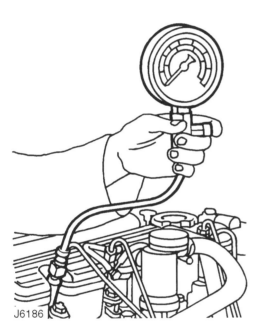

J6186

7. Fit dummy injector, from diesel compression tester kit **LRT-19-007**, into the cylinder head and clamp securely in position.
8. Connect flexible hose and gauge to dummy injector as shown above.
9. Crank engine for 10-20 seconds and note reading on gauge. The gauge will indicate the compression of the cylinder and maintain the reading until the pressure release valve on the gauge is depressed.
   Expected readings of a crank test, with vehicle battery fully charged, compression ratio 19.5:1 should be 24 bar (348 lbf/in$^2$).

10. Repeat test procedure for remaining clinders in turn.

> **NOTE: A variation in compression readings between cylinders is often a better indication of an engine problem than the absolute values of compression.**

11. If compression is appreciably less than correct reading, or varies by more than 10%, piston rings or valves may be worn or damaged. Low pressures in adjoining cylinders may indicate a faulty cylinder head gasket.

## ENGINE OIL PRESSURE TEST

**Service repair no - 12.90.09/01**

 **WARNING: Use suitable exhaust extraction equipment if an engine test is being carried out in a workshop.**

 **WARNING: If vehicle has been running, engine wil be hot; care must be taken when fitting test equipment to prevent personal injury.**

1. Check that engine lubricant is to correct level.
2. Remove oil pressure switch .

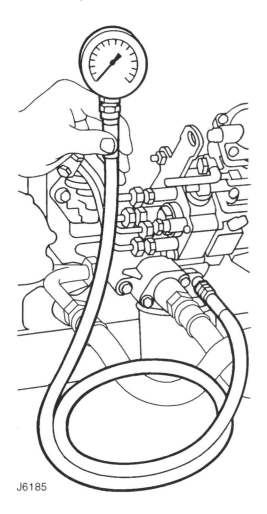

J6185

3. Connect pressure test gauge **LRT-12-052A**, as shown.
4. Start and run engine to normal operating temperature.
5. With engine running at idle check oil pressure, which should read 1.76 bar (25.87 lbf/in$^2$).

6. If pressure is low it can be caused by the following:-
   Thin or diluted oil.
   Low oil in sump.
   Choked oil strainer.
   Faulty oil pressure relief valve.
   Excessively worn or damaged oil pump displacement gears.
   Excessive crankshaft bearing clearance.
7. If excessive pressure is indicated it can be caused by :-
   Overfilling engine with lubricant.
   Sticking oil pressure relief valve.
   Blockage in breather system.

## ENGINE

Service repair no - 12.41.01

Remove

 NOTE: A chassis undertray may be fitted on some vehicle derivatives to conform to legal requirements. When under chassis remove and refit procedures are required, it may be necessary to remove the undertray and/or integral access panels.
*See CHASSIS AND BODY, Repair, Front undertray or Rear undertray*

 CAUTION: Seal all exposed pipe ends against ingress of dirt after disconnection.

1. Ensure vehicle is level and apply park brake.
2. Disconnect battery.

 NOTE: The vehicle may be fitted with an alarm and immobilisation system using a battery backed-up alarm sounder.
*See ELECTRICAL, Repair, battery*

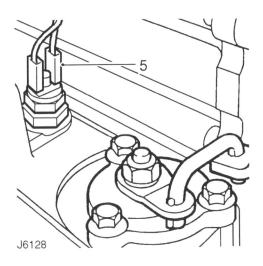

3. Remove bonnet.
4. Remove cable ties securing gearbox harness to breather pipes.
5. Disconnect harness from diff lock and reverse light switches.
6. Manouvre harness into engine bay.
7. Remove air cleaner. *See FUEL SYSTEM, Repair, Air cleaner*

8. Remove radiator assembly. *See COOLING SYSTEM, Repair, Radiator assembly*
If air conditioning is fitted the condenser will have to be removed, compressor pipes and heater matrix hoses disconnected.
*See AIR CONDITIONING, Repair, Condenser*
9. Remove rocker cover insulation.

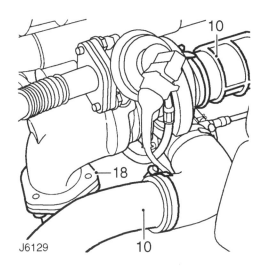

10. Remove feed pipe/hose from turbo-charger and intercooler.
11. Disconnect heater hoses from cylinder head and heater rails.

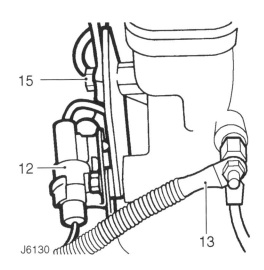

12. Disconnect electrical feed plug at rear of cylinder head.
13. Disconnect heater plug feed wire.

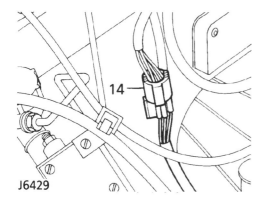

J6429

14. Disconnect engine harness multi-plug.
15. Remove single bolt securing transmission breather pipe clip to cylinder head and move breather pipes aside.

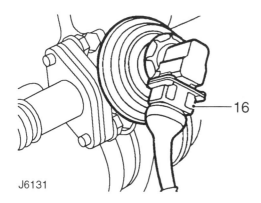

J6131

16. Disconnect multi-plug and vacuum pipe from EGR valve, if fitted.

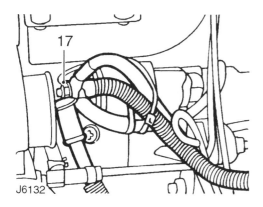

J6132

17. Remove starter motor cover and disconnect battery and fuse box leads.

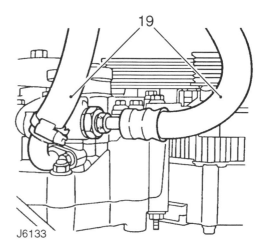

J6133

18. Remove 3 retaining nuts and disconnect exhaust down pipe.
19. Disconnect inlet and outlet hoses from power steering pump.
20. Disconnect bleed hose from thermostat housing.
21. Release bleed hose from retaining clips on front timing cover plate.

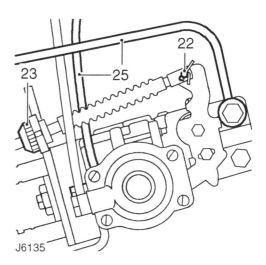

J6135

22. Remove split pin securing inner throttle cable to injector pump lever.
23. Depress tags on outer cable adjusting nut, remove cable from mounting bracket and move aside.
24. If fitted, release hand throttle cable from mounting bracket and injector pump lever and move aside.
25. Disconnect feed pipe and spill return pipe from injector pump.

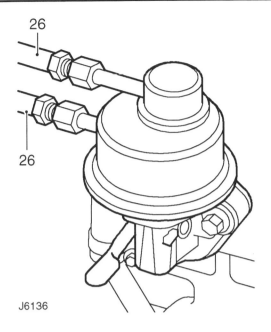

J6136

26. Disconnect both pipes from fuel lift pump.
27. Release fuel feed pipe from retaining clip on air cleaner bracket.

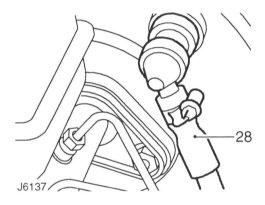

J6137

28. Disconnect vacuum hose from brake servo.

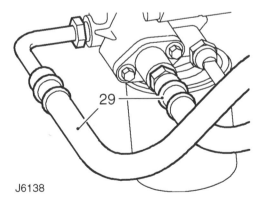

J6138

29. Remove oil pipes from oil filter adaptor.

30. Using suitable hoist, fit chains to lifting brackets and support engine.

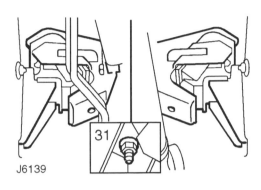

J6139

31. Remove nuts and plain washers securing front engine mountings to chassis.

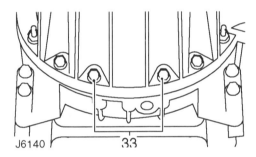

J6140

32. Support gearbox.
33. Remove engine to bell housing fixings, leaving starter motor attached to engine.
34. Carefully raise engine to release from gearbox.
35. Ensure all relevant connections to engine have been removed.
36. Remove engine.

**Refit**

37. Clean bell housing.
38. Apply Hylomar sealant to mating faces of bell housing and flywheel housing.
39. Lubricate splines of gearbox primary pinion with Rocol MV 3.
40. Carefully lower engine into position and locate primary pinion into clutch and engage bell housing dowels.
41. Fit engine to bell housing fixings. Tighten to *40 Nm (30 lbf/ft).*

42. Raise engine, and locate front engine mountings to chassis.
43. Remove gearbox support and lower engine.
44. Tighten front engine mounting to chassis fixings to **45 Nm (33 lbf/ft).**
45. Release chains from engine lifting brackets and remove hoist.
46. Connect oil cooler pipes to oil filter adaptor.
47. Fit vacuum hose to brake servo adaptor.
48. Secure fuel feed pipe in retaining clip on air cleaner bracket.
49. Fit fuel lift pump pipes.
50. Connect feed and spill return pipes to injector pump.
51. If fitted, reconnect hand throttle cable to mounting bracket and injector pump.
52. Fit outer cable adjusting nut into injector pump mounting bracket.
53. Fit inner throttle cable to injector pump and secure with clevis and split pin.
54. Secure bleed hose in retaining clips on front timing cover.
55. Fit bleed hose to thermostat housing.
56. Connect inlet and outlet hoses to power steering pump.
57. Fit down pipe to exhaust manifold and secure with 3 nuts.
58. Connect starter motor battery and fuse box leads.
59. If fitted, connect EGR valve multi-plug and vacuum pipe.
60. Secure breather pipe clip to cylinder head.
61. Connect engine harness multi-plug.
62. Fit heater plug feed wire.
63. Connect electrical feed plug at rear of cylinder head.
64. Fit heater hoses to cylinder head and heater rails.
65. Fit feed pipe/hose to turbo-charger and intercooler.
66. Fit rocker cover insulation.
67. Fit radiator assembly. **See COOLING SYSTEM, Repair, Radiator** If applicable, fit air conditioning condenser, compressor pipes and heater matrix hoses. **See AIR CONDITIONING, Repair, Condenser**
68. Fit bonnet.
69. Reconnect battery.

## CRANKSHAFT PULLEY

**Service repair no - 12.21.01**

**Remove**

1. Disconnect battery.
2. Drain coolant. **See COOLING SYSTEM, Repair, Drain and fill cooling system**
3. Remove top hose from radiator.
4. Remove intercooler to induction manifold hose.
5. Remove viscous coupling and fan. **See COOLING SYSTEM, Repair, Viscous coupling and fan**
6. Remove fan cowl. **See COOLING SYSTEM, Repair, Fan cowl**
7. Remove drive belt. **See ELECTRICAL, Repair, Auxiliary drive belt**

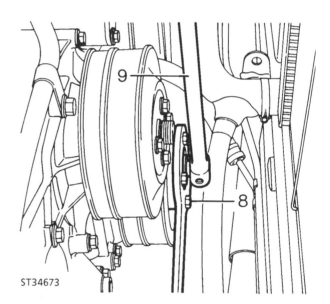

ST34673

8. Fit crankshaft pulley retainer **LRT-12-080** and secure with 4 bolts.
9. Remove crankshaft pulley retaining bolt anti-clockwise using socket and suitable long bar.
10. Remove pulley retainer.
11. Remove pulley, if necessary using extractor **LRT-12-049** with thrust pad from **LRT-12-031**.

**Refit**

12. Lightly grease pulley spigot and locate pulley onto cranshaft.
13. Fit pulley retaining bolt.
14. Fit pulley retainer **LRT-12-080** and secure with 4 bolts.
15. Tighten pulley nut to *80 Nm (59 lbf/ft)* + 90°.
16. Remove pulley retainer.
17. Fit drive belt. *See ELECTRICAL, Repair, Auxiliary drive belt renew*
18. Fit fan cowl. *See COOLING SYSTEM, Repair, Fan cowl*
19. Fit viscous coupling and fan. *See COOLING SYSTEM, Repair, Viscous coupling and fan*
20. Fit intercooler to induction manifold hose.
21. Fit radiator top hose.
22. Refill cooling system. *See COOLING SYSTEM, Repair, Drain and refill cooling system*
23. Reconnect battery.

## FRONT COVER PLATE AND SEAL

**Service repair no - 12.65.01**

**Remove**

1. Disconnect battery.
2. Drain coolant. *See COOLING SYSTEM, Repair, Drain and fill cooling system*
3. Remove top hose from radiator.
4. Remove intercooler to induction manifold hose.
5. Remove viscous coupling and fan. *See COOLING SYSTEM, Repair, Viscous coupling and fan*
6. Remove fan cowl. *See COOLING SYSTEM, Repair, Fan cowl*
7. Remove drive belt. *See ELECTRICAL, Repair, Auxiliary drive belt*
8. Remove crankshaft pulley. *See Crankshaft pulley*
9. Remove 14 bolts securing front cover plate. Note that top 2 bolts also retain thermostat hose clips.
10. Remove cover plate complete with gasket.
11. Remove small gasket from centre bolt boss.

**Seal replacement**

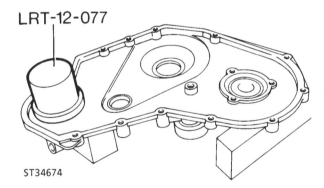

LRT-12-077

ST34674

12. Remove worn seal from cover and clean recess.
13. Support cover and fit new seal, open side fitted into recess, using special tool **LRT-12-077**.

## Refit

14. Fit gasket to centre bolt boss.
15. Locate new gasket and fit front cover plate using fixing bolts as shown. Tighten bolts to **25 Nm (18 lbf/ft).**

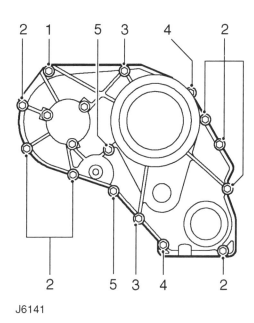

J6141

**1** - 25 mm, **2** - 35 mm, **3** - 50 mm, **4** - 100 mm, **5** - 110 mm

16. Fit crankshaft pulley. **See Crankshaft pulley**
17. Fit drive belt. **See ELECTRICAL, Repair, Auxiliary drive belt**
18. Fit fan cowl. **See COOLING SYSTEM, Repair, Fan cowl**
19. Fit viscous coupling and fan. **See COOLING SYSTEM, Repair, Viscous coupling and fan**
20. Fit intercooler to induction manifold hose.
21. Fit top hose to radiator.
22. Refill cooling system. **See COOLING SYSTEM, Repair, Drain and refill cooling system**
23. Reconnect battery.

## CAMSHAFT DRIVE BELT

**Service repair no - 12.65.18**

**Remove**

1. Remove front cover plate. **See Front cover plate**
2. Position engine at TDC on No. 1 cylinder.

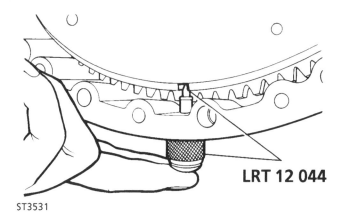

ST3531

3. Remove blanking plug from flywheel housing and insert timing tool **LRT-12-044.**
4. Engage timing tool pin with slot in flywheel.

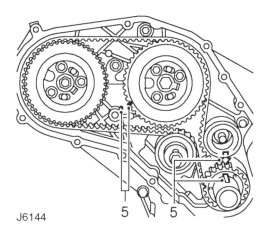

J6144

5. Check correct alignment of timing mark on camshaft gear and that crankshaft key aligns with cast arrow on housing.
6. Insert pin from special tool **LRT-12-045** in injection pump gear and through into pump flange.

NOTE: If the camshaft gear is to be removed during these operations its retaining bolt should be slackened before the timing belt is removed.

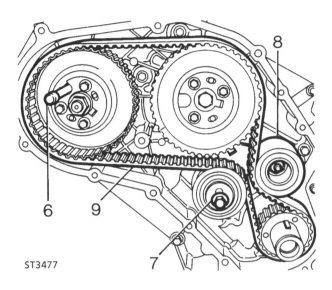

ST3477

7. Slacken belt tensioner bolt.
8. Remove idler pulley.
9. Remove timing belt.

NOTE: If excessive timing belt debris is evident in the front cover, this is probably due to the misalignment of the front timing cover caused by incorrect assembly of the fuel injection pump bracket. *See FUEL SYSTEM, Repair, Injector pump*

NOTE: During use, a belt develops a wear pattern relative to its running direction, if the original belt is to be re-used it must be refitted so that it rotates in the original direction. Mark belt direction of rotation, using soft chalk, to ensure correct refitment.

CAUTION: The belt must be stored on its edge on a clean surface and in such a manner that bends are not less than 50 mm (2.0in.) radius. Do not bend belts at an acute angle, otherwise premature failure could result.

Belt tensioner

NOTE: The belt tensioner need only be removed if it is being replaced or for access purposes to remove front cover.

10. Remove securing bolt and withdraw tensioner complete with spacer.

Refit

11. If necessary, fit belt tensioner and spacer. Tighten fixing bolt to *45 Nm (33lbf/ft).*

Timing belt fitting and tensioning

NOTE: It is important that belt tensioning is carried out carefully and accurately. The following procedure involves tensioning the belt twice to ensure that it is equally tensioned between each gear. New and original belts are tensioned to different figures.

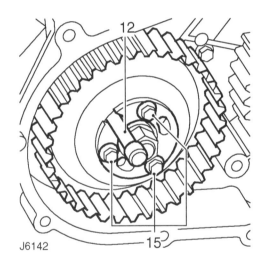

J6142

12. Ensure timing marks are correctly aligned, pin from special tool **LRT-12-045** is correctly inserted in injection pump gear and timing tool **LRT-12-044** is fitted to flywheel housing with pin located in flywheel slot.
13. Fit belt, observing rotational marks made during removal. Feed belt over gears keeping it tight on drive side.
14. Fit idler pulley.
15. Slacken injection pump gear retaining bolts.
16. Adjust belt to correctly sit in gears.

**17.** Slacken belt tensioner securing bolt to finger tight.
**18.** Insert 13 mm square drive extension bar in tensioner plate.

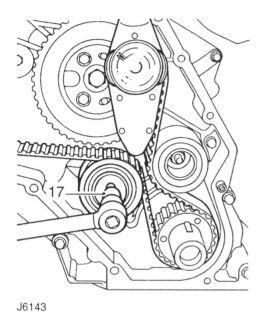

J6143

⚠ NOTE: Belt tensioning should be carried out using a dial type torque meter having a range not exceeding **60 Nm (44 lbf/ft)**. The torque meter should be used in the almost vertical position.

**19.** Apply a tension of **15 Nm (11 lbf/ft)** for a new belt or **12 Nm (9 lbf/ft)** for an original belt. When tension is correct, tighten clamp bolt.
**20.** Tighten injection pump gear bolts.
**21.** Remove pin from injection pump gear.
**22.** Disengage timing pin from timing slot in flywheel or ring gear.
**23.** Rotate crankshaft one and three quarter turns in a clockwise direction; then continue rotation until timing pin in timing tool can be engaged with slot in flywheel.
**24.** Disengage timing pin.
**25.** Insert pin from special tool **LRT-12-045** in injection pump gear and through into pump flange.
**26.** Slacken injection pump gear retaining bolts.
**27.** Slacken tensioner and retension belt.
**28.** Tighten injection pump gear retaining bolts.
**29.** Remove pin from injection pump gear.
**30.** Remove timing tool and refit plug.
**31.** Fit front cover plate using new gaskets.
*See Front cover plate and seal*

## CRANKSHAFT GEAR

**Service repair no - 12.65.25**

**Remove**

1. Remove camshaft drive belt. *See Camshaft drive belt*

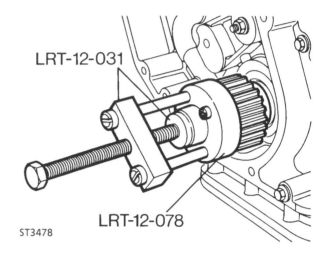

LRT-12-031

LRT-12-078

ST3478

2. If the crankshaft gear cannot be removed by hand, use special tool **LRT-12-078** with main body and thrust button from special tool **LRT-12-031**, as illustrated . Withdraw gear complete with 'O' ring seal.

**Refit**

3. Lubricate new 'O' ring seal with petroleum jelly and slide onto crankshaft, taking care not to damage seal on woodruff keys.
4. Fit crankshaft gear and tap fully home ensuring 'O' ring seal is properly seated.
5. Fit camshaft drive belt. *See Camshaft drive belt*

## CRANKSHAFT OIL SEAL

**Service repair no - 12.21.14**

**Remove**

1. Remove crankshaft gear. *See Crankshaft gear*
2. Prise out oil seal from front cover.

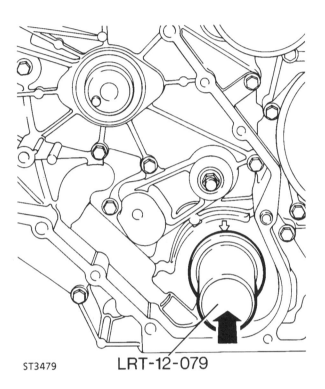

ST3479          LRT-12-079

**Refit**

3. Lubricate a new crankshaft oil seal with clean engine oil.
4. With lip side leading, drive in seal squarely using special tool **LRT-12-079**.
5. Fit crankshaft gear. *See Crankshaft gear*

## CAMSHAFT GEAR

**Service repair no - 12.65.24**

**Remove**

1. Remove camshaft drive belt. *See Camshaft drive belt*

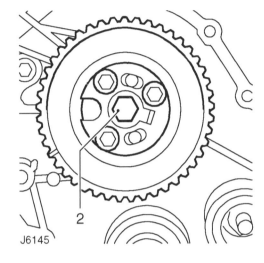

J6145

2. Remove centre bolt and withdraw camshaft gear, complete with hub and retaining plate.

**Refit**

3. Fit camshaft gear. Tighten bolt to *80 Nm (59 lbf/ft)* .
4. Fit camshaft drive belt. *See Camshaft drive belt*

## CAMSHAFT OIL SEAL

**Service repair no - 12.13.05**

**Remove**

1. Remove camshaft gear. *See Camshaft gear*

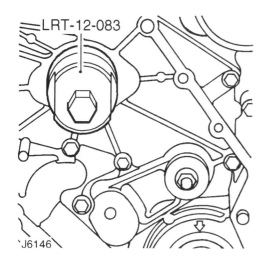

LRT-12-083

J6146

2. Remove camshaft oil seal from front cover using special tool **LRT-12-083**.

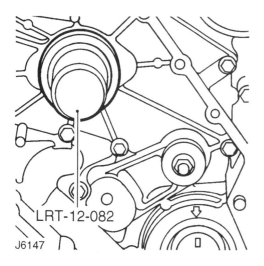

LRT-12-082

J6147

**Refit**

3. Lubricate a new camshaft oil seal with clean engine oil.
4. With lip side leading, drive in seal squarely using special tool **LRT-12-082**.
5. Fit camshaft gear. *See Camshaft gear*

## INJECTION PUMP GEAR

**Service repair no - 19.30.06**

**Remove**

1. Remove camshaft drive belt. *See Camshaft drive belt*

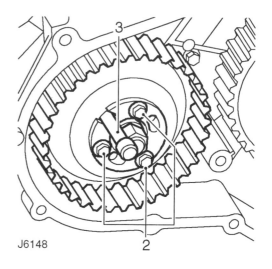

J6148

2. Slacken 3 bolts on front of injector pump gear.
3. Remove special tool pin from gear.
4. Remove 3 bolts and withdraw gear and retaining plate.

**Refit**

⚠ **CAUTION: It is important to ensure that when the injection pump is locked no attempt must be made to rotate it. Take care not to allow the crankshaft to be turned.**

5. Fit gear and retaining plate. Tighten bolts to **25 Nm (18 lbf/ft).**
6. Insert pin from special tool **LRT-12-045** in injection pump gear and through into pump flange.
7. Fit camshaft drive belt. *See Camshaft drive belt*

## FRONT COVER GASKET

**Service repair no - 12.65.10**

**Remove**

1. Remove camshaft drive belt. *See  Camshaft drive belt*
2. Remove crankshaft gear. *See  Crankshaft gear*
3. Remove camshaft gear. *See  Camshaft gear*
4. Remove injection pump gear. *See  Injection pump gear*
5. Remove fuel injection pump. *See FUEL SYSTEM, Repair,  Fuel injection pump*
6. Remove engine oil sump. *See  Engine oil sump*
7. Remove oil pick up strainer. *See  Oil pick-up strainer*
8. Remove 10 bolts securing timing gear housing to block.
9. Withdraw timing gear housing complete with gasket.
10. Clean all gasket material from mating faces.

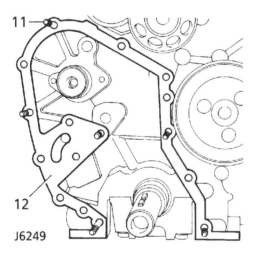

J6249

**Refit**

11. Fit slave guide studs to locate gasket.
12. Fit new gasket to cylinder block.
13. Align flats on oil pump with flats on crankshaft.
14. Fit front cover to block taking care not to damage oil seal.

15. Secure with bolts of correct length in locations where slave studs are not fitted, see J6149 .
16. Remove slave studs and fit correct length bolts.
17. Tighten all bolts to *25 Nm (18 lbf/ft).*

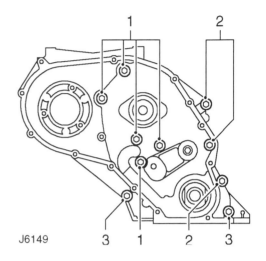

J6149

1 - 25 mm, **2** - 35 mm, **3** - 80 mm.

18. Fit oil pick-up strainer. *See  Oil pick-up strainer*
19. Fit oil sump. *See  Engine oil sump*
20. Fit fuel injection pump. *See FUEL SYSTEM, Repair,  Fuel injection pump*
21. Fit injection pump gear. *See  Injection pump gear*
22. Fit camshaft gear. *See  Camshaft gear*
23. Fit crankshaft gear. *See  Crankshaft gear*
24. Fit camshaft drive belt. *See  Camshaft drive belt*

## ENGINE OIL SUMP

**Service repair no - 12.60.44**

**Remove**

1. Disconnect battery.
2. Drain engine oil.

⚠ **NOTE: A chassis undertray may be fitted on some vehicle derivatives to conform to legal requirements. When under chassis remove and refit procedures are required, it may be necessary to remove the undertray and/or integral access panels.**
*See CHASSIS AND BODY, Repair, Front undertray or Rear undertray*

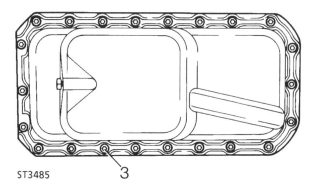

ST3485

3. Slacken sump securing bolts.
4. Break sealant around sump flange, using a sharp knife.
5. Remove 22 bolts and withdraw sump.

**Refit**

6. Clean mating faces of sump, timing gear housing and cylinder block.
7. Apply a 2,0 mm bead of 'Hylosil RTV102' to the sump flange, ensuring bead is applied inboard of the bolt holes.
8. Secure sump to block with 22bolts. Tighten to *25 Nm (18 lbf/ft).*
9. Refill engine oil. *See LUBRICANTS, FLUIDS AND CAPACITIES, Information, Lubricants, fluids and capacities*
10. Reconnect battery.

## OIL PICK-UP STRAINER

**Service repair no - 12.60.20**

**Remove**

1. Disconnect battery.
2. Drain engine oil.
3. Remove engine oil sump. *See Engine oil sump*

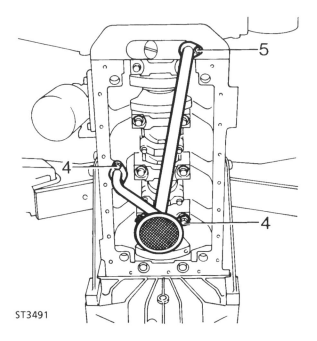

ST3491

4. Remove 2 bolts securing pipe support bracket to main bearing cap fixings.
5. Remove bolts from pipe flanges.
6. Withdraw pick-up strainer assembly.

**Refit**

7. Postion pick-up strainer assembly, fitting a new 'O' ring seal at oil pump connection.
8. Apply Loctite 242E to threads of bolts at main bearing cap. Fit bolts, tighten to *9 Nm (7 lbf/ft).*
9. Fit bolts to pipe flanges. Tighten to *25 Nm (18 lbf/ft).*
10. Fit sump. *See Engine oil sump*
11. Reconnect battery.

## FLYWHEEL

**Service repair no - 12.53.07**

**Remove**

1. Disconnect battery.
2. Remove gearbox. *See MANUAL GEARBOX, Repair, R380 gearbox*
3. Remove clutch. *See CLUTCH, Repair, Clutch assembly*

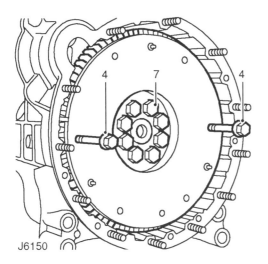

J6150

4. Fit 2, long, 8 mm bolts into the clutch bolt holes, as shown, to use as handles when lifting the flywheel off the crankshaft.
5. Remove fan cowl. *See COOLING SYSTEM, Repair, Fan cowl*
6. Fit crankshaft pulley retainer **LRT-12-080** and secure with 4 bolts, to restrain crankshaft while removing flywheel retaining bolts.
7. Remove bolts and lift off flywheel.

**Refit**

⚠ NOTE: To prevent excessive flywheel run-out, ensure that mating faces of flywheel and crankshaft are clean.

8. Locate flywheel on crankshaft, remove lifting bolts, and secure flywheel with new patched retaining bolts, progressively tighten to *147 Nm (108 lbf/ft).*

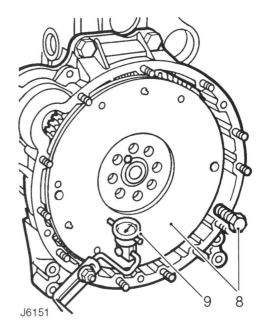

J6151

9. Check the flywheel for possible run-out by mounting a dial test indicator with the stylus in a loaded condition resting on the flywheel face at a radius of 114 mm (4.50 in.) from the centre.
10. Turn flywheel and check that run-out does not exceed 0,07 mm (0.003 in).
11. Should run-out be excessive, remove flywheel and check again for irregularities on crankshaft and flywheel mating faces and location dowel.
12. Remove crankshaft pulley retainer.
13. Fit fan cowl. *See COOLING SYSTEM, Repair, Fan cowl*
14. Fit clutch. *See CLUTCH, Repair, Clutch assembly*
15. Fit gearbox. *See MANUAL GEARBOX, Repair, R380 gearbox*
16. Reconnect battery.

## CRANKSHAFT REAR OIL SEAL

Service repair no - 12.21.20

Remove

⚠ NOTE: The crankshaft rear oil seal is retained in its own housing, if the seal requires replacing, the complete housing assembly (1) must be renewed. Housing and seal assemblies are supplied with their own former/seal guide (2) already fitted. This former must not be removed before fitting the assembly to the engine. If a seal and housing assembly is received without a former/guide fitted it must be returned to the supplier. Used formers/guides must be discarded immediately after use, under no circumstances should they be reused on other assemblies.

⚠ NOTE: A different rear oil seal housing, with integral 'O' ring seal and gasket, was fitted on earlier engines. They must be replaced with the current housing and gasket (3) shown below.

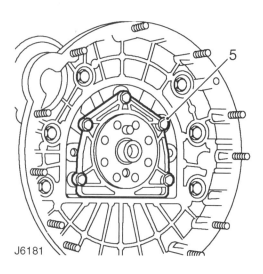

J6181

Refit

⚠ NOTE: The raised side of groove at the bottom of seal housing gasket must be fitted to cylinder block face.

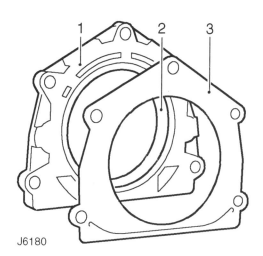

J6180

1. Disconnect battery.
2. Remove gearbox. *See MANUAL GEARBOX, Repair, R380 gearbox*
3. Remove clutch. *See CLUTCH, Repair, Clutch assembly*
4. Remove flywheel. *See Flywheel*
5. Remove 5 bolts and withdraw seal housing, complete with gasket.

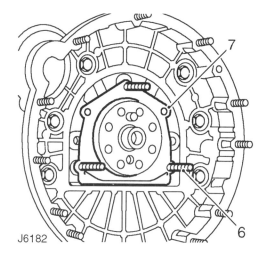

J6182

6. Insert slave studs to locate seal housing gasket.
7. Position new gasket over slave studs and crankshaft flange onto cylinder block.
8. Fit new seal housing assembly, with former/guide in-situ, over crankshaft flange. This action will eject former/guide.
9. Secure assembly to cylinder block, removing slave studs individually and inserting bolts. Tighten to *25 Nm (18 lbf/ft)*.
10. Refit flywheel. *See Flywheel*

11. Refit clutch. *See CLUTCH, Repair, Clutch assembly*
12. Refit gearbox. *See MANUAL GEARBOX, Repair, R380 gearbox*
13. Reconnect battery.

---

### CRANKSHAFT BEARING BUSH

**Service repair no - 12.21.45**

**Remove**

1. Disconnect battery.
2. Remove gearbox. *See MANUAL GEARBOX, Repair, R380 gearbox*
3. Remove clutch. *See CLUTCH, Repair, Clutch assembly*

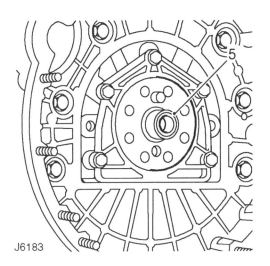

J6183

4. Remove flywheel. *See Flywheel*
5. Remove bearing bush.

 **NOTE: The bearing bush can be removed by using one of the following methods.**

**Method 1.**

Obtain a short length of steel rod of a diameter having a good slide fit in the bore of the bush. Pack the bore with grease and insert the steel rod into the end of the bore, give a sharp blow with a hammer and the grease should drive out the bush. It is recommended that the bush and rod be covered by a suitable cloth or rag to prevent grease from splashing.

**Method 2.**

Thread the bore of the existing bush and using a suitable bolt extract the bush. Thoroughly clean bush location ensuring all swarf is removed.

**Refit**

1. Fit new bush using a suitable shouldered drift, inserting bush flush with end of crankshaft.
2. Refit flywheel. *See Flywheel*
3. Refit clutch. *See CLUTCH, Repair, Clutch assembly*
4. Refit gearbox. *See MANUAL GEARBOX, Repair, R380 gearbox*
5. Reconnect battery.

## FLYWHEEL HOUSING

**Service repair no - 12.53.01**

**Remove**

1. Disconnect battery.
2. Remove gearbox. *See MANUAL GEARBOX, Repair, R380 gearbox*
3. Remove clutch. *See CLUTCH, Repair, Clutch assembly*
4. Remove flywheel. *See Flywheel*
5. Remove 3 fixings and withdraw starter motor.

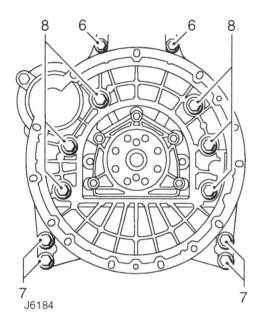

J6184

6. Remove 2 bolts from top of flywheel housing.
7. Remove 4 bolts securing bottom of flywheel housing to engine mounting brackets.
8. Remove inner bolts and lift off flywheel housing.

**Refit**

9. Clean rear face of housing and mating face on block, ensuring all old sealant is removed.

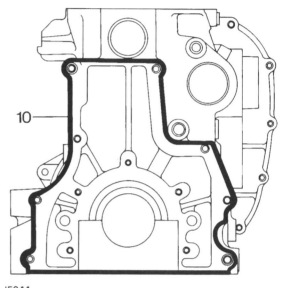

J5944

10. Apply sealant to flywheel housing mating face on cylinder block.
11. Fit housing to cylinder block. Tighten retaining bolts to *45 Nm (33 lbf/ft).*
12. Remove surplus sealant from block.
13. Fit starter motor.
14. Fit flywheel. *See Flywheel*
15. Fit clutch. *See CLUTCH, Repair, Clutch assembly*
16. Fit gearbox. *See MANUAL GEARBOX, Repair, R380 gearbox*
17. Reconnect battery.

## OIL FILTER

**Service repair no - 12.60.01**

**Remove**

1. Place drain tray under oil filter.
2. Unscrew filter anti-clockwise, using a strap wrench, if necessary.

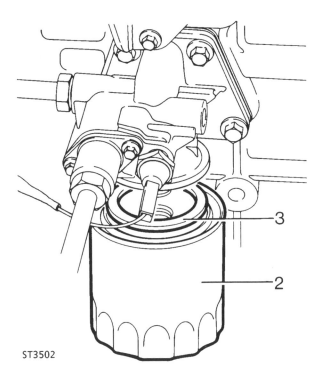

ST3502

**Refit**

3. Clean mating face of oil filter adaptor.
4. Coat rubber sealing ring of new filter with clean engine oil.
5. Screw on filter until sealing ring touches machined face, then tighten a further half turn by hand only. DO NOT over tighten.

## OIL TEMPERATURE CONTROL VALVE

**Service repair no - 12.60.69**

**Remove**

1. Clean adaptor housing.
2. Disconnect oil cooler feed pipe from thermostat extension housing and plug to prevent ingress of dirt.

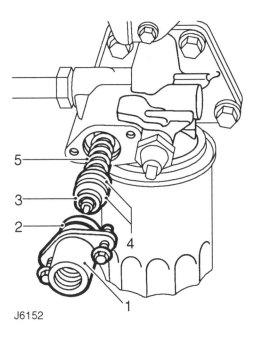

J6152

3. Remove 2 bolts and carefully withdraw thermostat extension housing (1) complete with 'O' ring seal (2), thermostat (3), 2 washers (4) and spring (5).
4. Inspect all parts and renew as necessary.

**Refit**

5. Fit thermostat to extension housing ensuring pin locates in hole.
6. Fit two washers and spring to thermostat.
7. Fit a new 'O' ring to extension housing.
8. Insert spring into adaptor and secure extension housing to adaptor. Tighten bolts to *9 Nm (7 lbf/ft).*

## OIL FILTER HEAD GASKET

**Service repair no - 12.60.03**

**Remove**

1. Clean filter head adaptor.
2. Disconnect oil cooler pipes and plug to prevent ingress of dirt.
3. Disconnect oil pressure switch lead.

J6153

4. Remove 4 bolts and withdraw filter head, complete with gasket.
5. Clean mating faces of filter head and cylinder block.
6. Fit head with new gasket.
7. Tighten bolts to *45 Nm (33 lbf/ft).*
8. Reconnect oil pressure switch lead.
9. Reconnect oil cooler pipes.

## CYLINDER HEAD GASKET

**Service repair no - 12.29.02**

**Remove**

1. Disconnect battery
2. Remove bonnet.
3. Drain coolant. *See COOLING SYSTEM, Repair, Drain and refill coolant*
4. Remove air cleaner. *See FUEL SYSTEM, Repair, Air cleaner*

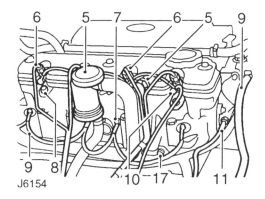

J6154

5. Detach crankcase ventilation valve and side breather hose from rocker cover and move to one side.
6. Remove fuel injectors and pipes. *See FUEL SYSTEM, Repair, Fuel injectors*
7. Remove heater plugs. *See FUEL SYSTEM, Repair, Heater plugs*

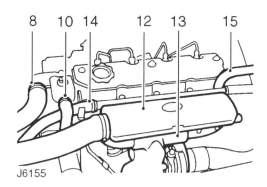

J6155

8. Disconnect radiator top hose from thermostat.
9. Disconnect bleed hose at thermostat.
10. Disconnect water pump hose at thermostat.
11. Disconnect water temperature sensor lead.

12. Remove induction manifold. *See MANIFOLD
AND EXHAUST SYSTEM, Repair, Induction
manifold*

13. Remove exhaust manifold and turbocharger
assembly.
*See MANIFOLD AND EXHAUST SYSTEM,
Repair, Exhaust manifold*

14. Disconnect heater hose from water pump and
move heater rail aside.

15. Disconnect heater hose from rear of cylinder
head.

16. Remove bolt securing air cleaner mounting
bracket to support strut.

17. Remove bolt securing harness bracket to
cylinder head.

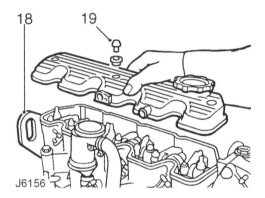

18. Remove rear engine lifting bracket. This will also
release clips securing transmission and engine
breather pipes and multi-plug. Note loose spacer
beneath inner clip.

19. Unscrew 3 bolts, with sealing washers and
remove rocker cover.

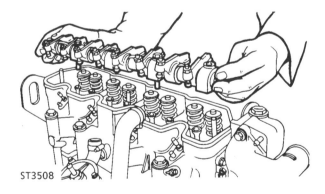

20. Remove 3 nuts and 2 bolts and lift rocker shaft
assembly from cylinder head.

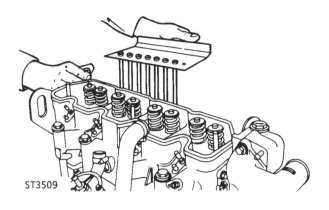

21. Remove push rods and store as an identified set
to allow refitment to same location.

22. Remove valve stem caps.

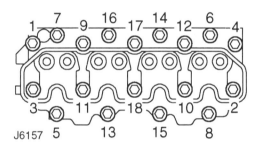

23. Evenly slacken and then remove cylinder head
to block retaining bolts in the sequence shown in
J6157. Two of the bolts also secure the air
cleaner mounting bracket.

24. Lift off cylinder head and remove gasket.

**Refit**

25. Thoroughly clean mating faces of cylinder block
and head.

26. Select new gasket of correct thickness.

⚠ **CAUTION: Three gaskets, of different
thicknesses, are available and can be
identified by the number of small holes
punched in the RH side of the gasket. One hole
identifies the thinnest gasket, two holes the
middle thickness and three holes the thickest.
When renewing a gasket it must be of the same
thickness as the one removed.**

27. Position gasket on cylinder block with
identification holes on RH side and TOP
identification mark uppermost.

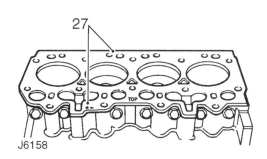

J6158

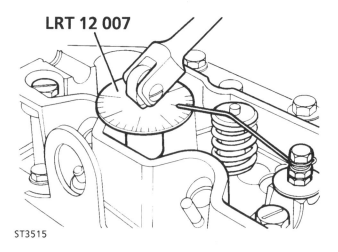

**LRT 12 007**

ST3515

28. Lower cylinder head onto block ensuring correct location with dowels.

 **NOTE: Cylinder head retaining bolts can be used up to a maximum of five times.**

29. Lubricate threads of bolts with light oil and fit to positions shown below. (Fit air cleaner mounting bracket at positions 6 and 14).

**Bolt sizes:**

M10 x 117mm locations 3, 5, 12, and 13.

M12 x 140mm locations 1, 2, 7, 8, 9, 10, 15, 16, 17, and 18.

M12 x 100mm locations 4, 6, 11, 14.

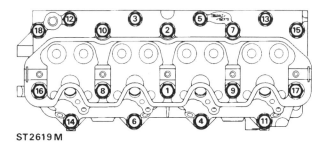

ST2619M

30. Tighten bolts so that underside of heads just make contact with cylinder head.
31. Following the sequence indicated, tighten all bolts to *40 Nm (30 lbf/ft)*.

32. Attach angle gauge **LRT-12-007**.
33. Make a suitable pointer from welding rod and attach to a bolt screwed into a rocker shaft securing bolt hole.
34. Tighten all bolts through 60°strictly in sequence illustrated.
35. Repeat 60°tightening procedure, again strictly in sequence illustrated.
36. Tighten the 10 longer bolts (M12 x 140mm) a further 20°, again following the sequence illustrated.

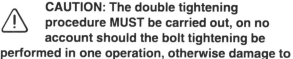 **NOTE: Repositioning of the pointer will be necessary to reach all bolts, the pointer can be fitted to the rocker shaft securing studs using 2 nuts.**

**CAUTION: The double tightening procedure MUST be carried out, on no account should the bolt tightening be performed in one operation, otherwise damage to the cylinder head may occur.**

37. Fit valve stem caps.
38. Fit push rods to locations from which they were removed.
39. Position rocker shaft assembly over locating studs and fit retaining nuts and bolts, but do not tighten at this stage.
40. Attach angle gauge **LRT-12-007**.
41. Make a suitable pointer and attach to one of the rocker shaft locating studs.
42. Tighten all fixings in turn to *5 Nm (4 lbf/ft)*. Then tighten a further 50°in same sequence.

 **NOTE: Repositioning of the pointer will be necessary to reach all fixings.**

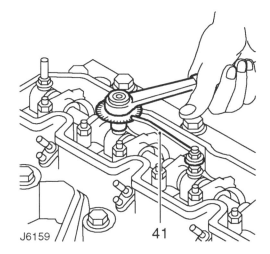

J6159       41

43. Check and adjust valve clearances.
*See Adjustment, Valve clearances - check and adjust*

44. Fit rocker cover, ensuring oil seal is satisfactory for continued use, and renew if necessary.

45. Secure rocker cover with special seal washers and nuts. Tighten to **10 Nm (7 lbf/ft).**

46. Fit rear engine lifting bracket, securing breather pipe and multi-plug retaining clips. Tighten fixing bolts to **25 Nm (18 lbf/ft).**

47. Fit engine harness bracket to cylinder head.

48. Secure air cleaner mounting bracket to support strut.

49. Connect heater hose to rear of cylinder head.

50. Position heater rail and connect hose from water pump.

51. Fit exhaust manifold and turbocharger assembly. *See MANIFOLD AND EXHAUST SYSTEM, Repair, Exhaust manifold*

52. Fit induction manifold. *See MANIFOLD AND EXHAUST SYSTEM, Repair, Induction manifold*

53. Connect water temperature sensor lead.

54. Connect water pump hose at thermostat.

55. Fit bleed hose at thermostat.

56. Connect radiator top hose at thermostat.

57. Fit heater plugs. *See FUEL SYSTEM, Repair, Heater plugs*

58. Fit fuel injectors. *See FUEL SYSTEM, Repair, Fuel injectors*

59. Fit crankcase ventilation valve and side breather hose.

60. Fit air cleaner. *See FUEL SYSTEM, Repair, Air cleaner*

61. Refill cooling system. *See COOLING SYSTEM, Repair, Drain and refill cooling system*

62. Fit bonnet.

63. Reconnect battery.

## OIL PUMP

**Service repair no - 12.60.26**

**Remove**

1. Remove engine front cover. *See Front cover gasket*

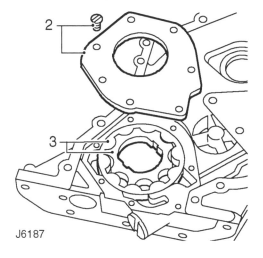

J6187

2. Remove 7 screws and release oil pump retaining plate from engine front cover.

3. Mark oil pump inner gear rotor, outer gear rotor and front cover housing for reassembly.

4. Check for rotor clearances:
   Outer rotor to housing, 0,025 - 0,075 mm (0.010 - 0.030 in).
   Inner rotor to outer rotor, 0,025 - 0,075 mm (0.010 - 0.030 in).
   Rotor end float, 0,026 - 0,135 mm (0.010 - 0.054 in).

5. Remove inner and outer rotors.

6. Check condition of oil pump components.

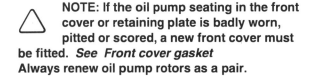 **NOTE: If the oil pump seating in the front cover or retaining plate is badly worn, pitted or scored, a new front cover must be fitted.** *See Front cover gasket*
**Always renew oil pump rotors as a pair.**

7. Clean sealant from pump retaining plate and front cover.

## Refit

8. Fit oil pump rotors in front cover.
9. Apply a bead of RTV sealant around retaining plate.
10. Fit oil pump retaining plate to front cover, securely tighten screws.
11. Fit front cover to cylinder block. *See Front cover gasket*

## OIL PRESSURE RELIEF VALVE

**Service repair no - 12.60.56**

### Remove

1. Remove engine oil sump. *See Engine oil sump*

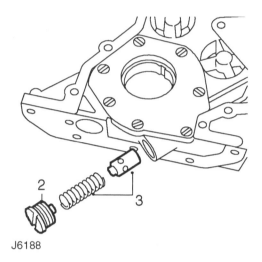

J6188

2. Unscrew relief valve retaining plug from base of front cover.
3. Withdraw valve spring and plunger and check for wear.
   Valve spring free length, 68.00 mm (2.68 in).

 **NOTE: If the valve plunger sleeve is badly worn, pitted or scored, a new front cover must be fitted.** *See Front cover gasket*
**Always renew valve spring and plunger as a pair.**

### Refit

4. Insert valve plunger and spring into sleeve in front cover and secure with retaining plug.
5. Fit engine oil sump. *See Engine oil sump*

---

## TORQUE VALUES

 **NOTE: Torque wrenches should be regularly checked for accuracy to ensure that all fixings are tightened to the correct torque.**

**Nm**

**Engine block**

Bearing cap .................................................................................. 133
Blanking plug, oil gallery, rear ..................................................... 37
Oil squirt jet assembly ................................................................. 17
Drain plug, cylinder block ............................................................ 25
Oil squirt jet, vacuum pump cam ................................................... 7
Connecting rod to cap .................................................................. 59
Oil pick up assembly to bearing cap .............................................. 9
Oil pick up assembly to front cover .............................................. 25
Camshaft thrust plate .................................................................... 9
Oil drain pipe to block (internal) ................................................. 25
Oil drain pipe to block (external) ................................................. 25
Sump to cylinder block and front cover ....................................... 25
Drain plug, oil sump .................................................................... 35
Tappet guide ............................................................................... 14
Breather side cover assembly ...................................................... 25
Baffle plate to breather side cover ................................................ 4
Vacuum pump .............................................................................. 25
Fuel lift pump .............................................................................. 25
Flywheel housing ......................................................................... 45
Flywheel housing clutch cover stud ............................................. 10
Plug, flywheel housing ................................................................ 12
Rear oil seal assembly ................................................................. 25
Oil filter adaptor .......................................................................... 45
Waxstat adaptor to oil filter adaptor .............................................. 9
Oil pressure switch ...................................................................... 17
Oil filter, spin on ......................................................................... 13
Oil cooler unions to filter adaptor ................................................ 45
Oil level tube ............................................................................... 25
Engine mounting foot to cylinder block ........................................ 85
Engine mounting foot to flywheel housing .................................... 45
Engine mounting foot rubber to mounting foot (bolt and nut) ...... 85

Flywheel to crankshaft ............................................................... 146
Clutch cover plate to flywheel ..................................................... 34
Flex drive plate to crankshaft (auto) .......................................... 146
Flex drive plate to ring gear (auto) .............................................. 25
Flex drive plate to torque converter (auto) ................................... 45

---

**Nm**

**Cylinder head**

Cylinder head to cylinder block
M10 x 117 ................................................................... 40 Nm + 60°
M12 x 100 ................................................................... 40 Nm + 60°
M12 x 140 ............................................................. 40 Nm + 60°+ 20°
Stub pipe heater feed ................................................ 22
Water temperature sensor .......................................... 14
Blanking plug cylinder head ....................................... 14
Engine lifting brackets .............................................. 25
Electrical harness clip bracket ................................... 25
Exhaust manifold stud .............................................. 10
Exhaust manifold nut ................................................ 45
Inlet manifold stud ..................................................... 8
Inlet manifold nut and bolt ........................................ 25
Air temperature sensor, inlet manifold ....................... 14
Blanking plug, inlet manifold ..................................... 14
Heatshield to inlet manifold ....................................... 6
Glow plug ................................................................ 20
Glow plug terminal nut .............................................. 2
Injector clamp (stud) ................................................. 8
Injector clamp (nut) .................................................. 25
Thermostat housing .................................................. 25
Water outlet elbow to thermostat housing ................... 25
Water temperature switch, thermostat housing ............ 11
Plug thermostat housing ............................................ 6
Rocker shaft pedestal bolt ..................................... 5 Nm + 50°
Rocker cover (stud) ................................................... 8
Rocker cover (fixing nut) ........................................... 10
Breather cyclone to rocker cover ............................... 9
Tappet adjusting nut ................................................. 16

Front cover to cylinder block ..................................... 25
Front cover plate to front cover ................................. 25
Static idler - timing belt (stud) .................................. 10
Static idler - timing belt (nut) ................................... 45
Tensioner (timing belt) .............................................. 45
Camshaft hub bolt .................................................... 80
Timing pulley to camshaft hub ................................... 25
Fuel injection pump (stud) ......................................... 8
Fuel injection pump (nut) ........................................... 25
Abutment bracket to injection pump ........................... 25
Support bracket injection pump to cylinder block ......... 25
Fuel injection pump access plate to front cover plate .... 25
Timing pulley to injection pump hub ........................... 25
TV Damper pulley bolt to crankshaft ..................... 80 Nm + 90°
Fan pulley to hub ..................................................... 25
Fan and viscous coupling to hub ................................ 45
Auto tensioner, auxiliary drive (stud) .......................... 14
Auto tensioner, auxiliary drive (nut) ........................... 45

Auxiliary mounting bracket to cylinder block (stud) ...... 8
Auxiliary mounting bracket to cylinder block (bolt and nut) ... 25
Water pump to block and mounting plate ..................... 25
Water pump pulley to hub .......................................... 25

Nm

Turbo charger oil drain adaptor to block ...................................................... 42
Oil drain pipe to turbocharger ........................................................................ 25
Turbocharger oil drain pipe to adaptor ......................................................... 38
Turbocharger oil feed pipe adaptor to block .................................................. 25
Turbocharger oil feed pipe to adaptor ........................................................... 25
Oil feed pipe to turbocharger ......................................................................... 19
Turbocharger to cylinder head (stud) ........................................................... 10
Turbocharger to cylinder head (nut) .............................................................. 45
Turbocharger to blanking plate ...................................................................... 25
Turbocharger to EGR valve ............................................................................ 25
EGR delivery tube to valve ............................................................................. 25
EGR delivery tube to mixing tube .................................................................. 25

Fuel lift pump to filter (union) ........................................................................ 15
Fuel filter from lift pump (banjo bolt) ............................................................ 33
Fuel filter to fuel injection pump (banjo bolt) ............................................... 33
Fuel injection pump from fuel filter (banjo bolt) ........................................... 25
Injector pipes to injectors and fuel injection pump ...................................... 29
Spill rail to injectors (banjo bolt) ................................................................... 10
Spill rail to injection pump (banjo bolt) ......................................................... 25
Boost pipe injection pump (banjo bolt) .......................................................... 10
Plug, rear of injection pump ........................................................................... 29
PAS pump to mounting plate .......................................................................... 25
PAS pump mounting plate to auxiliaries mounting bracket ......................... 25
PAS pump pulley to hub ................................................................................. 25
Starter motor (bolt and nut) ........................................................................... 45

**Air conditioning compressor**

Compressor mounting bracket to front cover ............................................... 45
Compressor to mounting bracket (stud) ......................................................... 8
Compressor to mounting bracket (nut) .......................................................... 25
Belt tensioner pulley to tensioner arm ........................................................... 45
Belt tensioner assembly to front cover plate ................................................ 25
Idler pulley to front cover plate ..................................................................... 45
Compressor belt guard (nut) .......................................................................... 25
Sensors to water outlet elbow (air/con) ......................................................... 25
Blanking plug, water outlet elbow (air/con) ................................................... 25

**Generator**

Generator mounting bracket to front cover .................................................. 45
Generator to mounting bracket ...................................................................... 85
Generator pulley to hub .................................................................................. 95
Generator belt guard ...................................................................................... 25
Generator to auxiliaries mounting bracket .................................................... 25
Tachometer electrical connection ................................................................... 4

**METRIC**                                                 **Nm**

| | Nm |
|---|---|
| M5 | 6 |
| M6 | 9 |
| M8 | 25 |
| M10 | 45 |
| M12 | 90 |
| M14 | 105 |
| M16 | 180 |

**UNC / UNF**

| | |
|---|---|
| 1/4 | 9 |
| 5/16 | 24 |
| 3/8 | 39 |
| 7/16 | 78 |
| 1/2 | 90 |
| 5/8 | 136 |

 **NOTE: Torque values above are to be used as a guide where no torque is specified.**

# 19 - FUEL SYSTEM

## CONTENTS

Page

# Notes

## DESCRIPTION

### Fuel system

The fuel system incorporates a supply and spill return line on all models as illustrated below.

On 90 models, see J6191, the fuel tank is mounted at the RH side of the vehicle chassis under the front seat.

On standard 110 and 130 models the fuel tank is located at the rear of the vehicle between the chassis longitudenal sections, as shown in J6192.

As an option, a twin tank system fitted with a combined change-over tap and 3 way fuel supply and return system , can be installed on both 110 and 130 models, see J6193.

The tank/s on all vehicles is vented by a 2 way valve in the filler cap.

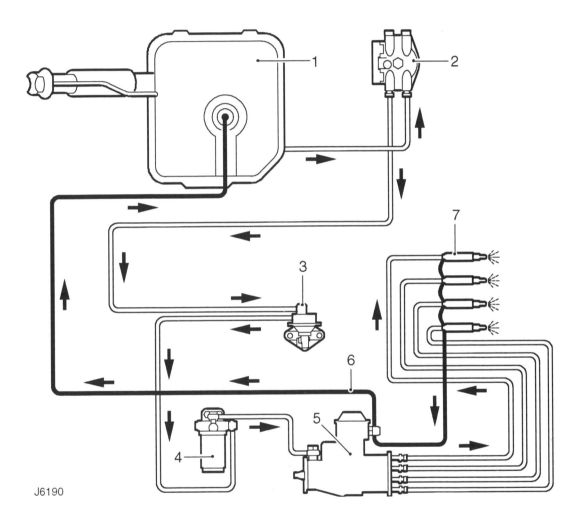

J6190

## FUEL SYSTEM LAYOUT

1. Fuel tank
2. Fuel sedimentor, if fitted
3. Fuel lift pump
4. Fuel filter

5. Fuel injection pump
6. Spill return line
7. Fuel injectors

A mechanical lift pump, with a hand priming facility, is driven by the camshaft, and is mounted on the RH side of the engine.

A fuel filter, with a replaceable element and incorporating a water separator, is mounted on the front RH side of the engine compartment.

A fuel sedimentor may be fitted when the vehicle is operating in more arduous conditions, and is used to minimise water deposits in the fuel system before reaching the fuel pump and filter.

Fuel injection is carried out by a Bosch direct injection pump, incorporating a cold start advance unit and a high idle setting. The pump is mounted on the RH side of the engine and is driven directly by gears in the front cover from the crankshaft. The pump meters and distributes fuel to 4 pintle type injectors located in pre-combustion chambers in the cylinder head. Four heater plugs, located in the cylinder head directly below each injector, are fitted to improve cold starting.

An optional hand throttle, for use with a centre power take off, is located on the fascia to the LH side of the fuse box, and is linked independently to the fuel injection pump throttle lever.

## Air intake

The air cleaner is mounted on the RH side of the engine and is connected by hoses to the cold air intake duct and turbocharger inlet. Fitted between the air cleaner and turbocharger is the crankcase breather hose which connects to a breather filter on the rocker cover.

A single stage turbocharger, fitted between the exhaust manifold and exhaust down pipe, is connected by hoses to the air cleaner and an intercooler which is mounted on the LH side of the radiator. The intercooler is connected by a hose to the inlet manifold. When an EGR valve is fitted to the turbocharger, additional pipes/hoses are used to connect the components.

**Exhaust gas recirculation (EGR), when fitted.**

Exhaust gas recirculation is controlled by an ECU mounted under the front centre seat or cubby box and receives the following inputs:
- Engine temperature from coolant temperature sender unit on LH side of cylinder head.
- Throttle position from potentiometer on injection pump.
- Engine speed from speedometer.

When all correct signals are received, the EGR solenoid allows vacuum to open EGR valve and recirculate a portion of the exhaust gas. See J6196 for the EGR system component location and 'Operation' for full system function.

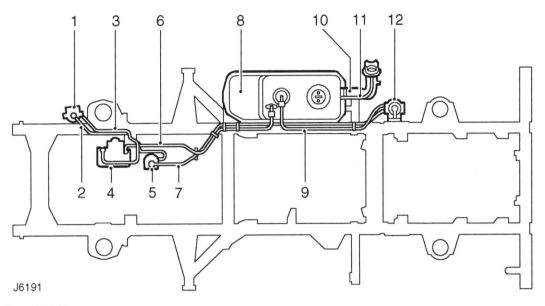

J6191

**90 FUEL SYSTEM**

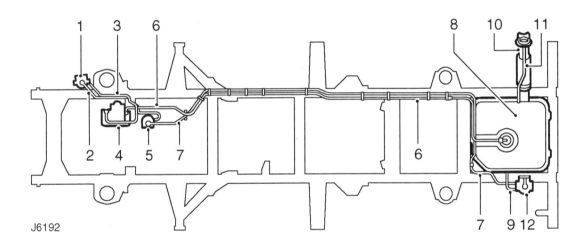

J6192

**110 FUEL SYSTEM**

1. Fuel filter
2. Supply pipe, lift pump to filter
3. Supply pipe, fuel filter to injection pump
4. Fuel injection pump
5. Fuel lift pump
6. Spill return pipe, injection pump to tank

7. Supply pipe, sedimentor to fuel pump
8. Fuel tank
9. Supply pipe, fuel tank to sedimentor
10. Fuel filler pipe
11. Breather pipe
12. Sedimentor, if fitted

 **NOTE: If a sedimentor is not fitted, the fuel supply pipe from the tank will connect directly to the fuel lift pump.**

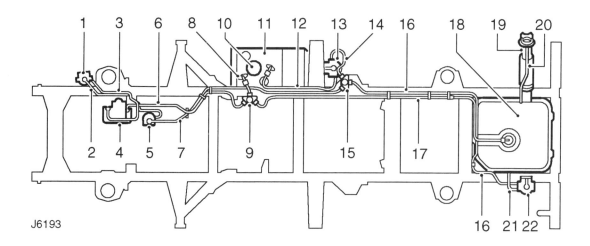

J6193

## 110/130 TWIN TANK FUEL SYSTEM - 5 DOOR VEHICLES

1. Fuel filter
2. Supply pipe, lift pump to filter
3. Supply pipe, filter to injection pump
4. Fuel injection pump
5. Fuel lift pump
6. Spill return pipe, injection pump to change-over tap
7. Supply pipe, fuel tank change-over tap to lift pump
8. Spill return pipe, change-over tap to side tank
9. Change-over tap, spill return
10. Fuel filler cap
11. Side fuel tank

12. Supply pipe, side tank to sedimentor
13. Sedimentor, if fitted, side tank
14. Supply pipe, sedimentor to fuel tank change-over tap
15. Change-over tap, side and rear tanks
16. Supply pipe, rear sedimentor to fuel tank change-over tap
17. Spill return pipe, change-over tap to rear tank
18. Rear fuel tank
19. Fuel filler pipe
20. Breather pipe
21. Supply pipe, rear tank to sedimentor
22. Sedimentor, if fitted, rear tank

 **NOTE: If sedimentors are not fitted, the fuel supply pipe from the side and rear tanks connects directly to the fuel tank change-over tap.**

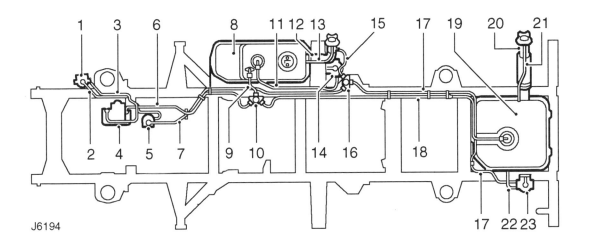

J6194

## 110/130 TWIN TANK FUEL SYSTEM - 2 DOOR VEHICLES

1. Fuel filter
2. Supply pipe, fuel lift pump to filter
3. Supply pipe, filter to injection pump
4. Injection pump
5. Fuel lift pump
6. Spill return pipe, injection pump to change-over tap
7. Supply pipe, fuel tank change-over tap to lift pump
8. Side fuel tank
9. Spill return pipe, change-over tap to side tank
10. Change-over tap, spill return
11. Supply pipe, side tank to sedimentor
12. Fuel filler pipe

13. Breather pipe
14. Sedimentor, if fitted, side tank
15. Supply pipe, sedimentor to fuel tank change-over tap
16. Change-over tap, fuel tanks
17. Supply pipe, rear sedimentor to fuel tank change-over tap
18. Spill return pipe, change-over tap to rear tank
19. Rear fuel tank
20. Fuel filler pipe
21. Breather pipe
22. Supply pipe, rear tank to sedimentor
23. Rear sedimentor, if fitted

 **NOTE: If sedimentors are not fitted, the fuel supply pipe from the side and rear tanks connects directly to the fuel tank change-over tap.**

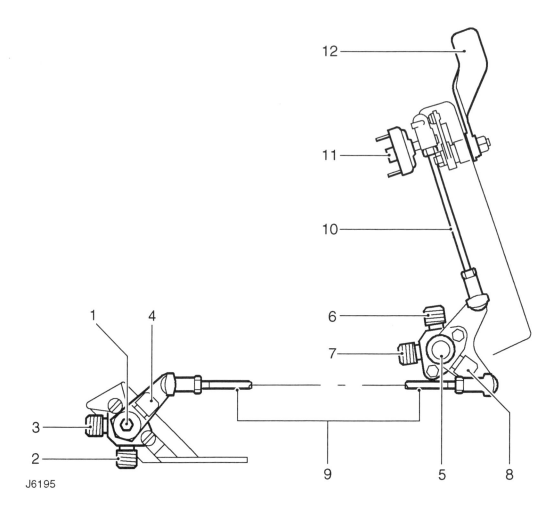

J6195

**TWIN TANK FUEL CHANGE - OVER MECHANISM**

1. Change-over tap, fuel tanks
2. Fuel supply, side tank
3. Fuel supply, rear tank
4. To fuel lift pump
5. Change-over tap, spill return
6. Spill return, side tank
7. Spill return, rear tank
8. Spill return, injection pump to change-over tap
9. Control rod, operating lever to fuel change-over tap
10. Control rod, change-over lever to spill return pivot bracket
11. Fuel tank change-over switch
12. Control lever

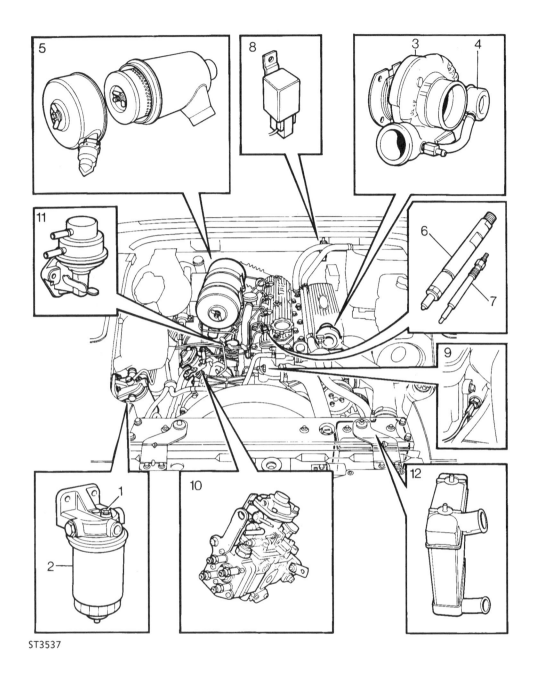

ST3537

## FUEL SYSTEM COMPONENT LOCATION

1. Fuel filter bleed screw
2. Fuel filter
3. Turbocharger
4. Actuator
5. Air cleaner
6. Fuel injector

7. Heater plug
8. Heater plug controller
9. Coolant temperature transmitter
10. Fuel injection pump
11. Fuel lift pump
12. Intercooler

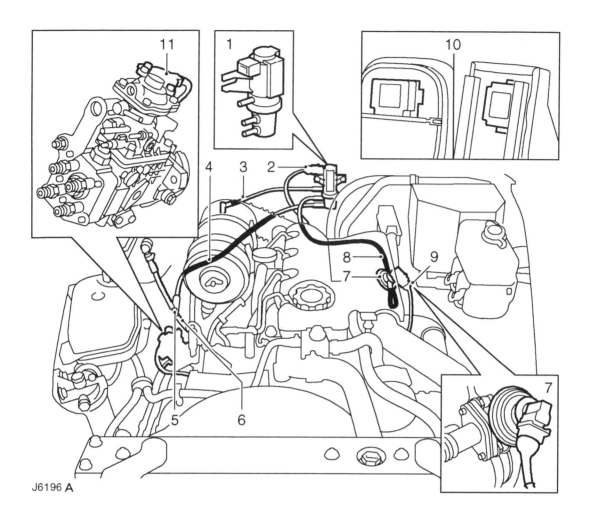

J6196 A

**EGR FUEL SYSTEM COMPONENT LOCATION, (when fitted)**

1. EGR modulator valve
2. Electrical harness plug
3. Vacuum spill pipe, modulator to air cleaner hose
4. Vacuum pipe, brake servo hose to modulator valve
5. 'T' piece connector
6. Vacuum pipe, vacuum pump to brake servo

7. EGR valve
8. Vacuum pipe, modulator valve to EGR valve
9. Multi-plug connector, EGR valve
10. EGR control unit (fixed on base of centre seat or cubby box)
11. EGR throttle position sensor

## OPERATION

Diesel engines operate by compression ignition. The rapid compression of air in the cylinder during the compression cycle heats the air and when fuel is injected into the heated air, it ignites instantaneously. During cold tarting, automatically controlled heater plugs assist in raising the temperature of the compressed air to ignition point.

A cold start advance unit advances the injection timing to further assist starting. Idle quality is improved by the high idle setting.

The engine is supplied with pre-compressed air by a single stage turbocharger.

Exhaust gases passing over a turbine cause it to rotate, driving a compressor mounted on the turbine shaft. Air drawn from the cold air intake passes, via the air cleaner, to the turbocharger where it is compressed. Compression in the turbocharger warms up the air considerably, so that it expands. As a result the air mass per cylinder is reduced, having a negative effect on power output. By fitting a charge-air intercooler, located on the LH side of the radiator, the air is cooled before reaching the cylinders. This increases power output through increased mass of oxygen in the combustion process, as well as maximising engine durability, through maintaining lower piston and head temperatures.

Fuel is drawn from the tank by a mechanical lift pump and passes to the injection pump via a filter. In addition to removing particle contamination from the fuel, the filter incorporates a water separator, which removes and stores water.

The sedimentor/s, when fitted, is located adjacent to the fuel tank/s and separates contamination and water particles in the fuel before reaching the fuel lift pump.

The injection pump meters a precisely timed, exact quantity of fuel to the injectors in response to throttle variations, injection timing varying with engine speed. Any excess fuel delivered to the injection pump is passed back to the tank via the spill return line.

Fuel is injected in a finely atomised form into the main combustion chamber, the burning fuel expands rapidly, creating extreme turbulence which mixes the burning fuel thoroughly with the compressed air, providing complete combustion.

Cold Starting is assisted by heater plugs, a cold start advance unit and a high idle setting.

### Heater plugs

Heater plug operation is controlled by a timer unit, start relay and resistor. When the ignition is turned on the timer unit is energised, the heater plugs start to operate and a warning light on the dashboard illuminates, remaining on until the heater plugs are automatically switched off.

The length of time the heater plugs will operate is dependent on under bonnet temperature, which is monitored by a sensor located in the timer unit.

Starting the engine results in the power supply to the heater plugs passing through the resistor, which reduces their operating temperature. The heater plugs are cut out either by the temperature sensor in the timer, or by a microswitch on the injection pump which operates when the throttle is depressed.

### Cold start advance

The cold start advance unit is connected to the engine cooling system via hoses. It contains a temperature sensitive element which is retracted when cold and pulls the advance lever, via cable, towards the rear of the pump against spring pressure. As coolant temperature rises, the cold start element expands releasing tension on the cable and allowing spring pressure to move the advance lever forwards.

### Exhaust gas recirculation (EGR), when fitted

Operation of the EGR system is dependent on the following:

- Engine temperature - must be between 20° C and 100° C approx.
- Engine speed - must be between 630 and 2850 rev/min.
- Engine load - calculated by throttle position sensor.
- EGR valve lift position.
- Duration of engine idling.

Under varying engine speed and load condition the control unit sends a signal to open the vacuum modulator which allows a vacuum to be applied above the EGR diaphragm. The vacuum supply is taken from a 'T' connector in the brake servo hose. This process is controlled by an engine speed/load map stored in the EGR control unit memory.

Engine speed is measured by monitoring the waveform present on one phase of the generator. Throttle position is measured via a sensor mounted on the fuel injection pump throttle lever. Closed loop control is achieved by allowing the control unit (ECU) to continually monitor EGR valve lift via the sensor mounted on the valve; this valve lift is compared with the actual valve lift required on the control unit map and adjusted, if necessary.

With coolant temperature between 20° C and 100° C, the engine having just returned to idle, EGR will shut off after 25-30 seconds idling.

## THROTTLE CABLE

**Adjust**

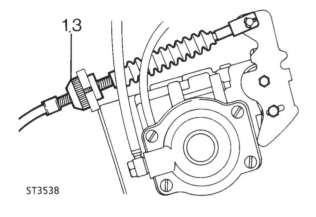

ST3538

1. Slacken throttle cable adjustment ferrule.
2. Hold throttle lever in fully closed position.
3. Adjust outer cable, by rotating ferrule, to give 1,57 mm (1/16 in) of deflection in the inner cable.
4. Check that throttle opens fully when the throttle is depressed.

## EGR THROTTLE POSITION SENSOR

**Check**

1. Run engine until normal operating temperature is reached.

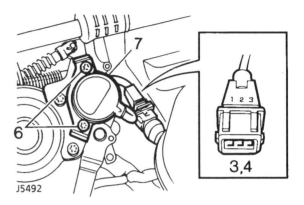

J5492

2. Switch off engine and disconnect throttle position sensor multi-plug.
3. Connect an Ohmmeter across pins 1 and 3 of multi-plug. Ohmmeter should read between 1K and 1.05K ohms.
4. Connect Ohmmeter across pins 1 and 2 of multi-plug. Ohmmeter should read between 850 and 900 ohms.
5. If readings are correct, reconnect multi-plug.
6. If readings are not obtained slacken 2 torx screws securing sensor.
7. Rotate sensor to obtain correct Ohmmeter reading, then tighten torx screws.
8. Re-check readings and fit multiplug.
9. If, after adjustment, Ohmmeter readings cannot be achieved, fit new sensor *See Repair, EGR throttle position sensor.*

## LOW AND HIGH IDLE SPEED ADJUSTMENT

⚠️ NOTE: The high idle speed (cold start idle) is automatically set by the setting of the low idle speed and cannot be adjusted individually.

1. Check and adjust throttle cable *See Throttle cable adjustment.*
2. Start engine and run it until normal operating temperature is reached.
3. Using a suitable tachometer, check the engine idle speed, *See ENGINE TUNING DATA, Information, 300Tdi.*

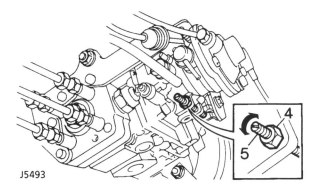

J5493

4. If adjustment is necessary, first slacken the locknut on injection pump.
5. Turn adjustment screw clockwise to increase engine speed or anti-clockwise to decrease the speed. Run engine at an increased speed for a few seconds then check idle speed again.
6. When correct speed has been achieved, hold adjuster screw steady while tightening locknut.

⚠️ NOTE: The low idle speed control is the only permitted adjustment in service. Any additional adjustments required must be entrusted to authorised Bosch agents.

## THROTTLE PEDAL ADJUSTMENT

**Adjust**

1. First ensure that throttle cable is correctly adjusted *See Throttle cable.*

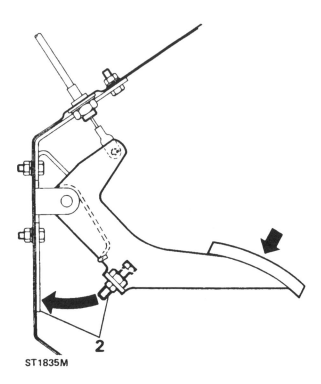

ST1835M

2. Depress throttle pedal, by hand, to full extent of injection pump lever travel. Slacken locknut and adjust throttle pedal stop screw to take up clearance between screw and bulkhead. Ensure no strain is placed upon throttle cable and pump lever.
3. Retighten locknut.

## INJECTION PUMP TIMING - CHECK AND ADJUST

**Service repair no - 19.30.01**

1. Viewing the valve mechanism through oil filler aperture, turn crankshaft clockwise until inlet valve of No.1 cylinder has just closed. No.1 cylinder is now just before TDC.

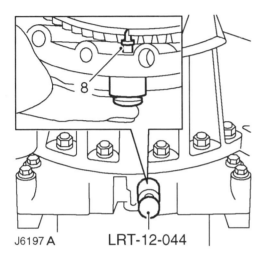

J6197 A     LRT-12-044

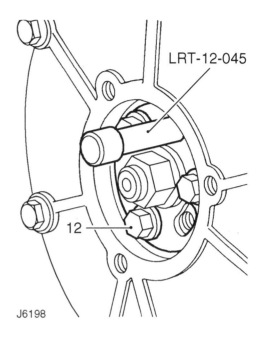

J6198

2. Remove blanking plug from flywheel housing and insert timing tool **LRT-12-044**, locating centre pin on flywheel.

⚠ **NOTE: A chassis undertray may be fitted on some vehicle derivatives to conform to legal requirements. When under chassis adjustments or remove and refit procedures are required, it may be necessary to remove the undertray and/or integral access panels** *See CHASSIS AND BODY, Repair, Front undertray or Rear undertray.*

3. Cearfully rotate crankshaft clockwise until centre pin engages timing slot in flywheel.
4. Remove injection pump access plate, complete with gasket, from front cover plate.
5. Fit locking pin **LRT-12-045/2** to injection pump gear. If difficulty is experienced in inserting pin, adjustments will be needed to correctly set injection pump timing as follows:
6. Support injection pump retaining nut to prevent strain on timing belt.
7. Slacken the 3 keeper plate retaining bolts.
8. Carefully turn fixing nut and keeper plate until locking pin can be inserted, without restriction, into injection pump gear.
9. Tighten keeper plate bolts to *25 Nm (18 lbf/ft)* and remove locking pin.

10. Refit injection pump access plate plate and gasket.
11. Remove flywheel timing tool and refit blanking plug.
12. Run engine until normal operating temperature is reached and check that idle speed adjustment *See low and high idle speed adjustment* and throttle cable adjustment *See Throttle cable adjustment* are correct.

## TURBOCHARGER BOOST PRESSURE - CHECK

**Service repair no - 19.42.06**

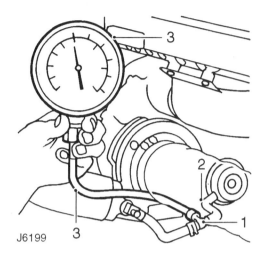

J6199

1. Disconnect actuator hose from turbocharger and insert a suitable 'T' piece connector.
2. Connect a short length of suitable hose to turbocharger and 'T'piece.
3. Connect further hose to 'T' piece and pressure gauge **LRT-12-011**. The pressure gauge hose must be long enough to reach into the vehicle cab so that the gauge can be observed by driver or passenger.
4. To check maximum boost pressure, drive vehicle normally, but in such a manner that full throttle can be maintained whilst climbing a hill with engine speed held steady between 2,500 and 3,000 rev/min. Under these circumstances boost pressure should read 0,95 - 1,09 Kgf/cm$^2$ (13.5 - 15.5 lb/in$^2$).

## PRIMING THE FUEL SYSTEM

**Service repair no - 19.50.01**

⚠️ **NOTE: If the fuel system has been completely drained carry out the procedures for priming both the sedimentor, if fitted, and fuel filter and injection pump.**

**Sedimentor and fuel filter**

If the sedimentor or fuel filter have been dismantled and air has entered the fuel system carry out the following procedure:

1. Slacken fuel filter bleed screw.
2. Operate hand priming lever on fuel lift pump until fuel, free from air, emerges from filter.

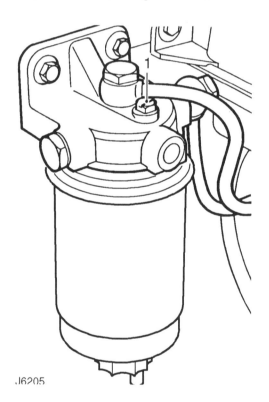

J6205

⚠️ **NOTE: Ensure that the fuel pump lever is on the bottom of operating cam when priming, otherwise maximum movement of the lever cannot be achieved.**

3. Tighten filter bleed screw whilst fuel is still emerging.

## Fuel injection pump

If the fuel injection pump has been removed or
renewed carry out the following:

1. Slacken fuel inlet pipe banjo bolt at injection
   pump.
2. Operate hand priming lever on fuel lift pump until
   fuel, free from air, emerges from injection pump.

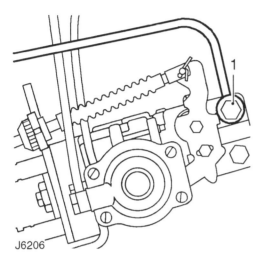

J6206

3. Tighten banjo bolt whilst fuel is still emerging.
4. Crank engine until fuel is drawn through the
   system and engine starts.
5. Check fuel connections for leaks.

# Notes

## FUEL INJECTION PUMP

**Service repair no - 19.30.07**

**Remove**

1. Disconnect battery.
2. Disconnect and remove high pressure fuel injection pipes, pump to injectors.
3. Viewing valve mechanism through oil filler cap aperture, turn crankshaft clockwise until No. 1 cylinder is just before TDC.

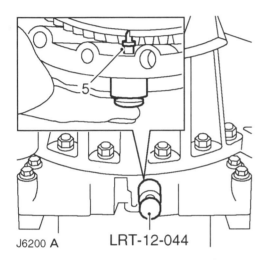

4. Remove blanking plug from flywheel housing and fit timing tool **LRT-12-044**, locating centre pin on flywheel.

⚠ NOTE: A chassis undertray may be fitted on some vehicle derivatives to conform to legal requirements. When under chassis adjustments or remove and refit procedures are required, it may be necessary to remove the undertray and/or integral access panels *See CHASSIS AND BODY, Repair, Front undertray or Rear undertray.*

5. Carefully rotate crankshaft clockwise until centre pin engages with timing slot in flywheel.
6. Remove injection pump access plate, complete with gasket, from front cover plate.
7. Fit pin from **LRT-12-045** to injection pump gear.

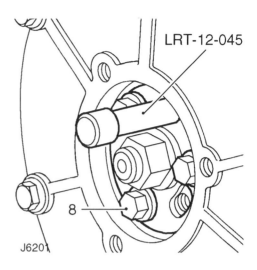

8. Restrain pulley nut to prevent straining timing belt and remove drive gear to pump hub fixing bolts and retaining plate.
9. Remove pin from pump gear.

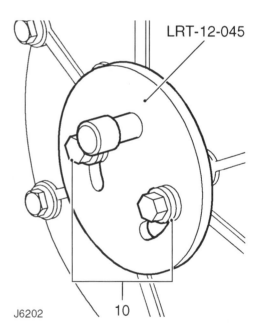

10. Fit gear retaining tool **LRT-12-045** with an 8 mm washer, 1,5 - 2 mm thick, under each bolt head in addition to the existing washer.
11. Remove throttle cable and hand throttle cable, if fitted.
12. Disconnect lead from fuel cut-off solenoid, and EGR throttle position sensor multi-plug, if fitted.

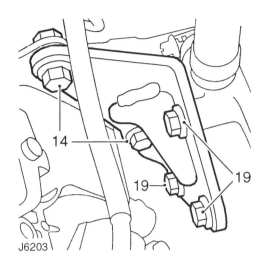

13. Remove banjo bolts securing spill return, main fuel and boost signal pipes, refit banjo bolts after disconnecting pipes.
14. Remove 2 bolts securing rear of pump to mounting bracket.
15. Remove 3 pump securing nuts at flange and withdraw pump and gasket.
16. Fit suitable caps to pipe connections to prevent ingress of dirt.

**Refit**

17. Clean mating faces of pump and front cover and fit new gasket into position over pump mounting studs.
18. Remove pump blanking plugs.
19. Slacken the 3 bolts, securing injection pump mounting bracket to cylinder block, sufficiently enough to allow bracket to move.
20. Fit pump to cover and secure with 3 nuts. Tighten to *25 Nm (18 lbf/ft)*.
21. Loosely attach pump to mounting bracket with nuts and bolts, then tighten bolts securing bracket to cylinder block and bolts securing pump to bracket, finger tight only.
22. To ensure correct fitting and alignment of injection pump, first tighten the 2 bolts securing pump to mounting bracket to *25 Nm (18 lbf/ft)*. Then tighten the 3 bolts securing mounting bracket to cylinder block, also to *25 Nm (18 lbf/ft)*.
23. Connect spill return and main fuel pipes and secure with banjo bolts. Tighten to *25 Nm (18 lbf/ft)*.
24. Connect boost signal pipe and secure with banjo bolt. Tighten to *10 Nm (7 lbf/ft)*.

25. Connect fuel cut-off solenoid lead and throttle position sensor multi-plug, if fitted.
26. Connect throttle cable and where applicable, hand throttle cable.
27. Remove pump gear retaining tool **LRT-12-045**.
28. Carefully turn the pump hub nut in a clockwise direction, sufficiently enough to enable timing tool pin to be inserted into injection pump.
29. Fit gear retaining plate and secure with 3 bolts. Tighten to *25 Nm (18 lbf/ft)*.
30. Remove timing pin.
31. Ensure flywheel timing pin is disengaged from slot in flywheel.
32. Turn crankshaft two complete revolutions, check timing pin from **RT-12-045** can be fully and easily inserted into the pump. At the same time check flywheel timing pin **LRT-12-044** can also be inserted in the flywheel slot.
33. If, with the flywheel timing pin located, the timing pin cannot be inserted cleanly into the injection pump, carry out the following:

   **a.** Ensure flywheel timing pin is disengaged from slot in flywheel.
   **b.** Slacken the 3 pump gear retaining bolts.
   **c.** Turn the pump hub nut in a clockwise direction, sufficiently to enable timing tool pin to be easily inserted into the injection pump.
   **d.** Keeping the tension on the hub nut, check that flywheel timing pin locates with slot in flywheel.
   **e.** Tighten the 3 pump gear retaining bolts to *25 Nm (18 lbf/ft)*.
   **f.** Remove timing pins from pump and flywheel housing.

34. Using a suitable anti-seize compound, fit the blanking plug to flywheel housing. Tighten to *12 Nm (9 lbf/ft)*.
35. Fit access plate with gasket to front cover plate. Tighten bolts to *25 Nm (18 lbf/ft)*.
36. Refit injector pipes.
37. Reconnect battery.

## FUEL INJECTORS

**Service repair no - 19.60.10**

**Remove**

⚠️ NOTE: When a fuel injector is considered to be the cause of irregular running and loss of power it will be necessary to fit a donor set of injectors to determine which injector is at fault. DO NOT attempt to dismantle or carry out spray tests on the fuel injectors. This work can only carried out by authorised Bosch dealers.

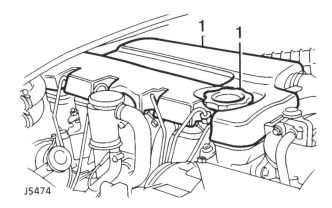

J5474

1. Remove oil filler cap and release sound insulation cover from top of engine.

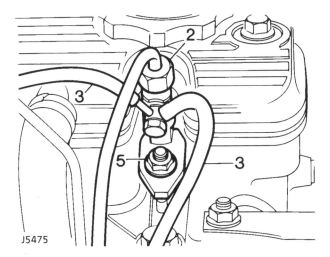

J5475

2. Disconnect high pressure fuel supply pipes from injectors and injection pump. Remove in pairs.
3. Disconnect spill return hose(s) from injectors.
4. Plug pipes and injector connections to prevent the ingress of dirt and foriegn matter.

5. Remove retaining nut and release each injector clamp plate from cylinder head.
6. Remove injector and discard copper washer.

**Refit**

7. Ensure injectors and seating in cylinder head are clean.
8. Lightly grease a new copper sealing washer and position on each injector.
9. Fit injectors in cylinder head with spill return outlets facing outward.
10. Secure injector with clamp plate and nut. Tighten nut to **25 Nm (18 lbf/ft).**

⚠️ NOTE: The clamp plates are slightly curved and should be fitted with the convex side uppermost.

11. Fit the spill return pipe with a single copper washer under the head of the banjo bolt and 2 copper washers fitted between the injector and the banjo. Tighten banjo bolt to **10 Nm (7 lbf/ft).**
12. Fit high pressure pipes to injectors and injection pump. Tighten union nuts to **28 Nm (21 lbf/ft).**
13. Fit sound insulation cover and oil filler cap.

## FUEL LIFT PUMP

**Service repair no - 19.45.09**

**Remove**

 **NOTE: Blank off pipe ends and connections to prevent ingress of dirt.**

1. Disconnect battery.
2. Remove high pressure fuel pipes, injection pump to injectors.

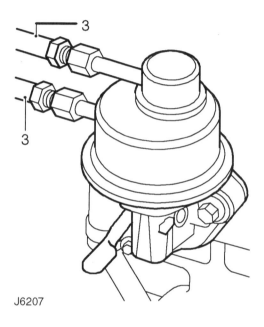

J6207

3. Disconnect fuel inlet and outlet pipes from lift pump.
4. Remove 2 bolts and withdraw lift pump and gasket from cylinder block.

**Refit**

5. Clean mating faces of pump and cylinder block.
6. Fit lift pump to cylinder block with a new gasket, ensure correct location of operating lever with camshaft.
7. Secure with bolts. Tighten to *25 Nm (18 lbf/ft)*.
8. Connect inlet and outlet pipes using new nuts and olives.
9. Refit injector pipes. Tighten union nuts to *28 Nm (21 lbf/ft)*.

## FUEL SEDIMENTOR

**Service repair no - 19.25.01**

**Remove**

1. Disconnect battery.

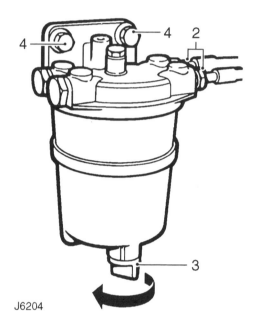

J6204

2. Disconnect inlet and outlet fuel pipes from sedimentor.
3. Slacken drain tap and allow sedimentor to completely drain.
4. Remove 2 bolts, washers and nuts and detach sedimentor from chassis mounting bracket.

**Refit**

5. Secure sedimentor to chassis mounting with fixing bolts.
6. Reconnect inlet and outlet fuel pipes to sedimentor.
7. Slacken drain plug until diesel free from air flows, then retighten plug.
8. Prime vehicle fuel system *See Adjustment, Priming the fuel system.*
9. Reconnect battery.

## FUEL FILTER ASSEMBLY

**Service repair no - 19.25.02**

**Remove**

1. Disconnect battery.

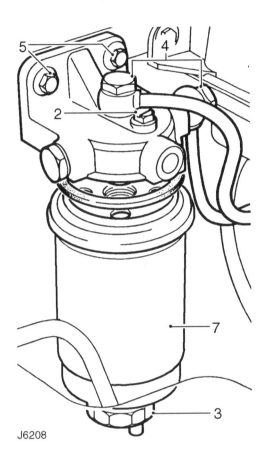

J6208

2. Place a suitable container under filter element and slacken filter bleed screw.
3. Slacken drain tap and allow fuel to drain from filter element.
4. Slacken fuel inlet and outlet banjo connections.
5. Remove 2 bolts and nuts securing filter head to inner wing.
6. Remove fuel inlet and outlet banjo bolts and detach fuel pipes.
7. Remove filter assembly from vehicle. Unscrew filter element, if necessary.
8. Plug fuel pipe ends to prevent ingress of dirt.

**Refit**

9. Position filter assembly and fit fuel inlet and outlet pipes using new copper sealing washers both sides of the banjo connections.
10. Secure filter head to inner wing.
11. Fully tighten banjo connections.
12. Prime fuel system to remove any air trapped in filter *See Adjustment, Priming the fuel system.*
13. Reconnect battery.

## FUEL FILTER ELEMENT

**Service repair no - 19.25.07**

For remove and refit procedure *See SECTION 10, Maintenance, Fuel filter element.*

## SIDE MOUNTED FUEL TANK

**Service repair no - 19.55.05**

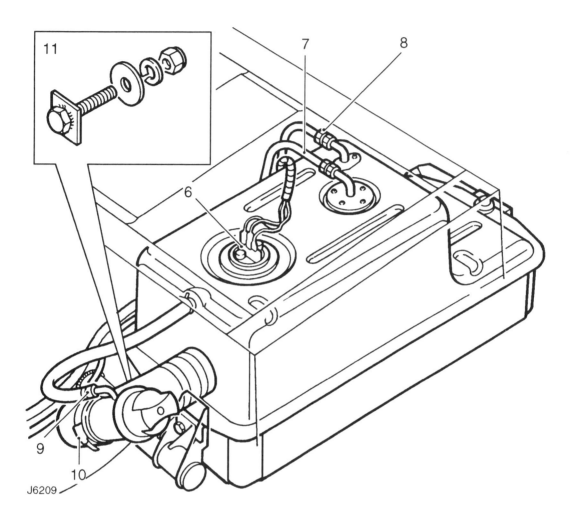

J6209

 **NOTE: This fuel tank is standard on 90 models and an option on 110/130 2 door vehicles fitted with twin tanks.**

**Remove**

 **WARNING: Before any attempt is made to start the removal procedure it is vital that the FUEL HANDLING PRECAUTIONS** *See INTRODUCTION, Information,* **are carefully studied and implemented in the interests of safety.**

1. Disconnect battery.
2. Remove fuel filler cap.
3. Remove fuel tank drain plug, allow fuel to drain into a clean container and refit plug.
4. Remove RH seat cushion.
5. Release retaining catch and remove seat base cover to gain access to fuel tank.
6. Disconnect electrical plug from fuel gauge unit.
7. Disconnect fuel supply pipe from tank.
8. Disconnect spill return pipe from fuel tank.
9. Disconnect breather pipe from fuel filler tube.
10. Slacken hose clip and remove filler hose from filler tube.
11. From rear of tank, remove 2 nuts and washers securing tank mounting to captive-headed bolts.
12. Support rear of fuel tank and remove captive bolts.

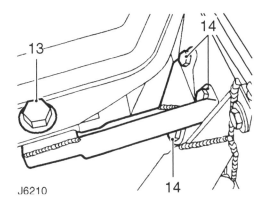

J6210

13. Remove single bolt fixing assembly securing front of tank to chassis mounted bracket.
14. Remove 3 bolts securing tank mounting bracket to chassis and release bracket.
15. Lower front of tank while turning anti-clockwise and remove from vehicle.
16. If required, remove tank gauge unit. *See INSTRUMENTS, Repair, Fuel gauge tank unit - side fuel tank* or *See INSTRUMENTS, Repair, Fuel gauge tank unit - rear fuel tank, 110/130*

### Refit

17. Fit filler hose and clip to tank but do not fully tighten. Position clip screw so that it is accessible when tank is fitted.
18. Fit breather hose and secure with clip.
19. Position fuel tank in vehicle and loosely secure front mounting bracket to tank with special bolt and rubber bushes.
20. Secure mounting bracket to chassis with 3 bolts and fully tighten to *20 Nm (15 lbf/ft).*
21. Secure rear of tank to chassis mounting and tighten captive bolt plate fixings to *20 Nm (15 lbf/ft).*
22. Fully tighten front fixing bolt assembly to *20 Nm (15 lbf/ft).*
23. Fit spill return and fuel supply pipes and secure union connections.
24. Fit fuel level unit electrical plug.
25. Fit hose to filler tube and tighten upper and lower clips.
26. Check that drain plug is secure and fill fuel tank.
27. Reconnect battery.
28. Prime fuel system *See Adjustment, Priming the fuel system* and start engine.
29. Check system for leaks and operation of fuel gauge.
30. Fit seat base cover and seat cushion.

### SIDE MOUNTED FUEL TANK - 5 DOOR VEHICLES

**Service repair no - 19.55.01**

⚠ NOTE: This fuel tank is used on 110/130 5 door vehicles fitted with a twin tank option.

⚠ WARNING: Before any attempt is made to start the removal procedure it is vital that the FUEL HANDLING PRECAUTIONS, *See INTRODUCTION, Information, Fuel handling precautions* are carefully studied and implemented in the interests of safety.

### Remove

1. Disconnect battery.
2. Remove tank drain plug, allow fuel to drain into a clean container, and refit plug.
3. Remove RH seat cushion.
4. Remove retaining catch and remove seat base cover to gain access to fuel tank.
5. Disconnect electrical plug from fuel gauge unit.
6. Disconnect fuel supply pipe from tank.
7. Disconnect spill return pipe from tank.
8. Remove 3 bolts securing tank to front mounting bracket.
9. Support front of tank and remove single fixing assembly securing tank to rear mounting bracket.
10. Remove tank from vehicle.
11. If required, remove fuel gauge unit. *See INSTRUMENTS, Repair, Fuel gauge tank unit - side fuel tank* or *See INSTRUMENTS, Repair, Fuel gauge tank unit - rear fuel tank, 110/130*

### Refit

12. Position fuel tank in vehicle and loosely secure to rear mounting bracket with special bolt and rubber bushes.
13. Secure tank to front mounting bracket and tighten fixings to *20 Nm (15 lbf/ft).*
14. Fully tighten rear fixing bolt assembly to *20 Nm (15 lbf/ft).*
15. Fit spill return and fuel supply pipes to fuel tank and securely tighten union connectios.
16. Fit electrical plug to fuel gauge unit.
17. Check that drain plug is secure and fill fuel tank.
18. Reconnect battery.
19. Prime fuel system. *See Adjustment, Priming the fuel system* and start engine.
20. Check system for leaks and operation of fuel gauge.
21. Fit seat base cover and seat cushion.

## REAR MOUNTED FUEL TANK - 110/130

**Service repair no - 19.55.26**

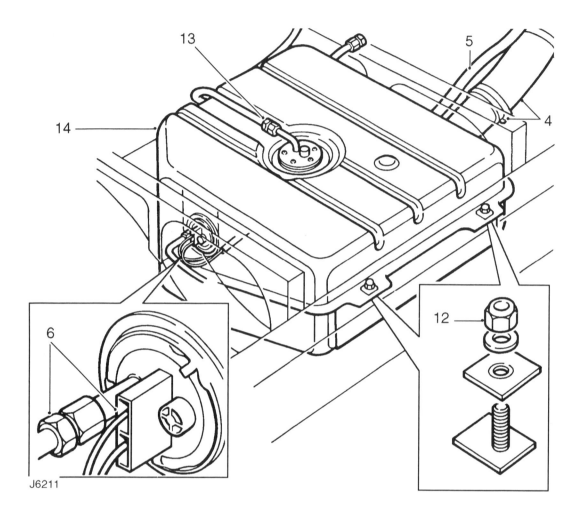

J6211

⚠️ **WARNING: Before any attempt is made to start the removal procedure it is vital that the FUEL HANDLING PRECAUTIONS** *See INTRODUCTION, Information, FUEL HANDLING PRECAUTIONS* **are carefully studied and implemented in the interests of safety.**

**Remove**

1. Disconnect battery.
2. Remove fuel filler cap.
3. Remove tank drain plug, allow fuel to drain into a clean container, and refit plug.
4. Slacken retaining clips and disconnect fuel filler hose from rear tank.

5. Disconnect breather hose from filler tube.
6. Disconnect electrical plug and fuel supply pipe ⟨ from outlet pipe union on fuel gauge unit.
7. If the vehicle is fitted with a tow ball drop-plate with support bars, the bars must be removed.
8. Remove anti-roll bar chassis mountings. *See REAR SUSPENSION, Repair, Anti-roll bar* and push roll bar down to provide access to the tank.
9. Remove LH lashing eye to assist access to tank.
10. Position a support under the tank, preferably one that can be progressively lowered.

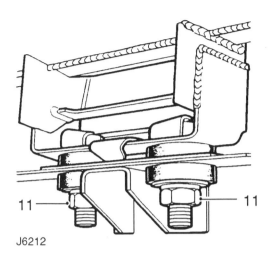

J6212

23. Fit anti-roll bar chassis mountings. *See REAR SUSPENSION, Repair, Anti-roll bar*
24. Check that drain plug is secure and fill fuel tank.
25. Reconnect battery.
26. Prime fuel system. *See Adjustment, Priming the fuel system* and start engine.
27. Check system for leaks and operation of fuel gauge.

11. Remove 2 nuts that secure front fixing assembly of the tank to chassis mounting bracket.
12. Remove tank rear mounting nuts.
13. With care, lower tank sufficiently to enable nut and olive of spill return to be disconnected from elbow in centre of tank.
14. Continue to lower tank until it can be removed from vehicle.

 NOTE: On later vehicles a separate stone guard is fitted and is attached to the tank with the existing front and rear fixings.

15. If required, remove tank gauge unit. *See INSTRUMENTS, Repair, Fuel gauge tank unit - side fuel tank* or *See INSTRUMENTS, Repair, Fuel gauge tank unit - rear fuel tank, 110/130*

**Refit**

16. If applicable, locate stone guard under tank.
17. Raise rear tank into position and connect spill return pipe to the elbow with the nut and olive.
18. Continue to raise tank so that front and rear mounting bolts locate in respective tank flange holes.
19. Fit and tighten fixings to *20 Nm (15 lbf/ft).*
20. Connect fuel suppnly pipe to the tank unit.
21. Fit fuel filler hose and breather pipe to filler tube and secure with retaining clips.
22. Fit LH lashing eye to chassis.

## TWIN TANK CHANGE-OVER TAP ASSEMBLY

**Service repair no - 19.43.50 - Fuel supply tap**
**Service repair no - 19.43.51 - Spill return tap**
**Service repair no - 19.43.52 - Fuel tank**
**change-over lever**

### Remove

1. Disconnect battery.
2. Remove RH front seat cushion.
3. Release retaining clip and remove access cover from seat base.

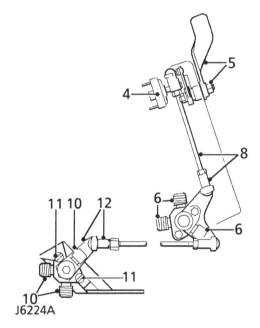

J6224A

4. Disconnect leads from fuel tank change-over switch.
5. Unscrew retaining nut and withdraw change-over lever and washers from pivot pin at heelboard.
6. Disconnect spill return pipes at spill change-over tap.
7. Remove 4 bolts, washers and nuts securing tap support bracket assembly to heel board.
8. Lift up support bracket assembly and disconnect control rod from spill tap lever.
9. Remove support bracket assembly from vehicle.
10. Disconnect fuel supply pipes at fuel change-over tap.
11. Remove 2 screws and release fuel tap from chassis mounted support bracket.

12. Remove fuel tap, complete with operating rod and lever.
13. Plug all connections to prevent ingress of dirt.
14. Dismantle spill return and fuel tap components as necessary.

### Refit

15. Fit fuel change-over tap, complete with operating rod and lever, to chassis mounted support bracket and fully tighten fixing screws.
16. Connect fuel supply pipes at fuel tap, ensuring they are fitted to correct ports.
17. Position support bracket assembly behind heelboard and connect operating rod to spill change-over tap lever.
18. With pivot pin bush correctly seated, secure support bracket assembly to heel board and tighten fixings to **8 Nm (6 lbf/ft).**
19. Connect spill return pipes to change-over tap, ensuring they are fitted to correct ports.
20. Secure change-over lever to pivot pin.
21. Fit leads to fuel tank change-over switch.
22. Reconnect battery.
23. Prime vehicle fuel system, **See Adjustment, Priming the fuel system** if necessary and check for leaks.
24. Fit access cover to seat base and seat cushion.

## HEATER PLUGS

**Service repair no - 19.60.31**

**Remove**

1. Disconnect battery.

**No.1 heater plug - air conditioning models:**

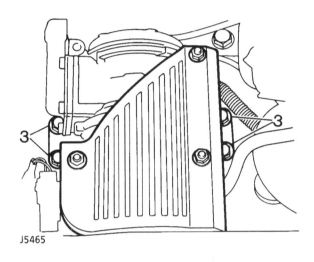

J5465

2. Release drive belt from compressor pulley *See AIR CONDITIONING, Repair, Compressor drive belt.*
3. Remove 4 bolts securing compressor to front cover, move compressor aside.

**No.3 heater plug:**

4. Remove retaining bolt and withdraw breather valve from rocker cover. Remove and discard 'O' ring.

**All heater plugs:**

5. Remove terminal nut and disconnect wire from heater plug terminal.
6. Unscrew heater plug.

**Refit**

7. Clean heater plug and seating.
8. Coat threads of heater plug with suitable anti-seize compound operational to a temperature of 1000° C.
9. Fit heater plug, tighten to *23 Nm (17 lbf/ft).*
10. Connect wire to heater plug terminal and secure with nut.

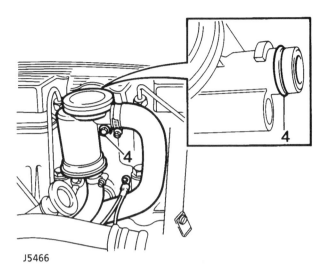

J5466

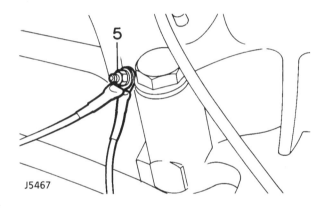

J5467

⚠ **NOTE: Feed wire must be connected to No. 4 heater plug terminal.**

**No. 3 heater plug:**

11. Lubricate new 'O' ring with engine oil and fit to breather valve.
12. Fit valve to rocker cover, tighten to bolt to *15 Nm (11 lbf/ft).*

**No. 1 heater plug - air conditioning models**

13. Position compressor to front cover, fit bolts and tighten to *25 Nm (18 lbf/ft).*
14. Fit drive belt to compressor pulley and adjust tension *See AIR CONDITIONING, Repair, Compressor drive belt.*

**All models:**

15. Reconnect battery.

## HEATER PLUG CONTROL UNIT

**Service repair no - 19.60.33**

**Remove**

1. Disconnect battery.

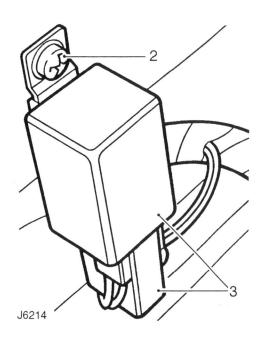

J6214

2. Remove screw securing control unit to bulkhead.
3. Disconnect multi-plug and release control unit.

**Refit**

4. Fit harness multi-plug to control unit.
5. Secure control unit to bulkhead.
6. Reconnect battery.

## AIR CLEANER

**Service repair no - 19.10.01**

**Remove**

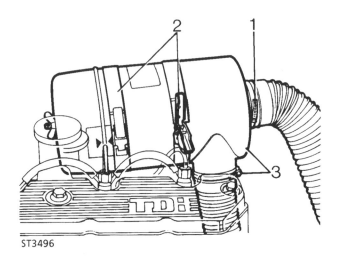

ST3496

1. Slacken hose clip and detach outlet hose.
2. Release clips and open air cleaner retaining straps.
3. Lift up air cleaner, slacken hose clip and detach inlet hose.
4. Remove air cleaner.

**Refit**

5. Position air cleaner and connect inlet hose.
6. Close air cleaner retaining straps and secure lock clips.
7. Connect outlet hose.

 **NOTE: If an EGR fuel system is fitted, ensure the modulator valve vacuum spill pipe is secure in the outlet hose.**

## AIR CLEANER ELEMENT

**Service repair no - 19.10.10**

For remove and refit procedure *See SECTION 10, Maintenance, Under bonnet maintenance.*

## THROTTLE CABLE

**Service repair no - 19.20.06**

**Remove**

1. Disconnect battery.

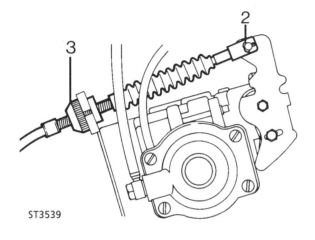

ST3539

2. Remove split pin and clevis pin securing throttle cable to injector pump throttle lever .
3. Depress ferrule retaining tags, release ferrule from abutment bracket and withdraw throttle cable.

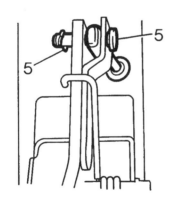

J5458

4. Release throttle cable from clip on bulkhead.
5. Remove pin and clevis pin securing throttle cable to pedal lever.
6. Release grommet from bulkhead.
7. Withdraw throttle cable from engine compartment.

**Refit**

8. Feed throttle cable through bulkhead from engine compartment and fit grommet.
9. Secure throttle cable to pedal lever. Use new split pin to secure clevis.
10. Secure throttle cable in bulkhead clip.
11. Guide throttle cable through abutment bracket and fit ferrule.
12. Secure cable to injection pump throttle lever. Use new split pin to secure clevis.
13. Adjust throttle cable *See Adjustment, Throttle cable adjustment.*

## THROTTLE PEDAL

**Service repair no - 19.20.01**

**Remove**

1. Remove throttle cable from pedal *See Throttle cable.*
2. Remove 6 bolts securing throttle pedal assembly to engine bulkhead.
3. Remove pedal assembly from footwell, complete with trim retainer.
4. Release return spring from pedal lever.
5. Remove roll pin securing pivot shaft to pedal assembly.
6. Withdraw pivot shaft and remove pedal from mounting bracket.
7. Remove return spring from pedal boss.

**Refit**

8. Fit return spring to pedal boss.
9. Fit pedal to mounting bracket and locate return spring.
10. Fit pivot shaft to pedal assembly and secure with roll pin.
11. Locate return spring on pedal lever.
12. Secure throttle pedal assembly and trim retainer to bulkhead. Tighten bolts to *9 Nm (7 lbf/ft).*
13. Fit throttle cable to pedal *See Throttle cable.*
14. Adjust pedal, if necessary *See Adjustment, Throttle pedal adjustment.*

## TURBOCHARGER INLET HOSE

**Service repair no - 19.42.11**

**Remove**

1. Disconnect battery.

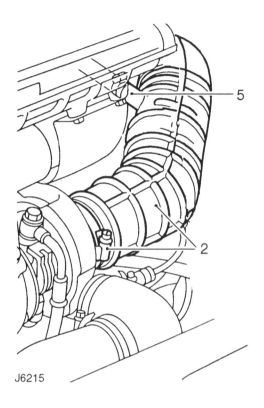

J6215

2. Slacken retaining clip and disconnect intake hose from turbocharger.
3. Slacken retaining clip and disconnect hose from air cleaner.
4. If fitted, disconnect EGR modulator valve vacuum spill pipe from inlet hose.
5. Slacken retaining clip and disconnect breather valve hose from inlet hose.
6. Remove inlet hose.

**Refit**

7. Fit inlet hose to air cleaner.
8. Fit cyclone breather hose to inlet hose.
9. If applicable, fit vacuum spill pipe to inlet hose.
10. Fit inlet hose to turbocharger.
11. Reconnect battery.

## TURBOCHARGER OIL FEED PIPE

**Service repair no - 19.42.14**

**Remove**

1. Disconnect battery.
2. Remove exhaust front pipe *See MANIFOLD AND EXHAUST SYSTEM, Repair, Exhaust front pipe.*

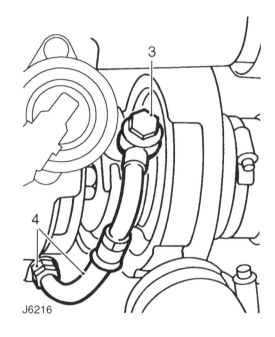

J6216

3. Remove banjo bolt securing oil feed pipe to turbocharger and discard 2 joint sealing washers.
4. Unscrew union and remove feed pipe from cylinder block.
5. Plug connections to prevent ingress of dirt.

**Refit**

6. Using new joint washer, fit oil feed pipe to cylinder block. Tighten union connector to *25 Nm (18 lbf/ft).*
7. Fit a new joint washer to both sides of banjo and secure feed pipe to turbocharger. Tighten banjo bolt to *20 Nm (15 lbf/ft).*
8. Fit exhaust front pipe *See MANIFOLD AND EXHAUST SYSTEM, Repair, Exhaust front pipe.*
9. Check/top-up engine oil level *See SECTION 10, Maintenance, Under bonnet maintenance.*
10. Reconnect battery.

## TURBOCHARGER OIL DRAIN PIPE

**Service repair no - 19.42.12**

**Remove**

1. Disconnect battery.
2. Remove exhaust front pipe *See MANIFOLD AND EXHAUST SYSTEM, Repair, Exhaust front pipe.*

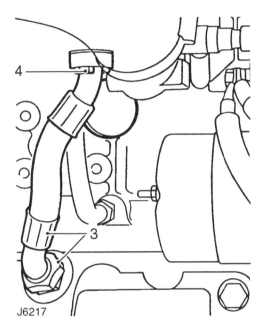

3. Unscrew union and disconnect oil drain pipe from cylinder block.
4. Remove 2 bolts securing oil drain pipe to turbocharger.
5. Remove drain pipe and discard gasket.
6. Plug connections to prevent ingress of dirt.

**Refit**

7. Ensure mating surfaces of oil pipe, turbocharger and engine block are clean.
8. Using new gasket, fit oil drain pipe to turbocharger. Tighten bolts to *25 Nm (18 lbf/ft).*
9. Fit drain pipe to cylinder block and tighten union connector to *38 Nm (28 lbf/ft).*
10. Fit exhaust front pipe *See MANIFOLD AND EXHAUST SYSTEM, Repair, Exhaust front pipe.*
11. Check/top-up engine oil level *See SECTION 10, Maintenance, Under bonnet maintenance.*
12. Reconnect battery.

## INTERCOOLER

**Service repair no - 19.42.15**

**Remove**

1. Disconnect battery.

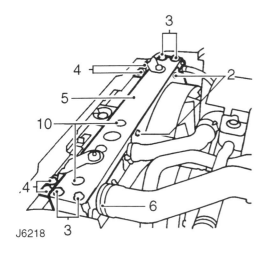

J6218

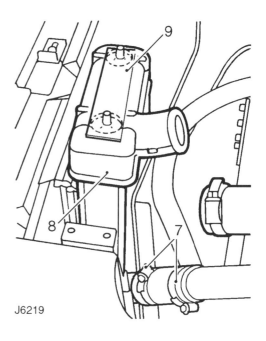

J6219

2. Remove 2 nuts securing fan cowl to radiator top cover.
3. Remove 4 bolts securing radiator top cover to side covers.
4. Remove 2 bolts from both sides, securing radiator top cover mounting brackets to bonnet platform.
5. Detach radiator top cover, complete with mounting brackets.
6. Slacken retaining clip and disconnect top hose from intercooler.
7. Slacken 2 clips and disconnect bottom hose from intercooler.
8. Manoeuvre intercooler upwards and remove from vehicle.
9. Check condition of foam pads fitted to top and bottom of intercooler and renew if necessary.
10. Check condition of intercooler locating grommets in radiator top cover and renew if necessary.

**Refit**

11. Manoeuvre intercooler into position at LH side of radiator.
12. Carefully lower intercooler and locate bottom lugs into radiator bottom support frame.
13. Fit bottom and top hoses to intercooler.
14. Fit radiator top cover and secure mounting brackets to bonnet platform.
15. Secure radiator top cover to side covers.
16. Fit fan cowl to top cover.
17. Reconnect battery.

## EGR VALVE

**Service repair no - 17.45.01**

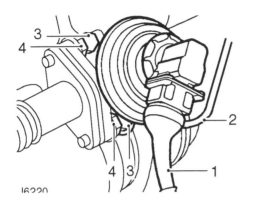

J6220

### Remove

1. Disconnect multi-plug from EGR valve.
2. Disconnect vacuum pipe from EGR valve.
3. Remove 2 Allen screws securing EGR valve to exhaust manifold.
4. Remove 2 bolts securing air inlet delivery tube to EGR valve.
5. Remove EGR valve and discard gaskets.

### Refit

6. Clean mating faces of EGR valve and exhaust manifold.
7. Position new gaskets and fit EGR valve to delivery tube and exhaust manifold. Tighten bolts to *25 Nm (18 lbf/ft).*
8. Fit vacuum pipe and multi-plug to EGR valve.

## EGR VALVE MODULATOR

**Service repair no - 17.45.04**

### Remove

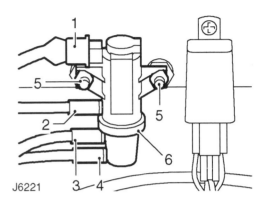

J6221

1. Disconnect multi-plug from modulator.
2. Disconnect spill pipe (green), modulator to air cleaner hose.
3. Disconnect vacuum pipe (blue), modulator to EGR valve.
4. Disconnect vacuum pipe (white), modulator to brake servo pipe.
5. Unscrew 2 nuts securing modulator to flexible mountings.
6. Remove modulator.

### Refit

7. Fit modulator to flexible mountings and tighten nuts to *8 Nm (6 lbf/ft).*
8. Fit modulator pipes, ensuring they are connected to correct ports.
9. Connect modulator multi-plug.

## EGR THROTTLE POSITION SENSOR

**Service repair no - 17.45.08**

**Remove**

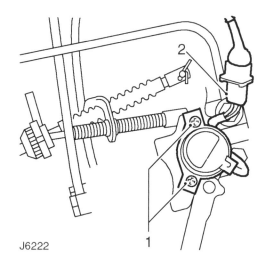

J6222

1. Remove 2 screws securing throttle position sensor mounting plate to injection pump.
2. Disconnect sensor multi-plug.
3. Remove sensor assembly.

**Refit**

4. Position sensor assembly on injection pump and secure with screws.
5. Connect multi-plug.
6. Adjust sensor *See Adjustment, EGR throttle position sensor.*

## EGR CONTROL UNIT

**Service repair no - 17.45.07**

**Remove**

1. Raise centre seat, or cubby box *See CHASSIS AND BODY, Repair, Cubby box* to gain access to EGR control unit harness.

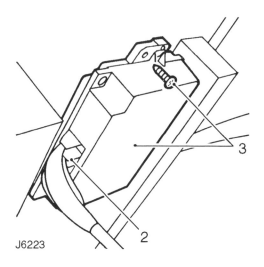

J6223

2. Disconnect control unit multi-plug and remove centre seat or cubby box.
3. Remove 4 screws and detach control unit from seat or cubby box base.

**Refit**

4. Secure EGR control unit to base of centre seat or cubby box.
5. Position centre seat or cubby box and connect control unit multi-plug.
6. Fit centre seat, or cubby box *See CHASSIS AND BODY, Repair, Cubby box.*

# 26 - COOLING SYSTEM

## CONTENTS

Page

**DESCRIPTION AND OPERATION**

**ADJUSTMENT**

**REPAIR**

# Notes

## ENGINE COOLING SYSTEM

### Description

The complete cooling system of the 300Tdi engine incorporates three independent functions:- Engine (coolant) cooling; Turbo (charge air) intercooling; Engine oil cooling.

The intercooler is a separate aluminium unit, located on the LH side of the engine compartment adjacent to the radiator, sharing the same upper and lower mountings. For details of turbo intercooling **See FUEL SYSTEM, Description and operation, Operation.** The oil cooler matrix is an integral part of the radiator. Pre-formed pipes/hoses are used to link the components within the separate systems as shown below.

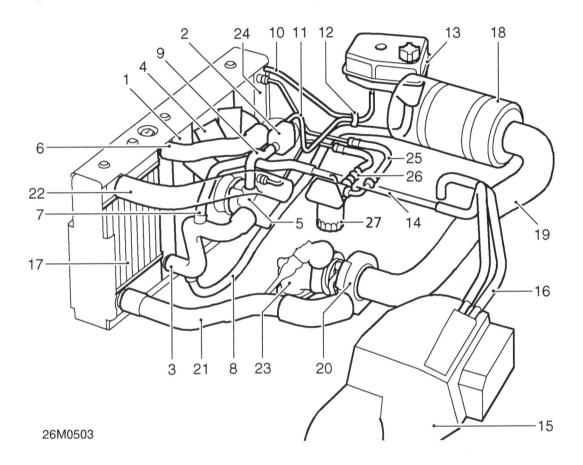

26M0503

### Engine cooling system

1. Radiator
2. Thermostat housing
3. Radiator bottom hose
4. Viscous fan
5. Water pump
6. Radiator top hose
7. Heater return hose
8. Coolant supply hose
9. By-pass hose
10. Radiator bleed (purge) hose
11. Bleed (purge) hose, thermostat housing
12. 'Y' piece ejector
13. Expansion tank

14. Heater rail
15. Heater unit
16. Heater feed hose
17. Intercooler
18. Air cleaner
19. Air feed hose
20. Turbocharger
21. Charge air supply pipe/hose
22. Cooled charge air supply hose
23. Exhaust manifold
24. Engine oil cooler
25. Feed pipe, engine oil cooler
26. Return pipe, engine oil cooler
27. Oil filter

## ENGINE (COOLANT) COOLING

### Description

The 300Tdi engine uses a pressurised cooling system and cross flow radiator which is supplied with coolant from an expansion tank mounted on the RH side of the engine compartment. A belt driven centrifugal water pump, fitted to an auxiliary mounting assembly, pumps coolant to the engine crankcase, cylinder head and vehicle heater unit.

An eleven bladed fan, incorporating a viscous coupling, is driven by an independent pulley secured to the front cover plate. The thermostat housing, bolted to the front of the cylinder head, is fitted with a vent valve that purges excessive air pressure and coolant back to the expansion tank.

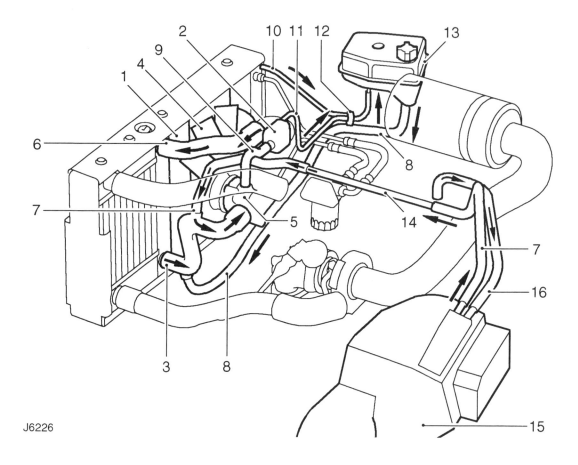

J6226

**Engine coolant circulation (engine warm - thermostat open).**

1. Radiator
2. Thermostat/housing
3. Radiator bottom hose
4. Viscous fan
5. Water pump
6. Radiator top hose
7. Heater return hose
8. Coolant supply hose
9. By-pass hose
10. Radiator bleed (purge) hose
11. Thermostat housing bleed (purge) hose
12. 'Y' piece ejector
13. Expansion tank
14. Heater rail
15. Heater unit
16. Heater feed hose

## COOLANT CIRCULATION

### Operation

When the engine is started from cold the thermostat (2) prevents coolant circulation through the radiator by closing off the top hose (6). During the engine warm up period the water pump (5) circulates coolant to the cylinders in the crankcase and through separate ports to the cylinder head. At the rear of the cylinder head a proportion of the flow is diverted through a heater feed pipe (16) to the matrix of the heater unit (15). The coolant is then carried, via a heater return rail (14) and hoses (7), back to the water pump. The remaining coolant flows through a by-pass hose (9) at the thermostat housing and back to the water pump to complete the first cycle.

When the normal engine running temperature is reached, the thermostat opens, closing off the by-pass hose (9). Coolant is then circulated via the top hose (6) and through the radiator, where it is cooled and drawn from the radiator bottom hose (3) by the water pump (5). The coolant circulation through the crankcase and cylinder head remains the same.

Two bleed pipes (10) and (11) help control the system pressure by purging excess air and coolant to the expansion tank via the 'Y'piece ejector (12).

## VISCOUS FAN

### Description

The viscous drive unit for the engine cooling fan, provides a means of controlling the speed of the fan relative to the running temperature of the engine. The viscous unit is a type of fluid coupling, which drives the fan blades by means of 'silicone fluid'.

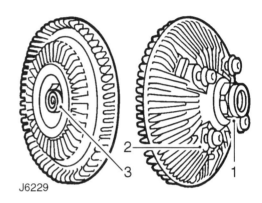

J6229

1.  Input (drive) member
2.  Output (driven) member
3.  Sensing mechanism (bi-metal coil)

The fan drive has to be engaged only periodically, between 5% and 10%, during normal operating conditions, because the engine is cooled by ram air for most of the time.

## Operation

To engage and disengage the fan drive the bi-metal coil senses air temperature behind the radiator. When a pre-determined temperature is reached, the coil opens a valve (5) which allows fluid to enter the drive area and, due to centrifugal force, circulates to the annular drive area.

There are two sets of annular grooves (3), one in the drive clutch and the other in the drive body, a specific clearance being provided between the two sets of grooves.

When this clearance is filled with viscous fluid, a shearing action, caused by the speed differential between the two drive components, transmits torque to the fan. The fluid is thrown to the outside of the unit by centrifugal force from where it is recirculated to the reservoir (10) via the pump plate (4) adjacent to the drive member.

If the engine speed is increased the amount of slip will also increase to limit the maximum fan speed.

When the air temperature from the radiator drops sufficiently, the bi-metal coil closes the valve and prevents fluid entering the drive area. The fluid that is in the drive area will gradually pump out into the reservoir (10) and the fan will return to an idle condition.

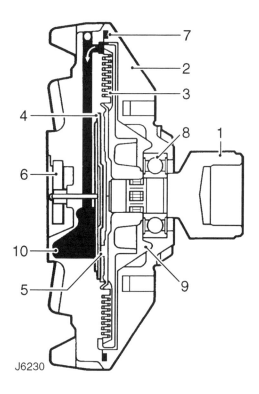

J6230

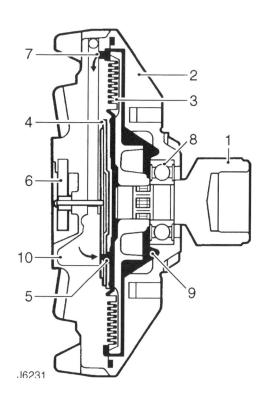

J6231

**Viscous unit disengaged (engine at normal running temperature)**

1. Input (drive) member
2. Output (driven) member
3. Running clearance
4. Pump plate
5. Valve (closed)
6. Sensing mechanism (bi-metal coil)
7. Fluid seal
8. Bearing, input member
9. Fluid chamber
10. Fluid reservoir

**Viscous unit engaged (hot running temperature)**

Bi-metal coil (6) expanded, valve (5) open.

## DRAIN AND REFILL COOLING SYSTEM

**Service repair no - 26.10.01**

**Draining**

⚠ WARNING: DO NOT remove caps or plugs when the engine is hot. The cooling system is pressurised and personal scalding could result.

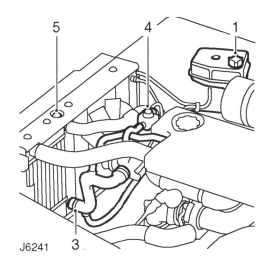

J6241  3

1. Remove expansion tank filler cap.
2. Position a clean container under radiator if coolant is to be reused.
3. Disconnect radiator bottom hose and allow coolant to drain.

△ NOTE: A chassis undertray may be fitted on some vehicle derivatives to conform to legal requirements. When under chassis remove and refit procedures are required, it may be necessary to remove the undertray and/or integral access panels *See CHASSIS AND BODY, Repair, Front undertray or Rear undertray.*

4. When expansion tank has emptied remove thermostat housing plug to assist drainage.
5. Similarly when coolant is below top of radiator, remove radiator plug.
6. Fit radiator bottom hose and fully tighten hose clip.

**Refill**

⚠ CAUTION: It is important that the correct procedure is followed when refilling or topping up the cooling system to avoid trapping air in the system.

7. Fill cooling system with 50% - 50% of water/anti-freeze mixture *See LUBRICANTS, FLUIDS AND CAPACITIES, Information, Recommended lubricants and fluids.*
8. Fill through expansion tank until radiator is full, with level in expansion tank the same as radiator.

△ NOTE: Care should be taken to avoid excess coolant spillage.

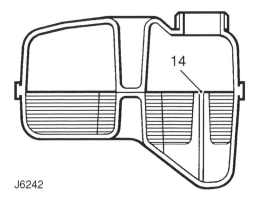

J6242

9. Fit plastic plug in radiator.
10. Add a further 1 litre (1.76 pints) of coolant into expansion tank and allow to settle.
11. Refit expansion tank cap and thermostat housing plug.
12. Run engine at idle speed for 5 minutes.
13. Switch off engine and allow to cool.
14. Check that coolant in expansion tank is level with top of indicator post. Top up if necessary.

# Notes

## VISCOUS COUPLING AND FAN

**Service repair no - 26.25.19 - Viscous coupling**
**Service repair no - 26.25.05 - Fan**

**Remove**

 **NOTE: The viscous coupling has a LH thread.**

1. Disconnect battery.
2. Using special pulley restraining tool **LRT-12-094** and special spanner **LRT-12-093** unscrew viscous coupling from pulley hub adaptor thread.

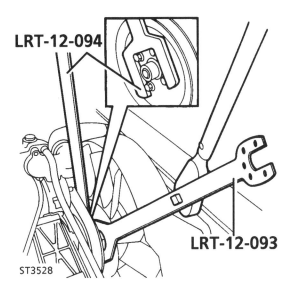

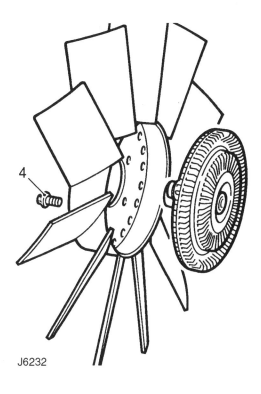

J6232

**Refit**

5. Fit viscous unit to fan blades.
6. If applicable, fit fan cowl *See Fan cowl.*
7. Carefully position viscous coupling and fit onto pulley hub adaptor thread.
8. Using special pulley retaining tool, spanner and a suitable torque wrench, tighten assembly to *45 Nm (33 lbf/ft).*

3. Remove viscous coupling and fan from vehicle.

 **NOTE: If air conditioning is fitted, the fan cowl will also need removing, *See Fan cowl*, with the viscous fan unit.**

4. If required, remove 4 screws and release viscous unit from fan blade.

## FAN COWL

**Service repair no - 26.25.11**

**Remove**

1. Disconnect battery.
2. Drain coolant *See Adjustment, Drain and refill cooling system .*

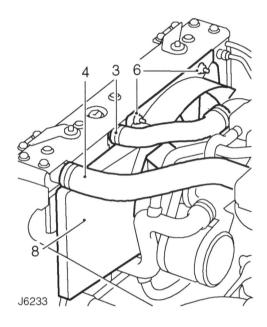

J6233

3. Slacken retaining clips and remove radiator top hose.
4. Slacken retaining clip and remove top hose from intercooler.

 **NOTE: On vehicles fitted with EGR system, remove complete intercooler top hose assembly.**

5. Remove viscous coupling and fan *See Viscous coupling and fan.*
6. Remove 2 nuts securing top of fan cowl.
7. Release expansion tank hose from clips at base of fan cowl.
8. Lift and remove cowl .

 **NOTE: On vehicles fitted with air conditioning, it will be necessary to remove the cowl and viscous fan unit together to enable clearance of the compressor.**

**Refit**

9. Position fan cowl.
10. Fit viscous fan unit *See Viscous coupling and fan.*
11. Fit expansion tank hose into fan cowl clips.
12. Secure top of fan cowl to radiator top cover.
13. Fit intercooler top hose.
14. Fit radiator top hose.
15. Refill cooling system *See Adjustment, Drain and refill cooling system.*
16. Reconnect battery.

## FAN PULLEY

**Service repair no - 26.25.04.**

**Remove**

1. Disconnect battery.
2. Remove viscous fan unit *See Viscous coupling and fan.*
3. Remove drive belt *See ELECTRICAL, Repair, Auxiliary drive belt.*

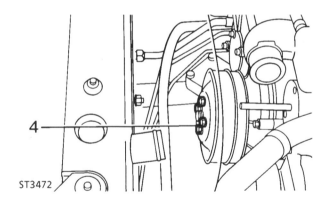

ST3472

4. Unscrew 4 bolts and remove pulley from adaptor boss.

**Refit**

5. Fit fan pulley to adaptor boss. Tighten bolts to *25 Nm (18 lbf/ft).*
6. Fit drive belt *See ELECTRICAL, Repair, Auxiliary drive belt.*
7. Fit viscous fan unit *See Viscous coupling and fan.*
8. Reconnect battery.

## WATER PUMP

**Service repair no - 26.50.01**

**Remove**

1. Disconnect battery.
2. Drain cooling system. *See Adjustment, Drain and refill cooling system*
3. Remove radiator top hose.
4. Remove intercooler top hose.
5. Slacken water pump and power steering pump pulley retaining bolts.
6. Remove drive belt. *See ELECTRICAL, Repair, Auxiliary drive belt*
7. Unscrew flange nut and remove belt tensioner.
8. Remove oil filler cap and remove rocker cover insulation.

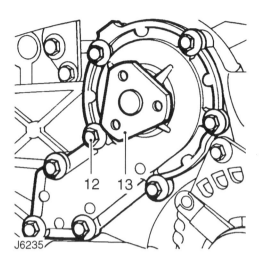

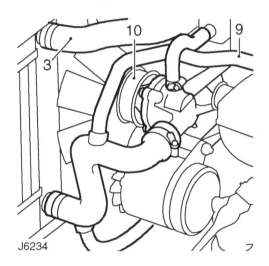

9. Slacken retaining clip and disconnect hose at heater rail.
10. Unscrew 3 bolts and remove water pump pulley.
11. Unscrew 3 bolts and remove power steering pump pulley.
12. Remove 8 bolts securing water pump, noting location of 3 through bolts into cylinder block.
13. Withdraw pump and gasket from auxiliary mounting bracket.
14. Clean all gasket material from mating faces.

**Refit**

15. Using new gasket, fit water pump to mounting bracket. Tighten bolts to *25 Nm (18 lbf/ft).*
16. Fit power steering pump pulley.
17. Fit water pump pulley. Tighten bolts of both pulleys to *25 Nm (18 lbf/ft).*
18. Fit drive belt. *See ELECTRICAL, Repair, Auxiliary drive belt*
19. Fit hose at heater rail.
20. Fit rocker cover insulation and oil filler cap.
21. Fit drive belt tensioner. Tighten retaining nut to *45 Nm (33 lbf/ft).*
22. Fit intercooler top hose.
23. Fit radiator top hose.
24. Refill cooling system. *See Adjustment, Drain and refill cooling system*
25. Reconnect battery.

## AUXILIARY MOUNTING BRACKET AND GASKET

**Service repair no - 26.50.04**

**Remove**

1. Disconnect battery.
2. Drain cooling system *See Adjustment, Drain and refill cooling system* .
3. Remove radiator top hose.
4. Remove intercooler top hose.
5. Remove viscous fan unit. *See Viscous coupling and fan*
6. Remove fan cowl. *See Fan cowl*
7. Slacken power steering pump pulley retaining bolts.
8. Remove drive belt. *See ELECTRICAL, Repair, Auxiliary Drive belt*

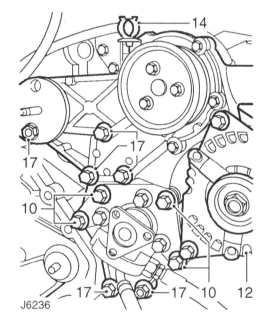

J6236

9. Unscrew 3 bolts and remove power steering pump pulley.
10. Remove 4 bolts securing power steering pump mounting bracket.
11. Lower pump and bracket. Do not disconnect fluid pipes.
12. Remove generator. *See ELECTRICAL, Repair, Generator*
13. Unscrew retaining nut and remove drive belt tensioner.
14. Release hose clip from bracket above water pump.

15. Disconnect bottom hose/heater return hose at water pump and heater rail.
16. Disconnect by-pass hose from water pump and thermostat housing.
17. Remove 5 bolts (one with nut) and single retaining nut, securing auxiliary mounting bracket to cylinder block.
18. Withdraw mounting bracket, complete with water pump.
19. Remove gasket and clean mating faces.

**Refit**

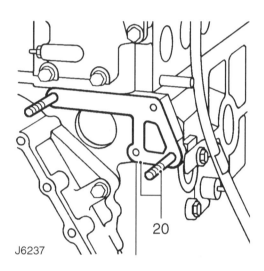

J6237

20. Using 2 slave studs, fit new gasket.

 NOTE: All fixing bolts and nuts should be tightened to *25 Nm (18 lbf/ft)* unless otherwise stated.

21. Locate mounting bracket, complete with water pump on slave studs and secure with 4 other fixings.
22. Remove slave studs and fit remaining bolts/nuts.
23. Fit by-pass hose to thermostat housing and water pump.
24. Fit bottom hose/heater return hose to water pump and heater rail.
25. Fit heater hose clip to mounting bracket.
26. Fit drive belt tensioner. Tighten nut to *45 Nm (33 lbf/ft)*.
27. Fit generator. *See ELECTRICAL, Repair, Generator* Do not fit drive belt at this stage.

28. Secure steering pump and bracket to auxiliary mounting bracket.
29. Fit steering pump pulley.
30. Fit drive belt *See ELECTRICAL, Repair, Auxiliary drive belt.*
31. Fit fan cowl *See Fan cowl.*
32. Fit viscous fan unit *See Viscous coupling and fan.*
33. Fit intercooler top hose.
34. Fit radiator top hose.
35. Refill cooling system *See Adjustment, Drain and refill cooling system.*
36. Reconnect battery.

## THERMOSTAT

**Service repair no - 26.45.01**

**Remove**

1. Partially drain cooling system, until coolant level is below thermostat housing.
2. Disconnect top hose from outlet elbow.

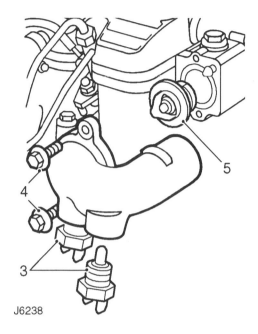

J6238

3. Disconnect electrical connections to water temperature switch.
4. Unscrew 2 bolts and remove outlet elbow.
5. Withdraw thermostat. Note 88° C rating of thermostat.
6. Place thermostat in a container half full of water. Heat water and observe temperature at which thermostat begins to open. Thermostat is satisfactory if it opens between 85° - 89° C.

**Refit**

7. Fit thermostat with jiggle pin/vent hole upwards.
8. Secure outlet elbow to thermostat housing. Tighten bolts to *25 Nm (18 lbf/ft).*
9. Fit water temperature switch connections.
10. Fit top hose to outlet elbow.
11. Refill cooling system *See Adjustment, Drain and refill cooling system.*

## RADIATOR

**Service repair no - 26.40.01**

**Remove**

1. Disconnect radiator bottom hose and drain cooling system **See Adjustment, Drain and refill cooling system** .
2. Disconnect radiator top hose.
3. Remove viscous fan unit **See Viscous coupling and fan** .
4. Remove fan cowl **See Fan cowl.**

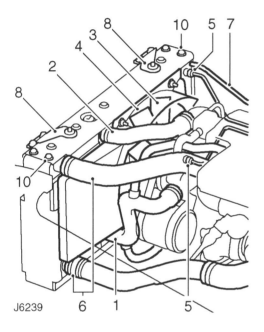

J6239

5. Disconnect oil cooler pipes. Plug all connections to prevent oil spillage and ingress of dirt.
6. Disconnect top and bottom intercooler hoses.
7. Disconnect bleed hose at radiator.
8. Remove 2 bolts from both sides securing radiator mounting brackets to bonnet platform.
9. Lift and remove radiator/intercooler assembly from vehicle.
10. Remove 2 bolts from both sides and detach radiator top cover from side covers.
11. Lift and remove radiator from intercooler and RH side frame.
12. Check condition of locating grommets in radiator top cover and lower mounting bushes. Renew if necessary.

**Refit**

13. Position radiator between intercooler and RH side frame.
14. Fit radiator top cover to side covers.
15. Lower radiator/intercooler assembly into position.
16. Secure radiator mounting brackets to bonnet platform.
17. Fit radiator bleed hose.
18. Fit top and bottom intercooler hoses.
19. Fit oil cooler pipes.
20. Fit fan cowl **See Fan cowl.**
21. Fit viscous fan unit **See Viscous coupling and fan.**
22. Fit radiator top hose.
23. Fit radiator bottom hose and refill cooling system **See Adjustment, Drain and refill cooling system.**

## EXPANSION TANK

**Service repair no - 26.15.01**

### Remove

1. Position container to collect coolant spillage.

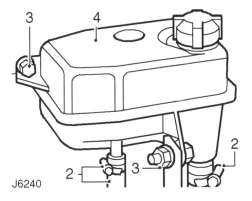

J6240

2. Slacken retaining clips and disconnect both hoses from base of expansion tank.
3. Remove 3 bolts securing expansion tank to inside wing and mounting bracket.
4. Remove expansion tank.

### Refit

5. Fit expansion tank to inside wing and mounting bracket.
6. Fit both hoses to base of tank.
7. Check and top up cooling system *See SECTION 10, Maintenance, Check/top up cooling system.*

# Notes

# 30 - MANIFOLD AND EXHAUST SYSTEM

## CONTENTS

Page

**DESCRIPTION AND OPERATION**

**REPAIR**

# Notes

## MANIFOLDS AND EXHAUST SYSTEM

### Description

The exhaust systems fitted on all models with the 300Tdi engine comprise three sections; front pipe assembly, intermediate silencer assembly, and tail pipe and silencer assembly. All sections, including silencers, are manufactured from luminised steel to give the system a durable working life under all conditions. Special clamps are provided to ensure

leak proof jointing between the various sections, which are supported by flexible rubber mountings.

### Catalytic convertor

When fitted, the catalytic converter is integral with the front pipe assembly, which also incorporates a flexible joint. The catalyst forms part of the engine emission control that can also include an EGR valve system *See FUEL SYSTEM, Description and operation, EGR fuel system component location.*

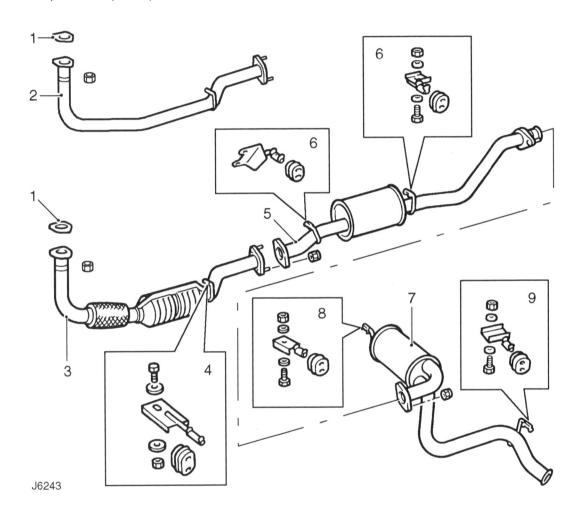

J6243

**Exhaust system - 90**

1. Gasket
2. Front pipe
3. Front pipe with catalytic converter
4. Front mounting bracket
5. Intermediate silencer
6. Intermediate mounting brackets
7. Tail pipe silencer*
8. Tail pipe silencer mounting
9. Tail pipe mounting
   * Deleted on later models

The catalyst comprises platinum coated ceramic elements. The Hydrocarbons (HC), Oxides of nitrogen (NOx) and Carbon monoxide (CO) emitted by the engine react with the catalytic element and exhaust temperature to convert the toxic gas into Nitrogen ($N_2$), Carbon dioxide ($CO_2$) and water vapour.

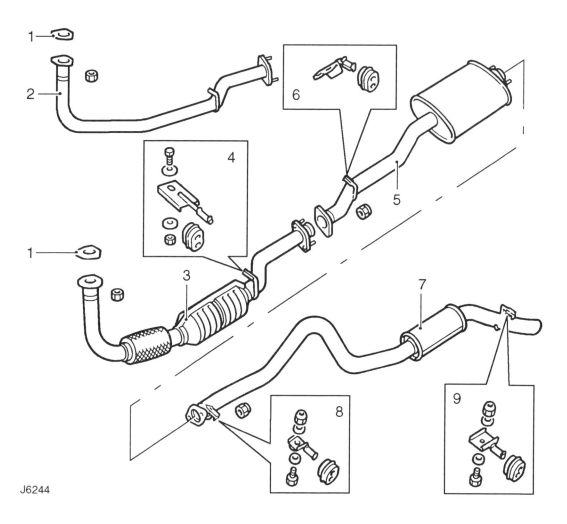

J6244

**Exhaust system - 110/130**

1. Gasket
2. Front pipe
3. Front pipe with catalytic converter
4. Front mounting bracket
5. Intermediate silencer
6. Intermediate mounting brackets
7. Tail pipe silencer
8. Tail pipe silencer mounting
9. Tail pipe mounting

## INDUCTION MANIFOLD

**Service repair no - 30.15.02**

### Remove

1. Disconnect battery.
2. Remove oil filler cap and remove rocker cover insulation.
3. Remove hose intercooler to induction manifold. If fitted, remove EGR valve *See FUEL SYSTEM, Repair, EGR valve.*
4. Remove 2 screws and release heat shield from induction manifold.
5. Slacken induction manifold lower securing nuts, located below exhaust manifold.

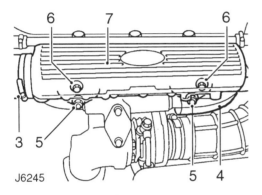

J6245

6. Remove induction manifold upper securing bolts.
7. Remove induction manifold. Plug apertures in cylinder head with clean rag to prevent any items falling into engine.
8. Check gasket is satisfactory for further use.

### Refit

9. Clean induction manifold mating face.
10. Position induction manifold and secure with upper and lower fixings.
11. Tighten securing nuts and bolts to *25 Nm (18 lbf/ft).*
12. Fit manifold heat shield.
13. Fit hose intercooler to induction manifold.
14. Fit rocker cover insulation.
15. Reconnect battery.

## INDUCTION/EXHAUST MANIFOLD GASKET

**Service repair no - 30.15.15**

### Remove

1. Remove induction manifold *See Induction manifold.*
2. Remove turbocharger outlet hose.
3. Raise vehicle and slacken exhaust front pipe to intermediate silencer flange nuts. Ensure pipe is free to turn.

⚠️ **NOTE: If removing exhaust manifold and turbocharger assembly from vehicle, remove manifold to exhaust front pipe nuts while working under vehicle.**

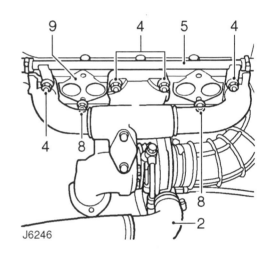

J6246

4. Remove exhaust manifold securing nuts, removing centre lower nut first.
5. Move heater rail clear of exhaust manifold.
6. With exhaust manifold and turbocharger still attached to exhaust front pipe, withdraw from head by turning front pipe until sufficient access is gained to remove gasket.
7. Suitably support exhaust manifold and turbocharger assembly to prevent damage.
8. Remove induction manifold lower nuts.
9. Remove gasket.
10. Clean mating faces.

**Refit**

11. Fit new gasket over manifold studs.
12. Loosely fit induction manifold lower nuts to studs.
13. Fit exhaust manifold and secure with central upper and lower nuts.
14. Locate heater rail to its correct position and secure with outer exhaust manifold nuts.
15. Tighten all exhaust manifold nuts to **45 Nm (33 lbf/ft).**
16. Tighten exhaust front pipe to intermediate silencer nuts to **50 Nm (37 lbf/ft).**
17. Fit turbocharger outlet pipe.
18. Fit induction manifold **See Induction manifold.**

## EXHAUST MANIFOLD/TURBOCHARGER ASSEMBLY

**Service repair no - 30.15.10**

**Remove**

1. Remove induction manifold **See Induction manifold.**
2. Disconnect turbocharger inlet hose.
3. Disconnect boost pressure pipe at turbocharger.

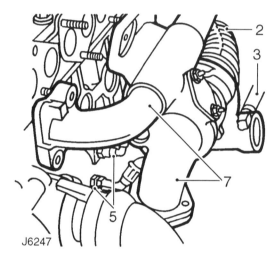

J6247

4. Remove intercooler bottom hose.
5. Place suitable container under engine and disconnect turbocharger oil feed and return pipes at cylinder block.
6. Remove 3 nuts securing exhaust front pipe to manifold flange.
7. Remove 7 nuts and lift exhaust manifold and turbocharger assembly from cylinder head.
8. Discard manifold gasket.

**Refit**

9. Fit new manifold gasket.
10. Position exhaust manifold assembly onto location studs and secure to cylinder head. Tighten nuts to **45 Nm (33 lbf/ft).**
11. Secure exhaust front pipe to manifold flange. Tighten fixings to **50 Nm (37 lbf/ft).**
12. Reconnect turbocharger oil feed and return pipes at cylinder block.
13. Fit intercooler bottom hose.
14. Fit boost pressure pipe at turbocharger.
15. Fit turbocharger inlet hose.
16. Fit induction manifold **See Induction manifold.**

## EXHAUST FRONT PIPE

**Service repair no - 30.10.09**

**Remove**

1. Disconnect battery.
2. Raise vehicle on ramp.

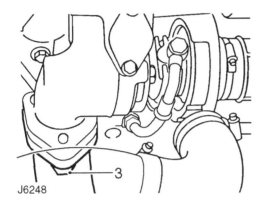

J6248

3. Remove 3 securing nuts at exhaust manifold flange.

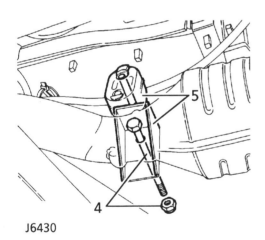

J6430

4. Remove through bolt securing front pipe mounting bracket to chassis.
5. Remove bracket and rubber mounting from exhaust pipe.

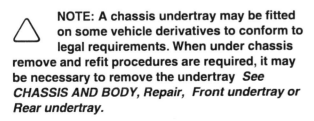

⚠ **NOTE: A chassis undertray may be fitted on some vehicle derivatives to conform to legal requirements. When under chassis remove and refit procedures are required, it may be necessary to remove the undertray** *See CHASSIS AND BODY, Repair, Front undertray or Rear undertray.*

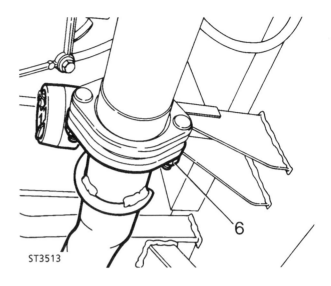

ST3513

6. Remove flange nuts securing front pipe to intermediate silencer assembly and separate flanges.
7. Release front pipe at manifold and remove gasket.
8. Move front pipe rearwards, lower front end and at the same time twist toward propeller shaft. Move pipe forward and withdraw from under vehicle.

**Refit**

9. Manouvre front pipe into position and secure to intermediate silencer flange. Do not fully tighten fixings at this stage.
10. Fit new gasket and secure front pipe to exhaust manifold. Tighten fixings to *50 Nm (37 lbf/ft).*
11. Fit front pipe bracket and mounting rubber to chassis.
12. Fully tighten front pipe to intermediate silencer flange nuts to *30 Nm (22 lbf/ft).*
13. Lower vehicle ramp and reconnect battery.

## INTERMEDIATE PIPE - 90

**Service repair no - 30.10.11**

**Remove**

1. Raise vehicle on ramp.
2. Release intermediate pipe from front mounting rubber, see J6243.
3. Remove 2 flange nuts securing intermediate pipe to tail pipe.
4. Release intermediate pipe from rear mounting rubber.
5. Remove 2 flange nuts securing intermediate pipe to front pipe.
6. Release intermediate pipe from front and tail pipe and remove.

**Refit**

7. Fit intermediate pipe to front and tail pipes.
8. Secure intermediate pipe to front and rear mounting rubbers.
9. Secure intermediate pipe to front pipe. Tighten nuts to *30 Nm (22 lbf/ft)*.
10. Secure intermediate pipe to tail pipe. Tighten nuts to *30 Nm (22 lbf/ft)*.
11. Lower vehicle.

## INTERMEDIATE PIPE - 110/130

**Service repair no - 30.10.11**

**Remove**

1. Raise vehicle on ramp.
2. Release intermediate pipe from mounting rubber, see J6244.
3. Remove 2 flange nuts securing intermediate pipe to tail pipe.
4. Remove 2 flange nuts securing intermediate pipe to front pipe.
5. Release intermediate pipe from front and tail pipe and remove.

**Refit**

6. Fit intermediate pipe to front and tail pipes.
7. Secure intermediate pipe to mounting rubbers.
8. Secure intermediate pipe to front pipe. Tighten nuts to *30 Nm (22 lbf/ft)*.
9. Secure intermediate pipe to tail pipe. Tighten nuts to *30 Nm (22 lbf/ft)*.
10. Lower vehicle.

## TAILPIPE - 90

**Service repair no - 30.10.22**

### Remove

1. Raise vehicle on ramp.
2. Remove 2 flange nuts securing tail pipe to intermediate pipe, see J6243.
3. Release tail pipe from inboard mounting rubber.
4. Release tail pipe from outboard mounting rubber and remove.

### Refit

5. Fit tail pipe to intermediate pipe.
6. Secure tail pipe to mounting rubbers.
7. Secure tail pipe to intermediate pipe. Tighten nuts to *30 Nm (22 lbf/ft).*
8. Lower vehicle.

## TAILPIPE - 110/130

**Service repair no - 30.10.22**

### Remove

1. Raise vehicle on ramp.
2. Remove 2 flange nuts securing tail pipe to intermediate pipe, see J6244.
3. Release tail pipe from front mounting rubber.
4. Release tail pipe from rear mounting rubber.
5. Release tail pipe from intermediate pipe and feed over rear axle.
6. Remove tail pipe.

### Refit

7. Feed tail pipe over rear axle and connect to intermediate pipe.
8. Secure tail pipe to mounting rubbers.
9. Secure tail pipe to intermediate pipe. Tighten nuts to *30 Nm (22 lbf/ft).*
10. Lower vehicle.

# Notes

# 33 - CLUTCH

## CONTENTS

# Notes

## DESCRIPTION

The clutch unit comprises a single dry plate friction disc and diaphragm spring clutch unit, secured to the engine flywheel.

## OPERATION

The unit is operated hydraulically by the clutch master cylinder (12) and a slave cylinder (13) attached to the transmission bell housing.

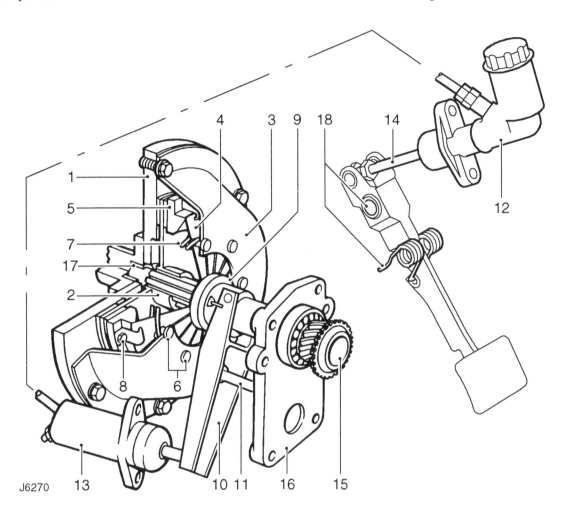

J6270

**Clutch components**

1. Crankshaft and flywheel
2. Friction plate
3. Clutch cover
4. Diaphragm spring
5. Pressure plate
6. Fulcrum posts (9) for diaphragm spring
7. Bearing rings (2) for diaphragm spring
8. Retraction links and bolts (3) for pressure plate
9. Release bearing

10. Release lever
11. Release lever pivot post
12. Master cylinder
13. Slave cylinder
14. Master cylinder pedal pushrod
15. Primary shaft and taper bearing (in gearbox)
16. Gearbox front cover
17. Primary shaft flywheel bush
18. Pedal pivot and return spring

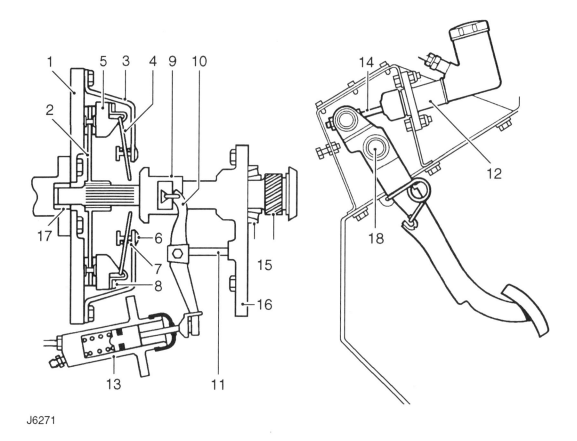

J6271

When the clutch pedal is depressed, hydraulic fluid transmits the movement via the slave cylinder, release lever (10), bearing (9), to the inner fingers of the diaphragm spring (4).

The diaphragm spring (4) pivots on the bearing rings (7) and fulcrum posts (6) causing the pressure plate (5) to release the clamping force on the friction plate and linings (2).

As the the clamping force is removed from the friction plate (2), the plate slides on the splines of the primary shaft (15) and takes up a neutral position between the flywheel (1) and the pressure plate (5), thus disconnecting the drive between the engine and the gearbox.

## CLUTCH ASSEMBLY CONDITIONS

For the clutch to operate correctly it is important the following conditions are satisfied:-

* The primary shaft (15) must be free in the crankshaft spigot bush (17).

* The friction plate (2) must be able to slide easily on the splines on the primary shaft (15), to a position where it does not contact either the flywheel or the pressure plate.

* The friction plate must not be distorted or the linings contaminated with oil, which may cause it to stick or continue to run in contact with the flywheel or pressure plate.

A number of faults can develop in the operation of the clutch for a variety of reasons and most faults are due to normal wear at high mileage. Problems can also occur if the unit has been renewed by an unskilled operator.

Recognising and diagnosing a particular clutch fault is therefore of paramount importance in ensuring that the problem is rectified at the first attempt.

Problems which develop in the clutch are as follows:-

* Clutch spin/drag

* Clutch slip

* Clutch judder/fierce

## CLUTCH SPIN - DRAG

**Symptoms**

Clutch spin is that, with engine running and clutch pedal depressed, the gears cannot be immediately engaged without making a grinding noise. This indicates the clutch is not making a clean break.

However, if the clutch pedal is held depressed for several seconds the friction plate will eventually break free from the engine and the gear will engage silently.

Clutch spin as it becomes more severe develops into clutch drag, making the silent engagement of a gear impossible, regardless of how long the pedal is held depressed.

## CLUTCH SLIP

**Symptoms**

Clutch slip is most evident climbing a hill or when the vehicle is moving off from stationary with a heavy load. As the clutch is released, slip occurs between the engine and the transmission, allowing the engine speed to increase without a corresponding increase in vehicle speed.

Clutch slip can develop to the stage where no power is transmitted through the clutch as the pedal is released.

## CLUTCH JUDDER - FIERCE

**Symptoms**

Clutch judder or fierce engagement, like slip, is most likely to occur when the vehicle is moving off from stationary. As the clutch pedal is released the vehicle will move rapidly or in a series of jerks, which cannot be controlled even by careful operation of the clutch by the driver.

It should be noted that a vehicle may display all the symptoms or any combination of the symptoms described, depending on the driving conditions vehicle load and operating temperatures.

## FAULT/SYMPTOM CHART

| Symptoms | | | | |
|---|---|---|---|---|
| Slip | Spin/Drag | Judder/Fierce | Fault | Item |
| * | * | * | Worn or oil on clutch linings | 2 |
| * | * | * | Mechanical damage | 4 5 6 7 8 |
| | * | * | Distorted clutch plate | 2 |
| | * | | Failed or air in hydraulic system | 12 13 |
| | * | * | Primary shaft tight fit in crankshaft bush | 15 17 |
| | * | | Clutch splines sticking | 2 15 |
| | | * | Weak clutch plate springs or insecure/worn engine/gearbox mountings | 6 |
| | | * | Insecure/worn propeller shafts | |
| | | * | Insecure/worn suspension components/rubber bushes | |

The items refered to in this chart relate to the clutch components shown in J6270 and J6271 *See Description and operation, Clutch.*

## CLUTCH NOISE - MECHANICAL FAULTS

**Noise from clutch or gearbox in neutral, which disappears when clutch is depressed.**

Suspect gearbox input/primary shaft bearings *See MANUAL GEARBOX, Fault diagnosis, Manual gearbox.*

**Noise from clutch or gearbox in neutral, which changes tone or becomes worse when the clutch is depressed.**

Suspect worn release bearing.

**Knocking/rattling from clutch or gearbox in neutral, which is reduced or disappears when the clutch is depressed.**

Suspect worn/weak release lever retainer or clutch unit.

**Noise from clutch or gearbox in neutral, which disappears when clutch is depressed.**

Suspect gearbox fault *See MANUAL GEARBOX, Fault diagnosis, Manual gearbox.*

## HYDRAULIC FAULTS

**Unable to dis-engage clutch, little or no pedal resistance.**

1. Check condition, specification and level of fluid.
2. Check pipes and cylinders for leaks.
3. Check that air vent in reservoir lid is clear. Suspect faulty master cylinder if no fluid leaks present *See Repair, Master cylinder.*

**Spongy pedal operation**

1. Check condition, specification and level of fluid.
2. Check that air vent in reservoir lid is clear. Suspect air in fluid *See Repair, Bleed hydraulic system.*

**Clutch is difficult to dis-engage and/or does not immediately re-engage when pedal is released.**

1. Check condition, specification and level of fluid.
2. Check that air vent in reservoir lid is clear. Suspect pedal pivot, master cylinder or slave cylinder seizure *See Repair, Master cylinder.*

## CLUTCH PEDAL AND MASTER CYLINDER SETTING

1. Remove 6 screws and detach pedal box top cover and gasket.
2. Slacken both locknuts on master cylinder push-rod.
3. Check distance from lower edge of clutch pedal to floor. Correct measurement is 140 mm (5.50 in) without floor mat.

7. Check operation of clutch pedal and ensure that there is a minimum of 6 mm (0.25 in) of free play before pressure is felt. If necessary, readust master cylinder push-rod.
8. Fit pedal box gasket and top cover.

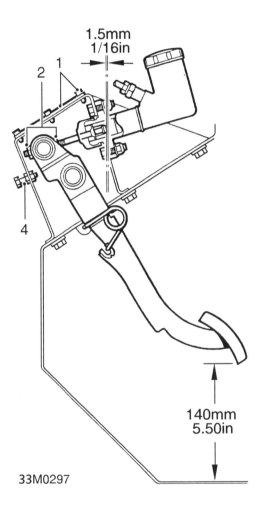

1.5mm
1/16in

140mm
5.50in

33M0297

4. Adjust pedal stop as necessary to obtain correct setting.
5. Adjust master cylinder push rod to obtain approximately 1,5 mm (1/16 in) free play between push-rod and master cylinder piston.
6. Tighten push-rod locknuts.

# Notes

## CLUTCH ASSEMBLY

**Service repair no - 33.10.01**

### Clutch pressure plate

Renew pressure plate if diaphragm spring fingers are worn or if pressure plate shows signs of wear, cracks or burning.

### Clutch driven plate

Renew driven plate if centre hub splines are worn or if lining is contaminated, burned or unevenly worn.

### Remove

1. Remove gearbox **See MANUAL GEARBOX, Repair, Gearbox.**
2. Mark position of clutch pressure plate to flywheel for reassembly.

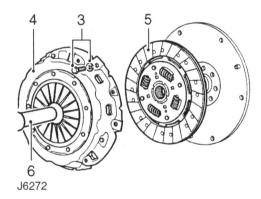

J6272

3. Remove pressure plate securing bolts, working evenly and diagonally.
4. Remove clutch assembly.
5. Withdraw clutch driven plate.

### Refit

 NOTE: To prevent driven plate sticking, lubricate splines using Rocol MV 3 or Rocol MTS 1000 grease.

6. Using centralising tool **LRT-12-040** to support clutch driven plate locate pressure plate on flywheel dowels. If fitting original pressure plate, align assembly marks.
7. Secure pressure plate cover fixings evenly, working in a diagonal sequence. Tighten to **34Nm (25 lbf/ft).**
8. Fit gearbox to engine **See MANUAL GEARBOX, Repair, Gearbox.**

## BLEED HYDRAULIC SYSTEM

**Service repair no - 33.15.01**

### Procedure

 NOTE: During bleed procedure, keep fluid reservoir topped up to avoid introducing air to system. For hydraulic fluid recommendations *See LUBRICANTS, FLUIDS AND CAPACITIES, Information, Recommended lubricants and fluids.*

1. Attach suitable tubing to slave cylinder bleed screw.

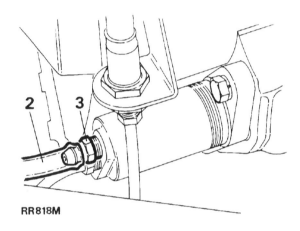

RR818M

2. Place free end of tube in a glass jar containing clutch fluid.
3. Loosen bleed screw.
4. Pump clutch pedal, pausing at end of each stroke, until fluid from tubing is free of air.

 NOTE: Keep free end of tube below surface of fluid.

5. Hold clutch pedal down, tighten bleed screw.
6. Top up fluid reservoir.

## MASTER CYLINDER

**Service repair no - 33.20.01/03**

 **NOTE: All hose and pipe connections and joints should be tightened to *15 Nm (11 lbf/ft).***

### Remove

1. Drain hydraulic fluid from system.
2. Disconnect fluid pipe at master cylinder. Plug master cylinder fluid port and seal end of hydraulic pipe to prevent ingress of dirt.
3. On RH drive vehicles, unclip air cleaner retaining straps, disconnect bottom hose, and move assembly aside.
4. From inside vehicle, remove fibre board closing panel above pedals.

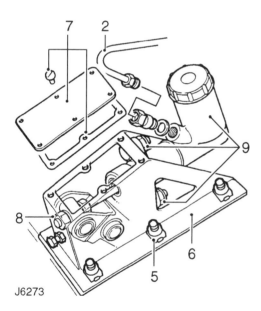

J6273

5. Remove 6 bolts securing pedal bracket to bulkhead.
6. Remove screw securing speedometer cable retaining bracket to top of pedal bracket.
7. Move pipework and cables aside and lift out pedal bracket, complete with master cylinder, turn through 90° to ensure pedal clears aperture in bulkhead.

8. Remove 6 screws and detach pedal box top cover and gasket.
9. Remove nut and washer securing master cylinder push rod to clutch pedal trunnion.
10. Remove 2 nuts and bolts and withdraw master cylinder from pedal bracket.

### Refit

11. Fit master cylinder to pedal bracket, engaging cylinder push rod through pedal trunnion.
12. Secure push rod to pedal trunnion.
13. Apply sealant to mating surfaces and fit pedal bracket to engine bulkhead.
14. Connect fluid pipe to master cylinder.
15. Bleed clutch hydraulic system *See Bleed hydraulic system.*
16. Check and adjust clutch pedal and master cylinder setting *See Adjustment, Clutch pedal and master cylinder setting.*
17. Fit top cover and gasket to pedal bracket.
18. On RH drive vehicles, refit air cleaner.

## CLUTCH PEDAL

**Service repair no - 33.33.02**

### Remove

1. Remove pedal bracket assembly and master cylinder **See Master cylinder.**
2. Release return spring from clutch pedal.

 **NOTE: If new pedal pivot bushes are required they must be reamed to 16 mm (0.625 in).**

### Refit

7. If removed, fit trunnion bush and trunnion to clutch pedal. Lubricate components with general purpose grease on assembly.
8. Fit pedal to bracket, insert pivot shaft and secure with new pin.
9. Fit pedal return spring.
10. Fit master cylinder and pedal bracket assembly **See Master cylinder.**
11. Adjust clutch pedal and master cylinder setting **See Adjustment, Clutch pedal and master cylinder setting.**

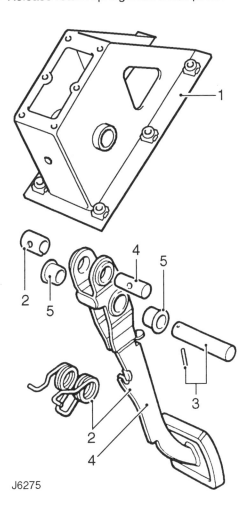

J6275

3. Using a suitable punch, drift out securing pin and withdraw pedal pivot shaft.
4. Withdraw clutch pedal, complete with trunnion and bush.
5. If necessary remove pivot bushes.
6. Examine components for wear and damage, renew as necessary.

## RELEASE BEARING ASSEMBLY

**Service repair no - 33.10.07**

**Remove**

1. Remove gearbox *See MANUAL GEARBOX, Repair, Gearbox.*
2. Remove clutch slave cylinder *See Slave cylinder.*

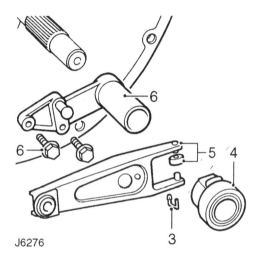

J6276

3. Remove release bearing sleeve retainer staple.
4. Withdraw bearing and sleeve.
5. Remove clutch release lever from bearing guide, complete with sliper pads.
6. If necessary, unscrew 2 bolts and remove bearing guide from bell housing.

**Refit**

7. If removed, fit bearing guide to bell housing. Tighten bolts to *25 Nm (18 lbf/ft).*
8. Prior to reassembly, grease pivot post, socket, slipper pads, pins, and ball end of slave cylinder push-rod.
9. Fit slipper pads onto release lever pins and locate lever on pivot post.
10. Smear release bearing sleeve inner diameter with molybdenum disulphide grease and fit to bearing guide, locating slipper pads to sleeve flats.
11. Fit new bearing sleeve retainer staple.
12. Fit clutch slave cylinder *See Slave cylinder.*
13. Fit gearbox *See MANUAL GEARBOX, Repair, Gearbox.*

## SLAVE CYLINDER

**Service repair no - 33.35.01**

 NOTE: All hose and pipe connections and joints should be tightened to *15 Nm (11 lbf/ft).*

**Remove**

1. Drain hydraulic fluid from system at slave cylinder bleed valve.
2. Disconnect fluid pipe.

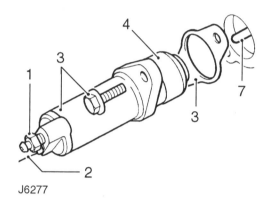

J6277

3. Remove 2 bolts and withdraw slave cylinder and backing plate.
4. If dust cover is not withdrawn with slave cylinder, withdraw it from bell housing.

 CAUTION: If removing slave cylinder with gearbox in situ, DO NOT detach push-rod and clip from clutch release lever in bell housing.

**Refit**

5. Coat both sides of backing plate with Hylomar P232M waterproof jointing compound.
6. Locate backing plate and dust cover in position on slave cylinder.
7. Fit slave cylinder, engaging push-rod through centre of dust cover and with bleed screw uppermost.
8. Reconnect fluid pipe.
9. Replenish and bleed clutch hydraulic system *See Bleed hydraulic system.*
10. Check for fluid leaks with pedal depressed and also with system at rest.

## MASTER CYLINDER - OVERHAUL

**Service repair no - 33.20.07**

**Dismantle**

1. Remove master cylinder from vehicle *See Repair, Mastercylinder.*

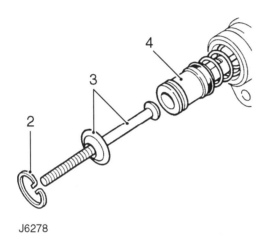

J6278

2. Remove circlip.
3. Withdraw push-rod and retaining washer.
4. Withdraw the piston assembly. If necessary, apply a low air pressure to outlet port to expel piston.

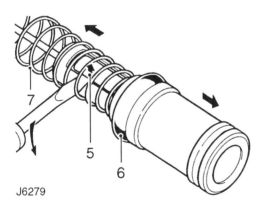

J6279

5. Prise locking prong of spring retainer clear of piston shoulder and withdraw piston.
6. Withdraw piston seal.
7. Compress spring and position valve stem to align with larger hole in spring retainer.

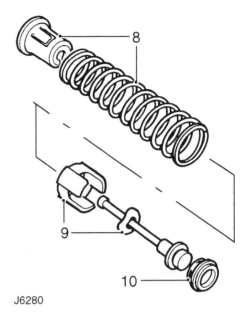

J6280

8. Withdraw spring and retainer.
9. Withdraw valve spacer and spring washer from valve stem.
10. Remove valve seal.

**Inspection**

11. Clean all components in new hydraulic fluid and allow to dry.
12. Examine cylinder bore and piston, ensure that they are smooth to touch with no corrosion, score marks or ridges. If there is any doubt, fit new components.
13. The seals should be renewed with seals from master cylinder overhaul kit.

**Assemble**

14. Smear seals with suitable rubber grease and remaining internal items with new hydraulic fluid.
15. Fit valve seal, flat side first, on end of valve stem.
16. Place bowed washer, domed side first, over small end of valve stem, see J6281.
17. Fit spacer to valve, legs first.

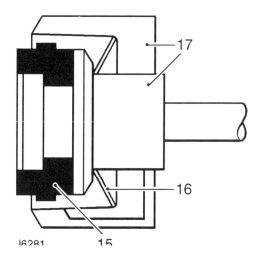

I6281    15

18. Place coil spring over valve stem.
19. Insert retainer into spring.
20. Compress spring and engage valve stem in keyhole slot in retainer.

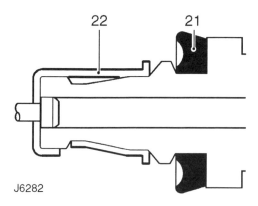

J6282

21. Fit seal, large diameter last, to piston.
22. Insert piston into spring retainer and engage locking prong.
23. Smear piston with suitable rubber grease and insert assembly, valve end first, into cylinder.
24. Fit push-rod, retaining washer and circlip.
25. Fit clutch master cylinder to vehicle *See Repair, Master cylinder.*

## SLAVE CYLINDER - OVERHAUL

**Service repair no - 33.35.07**

### Dismantle

1. Remove slave cylinder *See Repair, Slave cylinder.*

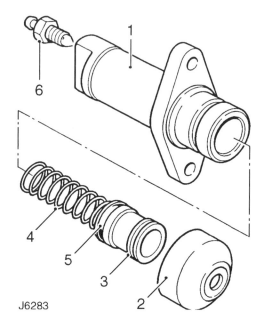

J6283

2. Withdraw dust cover.
3. Expel piston assembly, applying low pressure air to fluid inlet.
4. Withdraw spring.
5. Remove seal from piston.
6. Remove bleed valve.

### Inspection

7. Clean all components with new hydraulic fluid fluid and allow to dry.
8. Examine cylinder bore and piston, ensure that they are smooth to touch with no corrosion, score marks or ridges. If there is any doubt, fit new components.
9. Renew seal and dust cover from slave cylinder overhaul kit.

**Assemble**

10. Fit bleed valve to cylinder body, do not overtighten.
11. Lubricate seals, piston and bore with new hydraulic fluid.
12. Fit seal into piston groove with lip of seal towards fluid inlet end of cylinder.
13. Locate spring over front end of piston.
14. Fit assembly, spring first, into cylinder ensuring seal lip does not fold back.
15. Fill dust cover with suitable rubber grease and fit cover to cylinder.
16. Fit slave cylinder *See Repair, Slave cylinder.*

# Notes

# 37 - MANUAL GEARBOX

## CONTENTS

# Notes

## R380 GEARBOX

### Description

The all synchromesh five speed manual gearbox unit, is married to a two speed transfer gearbox.

All the gears, including reverse, run on needle roller bearings and the main, layshaft and primary shafts are supported by tapered roller bearings.

The whole of the geartrain is lubricated through drillings in the shafts, supplied by a low pressure pump driven from the rear of the layshaft. The gear change has a single rail selector and spool type interlock. The main and transfer gearboxes ventilate through nylon pipes, which terminate high up in the engine compartment to prevent water entry when the vehicle is operating in adverse conditions.

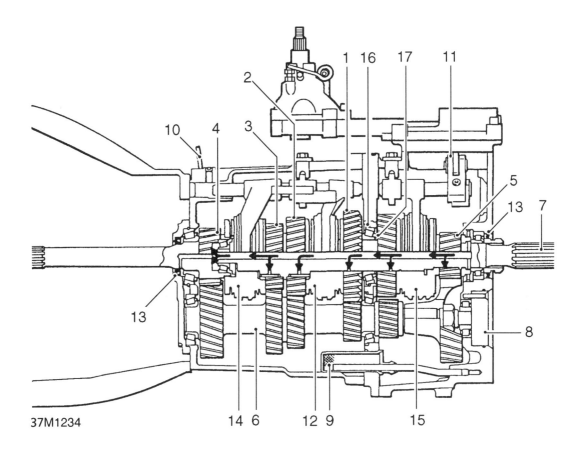

37M1234

### R380 Gearbox Components

1. Mainshaft 1st gear
2. Mainshaft 2nd gear
3. Mainshaft 3rd gear
4. Primary input shaft/4th gear
5. Mainshaft 5th gear
6. Layshaft
7. Mainshaft
8. Lubrication pump
9. Oil filter
10. Ventilation pipe
11. Single rail gear shift
12. 1st/2nd synchromesh
13. Oil seals
14. 3rd/4th synchromesh
15. 5th/reverse gear synchromesh
16. Selective spacers (mainshaft/layshaft end float)
17. Selective spacer (5th gear/reverse hub)

# Notes

## R380 GEARBOX

**Symptom - Gear jumps out of engagement (any forward gear)**

1. Check condition and security of transmission and engine mountings.
2. Check in situ, gear lever and selector adjustments *See Adjustment, Gear change lever bias spring adjustment* and *See Adjustment, Fifth gear stop screw adjustment.*
3. In situ, remove gearshift and check selector rail yoke security.
   Also check selector detent spring tension and both spool retainers.
   Suspect internal fault, see Overhaul Manual.
4. Check action/operation of main selector rail and forks.
5. Check condition of synchromesh and gear dog teeth.
6. Check main and layshaft end floats bearings and adjustments.
7. Check condition of all gearbox components, ensure clearances and adjustments are correct on reassembly.

**Symptom - Reverse gear only jumps out of engagment**

1. Check condition and security of transmission and engine mountings.
2. Check in situ, gear lever and selector adjustments *See Adjustment, Gear change lever bias spring adjustment* and *See Adjustment, Fifth gear stop screw adjustment.*
3. In situ, remove gearshift and check selector rail yoke security.
   Also check selector detent spring tension and both spool retainers.
   Suspect internal fault, see Overhaul Manual.
4. Check action/operation of main selector rail and reverse lever.
5. Check condition of reverse gear, angled bearings and shaft.
6. Check condition of all gearbox components, ensure clearances and adjustments are correct on reassembly.

**Symptom - Excessive force required to engage or change gear, vehicle stationary or moving.**

1. Check lubricant specification and level, if low do not top up at this stage.
2. In situ, lubricate gear mechanism, and check selector adjustments *See Adjustment, Gear change lever bias spring adjustment* and *See Adjustment, Fifth gear stop screw adjustment.*
3. In situ, remove gearshift and check selector rail is free and that the yoke is secure. Also check selector detent spring tension and both spool retainers.
4. Drain lubricant and check for contamination or metal particles.
   Suspect worn synchromesh unit or baulk rings on affected gears, see Overhaul Manual.

**Symptom - Noisy gear engagement, vehicle stationary** *See CLUTCH, Fault diagnosis, Clutch Noise - Mechanical Faults.*

**Symptom - Noisy gear selection, vehicle moving.**

1. Confirm that clutch operation is satisfactory.
2. Establish which gear/gears is causing noise.
3. Check lubricant specification and level, if low do not top up at this stage.
4. Drain lubricant and check for contamination or metal particles.
   Suspect worn synchromesh, see Overhaul Manual.
5. Check condition of synchromesh unit, springs and cones for distortion and wear. Also check dog teeth for damage and cone mating surface on gear for signs of overheating.
6. Check condition of all gearbox components, ensure clearances and adjustments are correct on reassembly.

**Symptom - Noise from gearbox in neutral, which changes tone or becomes worse when clutch is depressed,** *See CLUTCH, Fault diagnosis, Clutch Noise - Mechanical Faults.*

**Symptom - Noise from gearbox in neutral, which disappears when clutch is depressed.**

1. Check lubricant specification and level, if low do not top up at this stage.
2. Drain lubricant and check for contamination or metal particles.
   Suspect worn bearings on layshaft, primary shaft or front of main shaft, see Overhaul Manual.

**Symptom - Noise from gearbox in one or more gears when being driven.**

1. Check lubricant specification and level, if low do not top up at this stage.
2. Drain lubricant and check for contamination or metal particles.
   Suspect worn roller bearings on particular mainshaft gears, see Overhaul Manual.

## GEAR CHANGE LEVER BIAS SPRING - ADJUST

**Service repair no - 37.16.26**

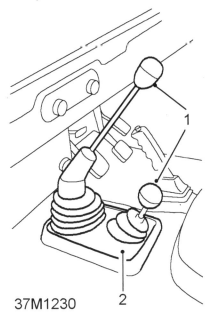

37M1230

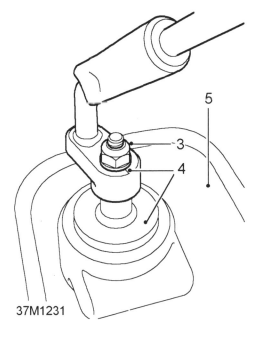

37M1231

1. Remove gear lever and transfer box lever knobs.
2. Remove gear lever cover.
3. Remove nut and washer securing gear lever.
4. Mark gear lever spline setting, remove lever and gaiter from lower lever.
5. Remove insulation pad from tunnel aperture.
6. Fit gear lever and select 3rd or 4th gear.
7. Slacken adjustment screw locknuts.
8. Adjust screws until both legs of bias springs are approximately 0.5mm clear of gear lever cross pin.
9. Apply a slight load to gear lever in a LH direction and adjust RH screw downward until RH spring leg just makes contact with cross pin.
10. Repeat procedure for LH adjustment screw.
11. Lower both adjustment screws equal amounts until radial play is eliminated.
12. Tighten locknuts.
13. Return gear lever to neutral position and rock across gate several times. The gear lever should return to 3rd and 4th gate.

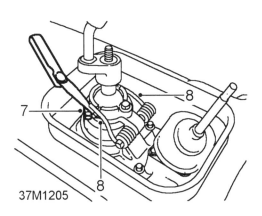

37M1205

14. Remove gear lever.
15. Fit insulation pad.
16. Locate gaiter over lower lever and bias springs.
17. Fit gear lever to lower lever spline, secure with new nyloc nut and tighten to *25 Nm (18 lbf/ft).*
18. Fit gear lever cover.
19. Fit gear lever and transfer box lever knobs.

## FIFTH GEAR STOP SCREW - ADJUST

**Service repair no - 37.16.67**

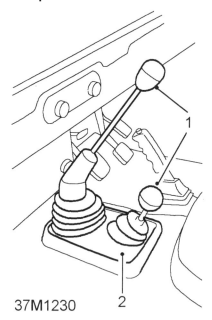

37M1230

1. Remove gear lever and transfer box lever knobs.
2. Remove gear lever cover.

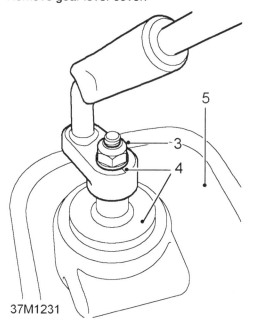

37M1231

3. Remove nut and washer securing gear lever.
4. Mark gear lever spline setting, remove lever and gaiter from lower lever.
5. Remove insulation pad from tunnel aperture.
6. Remove tunnel carpet.

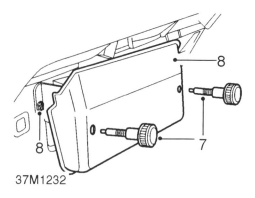

37M1232

7. Remove retaining screws and release fuse box cover.
8. Remove 2 screws and release fuse box from bulkhead to assist next operation.

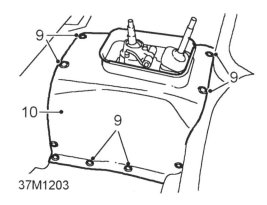

37M1203

9. Remove 16 screws securing tunnel cover to vehicle body.
10. Manouvre tunnel cover to clear handbrake lever and remove from vehicle.
11. Fit gear lever and knob and select reverse gear.

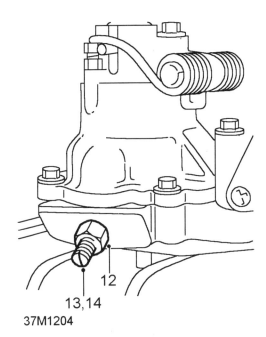

37M1204

12. Slacken stop screw locknut.
13. Apply light pressure to gear lever towards LH side and turn screw clockwise until it abuts yoke.
14. Turn screw anti-clockwise until 25 mm freeplay is felt at gear lever knob. Ensure 5th gear can be engaged.
15. Tighten stop screw locknut.
16. Check that all other gears are selectable.
17. Remove gear lever.
18. Manouvre tunnel cover into position and secure with 16 screws.
19. Fit fuse box and cover.
20. Fit tunnel carpet.
21. Fit insulation pad into tunnel aperture.
22. Locate gaiter over lower lever and bias springs.
23. Fit gear lever to lower lever spline, secure with new nyloc nut and tighten to *25 Nm (18 lbf/ft)*.
24. Fit gear lever cover.
25. Fit gear lever and transfer box lever knobs.

# Notes

## R380 GEARBOX

**Service repair no - 37.20.51**

**Remove**

The R380 gearbox should be removed from underneath the vehicle, using a hydraulic hoist and support plate **LRT-99-007**.

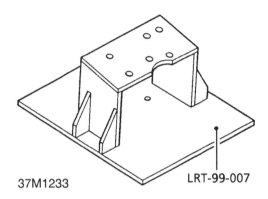

37M1233    LRT-99-007

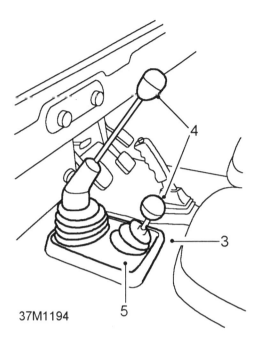

37M1194    5

⚠ **WARNING: Where the use of a transmission hoist is necessary, it is absolutely essential to follow the manufacturer's instructions to ensure safe and effective use of equipment.**

△ **NOTE: A chassis undertray may be fitted on some vehicle derivatives to conform to legal requirements. When under chassis remove and refit procedures are required, it may be necessary to remove the undertray** *See CHASSIS AND BODY, Repair, Front undertray or See CHASSIS AND BODY, Repair, Rear undertray*

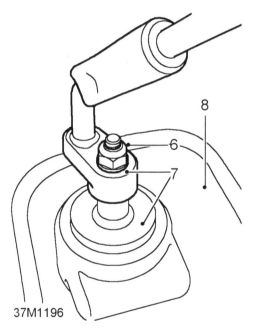

37M1196

1. Install vehicle on a ramp.
2. Disconnect battery.
3. Remove gearbox carpet.
4. Remove gear lever and transfer box lever knobs.
5. Remove gear lever cover.
6. Remove nut and washer securing gear lever.
7. Mark gear lever spline setting and remove lever and gaiter from the splined lower gear lever.
8. Release insulation pad from tunnel cover and gear levers and remove.
9. Select low range on transfer box lever to prevent lever from fouling tunnel when removing gearbox.

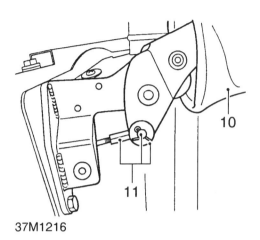

37M1216

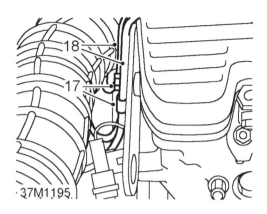

37M1195

10. Remove 3 trim studs and lift up handbrake gaiter.
11. Remove split pin, clevis pin, washer and disconnect cable from handbrake lever. Ensure handbrake is off.
12. Drain cooling system **See COOLING SYSTEM, Adjustment, Drain and refill cooling system** .
13. Remove viscous fan unit **See COOLING SYSTEM, Repair, Viscous coupling and fan** .

17. Remove bolt securing transmission breather pipe clip to rear of engine.
18. Release breather pipes.
19. Release ties securing gearbox harness to breather pipes.
20. Raise vehicle on ramp.
21. Position a suitable container under transmission and drain main gearbox and transfer box **See MAINTENANCE , Under vehicle maintenance**

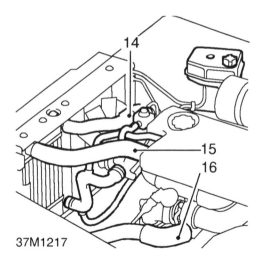

37M1217

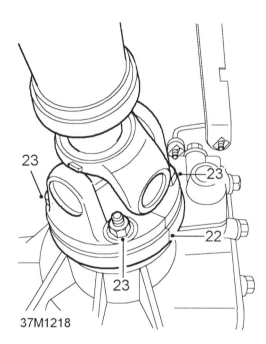

37M1218

14. Slacken retaining clip and disconnect radiator top hose at thermostat housing.
15. Slacken retaining clip and disconnect intake hose at induction manifold. If EGR system is fitted, slacken 2 retaining clips and disconnect intake hose at intercooler.
16. Slacken retaining clip and disconnect hose at turbocharger.

22. Mark front propeller shaft drive flange and transfer box output flange for reassembly.
23. Remove 4 nuts and disconnect propeller shaft from transfer box.

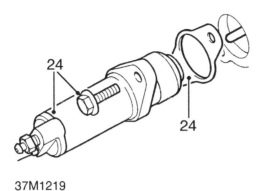

37M1219

24. Remove 2 bolts, withdraw clutch slave cylinder and backing plate from bell housing, and tie aside.

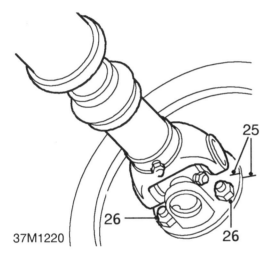

37M1220

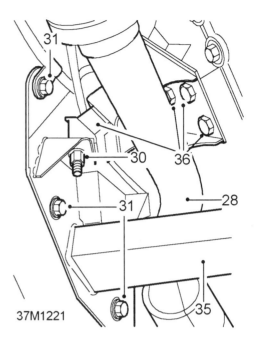

37M1221

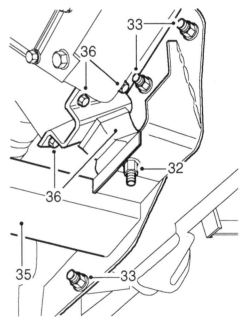

37M1222

25. Mark rear propeller shaft drive flange and transmission brake drum for reassembly.
26. Remove 4 nuts, disconnect propeller shaft from brake drum, and tie aside.
27. Remove front pipe from exhaust manifold *See MANIFOLD AND EXHAUST SYSTEM, Repair, Exhaust front pipe.*
28. Remove intermediate silencer *See MANIFOLD AND EXHAUST SYSTEM, Repair, Intermediate pipe and silencer.*
29. Temporarily support transmission.
30. Remove nut securing gearbox LH mounting rubber to chassis crossmember.
31. Remove 4 nuts and bolts securing crossmember to chassis longitudinals.
32. Remove nut securing transfer box mounting rubber to RH side of crossmember.

33. Remove 4 nuts and bolts securing crossmember to chassis longitudinals.
34. With assistance and using a body jack between chassis longitudinals, jack chassis sufficiently to enable removal of crossmember.
35. Remove chasss crossmember.
36. Remove 4 bolts from both sides and remove LH and RH mounting brackets.

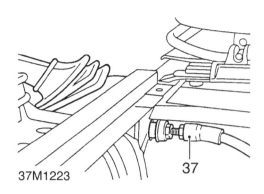

37M1223    37

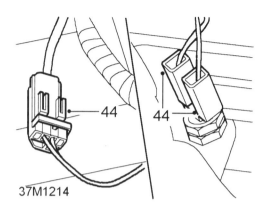

44    44

37M1214

**37.** Pull handbrake cable through heel board and tie aside.

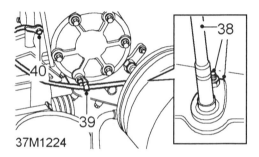

38

40

39

37M1224

**44.** Disconnect differential lock switch and reverse light connectors.

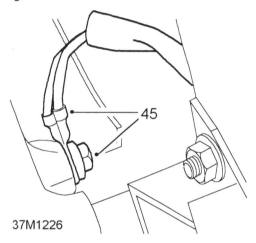

45

37M1226

**38.** Remove retaining nut, release clamp, and disconnect speedometer cable from transfer box.
**39.** Release speedometer cable from retaining clip on transfer box.
**40.** Remove retaining nut and release battery earth strap from transfer box.

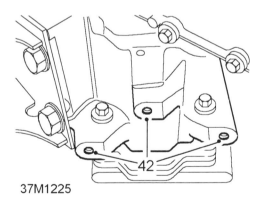

42

37M1225

**45.** Remove bolt and release earth leads from RH side of transfer box.

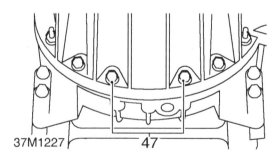

37M1227    47

**41.** Secure manufactured cradle **LRT-99-007** to a suitable hydraulic hoist.
**42.** Raise hoist and secure to gearbox with 3 bolts in location provided.
**43.** Lower hoist sufficiently to allow transfer lever to clear transmission tunnel aperture.

**46.** Support engine under sump with a jack.
**47.** Remove 14 bell housing to engine fixings.
**48.** Withdraw transmission whilst ensuring all connections to engine and chassis are released.
**49.** Lower hoist and remove gearbox assembly.

## Separating transfer gearbox from main gearbox

**50.** Remove transmission assembly from hoist cradle and position safely on a bench.

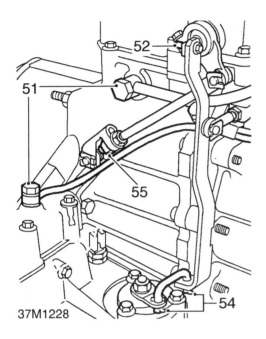

37M1228

**51.** Remove breather pipes. Discard pipe union sealing washers.
**52.** Remove 'Nyloc' nut, and remove bolt, securing lever to high/low shaft.
**53.** Collect spacer washer.
**54.** Remove 2 clips and remove differential lock lever link.
**55.** Remove lower locknut from high/low operating rod.
**56.** Place a sling round transfer box and attach to hoist.
**57.** Remove nut and 4 bolts securing transfer gearbox to extension housing.
**58.** Withdraw transfer gearbox.

## Assembling transfer gearbox to main gearbox

**59.** Clean extension housing and transfer gearbox mating faces.
**60.** Ensuring loose upper dowel is fitted, hoist transfer gearbox into position.
**61.** Secure transfer box to extension housing. Tighten fixings to *40 Nm (30 lbf/ft)*.
**62.** Connect high/low operating rod, fit and tighten locknut.

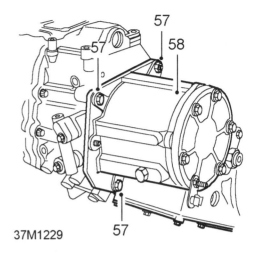

37M1229

**63.** Fit link to differential lock lever and secure with 2 clips
**64.** Align lever to high/low shaft, position washer, fit bolt and new Nyloc nut. Tighten to *2 Nm (1.5 lbf/ft)*.
**65.** Position breather pipes, secure pipe unions using new sealing washers. Tighten unions to *15 Nm (11 lbf/ft)*.

## Fitting transfer gearbox and main gearbox assembly

**66.** Position transmission assembly to hoist cradle.
**67.** Clean bell housing and engine mating faces. Apply sealant to both mating faces.
**68.** Temporarily fit gear lever and select any gear in main gearbox to facilitate entry of gearbox input shaft. Engage low range.
**69.** Position and raise hoist, fit transmission to engine whilst keeping harness and pipes clear to prevent trapping.
**70.** Secure transmission to engine. Tighten fixings to *45 Nm (33 lbf/ft)*.
**71.** Secure earth leads to RH side of transfer box.
**72.** Connect reverse lamp switch connectors and differential lock switch connectors.
**73.** Secure breather pipes to harness with clips.
**74.** Remove support from engine sump.
**75.** Position temporary support under transmission.
**76.** Secure LH and RH mounting brackets to gearbox. Tighten fixings to *55 Nm (41 lbf/ft)*.
**77.** With assistance and using a body jack between chassis longitudinals, jack chassis sufficiently to enable fitment of crossmember.

78. Position crossmember and locate over fixing studs of LH and RH gearbox mounting rubbers.
79. Align crossmember and secure to chassis with 4 nuts and bolts on each side.

 **NOTE: Fit battery earth strap retaining clip to LH top bolt.**

80. Fit intermediate silencer. *See MANIFOLD AND EXHAUST SYSTEM, Repair, Intermediate pipe - 90* or *See MANIFOLD AND EXHAUST SYSTEM, Repair, Intermediate pipe - 110/130*
81. Fit front pipe to exhaust manifold *See MANIFOLD AND EXHAUST SYSTEM, Repair, Exhaust front pipe* .
82. Fit rear propeller shaft to transmission brake drum. Tighten nuts to *47 Nm (33 lbf/ft).*
83. Remove 3 bolts securing support cradle to transmission and remove hoist.
84. Reconnect battery earth strap to transfer box fixing.
85. Connect speedometer cable to transfer box and secure with retaining clip.
86. Coat both sides of clutch slave clinder backing plate with Hylomar P232M waterproof sealant.
87. Locate backing plate on slave cylinder.
88. Fit slave cylinder to bell housing, engaging push-rod through centre of dust cover, and with bleed screw uppermost. Tighten bolts to *25 Nm (18 lbf/ft).*
89. Fit front propeller shaft to transfer box. Tighten nuts to *47 Nm (33 lbf/ft).*
90. Refill main gearbox and transfer box *See MAINTENANCE , Under vehicle maintenance*
91. Feed transmission brake cable through heel board and ensure grommet is correctly located.

 **NOTE: Apply a soap solution to aid fitment of cable.**

92. Lower vehicle on ramp.
93. Fit ties to secure gearbox harness to transmission breather pipes.
94. Fit breather pipe retaining clip to rear of engine.
95. Reconnect charge air hose at turbocharger.
96. Reconnect intake hose at induction manifold. If EGR system is fitted, reconnect intake hose at intercooler.
97. Reconnect radiator top hose at thermostat housing.
98. Fit viscous fan unit *See COOLING SYSTEM, Repair, Viscous coupling and fan* .
99. Reconnect battery.

100. Refill cooling system *See COOLING SYSTEM, Adjustment, Drain and refill cooling system* .
101. Connect cable clevis to handbrake lever and fit handbrake gaiter.
102. Locate insulation pad over gear levers and fit to tunnel cover.
103. Fit gear lever with gaiter to lower lever spline and secure with retaining nut.
104. Fit gear lever cover.
105. Fit gear lever and transfer box lever knobs.
106. Fit gearbox cover carpet.
107. Check operation of handbrake and adjust as necessary *See MAINTENANCE , Under vehicle maintenance* .

## TORQUE VALUES

 **NOTE: Torque wrenches should be regularly checked for accuracy to ensure that all fixings are tightened to the correct torque.**

|  | Nm |
|---|---|
| Slave cylinder to bell housing | 25 |
| Breather | 15 |
| Bell housing to cylinder block | 40 |
| High/low level to shaft | 2 |
| Transfer box to gearbox | 45 |

 **NOTE: Torque values below apply to all screws and bolts used unless otherwise specified.**

| METRIC | Nm |
|---|---|
| M5 | 6 |
| M6 | 9 |
| M8 | 25 |
| M10 | 45 |
| M12 | 90 |
| M14 | 105 |
| M16 | 180 |

| UNC / UNF |  |
|---|---|
| 1/4 | 9 |
| 5/16 | 24 |
| 3/8 | 39 |
| 7/16 | 78 |
| 1/2 | 90 |
| 5/8 | 136 |

# Notes

# 41 - TRANSFER GEARBOX

## CONTENTS

Page

**DESCRIPTION AND OPERATION**

**FAULT DIAGNOSIS**

**REPAIR**

**SPECIFICATIONS, TORQUE**

# Notes

## TRANSFER GEARBOX

### Description

The transfer gearbox is a permanent 4 wheel drive, two speed ratio reducing gearbox, incorporating high and low range outputs with mechanically lockable centre differential (diff-lock). High/low range and diff-lock selection are made via a single lever located forward of the main gear lever.

The transfer gearbox is mounted at the rear of the main gearbox, the mainshaft of which extends into the transfer casing. A transfer gear, supported on taper roller bearings and splined to the gearbox mainshaft, passes the drive to an intermediate gear cluster supported on a single shaft and rotating on taper roller bearings.

The intermediate gears pass the drive to high and low speed gears on the rear output shaft. The rear output shaft passes through the speedo drive housing, which also forms the mounting for the transmission brake. A worm gear fitted to the rear output shaft drives a pinion fitted in the speedo housing.

Integral with the output shafts is a differential assembly which compensates for speed differences between the front and rear prop shafts. To prevent all the power being transmitted to the axle offering the least resistance, a diff-lock is provided. The differential lock should only be engaged during severe off-road conditions and should be disengaged as soon as conditions permit. Selection of differential lock engages, through mechanical linkage, a dog clutch with the front output shaft, this action locks the centre differential and provides a fixed drive, giving equal power to the front and rear output shafts.

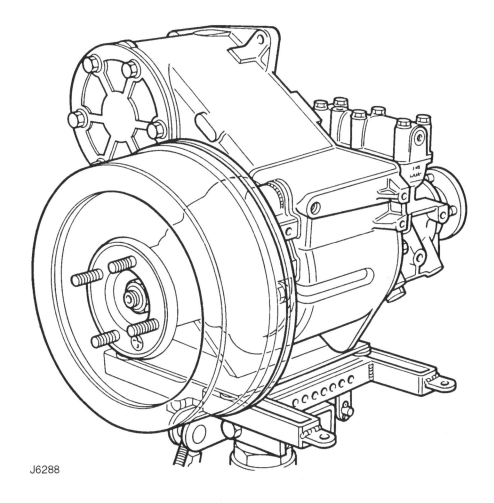

J6288

# Notes

## TRANSFER GEARBOX - OIL SEAL LOCATIONS

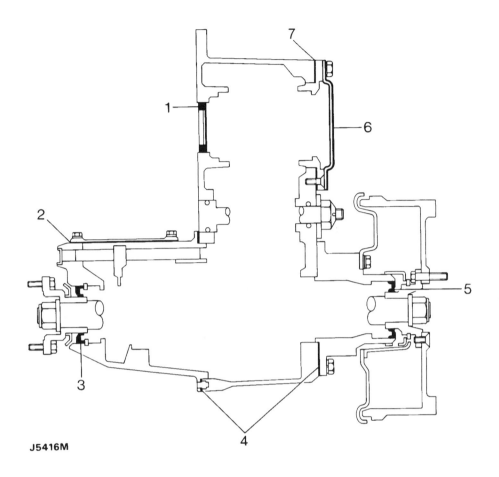

J5416M

1. Input seal.
2. Cover plate joints.
3. Front output seal.
4. Front and rear housing joint faces.

5. Rear output seal.
6. Power take off cover plate joint.
7. Bearing plate joint.

## OIL LEAKS

Verify that oil leak is from transfer box and not main gearbox before proceeding with checks.

### Prior to road test

1. Check oil level in transfer box is correct.
2. Check tightness of level and drain plugs.
3. Check breather system for blockage. To validate system pipe must be removed, inspected, rectified as necessary and refitted.
4. Remove all traces of oil from exterior of transfer box.

### Take vehicle for short road test.

5. Identify source of leaks and rectify as follows.

### Front or rear output seal leaking:-

1. Drain oil and remove leaking output flange.
2. Inspect seal track on flange for surface damage. If damaged renew component.
3. Remove and discard oil seal.
4. Inspect seal locating bore and remove any sharp edges which may damage new oil seal.
5. Fit new seal.
6. Fit output flange and all other parts.
7. Add oil to correct level into gearbox *See SECTION 10, Maintenance, Under vehicle maintenance.*

### Cover plate sealant leaking.

1. Drain oil and remove leaking cover plate.
2. Remove all traces of joint sealant from both joint faces.
3. Degrease all components and apply a thin film of Hylomar sealant, to both joint faces.
4. Apply thread sealant to bolts which come into contact with gearbox oil.
5. Refit cover plate.

 **CAUTION: Care must be taken not to overtighten fixings.**

### Leak between main and transfer gearboxes.

1. Site vehicle onto a ramp .
2. Select neutral in transfer box and select 4th gear in main gearbox.
3. Run engine at 2000 rpm with clutch/drive engaged.
4. Observe joint between main and transfer boxes.
5. If oil leak is found establish if it is gear oil.
6. If so, leak is originating from transfer box.
7. Check two inner (main/transfer) bolts are oil tight, as these holes are tapped into main transfer case.
8. Remove transfer box to inspect mainshaft collar seal track condition, and front face of transfer case for porosity *See Repair, Transfer gearbox.*
9. If these areas require servicing, transfer gearbox input seal must also be renewed.

 **CAUTION: Avoid damaging new seal lip and ensure seal is fitted flush with machined face. Also ensure new seal is not damaged when refitting transfer gearbox.**

10. If red ATF type oil is seen leaking during workshop test, investigate main gearbox for cause of leak.

### Detent plug or electrical switch leaks.

1. Detent plugs and electrical switches do not usually leak. It must be noted that they fit into open tapped holes in transfer case and therefore should be considered when looking for source of leak.

## TRANSFER GEARBOX

**Service repair no - 41.20.25**

**Remove**

The transfer gearbox should be removed from underneath the vehicle, using a hydraulic hoist and adaptor plate **LRT-99-010**.

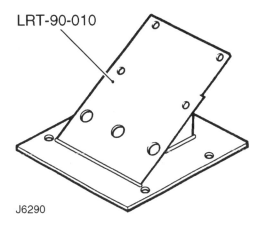

LRT-90-010

J6290

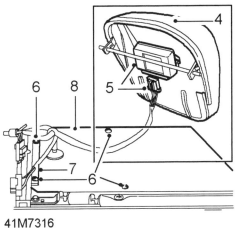

41M7316

**6.** Remove 4 screws securing centre access panel to seat or cubby box base.
**7.** Release EGR and alarm system diagnostic connector mounting bracket.
**8.** Lift up access panel, complete with diagnostic connector harness, and place aside.

> ⚠️ **WARNING: Where use of a transmission hoist is necessary, it is absolutely essential to follow the manufacturers' instructions to ensure safe and effective use of the equipment.**

> △ **NOTE: A chassis undertray may be fitted on some vehicle derivatives to conform to legal requirements. When under chassis remove and refit procedures are required, it may be necessary to remove the undertray** *See CHASSIS AND BODY, Repair, Front undertray or Rear undertray.*

**1.** Position vehicle on a ramp.
**2.** Select LOW range gear and leave vehicle in neutral.
**3.** Disconnect battery.
**4.** Remove front, centre, seat cushion, or cubby box *See CHASSIS AND BODY, Repair, Cubby box.*
**5.** If fitted, disconnect multi-plug from EGR control unit located on base of seat cushion or cubby box.

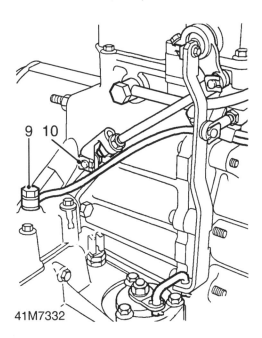

41M7332

**9.** Remove breather pipe union from transfer gearbox high/low cross-shaft housing.
**10.** Remove retaining clip and disconnect high/low lever from operating rod.

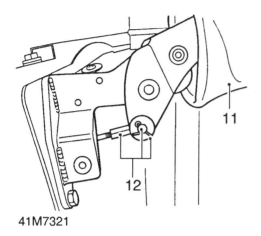

41M7321

11. Remove 3 trim studs and lift up handbrake
    gaiter.
12. Remove split pin, clevis pin, washer and
    disconnect cable from handbrake lever. Ensure
    handbrake is off.

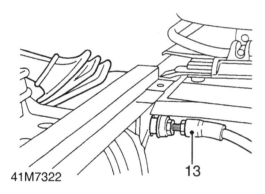

41M7322

13. Release handbrake outer cable from heelboard.
14. Remove fan cowl *See COOLING SYSTEM,*
    *Repair, Fan cowl.*
15. Raise vehicle on ramp.
16. Drain transfer box oil *See SECTION 10,*
    *Maintenance, Under vehicle maintenance.*
17. Remove intermediate silencer *See MANIFOLD*
    *AND EXHAUST SYSTEM, Repair,*
    *Intermediate pipe and silencer.*
18. Mark rear propeller shaft drive flange and
    transmission brake drum for reassembly.
19. Remove 4 nuts, disconnect propeller shaft from
    brake drum, and tie aside.

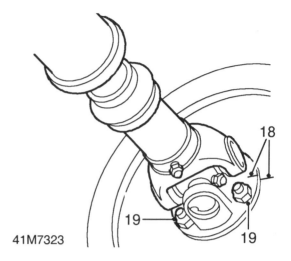

41M7323

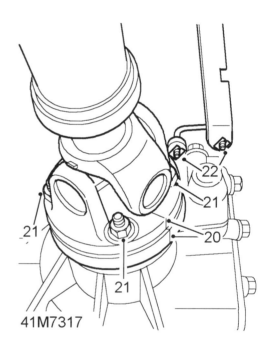

41M7317

20. Mark front propeller shaft drive flange and
    transfer box output flange for reassembly.
21. Remove 4 nuts, disconnect propeller shaft from
    transfer box, and tie aside.
22. Remove retaining clip at lower end of pivot arm
    and disconnect differential lock control operating
    rod.

23. Position 4, 30 mm (1.25 in), spacers between top of hoist and adaptor plate, **LRT-99-010**, at securing points and secure adaptor plate to hoist.

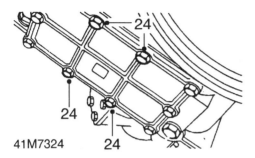

41M7324

24. Remove 4 central bolts from transfer box bottom cover, move hoist into position and secure adaptor plate to transfer box.
25. Adjust hoist to take weight of transfer box.

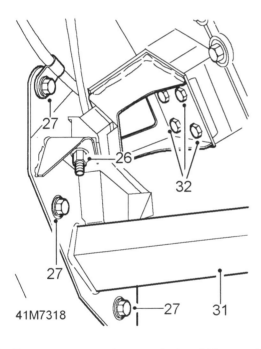

41M7318

26. Remove nut securing transfer box LH mounting rubber to chassis crossmember.
27. Remove 4 nuts and bolts securing chassis crossmember to chassis longitudinal.
28. Remove nut securing transfer box RH mounting rubber to chassis crossmember.
29. Remove 4 nuts and bolts securing chassis crossmember to chassis longitudinal.
30. With assistance and using a body jack between chassis longitudinals, jack chassis sufficiently to enable removal of crossmember.

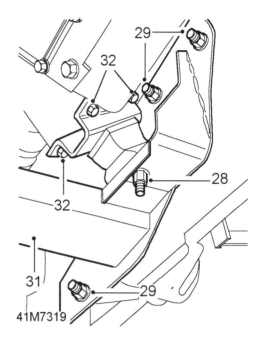

41M7319

31. Remove chassis crossmember.
32. Remove 4 bolts from both sides and remove LH and RH mounting brackets from transfer box.

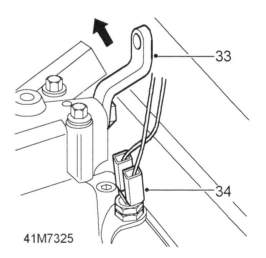

41M7325

33. Disconnect electrical leads from differential lock switch.
34. Move the small cranked lever, for high/low selector, upward to allow access to adjacent nut securing transfer box to main gearbox.
35. Position a jack to support main gearbox.

 **CAUTION: Use a block of wood or hard rubber pad to protect gearbox.**

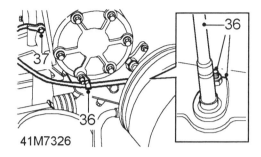

41M7326

36. Remove retaining nut, release clamp, and disconnect speedometer cable from transfer gearbox.
37. Remove battery earth strap retaining nut, 1 nut and 4 bolts, securing transfer box to main gearbox extension case.

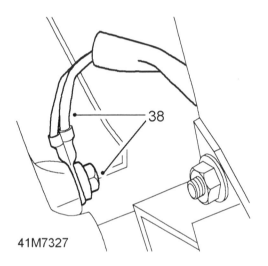

41M7327

38. Remove retaining nut securing earth leads to RH side of transfer box.
39. Fit three guide studs, **LRT-41-009**, through transfer box bolt holes to support it during removal.
40. Lower hoist and withdraw transfer box from main gearbox.
41. Remove transfer box.

**Refit**

42. Ensure joint faces of transfer box and main gearbox are clean and guide studs, **LRT-41-009**, are fitted to extension case.
43. Lubricate oil seal in joint face of transfer box.
44. Secure transfer box to adaptor plate on lifting hoist and raise hoist until transfer box can be located over guide studs.
45. Remove guide studs, fit battery earth strap, and secure transfer box to main gearbox extension case. Tighten fixings to *45 Nm (33 lbf/ft)*.
46. Fit electrical leads to differential lock switch.
47. Raise hoist and remove wooden block supporting main gearbox.
48. Secure LH and RH mounting brackets to gearbox and tighten fixings to *55 Nm (41 lbf/ft)*.
49. With assistance and using a body jack between chassis longitudinals, jack chassis sufficiently to enable fitment of crossmember.
50. Position chassis crossmember and locate over fixing studs of LH and RH gearbox mounting rubbers .
51. Align crossmember and secure to chassis with 4 nuts and bolts on each side.

⚠ **NOTE: Fit battery earth strap retaining clip to LH top bolt.**

52. Remove body jack.
53. Fit retaining nut to LH and RH mounting rubbers. Tighten to *21 Nm (15 lbf/ft)*.
54. Remove 4 bolts securing hoist adaptor plate to transfer box bottom cover.
55. Lower hoist and move aside.
56. Clean threads of the 4 bolts, coat with Loctite 290, and fit to transfer box bottom cover. Tighten to *25 Nm (18 lbf/ft)*.
57. Fit earth leads to RH side of transfer box.
58. Connect differential lock control operating rod to pivot arm.
59. Fit speedometer cable to transfer box.
60. Fit front and rear propeller shafts to transfer box. Tighten nuts to *47 Nm (33 lbf/ft)*.
61. Fit intermediate silencer *See MANIFOLD AND EXHAUST SYSTEM, Repair, Intermediate silencer.*
62. Refill transfer box with recommended oil *See SECTION 10, Maintenance, Under vehicle maintenance.*

63. Feed transmission brake cable through heel board. Ensure cable grommet is correctly located.

 **NOTE: Apply a soap solution to aid fitment of cable.**

64. Lower vehicle ramp.
65. Connect cable clevis to handbrake lever and fit handbrake gaiter.
66. Connect high/low lever to operating rod.
67. Fit breather pipe banjo union to high/low cross-shaft housing.
68. Fit centre access panel to seat base. If fitted, secure EGR and alarm system diagnostic connector mounting bracket to front of access panel.
69. If fitted, reconnect multi-plug to EGR control unit on base of centre seat cushion or cubby box.
70. Fit seat cushion or cubby box *See CHASSIS AND BODY, Repair, Cubby box* .
71. Reconnect battery.
72. Check operation of handbrake and adjust as necessary *See MAINTENANCE , Handbrake cable* .

# Notes

## TORQUE VALUES

 **NOTE: Torque wrenches should be regularly checked for accuracy to ensure that all fixings are tightened to the correct torque.**

Nm

**Transfer gearbox**

| | |
|---|---|
| Pinch bolt - operating arm to crank arm | 9 |
| End cover gear change housing | 9 |
| Bottom cover to transfer case | 25 |
| Front output housing to transfer case | 25 |
| Cross shaft housing to front output housing | 25 |
| Gear change housing | 25 |
| Pivot shaft to link arm | 25 |
| Connecting rod to adjustable clevis | 25 |
| Anti-rotation plate intermediate shaft | 25 |
| Front output housing cover | 25 |
| Pivot bracket to extension housing | 25 |
| Finger housing to front output housing | 25 |
| Bearing housing to transfer case | 25 |
| Brake drum to coupling flange | 25 |
| Bearing housing cover to transfer gearbox | 45 |
| Rear output speedometer housing to transfer gearbox | 45 |
| Selector finger to cross shaft high/low | 25 |
| Selector fork, high/low to shaft | 25 |
| Transmission brake to speedometer housing | 72 |
| Gate plate to grommet plate | 9 |
| Gearbox to transfer case | 45 |
| Oil drain plug | 30 |
| Oil filler/level plug | 30 |
| Differential case (front to rear) | 60 |
| Output flanges | 162 |
| Differential case rear stake nut | 72 |
| Transfer breather | 15 |
| Transfer box front drive flange to drive shaft | 45 |
| Transfer box rear drive flange to drive shaft | 45 |
| Transfer gearbox mounting brackets to chassis | 30 |
| Mounting brackets to transfer gearbox | 55 |
| Mounting rubbers to mounting brackets | 21 |

# Notes

# 47 - PROPELLER SHAFTS

## CONTENTS

Page

# Notes

## PROPELLER SHAFT

### Description

The front and rear propeller shafts have non-constant velocity type universal joints, with needle roller bearings. The bearing cups are pre-packed with lubricant on assembly and a grease nipple is fitted for servicing as specified, in maintenance section.

Both shafts have Rilsan coated sliding splines to accommodate the variation in distance between the axles and transmission. The splines are pre-packed with lubricant and protected by a rubber gaiter. A grease nipple is also fitted for servicing requirements.

The front shaft which is shorter than the rear is 'phased', with the joints at each end, A and B mis-aligned as shown.

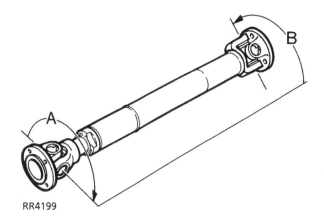

RR4199

The phasing is necessary on the front shaft only to allow for greater variation in angular changes.

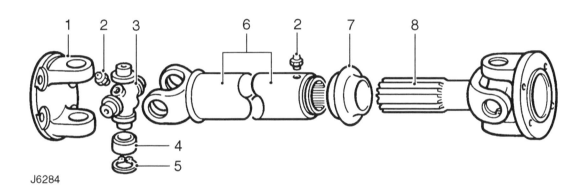

J6284

### Propeller shaft

1. Flanged yoke
2. Grease nipple
3. Journal spider
4. Needle roller bearing
5. Circlip
6. Splined shaft
7. Rubber gaiter (dust cap)
8. Splined shaft

# Notes

## VIBRATION HARSHNESS

Check that the propeller shaft universal joints and
sliding splines are not siezed or worn and that the
shafts are correctly aligned.

⚠ **NOTE: In the event that both shafts are
satisfactory, but the vibration/harshness is
still present, the transfer box operation
and balance of the road wheels should be
checked.**

For transfer box operation **See TRANSFER
GEARBOX, Fault diagnosis, Transfer Gearbox -
Oil Leaks** .

For balance of road wheels **See WHEELS AND
TYRES, Repair, Wheel Balancing** .

# Notes

## PROPELLER SHAFT

**Service repair no - 47.15.02 - Front**
**Service repair no - 47.15.03 - Rear**

**Remove**

1. Place vehicle on ramp.

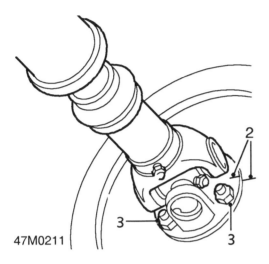

47M0211

2. Mark drive flanges at each end of propeller shaft for reassembly.
3. Remove 4 bolts/nuts from each end and remove propeller shaft.

⚠ **NOTE: A chassis under tray may be fitted on some vehicle derivatives to conform to legal requirements. When under chassis remove and refit procedures are required, it may be necessary to remove the under tray** *See CHASSIS AND BODY, Repair, Front under tray* **or** *See CHASSIS AND BODY, Repair, Rear under tray.*

**Refit**

4. Fit propeller shafts to vehicle with sliding joints to transfer box and tighten nuts to *47 Nm (35 lbf/ft).*

# Notes

## PROPELLER SHAFT

**Service repair no - 47.15.11 - Front**
**Service repair no - 47.15.12 - Rear**

1. Thoroughly examine universal joint for signs of damage or wear. Replace if necessary.

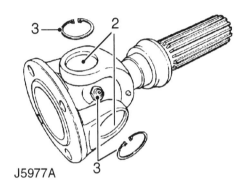

J5977A

2. Clean universal joint bearing cups and circlips.

⚠️ **CAUTION: To ensure correct assembly and reduce possibility of imbalance, mark position of spider pin lubricator relative to journal yoke ears, before removing propeller shaft joint.**

3. Remove circlips, and grease nipple.

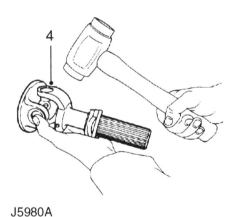

J5980A

4. Tap yokes to eject bearing cups.

5. Remove bearing cups and spider.
6. Repeat instructions 4 to 7 for opposite end of propeller shaft if necessary.
7. Clean yokes and bearing cup locations.

### Assembly

8. Remove bearing cups from new spider.
9. Check all needle rollers are present and positioned in bearing cups.
10. Ensure bearing cups are one-third full of lubricant *See LUBRICANTS, FLUIDS AND CAPACITIES, Information, Recommended lubricants and fluids* .
11. Enter new spider with seals into yokes of sliding member flange.
12. Partially insert one bearing cup into flange yoke and enter spider trunnion into bearing cup.
13. Insert opposite bearing cup into flange yoke.
14. Press both cups into place.

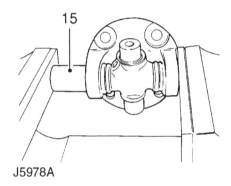

J5978A

15. Press each cup into its respective yoke up to lower land of circlip grooves. Damage may be caused to cups and seals if cups pass this point.
16. Fit circlips and check no end float exists.

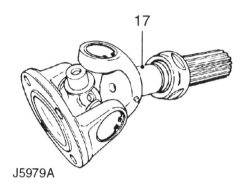

J5979A

17. Engage spider in yokes of sliding member. Fit bearing cups and circlips as described in instructions 14 to 19.
18. Fit grease nipples to spider and sliding member.
19. Apply instructions 14 to 19 to opposite end of propeller shaft.
20. Fit grease nipple and lubricate.

# 51 - REAR AXLE AND FINAL DRIVE

## CONTENTS

Page

**DESCRIPTION AND OPERATION**

# Notes

## DESCRIPTION

The welded steel rear axle casing houses a separate spiral bevel type differential unit, which is off set to the right of the vehicle centre line. The differential unit drives the rear wheels via the axle shafts and fully floating hubs which are mounted on tapered roller bearings.

### Lubrication

The differential is lubricated with oil and the hub bearings with grease.

The hub bearings are fitted with inner and outer seals. The outer seals prevent the differential oil mixing with the hub grease and the inner seals prevent dirt ingress into the hub.

### Ventilation

Ventilation of the hub bearings is through the outer oil seals and the differential ventilation pipe, which terminates at a high level.

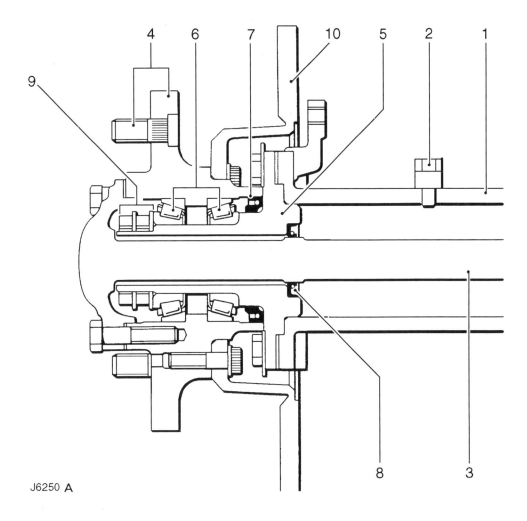

J6250 A

**Rear axle hub - 90**

1. Axle casing
2. Ventilation pipe
3. Axle shaft
4. Wheel studs and hub
5. Wheel bearing stub axle

6. Wheel bearings
7. Inner hub seal
8. Outer hub/axle shaft seal
9. Hub lock plate, thrust washer and nuts
10. Brake disc

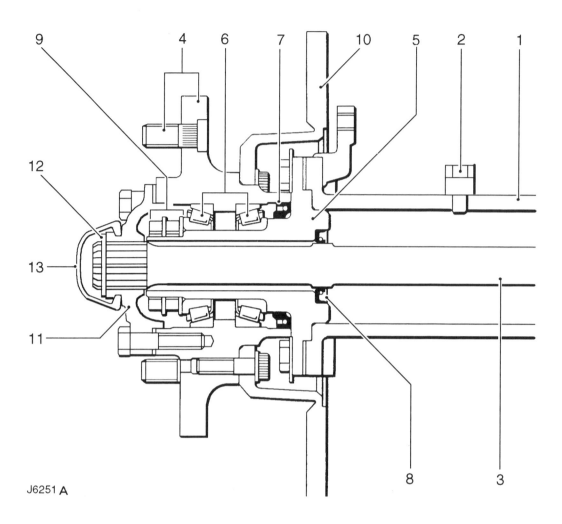

J6251 A

**Rear axle hub - 110/130**

1. Axle casing
2. Ventilation pipe
3. Axle shaft
4. Wheel studs and hub
5. Wheel bearing stub axle
6. Wheel bearings
7. Inner hub seal

8. Outer hub/axle shaft seal
9. Hub lock plate, thrust washer and nuts
10. Brake disc
11. Drive flange
12. Drive shaft circlip
13. Dust cap

## FAULT DIAGNOSIS

### Complaint - Oil leaks

An external leak of lubrication from the hub seals can be caused by a faulty internal seal. For example, if the seals which separate the differential from the hubs are faulty and the vehicle is operating or parked on an embankment, oil from the differential may flood one hub resulting in a lack of lubrication in the differential.

When a seal is found to be leaking check the axle ventilation system, as a blockage can cause internal pressure to force oil past the seals.

See 'Description and Operation' for illustrations of oil seal locations.

When investigating hub seal leaks check the grease for dilution with oil. Also check the differential oil level, for signs of metal particles in the oil and the condition of internal seals.

If the vehicle is driven in deep water with defective oil seals, water may contaminate the lubricants and raise the differential oil level, giving a false impression that the housing has been overfilled.

**Do not assume that a high oil level in the differential is due to over filling or, that a low level is because of an external leak.**

# Notes

## REAR AXLE

**Service repair no - 51.25.01**

**Remove**

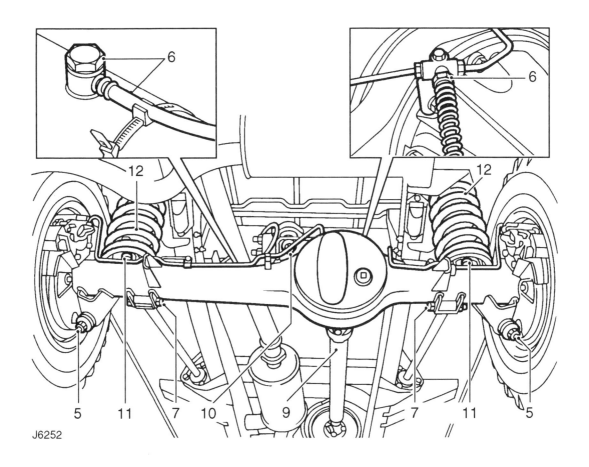

J6252

 **WARNING: Remove and refit of axle requires a further two persons to steady the axle when lowering or repositioning axle.**

1. Drain brake system.
2. Support chassis rear.
3. Remove road wheels.
4. Support axle weight with hydraulic jack.
5. Disconnect shock absorbers.
6. Disconnect flexible brake hose at RH chassis side member and breather hose at banjo connection on axle casing.
7. Disconnect lower links at axle.

8. Mark differential and propeller shaft flanges with identification marks for assembly.
9. Remove 4 nuts and bolts, lower propeller shaft and tie to one side.
10. Disconnect pivot bracket ball joint at axle bracket.
11. Release bolts and remove coil spring retaining plates.
12. Lower axle and remove road springs.
13. If applicable, remove anti-roll bar links at axle *See REAR SUSPENSION, Repair, anti-roll bar* .
14. Remove axle assembly.

**Refit**

15. Position axle and fit lower links. Tighten fixings to *176 Nm (130 lbf/ft).*
16. If applicable, fit anti-roll bar links to axle *See REAR SUSPENSION, Repair, Anti-roll bar links* .
17. Raise axle and locate road springs.
18. Fit coil spring retaining plates and secure with fixing bolts.
19. Secure pivot bracket ball joint to axle bracket. Tighten fixing to *176 Nm (130 lbf/ft).*
20. Align propeller shaft to differential drive flange and tighten fixings to *47 Nm (35 lbf/ft).*
21. Reconnect flexible brake hose and axle breather hose.
22. Refit shock absorbers.
23. Fit road wheels and tighten to correct torque:
    Alloy wheels - *130 Nm (96 lbf/ft)*
    Steel wheels - *100 Nm (80 lbf/ft)*
    Heavy Duty wheels - *170 Nm (125 lbf/ft)*
24. Remove rear chassis support.
25. Bleed brake system *See BRAKES, Repair, brake system bleed* .

## REAR HUB ASSEMBLY - 90

**Service repair no - 64.15.01**

**Remove**

1. Place rear axle onto axle stands and remove road wheel.
2. Release brake hose clips and remove brake caliper bolts. Secure to one side.

 **WARNING: Take care not to kink brake hose.**

3. Remove 5 bolts and withdraw axle shaft.
4. Remove joint washer.
5. Bend back lock washer tabs.
6. Remove locknut and lock washer.
7. Remove hub adjusting nut.
8. Remove spacing washer.
9. Remove hub and brake disc assembly complete with bearings.

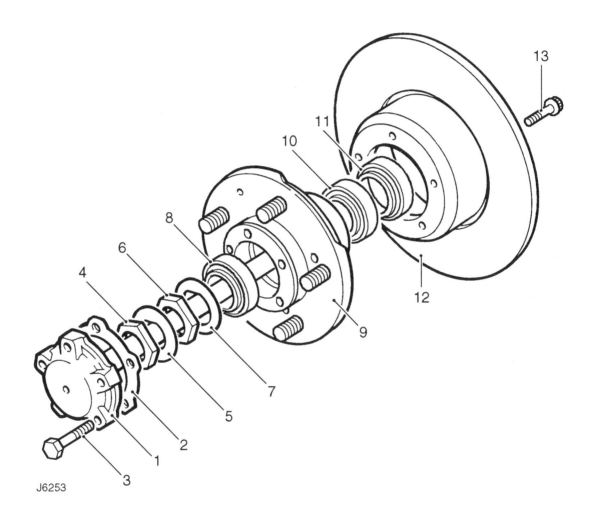

J6253

**Rear hub components - 90**

1. Axle shaft.
2. Axle shaft joint washer.
3. Axle shaft retaining bolt.
4. Lock nut.
5. Lock washer.
6. Hub adjusting nut.
7. Spacing washer.

8. Outer bearing.
9. Hub.
10. Inner bearing.
11. Grease seal.
12. Brake disc.
13. Disc retaining bolt.

**Refit**

10. Clean stub axle.
11. Fit hub assembly to stub axle.

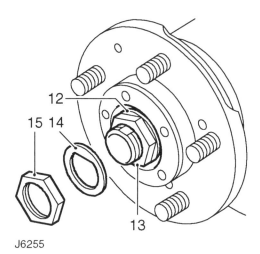

J6255

12. Fit spacing washer.
13. Fit hub adjusting nut. Tighten to **50 Nm (37 lbf/ft).** Ensure hub is free to rotate with no bearing play. Back off adjusting nut 90° and tighten to **10 Nm (7 lbf/ft).**
14. Fit a new lock washer.
15. Fit locknut. Tighten to **50 Nm (37 lbf/ft).**
16. Tab over lock washer to secure adjusting nut and locknut.
17. Using a new joint washer fit axle shaft to hub. Tighten bolts to **65 Nm (48 lbf/ft).**
18. Fit brake caliper. Tighten bolts to **82 Nm (61 lbf/ft).** Secure brake pipes to axle casing.
19. Fit road wheel, remove axle stands and tighten road wheel nuts to correct torque:
    Alloy wheels - **130 Nm (96 lbf/ft)**
    Steel wheels - **100 Nm (80 lbf/ft)**
    Heavy duty wheels - **170 Nm (125 lbf/ft)**
20. Operate footbrake to locate brake pads before driving vehicle.

## REAR HUB ASSEMBLY - 110/130

**Service repair no - 64.15.01**

**Remove**

1. Loosen rear wheel nuts, jack up vehicle and lower onto axle stands. Remove road wheel.
2. Release brake pipe clips, remove brake caliper and brake disc shield bolts. Secure to one side.

 **WARNING: Take care not to kink brake hose.**

3. Lever off dust cap.
4. Remove circlip from driveshaft.
5. Remove 5 bolts and withdraw driving member and joint washer.
6. Bend back lock washer tabs.
7. Remove locknut and lock washer.
8. Remove hub adjusting nut.
9. Remove spacing washer.
10. Remove hub and brake disc assembly complete with bearings.

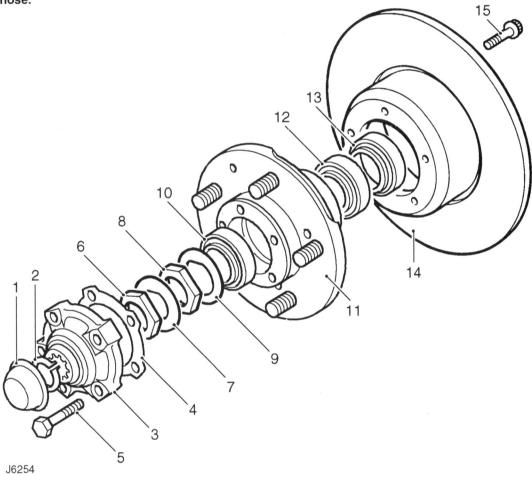

J6254

**Hub components**

1. Dust cap.
2. Drive shaft circlip.
3. Drive member.
4. Drive member joint washer.
5. Drive member retaining bolt.
6. Lock nut.
7. Lock washer.
8. Hub adjusting nut.
9. Spacing washer.
10. Outer bearing.
11. Hub.
12. Inner bearing.
13. Grease seal.
14. Brake disc
15. Disc retaining bolt.

**Refit**

11. Clean stub axle and drive shaft and fit hub assembly to axle.

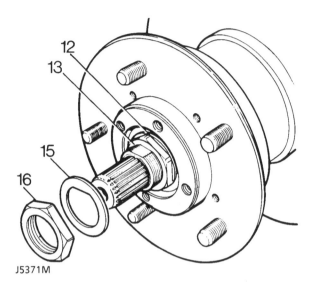

J5371M

12. Fit spacing washer.
13. Fit hub adjusting nut. Tighten to **50 Nm (37 lbf/ft).** Ensure hub is free to rotate with no bearing play.
14. Back off adjusting nut 90°and tighten to **10 Nm (7 lbf/ft).**
15. Fit a new lock washer.
16. Fit locknut. Tighten to **50 Nm (37 lbf/ft).**
17. Tab over lock washer to secure adjusting nut and locknut.
18. Fit a new joint washer to driving member and fit member to hub. Tighten bolts to **65 Nm (48 lbf/ft).**
19. Fit circlip and dust cap.
20. Fit brake disc shield and brake caliper. Tighten bolts to **82 Nm (61 lbf/ft).**
21. Bleed brake system **See BRAKES, Repair, Brake system bleed** .
22. Fit road wheel, remove axle stands and tighten road wheel nuts to correct torque:
    Alloy wheels - **130 Nm (96 lbf/ft)**
    Steel wheels - **100 Nm (80 lbf/ft)**
    Heavy duty wheels - **170 Nm (125 lbf/ft)**
23. Operate footbrake to locate brake pads before driving vehicle.

## DIFFERENTIAL ASSEMBLY - 90

**Service repair no - 51.15.01**

**Remove**

1. Using suitable container, drain axle oil.
2. Mark differential and propeller shaft flanges to facilitate reassembly.

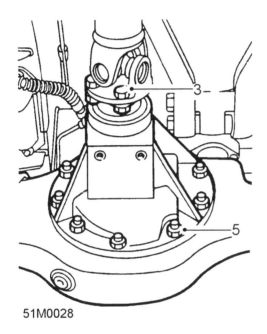

51M0028

3. Remove 4 bolts and disconnect propeller shaft from differential. Tie aside.
4. Remove 5 hub drive member bolts and withdraw axle half shafts sufficiently to disengage from differential unit.
5. Remove 10 nuts securing differential to axle case.
6. Withdraw differential unit.

⚠ **NOTE: The differential unit can only be serviced as a complete assembly with matching drive pinion. For advice ring Land Rover Service Department.**

**Refit**

7. Ensure mating faces are clean and apply a bead of RTV sealant to axle case.
8. Support differential unit and position on axle casing.
9. Secure with self locking nuts and tighten to *40 Nm (30lbf/ft)*.
10. Align marks on flanges and secure propeller shaft to differential. Tighten bolts to *48 Nm (35 lbf/ft).*
11. Refit half shafts, using new drive member gaskets. Tighten bolts to *65 Nm (48 lbf/ft).*
12. Refill axle oil with approved lubricant *See LUBRICANTS, FLUIDS AND CAPACITIES, Information, Recommended lubricants and capacities*

# Notes

## DIFFERENTIAL ASSEMBLY - 110/130

**Service repair no - 51.15.07**

**Overhaul**

1. Drain off differential lubricating oil, and refit plug.
2. Remove rear axle assembly from vehicle *See Repair, Rear axle.*
3. Remove hub driving member fixings.
4. Withdraw driving member and axle shaft sufficiently to disengage differential.
5. Repeat instruction 4 for other axle shaft.

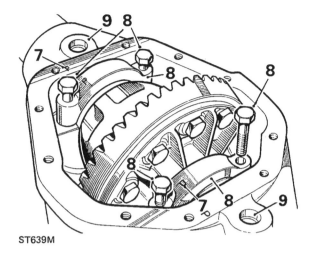

ST639M

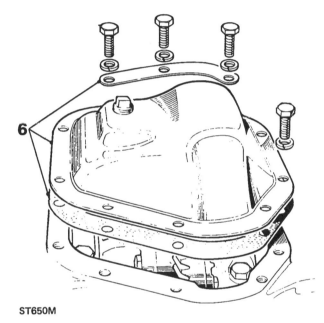

ST650M

6. Remove fixings and support strip at differential cover and withdraw cover and joint washer.
7. Note relationship marking on bearing caps and axle casing to ensure correct refitting.
8. Remove fixings and withdraw differential bearing caps.
9. Clean out and examine spreader tool pegholes provided in gear casing face; ensure that holes are free from dirt and burrs and damage.
10. Ensure that turnbuckle adjuster is free to turn.

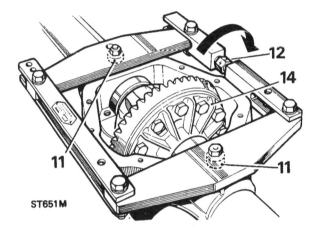

ST651M

**Using axle spreader 18G31C**

11. Fit axle spreader to engage peg holes. (Spreader **18G131C**, Adaptor pegs **18G131F**)
12. Using a spanner, turn adjuster until all free play between spreader and casing is taken up, denoted by adjuster becoming stiff to turn.
13. Check that side members of spreader are clear of casing.
14. Stretch casing, rotating adjuster by one flat at a time, until differential assembly can be levered out. Do not lever against spreader; use suitable packing under levers to avoid damage to casing.

⚠ CAUTION: To prevent permanent damage to the gear carrier case, it must not be over-stretched. Each flat on the turnbuckle is numbered to enable a check to be made on the amount turned. The maximum stretch permitted is 0,30 mm, equivalent to three flats.

15. Ease off adjuster and remove spreader.

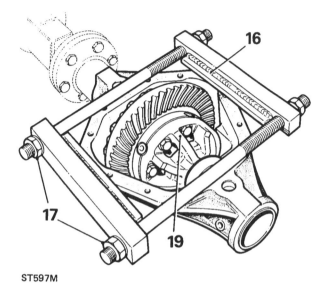

ST597M

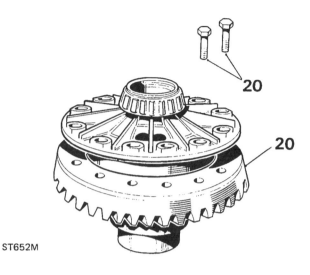

ST652M

**Dismantle differential**

20. Add alignment marks between crown wheel and differential case for reassembly purposes, n remove fixings and withdraw crown wheel.

**Using axle compressor LRT-51-503 (GKN 131)**

16. Place tool on to differential casing, as illustrated, with weld seam uppermost. Ensure that plates rest squarely on differential machined surface and end bars butt against edges of casing.
17. Tighten adjusting nuts by hand only, until all slack is taken up.
18. Continue to tighten both nuts alternately with a spanner, one flat at a time, to a maximum of three flats.
19. Carefully lever-out differential assembly.

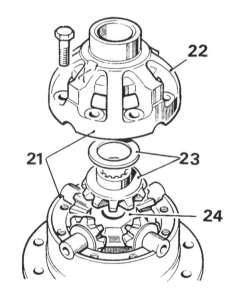

ST653M

21. Note alignment markings on two differential casings to ensure correct refitting, n remove fixings.
22. Lift off upper case.
23. Withdraw upper differential wheel and thrust washer.
24. Lift out cross-shaft and pinions.

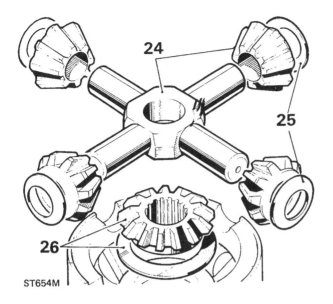

ST654M

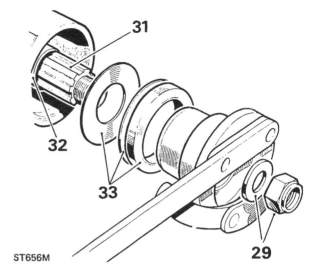

ST656M

**25.** Withdraw four dished thrust washers.
**26.** Withdraw lower differential wheel and thrust washer.

**Remove final drive pinion**

**29.** Using **LTR-51-003** to prevent coupling flange from rotating, remove flange locknut and plain washer.
**30.** Support drive pinion and remove coupling flange by tapping with a hide hammer.
**31.** Withdraw drive pinion toger with inner bearing cone.
**32.** Withdraw and discard collapsable bearing spacer.
**33.** Withdraw oil seal, gasket and oil thrower.

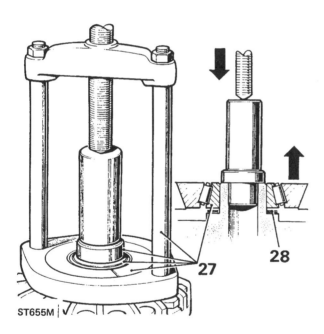

ST655M

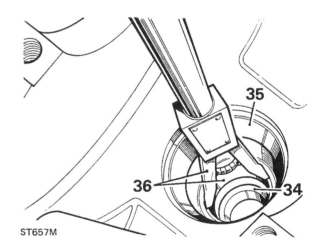

ST657M

**27.** Remove differential bearing cones using **LRT-51-500**, adaptors 1 and 2 and press **LRT-99-002**.
**28.** Withdraw shim washers fitted between bearing cones and differential casings.

**34.** Withdraw outer bearing cone.
**35.** Using **LRT-51-502**, extract pinion inner bearing cup and shim washers from casing. Note shim washer thickness. .
**36.** Extract pinion outer bearing cup from casing using **LRT-51-502**.

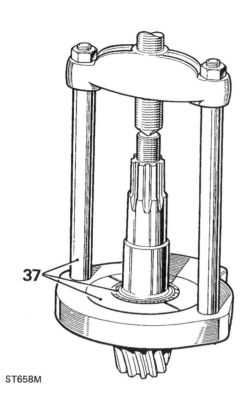

ST658M

**37.** Using **LRT-51-500** and press **LRT-99-002**, remove inner bearing cone from pinion.

## INSPECTION

**38.** Examine all components for obvious wear or damage.
**39.** Bearing cones must be a press fit on ir locations, except drive pinion flange and bearing which is a slide fit.
**40.** The crown wheel and pinion are supplied as a matched pair and must not be interchanged separately. A new crown wheel and pinion matched pair may be fitted to an original gear carrier casing if sound. original crown wheel and pinion, if sound, may be fitted into a replacement casing.
**41.** The two parts of differential unit casing are matched and must not be replaced separately.
**42.** Discard and renew all thrust washers.
**43.** Differential housings with worn thrust washer seatings must be replaced as a pair.
**44.** Examine differential case to crown wheel joint face for burrs and damage which could lead to crown wheel run-out when fitted.

## ASSEMBLE

### Differential

**45.** Fit differential lower wheel and thrust washer to differential case. See illustration following instruction 23.
**46.** Fit dished thrust washers.
**47.** Fit cross-shaft and pinions.
**48.** Fit differential upper wheel and thrust washer.
**49.** Fit differential upper case lining-up marks.
**50.** Secure assembly with bolts using Loctite 'Studlock' grade CVX on threads and tighten evenly and diametrically to *95 Nm (70 lbf/ft)*.

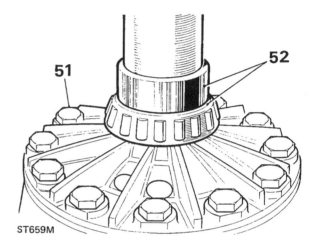

ST659M

**51.** Fit crown wheel to differential casing. Use Loctite 'Studlock' grade CVX on fixing bolt threads and tighten to correct torque.
**52.** Press on differential roller bearing cones less shim washers, using **LRT-51-504**, and leave to one side until required for instruction 96.
**53.** Fit bearing cups to differential.
**54.** Fit differential unit and bearings to gear carrier casing, and rotate unit to centralize bearings. Do not fit bearing caps.

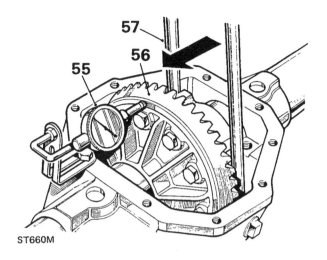

ST660M

55. Position a suitable dial gauge indicator on casing with stylus registering on back face of crown wheel.
56. Rotate differential and check total indicated run-out on crown wheel back face. This must not exceed 0,05 mm. If run-out is excessive, check mating faces for dirt and damage; if necessary, select a new radial position for crown wheel. When satisfactory, continue with following check.

**Differential bearing adjustment**

57. Insert two levers between casing and differential unit at one side.
58. Move differential unit fully to one side of casing; do not tilt unit.
59. Rotate differential unit to settle bearings, continue to lever differential to side, n zero dial gauge indicator.
60. Lever assembly fully to other side of casing, rotate unit to settle bearings, then note total indicator reading.
61. Add 0,127 mm, for bearing pre-load, to total noted in preceding instruction. The sum is then equal to nominal value of shims required for differential bearings. Shims are available in range 0,07 mm, 0,12 mm, 0,25 mm and 0,76 mm. Select total value of shims required.
62. Remove differential unit and bearings and place aside. Do not fit shim washers until subsequent 'Differential backlash' checks have been made, instructions 96 to 102.

**Fit drive pinion**

63. Select shim washers of same thickness value as those removed from under pinion inner cup, instruction 35, and place ready for fitting.

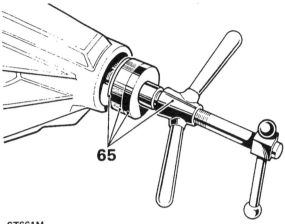

ST661M

64. Position outer bearing replacer **LRT-51-505**, detail 2, and outer bearing cup on press **LRT-99-502**.
65. Locate assembly into pinion housing nose.
66. Place selected shim washers on to inner bearing cup seating.

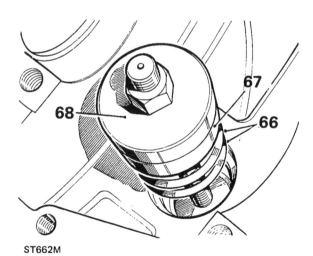

ST662M

67. Position inner bearing cup in casing.
68. Position inner bearing replacer **LRT-51-505**, detail 1, onto **LRT-99-502** and secure with fixing nut.
69. Hold still centre screw and turn butterfly lever to draw in bearing cups.

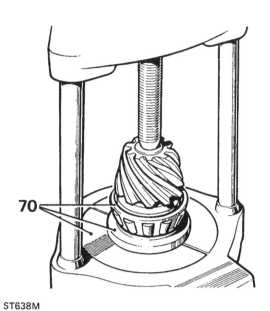

ST638M

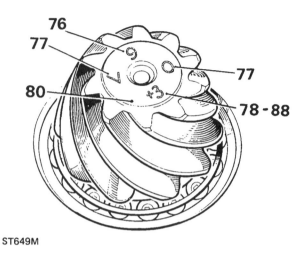

ST649M

**79.** The nominal setting dimension is represented by setting gauge block **18G191P** or **LRT-54-503**, which is referenced from pinion end face to bottom radius of differential bearing bore. The latter gauge is illustrated following instruction 85.

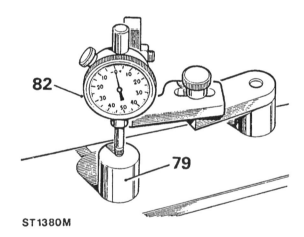

ST1380M

**70.** Press inner bearing cone onto drive pinion using, **LRT-51-502** details 1 and 2 and press **LRT-99-002**.
**71.** Position pinion and bearing in casing; omit collapsable spacer at this stage.
**72.** Fit outer bearing cone onto pinion.
**73.** Fit coupling flange and plain washer and loosely fit flange nut.
**74.** Tighten coupling flange locknut to remove end-float from pinion.
**75.** Rotate pinion to settle bearings and slowly tighten flange locknut. Use a spring balance to obtain a torque resistance of 11 Kgf/cm (18 lbf/in). to rotate pinion.

**Drive pinion markings**

**76.** Check that serial number marked on pinion end face matches that marked on crown wheel.
**77.** The markings on end face adjacent to serial number are of no significance during servicing.
**78.** The figure marked on end face opposite to serial number indicates, in thousandths of an inch, deviation from nominal required to correctly set pinion. A pinion marked plus (+) must be set below nominal, a minus (-) pinion must be set above nominal. An unmarked pinion must be set at nominal.

**Drive pinion adjustment**

**80.** Ensure that pinion end face is free of raised burrs around etched markings.
**81.** Remove keep disc from magnetized base of dial gauge tool **18G191**.
**82.** Place dial gauge and setting gauge **18G191P** or **LRT-54-503** on a flat surface and zero dial gauge stylus on to setting gauge.

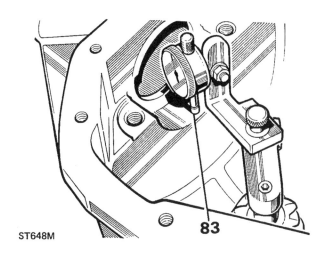

ST648M

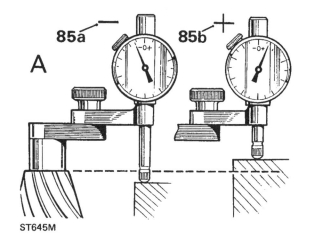

ST645M

**83.** Position dial gauge centrally on pinion end face with stylus registering on lowest point on one differential bearing bore. Note dial gauge deviation from zeroed setting.

**84.** Repeat on other bearing bore. Add together readings, then halve sum to obtain mean reading. Note whether stylus has moved up or down from zeroed setting.

**Example 1**

Reading obtained LH side.............. + 0.1524mm
Reading obtained RH side............. - 0.0762mm

Add + 0.1524mm - 0.0762mm = + 0.0762mm

Divide by 2 (0.0762 divided by 2)= 0.0381mm

Therefore subtract 0.0381mm from shim thickness behind pinion inner bearing track.

**Example 2**

Reading obtained LH side............. + 0.1524mm
Reading obtained RH side............ - 0.2032mm

Add + 0.1524mm - 0.2032mm = + 0.0508mm

Divide by 2 (0.0508 divided by 2)= 0.0254mm

Therefore add 0.0254mm from shim thickness behind pinion inner bearing track.

**B**

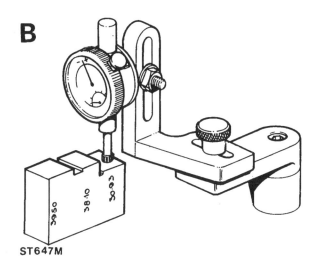

ST647M

**85.** Where stylus has moved down (85a), amount is equivalent to thickness of shims that must be removed from under pinion inner cup to bring pinion down to nominal position. Where stylus has moved up (85b), amount is equivalent to additional thickness of shims required to bring pinion up to nominal position.

Illustration A. Using setting gauge **18G191P**.

Illustration B. Using universal setting block **LRT-54-503**. This setting block has 3 setting heights.

Ensure that height marked 30.93 mm is used for this differential.

86. Before adjusting shim thickness, check pinion face marking and if it has a plus (+) figure, subtract that from shim thickness figure obtained in previous instruction. Alternatively if pinion has a minus (-) figure, add amount to shim thickness figure.

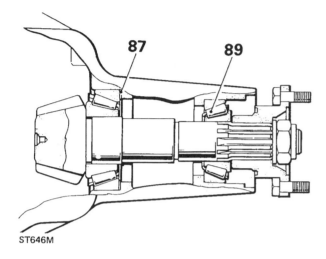

ST646M

87. Adjust shim thickness under pinion inner cup as necessary, by amount determined in instructions 85 and 86.
88. Recheck pinion height setting instructions 82 to 84. If setting is correct, mean reading on dial gauge will agree with figure marked on pinion end face. For example, with an end face marking of +3, dial gauge reading should indicate that pinion is 0.003 in (0.0762 mm) below nominal.
89. When pinion setting is satisfactory, temporarily remove pinion outer bearing.
90. Fit a new collapsable bearing spacer, flared end outward, to drive pinion and refit outer bearing.
91. Fit pinion oil slinger.
92. Fit oil seal gasket.
93. Fit pinion oil seal, lipped side first, using general purpose grease or, where available, a molybdenum disulphide based grease on seal lip, using **LRT-51-002** to drift in seal.
94. Fit coupling flange and plain washer and loosely fit a new flange nut. Secure **LRT-51-003** to coupling flange, using slave fixings.

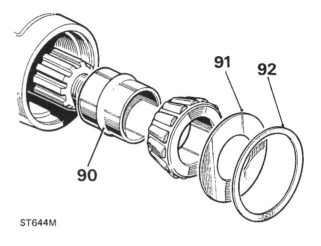

ST644M

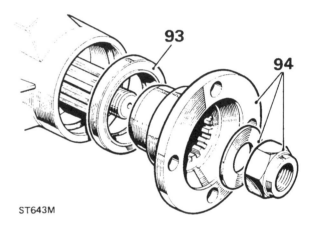

ST643M

95. Alternately tighten flange nut and check drive pinion resistance to rotation until following figures are achieved, as applicable:
    **A.** Assemblies re-using original pinion bearings: 17,3 to 34,5 kgf cm.
    **B.** Assemblies with new pinion bearings: 34,5 to 46,0 kgf cm.

⚠ **NOTE: Once the bearing spacer has started to collapse the torque resistance build-up is rapid, therefore check frequently, using a spring balance, to ensure the correct figures are not exceeded, otherwise a new collapsable bearing spacer will be required.**

**Differential backlash checks**

96. Pick up differential unit as left after instruction 52.

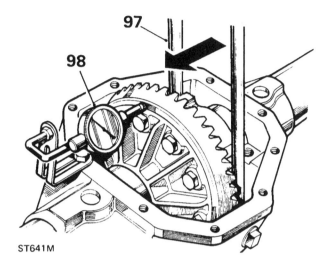

ST641M

97. Fit differential unit and lever unit away from drive pinion until opposite bearing cup is seated against housing. Do not tilt unit.
98. Install a dial gauge on casing with its stylus resting on back face of crown wheel. Zero the gauge.
99. Lever differential unit to engage crown wheel teeth in full mesh with drive pinion teeth. Do not tilt unit.
100. Note total reading obtained on dial gauge.
101. From this figure subtract 0,25 mm to obtain correct crown wheel backlash when fitted. The result indicates value of shimming to be fitted between differential case and bearing cone at crown wheel side of differential.
102. Fit shim value determined in instruction 101, taking shims from pack previously determined during 'Differential bearing adjustment' checks, instructions 57 to 62 **LRT-51-500** details 1 and 2, press **LRT-99-002**, and **LRT-51-504**.
103. Fit remaining shims from instruction 101 to opposite side of differential. **LRT-51-501** details 1 and 2, press **LRT-99-002**, and **LRT-51-504**.
104. Fit differential unit with shims and bearings to axle casing, using axle spreader **LRT-51-503** with pegs **18G131F**.
105. Remove axle spreader.

106. Fit bearing caps in their correct position, referring to relationship markings on caps and on axle casing.
107. Tighten bearing caps fixings to **135 Nm (100 lbf/ft).**

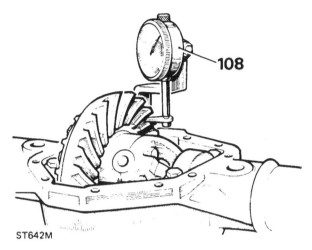

ST642M

108. Mount a dial gauge on axle casing with stylus resting on a crown wheel tooth.
109. Prevent drive pinion from rotating and check crown wheel backlash which must be 0,15 to 0,27 mm. If backlash is not within specified limits, repeat differential backlash checks, instructions 96 to 102 looking for possible errors.
110. Fit differential cover and new gasket, coating both sides of gasket with Hylomar PL 32M or an equivalent non-setting sealant. Torque load for fixings is **30 Nm (22 lbf/ft).**
111. Reverse instructions 3 to 5 and coat threads of hub driving member bolts with Loctite 'Studlock' grade CVX and fit and tighten bolts evenly to correct torque.
112. Fit rear axle assembly to vehicle **See Repair, Rear axle.**
113. Replenish differential with recommended lubricant **See LUBRICANTS, FLUIDS AND CAPACITIES, Information, Recommended lubricants and fluids** . After initial axle run, check oil level and replenish as necessary to filler/level plug hole.
114. Where major running parts have been replaced during servicing, it is a recommended practice to allow axle assembly to 'run in' by avoiding, where possible, heavy loads and high speeds during initial running.

## REAR HUB ASSEMBLY - 90

**Service repair no - 64.15.13.**

1. Remove rear hub *See Repair, Rear hub assembly.*
2. Remove outer bearing.
3. Mark, for reassembly, position of hub to brake disc.

4. Remove 5 bolts and separate hub from brake disc.

 **WARNING: A maximum of two road wheel retaining studs can be renewed. Should more studs be unserviceable fit new hub with studs.**

5. Remove grease seal and inner bearing from hub.
6. Remove inner and outer bearing tracks.

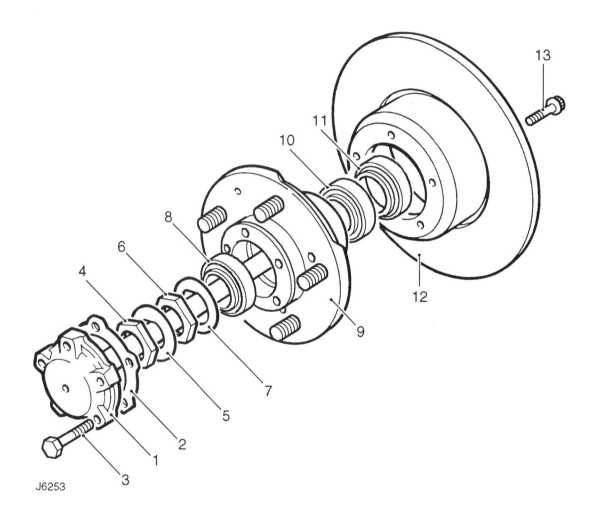

J6253

## REAR HUB COMPONENTS - 90

1. Axle shaft.
2. Axle shaft joint washer.
3. Axle shaft retaining bolt.
4. Lock nut.
5. Lock washer.
6. Hub adjusting nut.
7. Spacing washer.

8. Outer bearing.
9. Hub.
10. Inner bearing.
11. Grease seal.
12. Brake disc.
13. Disc retaining bolt.

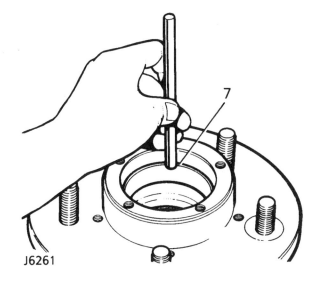

J6261

10. Assemble brake disc to hub, line up reassembly marks. Applying Loctite 270, fit and tighten retaining bolts to **73 Nm (54 lbf/ft)**.
11. Pack hub outer bearing with grease and fit to hub.
12. Fit rear hub assembly **See Repair, Rear hub assembly.**

**Refit**

7. Clean hub and fit inner and outer bearing tracks.
8. Pack hub inner bearing with grease and fit to hub.

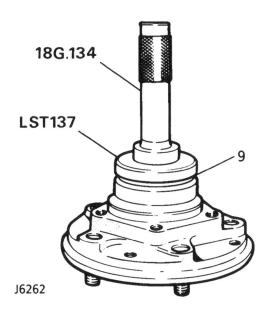

**18G.134**

**LST137**

9

J6262

9. With lip side leading, fit a new seal flush with rear face of hub. Using service tool **LRT-54-003 (LST137)** seal replacer and drift. Apply grease between seal lips.

## REAR STUB AXLE - 90

**Service repair no - 64.15.22.**

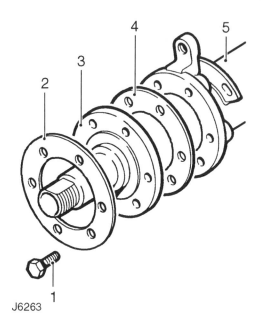

J6263

### STUB AXLE COMPONENTS

1. Stub axle to axle casing bolt.
2. Mudshield.
3. Stub axle.
4. Stub axle joint washer.
5. Axle case.

## Overhaul

1. Remove hub assembly **See Repair, Rear hub assembly.**
2. Remove six bolts from stub axle to axle casing.
3. Remove mudshield.
4. Remove stub axle and joint washer.

### Renew rear stub axle oil seal

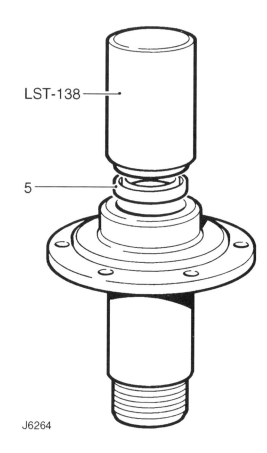

LST-138

J6264

5. Remove and discard oil seal. Lubricate seal and lip with EP90 oil. Using special tool **LRT-51-004 (LST 138)** fit new oil seal lip side trailing so that seal is flush with rear face of stub axle.

### Refit

6. Fit new joint washer, stub axle and mudshield bolts. Tighten bolts to **65 Nm (48 lbf/ft).**
7. Refit hub assembly **See Repair, Rear Hub Assembly.**

**REAR HUB - 110/130**

**Service repair no - 64.15.14.**

**Overhaul**

1. Remove rear hub assembly *See Repair, Rear hub assembly* .

2. Remove outer bearing.
3. Mark, for reassembly, relationship between hub and brake disc, if original hub is to be refitted.
4. Remove 5 bolts and separate hub from brake disc.
5. Drift out grease seal and inner bearing from hub and discard seal.

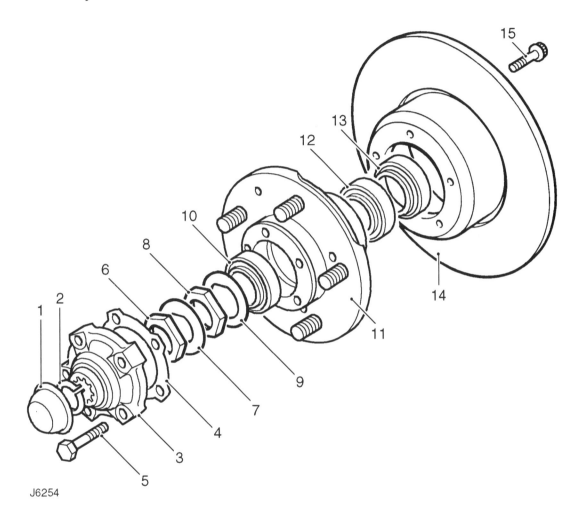

J6254

**HUB COMPONENTS**

1. Dust cap.
2. Drive shaft circlip.
3. Drive member.
4. Drive member joint washer.
5. Drive member retaining bolt.
6. Lock nut.
7. Lock washer.
8. Hub adjusting nut.

9. Spacing washer.
10. Outer bearing.
11. Hub.
12. Inner bearing.
13. Grease seal.
14. Brake disc.
15. Disc retaining bolt.

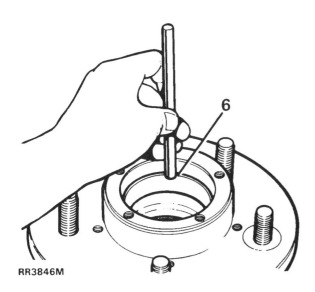

RR3846M

10. Fit brake disc to hub, lining up to marks made during dismantling. apllying Loctite 270, fit retaining bolts. Tighten to **73 Nm (54 lbf/ft).**
11. Grease and fit outer bearing to hub.
12. Fit hub assembly *See Repair, Rear hub assembly.*

6. Drift out inner and outer bearing tracks.
7. Clean hub and drift in inner and outer bearing tracks.
8. Pack hub inner bearing with recommended grease and fit to hub.

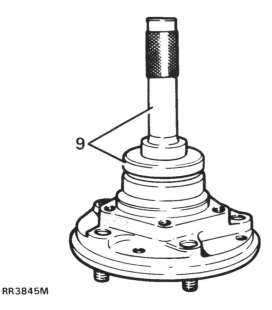

RR3845M

9. With lip side leading, fit new seal to hub using special tool **LRT-54-003** (LST 137) seal replacer and drift **18G 134** . Drive in seal flush with rear face of hub. Apply grease between seal lips.

## REAR STUB AXLE - 110/130

**Service repair no - 64.15.22**

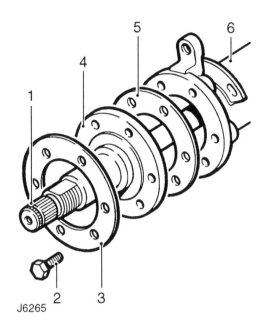

J6265

### STUB AXLE COMPONENTS

1. Rear axle shaft
2. Stub axle to axle casing bolt
3. Mudshield
4. Stub axle
5. Stub axle joint washer
6. Axle case

**Overhaul**

1. Remove hub assembly *See Repair, Rear hub assembly.*
2. Remove 6 bolts from stub axle to axle casing.
3. Remove mudshield.
4. Remove stub axle and joint washer.
5. Remove rear axle shaft from axle casing.

**Renew rear stub axle oil seal**

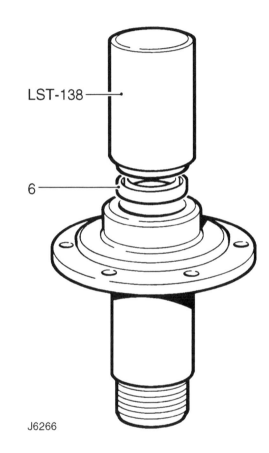

LST-138

6

J6266

6. Remove and discard oil seal. Lubricate seal and lip EP90 oil. Using special tool **LRT-51-004** (LST138) fit new seal lipside trailing so that seal is flush with rear face of stub axle.

**Refit**

7. Fit new joint washer, stub axle and mudshield. Tighten bolts to *65 Nm (48 lbf/ft).*
8. Fit rear axle shaft, avoid damaging stub axle seal.
9. Refit hub assembly *See Repair, Rear hub assembly.*

# Notes

---

**TORQUE VALUES**

 **NOTE: Torque wrenches should be regularly checked for accuracy to ensure that all fixings are tightened to the correct torque.**

**Nm**

**REAR AXLE**

| | |
|---|---|
| Pinion housing to axle case | 41 |
| Crown wheel to differential case | 58 |
| Differential bearing cap to pinion housing | 90 |
| Differential drive flange to drive shaft | 47 |
| Bevel pinion nut | 129 |
| Lower link to axle | 176 |
| Pivot bracket ball joint to axle | 176 |

---

# Notes

# 54 - FRONT AXLE AND FINAL DRIVE

## CONTENTS

Page

# Notes

## DESCRIPTION

The welded steel front axle casing houses a separate spiral bevel type differential unit, which is off-set to the right of the vehicle centre line. The differential unit drives the front wheels via the axle shafts and constant velocity joints which are totally enclosed in the spherical and swivel housings.

The front wheels are pivoted on tape roller bearings at the top and bottom of the swivel housing. The wheel hubs on all axles are supported by two taper bearings and driven by drive flanges which are splined to the one piece, stub shaft/constant velocity joint.

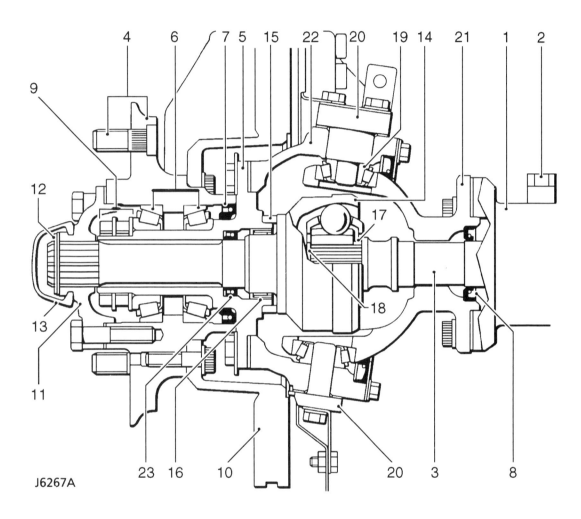

J6267A

**Front axle hub and swivel housing**

1. Axle casing
2. Ventilation pipe
3. Axle shaft
4. Wheel studs and hub
5. Stub axle
6. Wheel bearings
7. Inner and outer hub seals
8. Axle shaft seal
9. Hub lock plate, thrust washer and nuts
10. Brake disc
11. Drive flange
12. Shim washer and circlip

13. Dust cap
14. Constant velocity joint/shaft
15. Thrust collar for CV joint
16. Roller bearing
17. Spacer
18. Circlip
19. Top and bottom swivel taper bearing
20. Top and bottom swivel pins
21. Spherical housing, seal and retainer
22. Swivel housing
23. Constant velocity shaft seal

## Lubrication

The differential, swivel pin housing and wheel hubs
are indiviudally lubricated and separated by oil seals
(7) and (8), see J6267A, to prevent oil transfer across
the axle when the vehicle is traversing steep inclines.
The wheel bearings are lubricated with grease and the
swivel housing and differential with oil. On later
vehicles, identified by having only a filler plug in the
swivel housing, grease is used to lubricate the
housing assembly,

## Ventilation

Ventilation of the differential is through a plastic pipe
(2) which terminates at a high level in the vehicle axle.
The swivel housings ventilate through axle shaft oil
seals (8) into the differential and the hub bearings
vent via the oil seals into the swivel housing.

## FAULT DIAGNOSIS

### Complaint - Oil leaks

An external leak of lubrication can be caused by a faulty internal seal. For example, if the seals which separate the differential from the swivel housings are faulty and the vehicle is operating or parked on an embankment, oil may leak across the axle leaving one swivel with a high level and the opposite swivel and differential lacking lubrication.

See 'Description and Operation' for illustrations of oil seal locations.

When investigating leaks or checking oil levels, it is essential that all the lubrication is drained from any housing with a high level and that the other levels are checked.

Swivel oil should be checked for signs of grease leaking from the hub bearings and oil contamination of the hub grease.

Check that the axle ventilation system is clear, as a blockage can cause internal pressure to force oil past the seals.

If the vehicle is driven in deep water with defective oil seals, water may contaminate the lubricants and when checked, give a false impression that the housing has been overfilled with oil.

**Do not assume that a high oil level is due to over filling or, that a low level is because of an external leak**.

# Notes

## FRONT AXLE ASSEMBLY

**Service repair no - 54.10.01**

**Remove**

 **WARNING: Remove and refit of axle requires a further two persons to steady axle when lowering or repositioning axle.**

1. Support chassis front.
2. Remove road wheels.
3. Support axle weight with hydraulic jack.

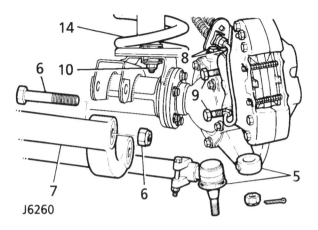

J6260

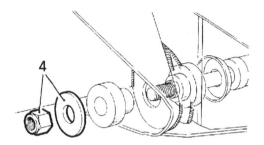

RR983

4. Remove radius arms to chassis frame nuts.
5. Disconnect steering damper from track rod. Using a extractor remove track rod links from swivel pin arms.
6. Remove four nuts and bolts securing radius arms to axle bracket.
7. Remove radius arms.
8. Remove bolts securing brake hose brackets . Refit bolts to prevent oil leakage.
9. Remove bolts from brake calipers and tie to one side.
10. Remove nuts and washers securing shock absorbers to axle.
11. Disconnect drag link from swivel pin housing arm.
12. Remove two nuts and bolts securing panhard rod to axle bracket. Lift rod clear of axle.
13. Mark for reassembly drive shaft flanges. Remove four nuts and bolts, tie propeller shaft to one side.

14. Release axle ventilation pipe banjo and lower axle assembly. Remove road springs.
15. Disconnect anti-roll bar link *See FRONT SUSPENSION, Repair,  Anti-roll bar ball* .
16. Remove axle assembly.

**Refit**

17. Position axle under vehicle, supporting left side of axle, and fit anti-roll bar links *See FRONT SUSPENSION, Repair,  Anti-roll bar links* .
18. Fit propeller shaft. Tighten bolts to *47 Nm (35 lbf/ft)*.
19. Fit panhard rod to axle bracket. Tighten bolts to *88 Nm (65 lbf/ft)*.
20. Fit drag link to swivel pin arm. Tighten fixings to *40 Nm (30 lbf/ft)*.
21. Fit shock absorbers to axle.
22. Fit brake calipers. Tighten bolts to *82 Nm (60 lbf/ft)*.
23. Tighten upper swivel pin bolts to *78 Nm (58 lbf/ft)*.
24. Fit radius arms to axle brackets. Tighten bolts to *197 Nm (145 lbf/ft)*.
25. Fit steering damper to track rod.
26. Fit radius arms to chassis side member. Tighten fixings to *197 Nm (145 lbf/ft)*.
27. Tighten track rod end to *40 Nm (30 lbf/ft)* and fit new split pin.
28. Remove chassis supports, fit road wheels and tighten to correct torque:
   Alloy wheels - *130 Nm (96 lbf/ft)*
   Steel wheels - *100 Nm (80 lbf/ft)*
   Heavy duty wheels - *170 Nm (125 lbf/ft)*

## FRONT HUB ASSEMBLY

**Service repair no - 60.25.01.**

**Remove**

1. Loosen front wheel nuts, jack up vehicle and lower onto axle stands and remove road wheel.
2. Release brake hose clips and remove brake caliper and brake disc shield bolts. Secure to one side.
3. Lever off dust cap.
4. Remove circlip and drive shaft shim from driveshaft.
5. Remove 5 bolts and withdraw driving member and joint washer.
6. Bend back lock washer tabs.
7. Remove locknut and lock washer.
8. Remove hub adjusting nut.
9. Remove spacing washer.
10. Remove hub and brake disc assembly complete with bearings.

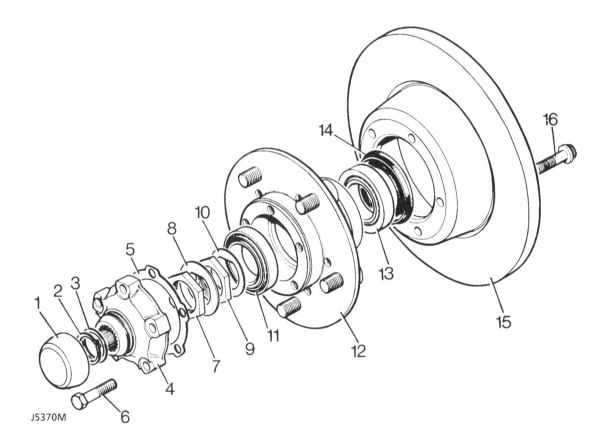

J5370M

## HUB COMPONENTS

1. Dust cap.
2. Drive shaft circlip.
3. Drive shaft shim.
4. Drive member.
5. Drive member joint washer.
6. Drive member retaining bolt.
7. Lock nut.
8. Lock washer.
9. Hub adjusting nut.
10. Spacing washer.
11. Outer bearing.
12. Hub.
13. Inner bearing.
14. Grease seal.
15. Brake disc
16. Disc retaining bolt.

**Refit**

11. Clean stub axle and drive shaft and fit hub assembly to axle.

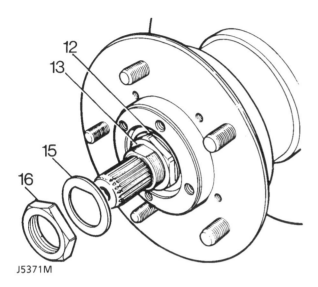

J5371M

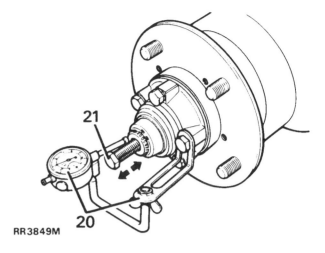

RR3849M

12. Fit spacing washer.
13. Fit hub adjusting nut. Tighten to **50 Nm (37 lbf/ft).** Ensure hub is free to rotate with no bearing play.
14. Back off adjusting nut 90° and tighten to **10 Nm (7 lbf/ft).**
15. Fit a new lock washer.
16. Fit locknut. Tighten to **50 Nm (37 lbf/ft).**
17. Tab over lock washer to secure adjusting nut and locknut.
18. Fit a new joint washer to driving member and fit member to hub. Tighten bolts to **65 Nm (48 lbf/ft).**
19. Fit original drive shaft shim and secure with a circlip.

20. To check drive shaft end play, mount a dial gauge using bracket **LRT-99-503** and rest pin in a loaded condition on end of drive shaft.
21. Fit a suitable bolt to threaded end of drive shaft. Move drive shaft in and out noting dial gauge reading. End play should be between 0,08 to 0,25 mm.
22. If end play requires adjustment, remove circlip, measure shim thickness and fit an appropriate shim to give required end-play.
23. Remove bolt from drive shaft, fit circlip and dust cap.
24. Fit brake disc shield and brake caliper. Tighten fixings to **82 Nm (60 lbf/ft).**
25. Bleed brake system **See BRAKES, Repair, Brake system bleed** .
26. Fit road wheel, remove axle stands and tighten road wheel nuts to correct torque:
    Alloy wheels - **130 Nm (96 lbf/ft)**
    Steel wheels - **100 Nm (80 lbf/ft)**
    Heavy duty wheels - **170 Nm (125 lbf/ft)**
27. Operate footbrake to locate brake pads before driving vehicle.

# Notes

## FRONT DIFFERENTIAL

**Service repair no - 54.10.07.**

**Overhaul**

⚠ NOTE: The front axle differential, for all models, is the same as that fitted to the 90 rear axle and can only be serviced as a complete assembly *See REAR AXLE AND FINAL DRIVE, Repair, Rear differential - 90.*

## FRONT HUB

**Service repair no - 60.25.14.**

**Overhaul**

1. Remove hub assembly *See Repair, Front hub assembly.*
2. Remove outer bearing.
3. Mark, for reassembly, relationship between hub and brake disc, if original hub is to be refitted.
4. Remove 5 bolts and separate hub from brake disc.
5. Drift out grease seal and inner bearing from hub and discard seal.

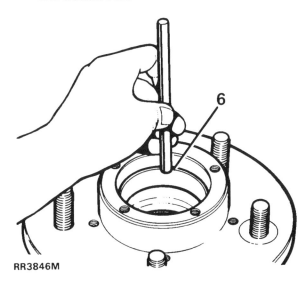

RR3846M

6. Drift out inner and outer bearing tracks.
7. Clean hub and drift in inner and outer bearing tracks.
8. Pack hub inner bearing with recommended grease and fit to hub.

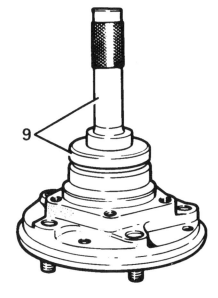

RR3845M

9. With lip side leading fit new seal to hub using special tool **LST 137** seal replacer and drift **18G 134**. Drive in seal flush with rear face of hub. Apply grease between seal lips.
10. Fit brake disc to hub, lining up to marks made during dismantling. Applying Loctite 270, fit retaining bolts. Tighten to **73 Nm (54 lbf/ft).**
11. Grease and fit outer bearing to hub.
12. Fit hub assembly *See Repair, Front hub assembly.*

## FRONT STUB AXLE, CONSTANT VELOCITY JOINT AND SWIVEL PIN HOUSING

**Service repair no - 60.15.43.**

**Remove stub axle, axle shaft and constant velocity joint.**

1. Remove front hub assembly *See Repair, Front hub assembly.*
2. Drain swivel pin housing and refit plug.

**NOTE: On later vehicles the swivel pin housing is filled with grease for life, the level and drain plugs being deleted.**

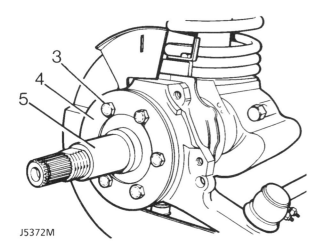

J5372M

3. Remove 6 bolts retaining stub axle to swivel housing.
4. Remove mud shield.
5. Remove stub axle and joint washer.

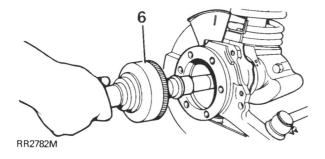

RR2782M

6. Wthdraw axle shaft and constant velocity joint from axle casing.

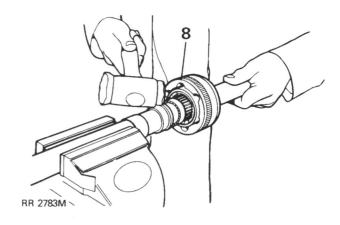

RR 2783M

### Remove constant velocity joint from axle shaft

7. Hold axle shaft firmly in a soft jawed vice.
8. Using a soft mallet drive constant velocity joint from shaft.
9. Remove circlip and collar from axle shaft.

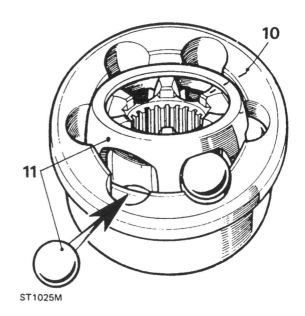

ST1025M

### Constant velocity joint

10. Mark positions of constant velocity joint, inner and outer race and cage for reassembly.
11. Swivel cage and inner race to remove balls.

12. Examine all components, in particular, inner and outer track, cage balls and bearing surfaces for damage and excessive wear.
13. Maximum acceptable end-float on assembled joint 0,64mm. Renew if worn or damaged. Lubricate with a recommended oil during assembly.

**Fit constant velocity joint to axle**

14. Fit collar and a new circlip.
15. Engage constant velocity joint on axle shaft splines and using a soft mallet, drive joint in fully.

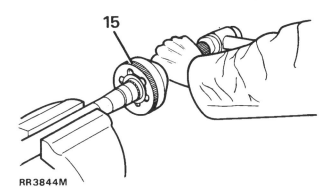

RR3844M

**Renew stub axle, thrust ring, oil seal and bearing**

16. Drill and chisel off thrust ring taking care to avoid damaging stub axle.

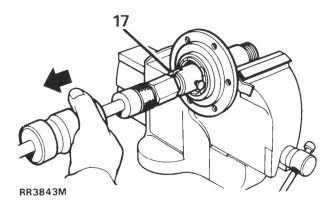

RR3843M

17. Remove bearing and oil seal using special tool **TRT-37-004** and slide hammer **LRT-99-004**. Ensure lip of tool locates behind bearing to to drive it out.
18. Repeat instruction for removal of oil seal.

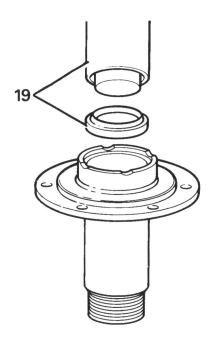

RR3840M

19. Lubricate seal and lip with EP90 oil and with cavity side leading press in a new oil seal using special tool **LRT-54-004**.

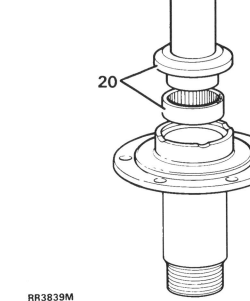

RR3839M

20. Using special tool **LRT-54-005**, fit bearing with its part number visible when fitted, and flush with end face of stub axle.
21. Press fit a new thrust ring onto stub axle.

## Swivel pin housing

22. Remove bolts securing oil seal retaining plate and joint washer. Release assembly from swivel pin housing.

 **NOTE: Removal of oil seal and retaining plate is achieved when swivel bearing housing is removed.**

23. Remove 2 bolts, retaining lower swivel pin to housing.
24. Remove brake disc shield bracket.
25. Tap lug to remove lower swivel pin and joint washer.
26. Remove two bolts retaining brake hose bracket and top swivel pin.
27. Remove bracket, top swivel pin and shims.
28. Remove swivel pin housing while retrieving lower and upper bearings.

## Swivel bearing housing

29. Remove lower bearing track from swivel bearing housing.

 **NOTE: Use upper bearing opening to gain access to lower bearing track.**

30. Remove 7 bolts retaining swivel bearing housing to axle case.
31. Remove inner oil seal from back of housing.
32. Remove top bearing track from swivel bearing housing.

 **NOTE: Use lower bearing opening to gain access to upper bearing track.**

33. If worn, pitted or damaged, renew housing.
34. Fit upper and lower bearing tracks into swivel bearing housing.

 **CAUTION: Ensure bearing tracks are fitted square or damage could occur.**

35. With seal lips trailing, fit swivel housing inner oil seal into rear of housing. Grease seal lips.

## Fit swivel pin housing

36. Coat swivel bearing housing to axle casing bolts with Loctite 270 or equivalent.
37. Coat both sides of joint washer with a sealing compound. Position swivel bearing housing to axle mating face.

## Swivel assembly components

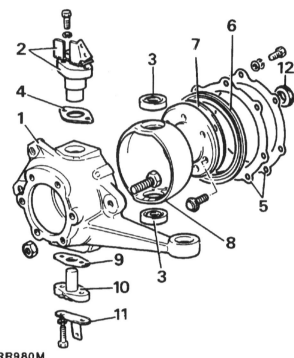

**RR980M**

1. Swivel pin housing
2. Top swivel pin and brake hose bracket
3. Upper and lower swivel pin bearings
4. Shim
5. Retaining plate and washer
6. Oil seal
7. Joint washer
8. Swivel bearing housing
9. Joint washer
10. Lower swivel pin
11. Mudshield bracket
12. Swivel housing inner oil seal

38. Place retaining plate, joint washer and oil seal over axle flange ready for assembly.
39. Fit swivel bearing housing to axle flange with 7 bolts. Tighten to *73 Nm (54 lbf/ft)*.
40. Grease and fit upper and lower swivel pin taper roller bearings.
41. Position swivel pin housing over swivel bearing housing.
42. Coat joint washer both sides with sealing compound and position on lower swivel pin.
43. Loosely fit brake shield bracket plus lower swivel pin with lug outboard to swivel pin housing.
44. Loosely fit top swivel pin plus existing shims and brake hose bracket to swivel pin housing.
45. Apply Loctite 270 or equivalent to lower swivel pin bolts. *78 Nm (58 lbf/ft)* , bend over lock tabs.
46. Tighten top swivel pin bolts to *78 Nm (58 lbf/ft)*.

**Check and adjust preload on bearings**

 **NOTE: Swivel housing oil seal and axle should not be fitted.**

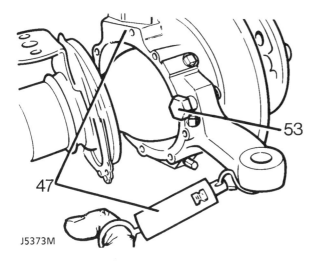

J5373M

47. Attach a spring balance to ball joint bore and pull balance to determine effort required to turn swivel pin housing.
    Resistance, once initial inertia has been overcome, should be **1.16 to 1.46 kg.** Adjust by removing or adding shims to top swivel pin.
48. When setting is correct remove top swivel bolts, apply Loctite 270 or equivalent. Refit bolts and tighten to *78 Nm (58 lbf/ft),* and bend over lock tabs.
49. Apply recommended grease between lips of swivel oil seal.

50. Fit oil seal, joint washer and retaining plate with 7 bolts and spring washers. Tighten to *11 Nm (8 lbf/ft)*.
51. Fit tie rod and drag link and secure with new cotter pins. Tighten fixing to *40 Nm (30 lbf/ft)*.
52. Fit brake disc shield.
53. Loosely fit lock stop bolt and nut.
54. Apply a recommended grease between lips of swivel housing oil seal.
55. Secure oil seal with retaining plate and securing bolts. Tighten to *11 Nm (8 lbf/ft)*.
56. Fit track-rod and drag link and secure with new cotter pins.
57. Loosely fit lock stop bolt for later adjustment.
58. Fit brake disc shield.

**Fit driveshaft and stub axle**

59. Insert axle shaft, and when differential splines are engaged, push assembly in fully.

 **CAUTION: Take care not to damage axle shaft oil seals.**

60. Place a new joint washer in position on swivelpin housing to stub axle mating face. Coat threads of stub axle bolts with Loctite 270.
61. Fit stub axle with flat at 12 O'clock position.

 **CAUTION: Ensure that constant velocity joint bearing journal is butted against thrust ring on stub axle before stub axle is secured.**

62. Place mud shield in position and secure stub axle to swivel pin housing with 6 bolts and tighten evenly to *65 Nm (48 lbf/ft)*.
63. Fit brake jump hoses to brake jump hose bracket.
64. Fit complete front hub assembly *See Repair, Front hub assembly.*
65. Check swivel pin housing oil drain plug is fitted.
66. Fill swivel assembly to correct level, with new oil *See SECTION 10, Maintenance, Under vehicle maintenance.*

 **NOTE: On later vehicles fill swivel pin housing with 0.33 Litres of Molytex EP 00 grease.**

67. Set steering lock stop bolts *See STEERING, Adjustment, Steering lock stops.*

# Notes

## TORQUE VALUES

 NOTE: Torque wrenches should be regularly checked for accuracy to ensure that all fixings are tightened to the correct torque.

**Nm**

### FRONT AXLE

| | |
|---|---|
| Hub driving member to hub | 65* |
| Brake disc to hub | 73 |
| Stub axle to swivel pin housing | 65* |
| Brake caliper to swivel pin housing | 82 |
| Upper swivel pin to swivel pin housing | 78* |
| Lower swivel pin to swivel pin housing | 78* |
| Oil seal retainer to swivel pin housing | 11 |
| Swivel bearing housing to axle case | 73* |
| Pinion housing to axle case | 41 |
| Crown wheel to differential housing | 58 |
| Differential bearing cap to pinion housing | 90 |
| Differential drive flange to drive shaft | 47 |
| Mudshield to bracket lower swivel pin | 11 |
| Bevel pinion nut | 130 |
| Draglink to hub arm | 40 |
| Panhard rod to axle bracket | 88 |
| Radius arm to axle | 190 |
| Radius arm to chassis side member | 190 |

 NOTE: * These bolts to be coated with Loctite 270 prior to assembly.

# Notes

# 57 - STEERING

## CONTENTS

# 57 - STEERING

## CONTENTS

Page

## DESCRIPTION

The steering system incorporates a compression joint in the lower shaft and is designed to collapse on impact. The mis-alignment of the upper steering column with the steering box and the inclusion of two universal joints, is also designed to prevent the column moving toward the driver under frontal impact.

The steering box is located behind the first chassis cross member and is connected to the road wheel swivel housing by a drag link and track rod. A hydraulic damper absorbs shocks in the steering, caused by road wheel deflections when operating on rough terrain.

## Power steering system

The power steering system comprises a hydraulic pump which is belt driven from the engine and supplied with fluid from a reservoir that also acts as a cooler.

The steering box houses a self neutralizing rotary valve which is part of the worm/valve assy and an hydraulic piston/rack to assist the mechanical operation. The rotary valve which is operated by movement of the steering wheel, directs fluid pressure to the appropriate side of the hydraulic piston/rack to provide assistance.

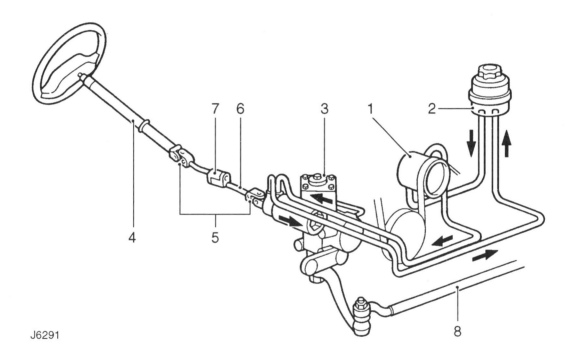

J6291

## Power steering system

1. Hydraulic pump
2. Fluid reservoir
3. Steering box
4. Upper column

5. Universal joints
6. Lower shaft
7. Compression joint
8. Drag link

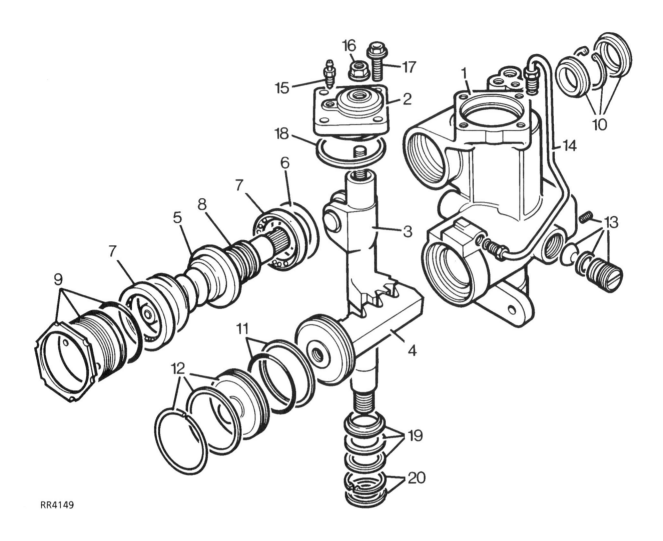

RR4149

**Power steering box components**

1. Housing complete with sector shaft bearings
2. Cover plate complete with bearing
3. Sector shaft
4. Hydraulic piston/rack
5. Worm/valve and torsion bar assembly
6. Shims for centralizing worm/valve
7. Ball race
8. 'Teflon' seals for valve sleeve
9. Bearing adjuster, locknut and seal
10. Worm shaft pressure seal, circlip and dirt excluder

11. 'Teflon' and rubber seal for piston
12. End cover seal and snap ring
13. Adjustment components for piston/rack
14. Hydraulic pipe
15. Bleed screw
16. Sector shaft adjustment lock nut with seal
17. Cover plate bolts
18. Cover plate seal
19. Seal, washer and backup seal
20. Circlip and dust cover

## Rotary valve operation

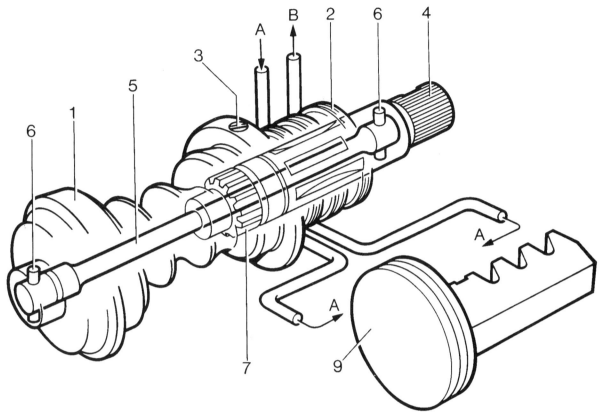

RR3620M

### Rotary valve at neutral

The rotary valve assembly comprises a worm (1), valve sleeve (2), input shaft (4) and torsion bar (5).

The valve sleeve is retained inside the worm by a trim screw (3), and incorporates valve ports in its inner bore. The input shaft is attached to the steering wheel via a steering shaft and steering column and incorporates valve ports in its outer diameter to align with those in the sleeve.

The torsion bar, which is secured to the worm and input shaft with pins (6) at each end, holds the valve ports in neutral alignment when there is no demand for assistance.

### No demand for assistance (Valve at neutral)

When there is no demand for assistance the torsion bar holds the input shaft and sleeve valve ports in neutral relationship to one another, allowing equal pump pressure (A) to both sides of the piston/rack (9). Any excess fluid flow from the pump returns to the reservoir via (B).

**Rotary valve misaligned**

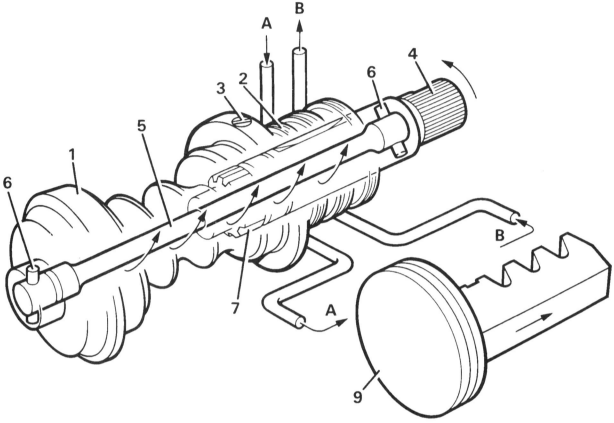

RR3621M

### Demand for assistance (Valve misaligned)

When the steering wheel and input shaft is turned, steering resistance transmitted to the worm causes the torsion bar to be twisted and the valve ports to be misaligned for a right or left turn. The misalignment of the valve ports directs all fluid pressure A to one side of the piston only and allows displaced fluid B on the other side.

When demanding maximum assistance, any excessive fluid output from the pump due to high pump speed, will circulate through the regulator valve located in the pump unit, causing the temperature of the fluid and the pump to rise rapidly.

 **CAUTION: To avoid excessive fluid temperatures which could damage the oil seals, the steering must not be held on full lock for more than 30 seconds in one minute.**

Only when the steering wheel, and the demand for assistance, is released, will the torsion bar return the valve to neutral, allowing the fluid to circulate through the reservoir where it is cooled.

In the unlikely event of mechanical failure of the torsion bar, a coarse splined connection (7) between the input shaft and worm, ensures steering control is maintained sufficient to allow the vehicle to be recovered.

### Pump and regulator valve operation

The pump which is belt driven from the engine is an eccentric roller type and also houses the pressure regulator and flow control valve. The pressure is controlled by a spring loaded ball valve (3) which is housed inside the flow control valve piston (4).

### No demand for assistance High flow through box - Low pressure

With no demand for assistance the rotary valve in the steering box acts as a pressure relief valve, allowing fluid (A) to flow freely through the steering box and back to the reservoir and pump inlet (B).

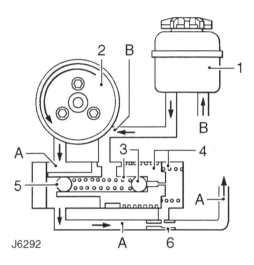

J6292

### No demand for assistance

1. Reservoir
2. Pump
3. Pressure control ball valve and spring
4. Flow control valve and spring
5. Press fit plug (ball bearing)
6. Restrictor

**The ball plug (5) is pressed into the valve (4) during manufacture and determines the opening pressure of pressure relief valve (3).**

### No flow, through box - High pressure

When the steering is turned, the rotary valve effectively stops all fluid flow through the steering box, thus causing an increase in pressure (A). This increase in pressure is felt in the flow control valve spring chamber where, at a pre-determined pressure the relief valve (3) will open and allow the pressure to escape. The fall in pressure in the flow control spring chamber, allows the flow control valve to move to the right, which in turn allows pump output (A) to escape directly into the pump inlet (B).

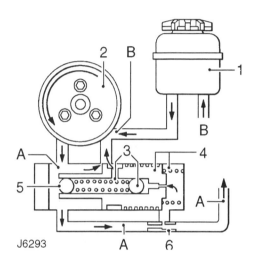

J6293

### Assistance demanded

As soon as the steering wheel is released after making a turn, the system reverts to the condition seen in J6292 and the road wheels are returned to the straight ahead position by the mechanical steering geometry.

In the event of any hydraulic failure, steering control, though heavy, will be maintained through the mechanical components in the steering box.

# Notes

## INSUFFICIENT POWER ASSISTANCE

1. Is fluid level correct?
   YES - go to 3.
   NO - Fill/bleed sytem

2. Is problem a leak?
   YES - Diagnose *See  Power Steering Fluid Leaks.*
   NO - continue

3. Is drive belt tension correct?
   YES - go to 5.
   NO - Is drive belt worn or contaminated with oil? *See ELECTRICAL, Repair,  Auxiliary drive belt.*

4. Is problem resolved?
   YES - end
   NO - continue

5. Carry out pressure test at idle and 1000 rev/min. *See  Power Steering System - Test.*

6. Is correct pressure achieved?
   YES - steering box defective
   Not at any speed go to 9.
   Not at idle go to 7.

7. Is idle speed correct?
   YES - Go to 8.
   NO - Correct idle speed - *See ENGINE TUNING DATA, Information,  300 Tdi Engine.*

8. Is problem resolved?
   YES - end
   NO - go to 9.

9. Bypass steering box using adaptor tap **LRT-57-001**

10. Is correct pressure obtained?
    YES - defective steering box
    NO - defective steering pump

 **CAUTION: Do not hold steering wheel on full lock for more than 30 seconds in any one minute to avoid overheating fluid and possibly damaging seals.**

**NOTE: 1. Excessive pressure in the system is almost always caused by a faulty relief valve in the PAS pump.**

**NOTE: 2. Insufficient pressure in the system is usually caused by low fluid level or PAS pump drive belt slip, or one of the following: PAS system leaks, faulty PAS pump relief valve, fault in steering box valve and worm assembly, leak at piston in steering box, worn components in PAS pump or box.**

## POWER STEERING SYSTEM - TEST

⚠️ **NOTE: If steering lacks power assistance. Check pressure of hydraulic pump before fitting new components. Use fault diagnosis chart to assist in tracing faults.**

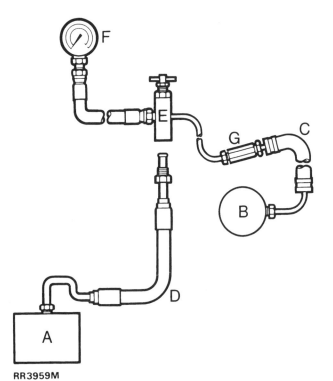

RR3959M

A. Steering box.
B. Steering pump.
C. Existing hose, steering box to pump.
D. Hose **LRT-57-030**.
E. Test adaptor **LRT-57-001**.
F. Pressure gauge **LRT-57-005**.
G. Thread adaptor **LRT-57-004**.
H. Thread adaptor **LRT-57-022**.

## Procedure

1. A hydraulic pressure gauge and test adaptor is used to test power steering system. This gauge is able to measure 140 kgf/cm$^2$. The maximum power steering system pressure is 77 kgf/cm$^2$.
2. Under certain fault conditions of the hydraulic pump it is possible to obtain pressures up to 105 kgf/cm$^2$. It is important to realise that pressure on gauge is same pressure being exerted upon steering wheel. When testing, turn steering wheel gradually while reading pressure gauge.
3. Check and maintain maximum fluid level of reservoir.
4. Examine power steering units and connections for leaks. All leaks must be rectified before attempting to test the system.
5. Check steering pump drive belt tension and renew belt if necessary, *See ELECTRICAL, Repair, Auxiliary drive Belt.*
6. Assemble test equipment and fit to vehicle, as shown in RR3959M.
7. Open tap of adaptor.
8. Bleed system, take care not to overload pressure gauge.
9. With system in good condition, pressures should be:
   (A) Steering wheel held on full lock and engine running at 1,000 rev/min, 70 to 77 kgf/cm$^2$.
   (B) Steering wheel held on full lock and engine idling, 28 kgf/cm$^2$.
   Checks should be carried out on both full lock positions.

⚠️ **CAUTION: Do not maintain this pressure for more than 30 seconds in any one minute to avoid overheating fluid and possibly damaging seals.**

10. Release steering wheel and with engine idling. Pressure should read below 7 kgf/cm$^2$.
11. If pressures differ to those given a fault exists.
12. To determine if fault is steering box or pump. Close adaptor tap for a maximum five seconds.
13. If gauge does not register specified pressure, pump is faulty.
14. Fit a new pump, bleed system and repeat test. If low pressure or a substantial imbalance exists, fault is in steering box valve and worm assembly.

## STEERING DAMPER

The power steering system, as well as reducing the effort required to manoeuvre the vehicle when parking, also helps to dampen any deflections of the road wheels, being transmitted back to the steering wheel.

When operating the vehicle off road, the road wheels are often deflected by ruts and boulders causing the steering wheel to turn left and right. This phenomenon is known as 'steering kickback'. To subdue the effects of 'steering kickback', a hydraulic damper is fitted in the steering linkage between the track rod and the differential casing. The damper, which offers the same resistance in extension and compression, is sealed for life.

### Steering damper check

Check the condition operation of the hydraulic steering damper as follows:

### Check procedure

1. Inspect damper for casing damage or leaks.
2. Clamp one end of the damper horizontally in a vice using soft jaws. Compress and extend the unit by hand. Resistance should be equal in both directions.
3. If it is felt that the unit is outside acceptable limits, fit a new steering damper

## STEERING FAULTS

**Symptom:-**

**Excessive kickback through steering wheel - when driven on rough terrain.**

1. Is the steering damper in good working order? *See Steering Damper.*
   NO - Renew unit *See Repair, Steering Damper.*
   YES - Continue.

2. Is there any looseness or free play in the steering ball joints and linkage?
   YES - *See Steering Linkage Inspect.*
   NO - Continue.

3. Is there any looseness or worn bushes in front suspension?
   YES - *See FRONT SUSPENSION, Repair, Radius Arm.*

 **NOTE: When replacing suspension bushes ALL bushes and fixings must be replaced.**

   NO - Continue.

4. Is the steering exceptionally light/sensitive when driven on good road surface?
   YES - See fault symptom - **Steering excessively light/sensitive and freeplay at steering wheel**.
   NO - Suspect axle swivel resistance.

5. Check the resistance of the axle swivels *See FRONT AXLE AND FINAL DRIVE, Overhaul, Front Stub Axle, Constant Velocity Joint and Swivel Pin Housing .*

**Symptom:-**

**Fluid leaks from steering box seals.**

 **CAUTION: The steering wheel must not be held on full lock for more than 30 seconds in one minute, as this may overheat the fluid and cause damage to the oil seals.**

1. Check fluid level *See Repair, Power Steering Fluid Reservoir* .
Check fluid pressure *See Power Steering System - Test* .

2. Is pressure high?
YES - Renew pump *See Repair, Power steering Pump.*
If oil seal leaks persist after renewing the pump *See Overhaul, Power Steering Box.*
NO - *See Overhaul, Power Steering Box.*

**Symptom:-**

**Insufficient power assistance - castor return action normal.**

1. Are tyres correct type and pressure?
NO - *See GENERAL SPECIFICATION DATA, Information, Wheels and Tyres.*
YES - Continue.

2. Is fluid level correct?
NO - Check fluid level *See Repair, Power Steering Fluid Reservoir.*
YES - Check system for air locks *See Repair, Power Steering System - Bleed.*

3. Is pressure correct?
NO - Check fluid pressure *See Power Steering System - Test* .
If pressure is not correct after bleeding the system, renew pump *See Repair, Power Steering Pump.*
YES - *See Overhaul, Power Steering Box.*

**Symptom:-**

**Steering heavy - stiff, poor castor return action.**

1. Are tyres correct type and pressure?
NO - *See GENERAL SPECIFICATION DATA, Information, Wheels and Tyres.*
YES - Check universal joints for seizure and correct alignment *See Repair, Lower Steering Shaft and Universal Joints.*
Check power steering box adjustments *See Overhaul, Power Steering Box.*

2. Is the power assistance satisfactory?
NO - See fault symptom **Insufficient assistance, (castor return action normal)**.
YES - Disconnect drag link from drop arm and check steering column and box for stiffness *See Repair, Drag Link and Drag Link Ends.*

3. Is the steering stiff with the drag link disconnected?
NO - Check steering ball joints for seizure and axle swivels lubrication and resistance *See Repair, Drag Link and Drag Link Ends, See FRONT AXLE AND FINAL DRIVE, Overhaul, Front Stub Axle, Constant Velocity Joint and Swivel Pin Housing.*
YES - Disconnect the lower steering shaft and check the column and box for stiffness *See Repair, Lower Steering Shaft and Universal Joints.*

4. Is the steering column stiff to turn when disconnected from the box?
NO - Remove and overhaul box *See Overhaul, Power Steering Box* .
YES - Adjust steering column *See Stiff Steering Checklist.*

**Symptom :-**

**Steering excessively light/sensitive. Excessive freeplay at steering wheel.**

1. Are steering box adjustments correct?
   NO - *See Adjustment, Power Steering Box* .

    **WARNING: Adjustments of steering box should not be required while in warranty period. If box is within warranty, it must be returned to manufacturer. No attempt must be made to introduce backlash.**

   YES - Suspect worn panhard rod or radius arm bushes. Check condition of ball joints and the lower steering column shaft universal joints for wear *See Repair, Lower Steering Shaft and Universal Joints* .

**Symptom :-**

**Steering vibration, road wheel shimmy - wobble.**

Vibration through the steering linkage powerful enough to induce high frequency oscillation of the steering wheel, is generally caused by out of balance road wheels. However there are a number of other possible causes of this symptom which if severe, may be described as shimmy or wobble. Regardless of the terminology used by the owner/driver to describe the symptoms, the following diagnostic checks should be carried out in the order presented.

1. Check the tyres and balance of the road wheels *See GENERAL SPECIFICATION DATA, Information, Wheels and Tyres* , *See WHEELS AND TYRES, Fault diagnosis, Fault - Symptoms* *See WHEELS AND TYRES, Repair, Wheel Balancing* .

2. Check the steering hydraulic damper function *See Steering Damper.*

3. Check steering column universal joints for wear and correct alignment *See Repair, Lower Steering Shaft and Universal Joints* .

4. Check steering linkage ball joints for wear, correct alignment and security, including steering box and tie rod *See Steering Linkage Inspect*

5. Check all front suspension rubbers for wear. Check all fixing torques, including radius arm bushes, panhard rod and anti-roll bar *See FRONT SUSPENSION, Repair, Panhard Rod* , *See FRONT SUSPENSION, Repair, Radius Arm* , *See FRONT SUSPENSION, Repair, Anti-Roll Bar* , *See FRONT SUSPENSION, Repair, Front Shock Absorber* .

6. Fit new radius arm bushes using NTC 6781. Fit new nuts, bolts and washers.

7. If problem persists fit damper kit STC 288 - 90, STC 290 - 110/130 (2 off front) and STC 289 - 90, STC 291 - 110 levelled, STC 292 - 110 unlevelled, STC 293 - 130 (2 off rear). Road test vehicle.

8. Check the power steering box adjustments and operation *See Overhaul, Power Steering Box.*

9. Check the hub bearing end floats and determine the condition of the hub bearings as applicable *See FRONT AXLE AND FINAL DRIVE, Repair, Front Hub Assembly* .

10. Check the resistance and condition of the swivels *See FRONT AXLE AND FINAL DRIVE, Description and operation, Description* . If problem is not diagnosed: Repeat checks starting at 1.

11. Carry out a full steering geometry check *See GENERAL SPECIFICATION DATA, Information, Steering* .

## STEERING STABILITY AND VEER UNDER BRAKING

**Possible cause:**

Incorrectly set, swivel pin bearing preload.

**Remedy.**

1. Follow instructions to overhaul front stub axle, constant velocity joint and swivel pin *See FRONT AXLE AND FINAL DRIVE, Overhaul, Front Stub Axle, Constant Velocity Joint and Swivel Pin Housing* .

## 1. GENERAL STEERING

1. Carry out visual and safety checks *See Visual and Safety Checks* .

2. Road test vehicle *See Road Test Procedure* .

3. Is problem resolved?
   YES - end
   NO - continue

4. Is problem stiff steering?
   YES - *See Stiff Steering Checklist* .
   NO - Go to 6.

5. Is problem resolved?
   YES - end
   NO - go to 8.

6. Is problem steering niggle ?
   YES - Replace radius arm bushes, arm and axle *See FRONT SUSPENSION, Repair, Radius Arm* .
   NO - go to 8.

7. Is problem resolved?
   YES - end
   NO - continue.

8. Centralise steering box *See Adjustment, Centralise Steering Box* .

9. Is problem resolved?
   YES - end
   NO - continue.

10. Check, adjust if necessary, steering geometry.

11. Is problem resolved?
    YES - end
    NO - continue.

12. Categorise the remaining problems into one or more of the following descriptions:
    *See 2. Steering Veer* .
    *See 3. Veer Under Braking* .
    *See 4. Directional Stability* .

## 2. STEERING VEER

From 1. GENERAL STEERING:

1. Vehicle veers, not under braking, swap front
   tyres side to side.

2. Is problem resolved?
   YES - end
   NO - continue.

3. Does vehicle now veer in other direction?
   YES - fit new tyres
   NO - continue.

4. Recentralise steering box *See Adjustment,
   Centralise Steering Box* .

5. Is problem resolved?
   YES - end
   NO - contact local technical office.

## 3. VEER UNDER BRAKING

From 1. GENERAL STEERING:

1. Vehicle veers under braking, bleed brake
   system.

2. Is problem resolved?
   YES - end
   NO - continue.

3. Check brake pads for glazing, and discs, axles
   etc for contamination.

4. Is problem resolved?
   YES - end
   NO - continue.

5. Check brake lines and hoses for deterioration.
   Replace as necessary.

6. Is problem resolved?
   YES - end
   NO - continue.

7. Contact local technical office.

## 4. DIRECTIONAL STABILITY

From 1. GENERAL STEERING:

1. Is directional stability concern when vehicle is towing?
   YES - Check towing/vehicle loading parameters in Owner's Handbook.
   NO - go to 3.

2. Is problem resolved?
   YES - end
   NO - continue.

3. Check condition of rear trailing link/chassis bushes.

4. Is problem resolved?
   YES - end
   NO - continue.

5. Check condition of front and rear shock absorbers. If necessary, change units in pairs, side to side.

6. Is problem resolved?
   YES - end
   NO - continue.

7. Check steering damper *See Steering Damper.*

8. Is problem resolved?
   YES - end
   NO - continue.

9. Check wheel balance

10. Is problem resolved?
    YES - end
    NO - contact local technical office.

## POWER STEERING FLUID LEAKS

1. Is fluid level correct?
   YES - go to 3.
   NO - Refill or drain to correct level. Bleed system, check for leaks *See Repair, Power Steering System - Bleed.*

2. Is problem resolved?
   YES - end
   NO - continue.

3. Are hoses or joints leaking? Check on full lock with engine at 2000 rev/min.
   YES - loosen and retorque joints.
   NO - go to 6.

4. Does leak remain?
   YES - change PAS pipe.
   NO - end.

5. Does leak remain?
   YES - suspect seal in component. Check and replace as necessary.
   NO - end.

6. Is oil escaping from filler cap?
   YES - bleed system *See Repair, Power Steering System - Bleed .*
   NO - go to 8.

7. Is oil still escaping from filler cap?
   YES - go back to 1.
   NO - end.

8. Is oil leaking from PAS pump?
   YES - go to 10.
   NO - continue.

9. Is oil leaking from PAS box?
   YES - go to 10.
   NO - end.

10. Clean unit, add tracer dye to system. Retest

11. Is oil still leaking?
    YES - establish leak point. Repair or replace unit as necessary.
    NO - end.

## POWER STEERING SYSTEM - EXCESSIVE NOISE

1. Is fluid level correct?
   YES - go to 3.
   NO - Refill or drain to correct level. Bleed system, check for leaks *See Repair, Power Steering System - Bleed* .

2. Is problem resolved?
   YES - end
   NO - continue.

3. Is pressure hose from pump to box touching body in a hard foul condition?
   YES - route hose away from body.
   NO - go to 5.

4. Does noise remain?
   YES - continue.
   NO - end.

5. Is noise a whistle or hiss on full lock?
   YES - noise is not a fault unless excessive. Compare with other vehicles
   NO - go to 8.

6. Is noise excessive?
   YES - continue.
   NO - end.

7. Change steering box and/or pump.

8. Is noise a squeal on full lock?
   YES - check drive belt tension and remove belt if necessary *See ELECTRICAL, Repair, Auxiliary drive Belt* .
   NO - go to 10.

9. Does squeal remain?
   YES - drive belt contaminated, change belt.
   NO - end.

10. Is noise a continuous moan?
    YES - bleed PAS system *See Repair, Power Steering System - Bleed* .
    NO - go to 13.

11. Does moan remain?
    YES - do figure 8 manoeuvres.
    NO - end.

12. Does moan remain?
    YES - continue
    NO - end.

13. Is noise an intermittent "grunt"?
    YES - *See Power Steering System - Grunt* .
    NO - continue.

14. Is it a clunking noise?
    YES - check drive belt tension and renew belt if necessary *See ELECTRICAL, Repair, Auxiliary drive Belt* .
    NO - contact local technical office.

15. Does noise remain?
    YES - Suspect suspension or drive train.
    NO - end.

## POWER STEERING SYSTEM - GRUNT

**Steering box grunts intermittently when turning from lock to lock:**

1. Is fluid level correct?
   YES - go to 3.
   NO - refill or drain to correct level. Bleed system, check for leaks *See Repair, Power Steering System - Bleed* .

2. Does grunt remain?
   YES - continue
   NO - end.

3. Is correct low pressure hose, steering box to reservoir, fitted?
   YES - go to 5.
   NO - Fit correct hose.

4. Does grunt remain?
   YES - continue
   NO - end.

5. Purge box by doing figure 8 manoeuvres e.g. on car park, followed by 10 minutes normal road use.

6. Does grunt remain?
   YES - Contact local technical office
   NO - end.

## VISUAL AND SAFETY CHECKS

 **WARNING: Before taking vehicle out on the public highway for road test, it is important that the following basic visual checks are carried out to ensure that the vehicle complies with legal requirements.**

### Tyres and wheel rims

1.  Check and adjust tyre pressures *See GENERAL SPECIFICATION DATA, Information, Tyre Pressures*.
    Note that this information refers to standard tyres fitted as original equipment.

2.  Check condition of tyres. Inspect for signs of uneven wear, damage and feathering. Check tread depth.

3.  Ensure that the tyre make, type and general condition are common across each axle.

4.  Check wheel rims for signs of damage and excessive run out.

5.  Carry out road test *See Road Test Procedure*

## ROAD TEST PROCEDURE

General steering/handling problems can usually be classified into one of the categories listed and ARE GENERALLY RELATED TO THE AGE, CONDITION AND USE OF THE VEHICLE.

 **WARNING: Ensure that all road tests are conducted by suitably qualified drivers in a safe and legal manner, and where local traffic conditions allow.**

1.  Carry out visual and safety checks *See Visual and Safety Checks*.

Confirm general nature of complaint with customer, simulating where possible the conditions under which the problem occurs. Carry out following road test procedure to establish the problem.

2.  Steering load assessment - drive at 16 km/h (10 mph). Put 90°turn input into steering wheel, check self centering. The self centering should be equal on each lock but not necessarily return to exactly straight ahead without assistance from the driver.

3.  Steering assessment - drive at 64 km/h (40 mph) on a staight FLAT road (no camber), check for steering veer. The vehicle should follow a straight path with NO tendency to follow a curved path. If vehicle veers towards the kerb, vehicle may be 'camber sensitive'. A small amount of veer in direction of camber is acceptable.

4.  Directional stability assessment - drive at 112 km/h (70 mph) or maximum legal speed on a straight flat road. Carry out a normal lane change. Vehicle should quickly settle into a new straight path.

5.  Braking assessment (medium effort) - drive at 96 km/h (60 mph) on a straight flat road. Apply steady medium braking effort, noting any tendency to veer. Carry out brake test three times, if a veer is consistently noted carry out a braking efficiency test on a rolling road.

6.  Braking assessment (full effort) - drive at 96 km/h (60 mph) on a straight flat road. Apply full braking effort, noting any tendency to veer. Carry out brake test three times, if a veer is consistently noted carry out a braking efficiency test on a rolling road.

If the symptom described by the customer is stiff steering or steering niggle, carry out stiff steering procedure *See Stiff Steering Checklist*.

If not, proceed with basic checks and adjustments *See Visual Check and Basic Adjustments*.

## STIFF STEERING CHECKLIST

 **NOTE: Having completed visual checks and steering assessment and confirmed that vehicle steering load is incorrect carry out the following procedure in order shown.**

### Steering wheel 'torque to turn' loads

1. Raise vehicle so both front wheels free.

2. With engine off, centralise steering wheel, and remove steering wheel decal. Using torque wrench on column nut, check torque required to turn the steering wheel one turn in each direction.

3. Record readings obtained in each direction. Reading should be *4.40 Nm (3.5 lbf/ft).*

△ **NOTE: If figures are in excess of that specified carry out steering box tie bar reset below. If figures are as specified** *See Visual Check and Basic Adjustments .*

### Steering box tie bar reset

1. Loosen the tie bar fixings one complete turn.

2. Drive vehicle carefully a short distance (within the dealership) applying full lock in both directions in order to settle steering components. Drive vehicle over speed bumps and include harsh braking if possible.

⚠ **WARNING: Do not drive on public highway.**

3. Near end of operation 2. ensure vehicle is driven in a straight line on level ground and halted.

4. Tighten panhard rod mounting arm nut to *110 Nm (81 lbf/ft).*

5. Tighten the 2 fixings, tie bar to steering box, to *81 Nm (60 lbf/ft).*

6. Recheck steering wheel torque to turn. If torque reading is still greater than specified, carry out steering shaft universal joint lubrication.

### Lower steering shaft universal joint lubrication

1. Check lower steering shaft is correctly phased *See Repair, Lower Steering Shaft and Universal Joints .*

2. Lubricate universal joints with an anti-seizure type penetrating spray. Work the joints to ensure full penetration of the spray by driving vehicle and steering from lock to lock.

3. If steering stiffness still persists carry out swivel pin preload setting.

### Swivel pin preload setting

1. The swivel pin preload setting must be checked and set *See FRONT AXLE AND FINAL DRIVE, Overhaul, Front Stub Axle, Constant Velocity Joint and Swivel Pin Housing .*
Note that a pull load of 1.16 - 1.46 kg is required after the axle shaft and swivel housing seal have been removed.

### Steering box adjustment

1. Check steering box adjustment *See Adjustment, Power Steering Box .*

### Steering damper check

1. Check condition of steering damper *See Steering Damper .*

## VISUAL CHECK AND BASIC ADJUSTMENTS

 **NOTE: It is important that the following instructions are carried out in the sequence shown and the results recorded.**

1. Road springs - check that road springs are correctly seated and are to correct specification for vehicle. For spring specification *See GENERAL SPECIFICATION DATA, Information, Road Spring Data* .

2. Ride height - measure trim height from wheel centre to wheelarch eyebrow. Record results on data sheet.

3. Check/top up power steering fluid *See Repair, Power Steering Fluid Reservoir* .

4. Check tension and condition of drive belt *See ELECTRICAL, Repair, Auxiliary drive belt* .

5. Track rod/drag link - check condition of track rod, drag link and ball joints *See Repair, Drag Link and Drag Link Ends* .
   If either component is damaged, check operation of steering damper and steering box for smoothness. Replace all damaged or worn components that impair the operation of the steering system.

6. Suspension bushes - examine all steering and suspension bushes for signs of wear and deterioration. Also check all fixings for torque relaxation. Tighten to correct torque value *See FRONT SUSPENSION, Specifications, torque, Torque Values* .

7. Oil leaks - check front and rear axle hubs for leak and repair as necessary.

8. Brake system - check brake system for leaks, pipe condition, pad wear/contamination, disc wear/condition.

9. Hub end float - check movement in the hubs by rocking the wheels.

10. Check front wheel alignment. Vehicles displaying a tendency to veer more than considered allowable, it is permissible to set the front track to parallel.

11. Having completed all the above checks and adjustments, road test vehicle *See Road Test Procedure* .
    Attempt to reproduce the symptoms established earlier. If symptoms still exist refer to relevant Diagnostic Chart.

## STEERING LINKAGE INSPECT

 **NOTE: When inspecting steering linkages and ball joints for wear the following items must be checked.**

### Steering ball joints

1. Check ball joint rubber boots for security, signs of cracking or deterioration.

2. Check ball joint assemblies for seizure i.e. no movement on ball joint and associated assemblies.

3. Check for excessive wear. This will be evident as extreme movement on track rod and steering linkages. Renew parts as necessary *See Repair, Track Rod and Linkage* , *See Repair, Drag Link and Drag Link Ends* .

### Steering linkages

1. Check all linkages for wear, deterioration and damage. Renew parts as necessary *See Repair, Track Rod and Linkage* , *See Repair, Drag Link and Drag Link Ends* .

## POWER STEERING BOX - ADJUST

**Service repair no - 57.35.01**

 **WARNING: Adjustments of steering box should not be required while in warranty period. If box is stiff or tight and within warranty, it must be returned to manufacturer. No attempt must be made to introduce backlash.**

1. Apply park brake brake, chock wheels and Jack up front of vehicle until wheels are clear of ground.
2. Support chassis front on axle stands.
3. Disconnect drag link from steering drop arm.
4. Check torque to turn **See Fault diagnosis, Stiff Steering Checklist.**
5. Centralise steering box **See Centralise Steering Box.**

 **NOTE: Only check for no backlash when steering box is in central position.**

 **NOTE: If steering wheel is not straight, it should be repositioned See Repair, Steering Wheel.**

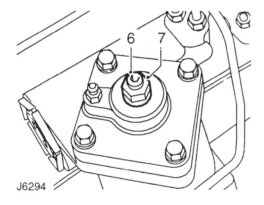

J6294

6. Adjustment is obtained by rocking the drop arm about centre whilst an assistant slowly tightens the steering box adjuster screw.
7. Tighten locknut when all backlash has been removed.

8. Repeat the check for backlash. If backlash exists loosen locknut and repeat adjustment procedure.
9. Turn steering wheel lock to lock and check no tightness exists.
10. Ensure front wheels are aligned and in straight ahead position.
11. Adjust drag link 924 mm between ball joint centres.
12. Connect drag link and tighten to **40 Nm (30 lbf/ft).**
13. Lower vehicle to ground level and remove chocks.
14. Road test vehicle **See Fault diagnosis, Road Test Procedure.**

### Drag link adjust

1. RH drive vehicles - if steering wheel is to right, drag link is too long. If steering wheel is to left drag link is too short.
   LH drive vehicles - if steering wheel is to right, drag link is too short. If steering wheel is to left drag link is too long.
2. Adjust drag link until steering wheel points straight ahead when vehicle is travelling in a straight line.

## CENTRALISE STEERING BOX

**Service repair no - 57.35.05**

### LH drive vehicle

1. Disconnect drag link from drop arm **See Repair, Drag link and drag link ends.**
2. Turn steering wheel on full RH lock.
3. Turn steering wheel back exactly two turns.
4. Fit drag link **See Repair, Drag link and drag link ends.**

### RH drive vehicle

1. Repeat operation for LH drive vehicle but turn steering wheel on full LH lock.

## STEERING LOCK STOPS

**Service repair no - 57.65.03**

**Check**

1. Measure clearance between tyre wall and radius arm at full lock. This must be not less than 20 mm.

**Adjust**

2. Loosen stop bolt locknut.
3. Turn stop bolt as required.
4. Tighten locknut.
5. Check clearance between tyre wall and radius arm on each lock.

 **NOTE: Alternatively lock stop adjustment may be carried out using following procedure.**

**Check**

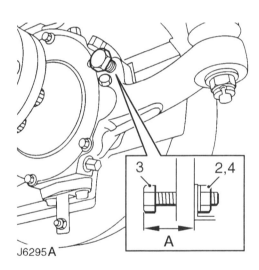

J6295A

1. Measure stop bolt protrusion 'A'. Refer to table for correct setting.

**Adjust**

2. Loosen stop bolt locknut.
3. Turn stop bolt as required.
4. Tighten locknut.
5. Check wheel position at full lock.

## LOCK STOP SETTINGS

**Tyre & wheel size - alloys**

| Make | Size | Setting |
|---|---|---|
| BF Goodrich Mud Terrain | 265 | 59,7 mm |
| Goodyear GT+4 | 235 | 55,7 mm |
| Michelin M+S 4x4 | 235 | 54,2 mm |

**Tyre & wheel size - steel**

| Make | Size | Setting |
|---|---|---|
| Goodyear | 205 | 52,2 mm |
| Michelin | 205 | 52,2 mm |
| Avon | 7.50 | 56 mm |
| Michelin | 7.50 | 56 mm |
| Goodyear | 7.50 | 56 mm |

## FRONT WHEEL ALIGNMENT

**Service repair no - 57.65.01**

**Checking Toe-out dimensions**

⚠️ NOTE: Recognised front wheel alignment and tracking equipment should be used for this operation. Only the use of basic equipment is described below. No Adjustment is provided for castor, camber or swivel pin inclinations.

1. Set vehicle on level ground with road wheels positioned straight ahead.
2. Push vehicle back and forwards to settle linkage.
3. Set up the equipment to manufacturers instructions and check alignment as advised by equipment supplier.
4. Position trammel probes on inner face of wheel, not the rims, if the latter are damaged.

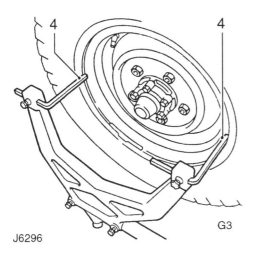

J6296

5. Measure toe-out at horizontal centre-line of wheels.
6. Check tightness of clamp bolt fixings. Tighten to **14 Nm (10lbf/ft).**

**Adjust**

7. Slacken clamps at both ends of track rod.
8. Rotate track rod to increase or decrease its effective length until correct toe-out is obtained **See GENERAL SPECIFICATION DATA, Information, Steering.**

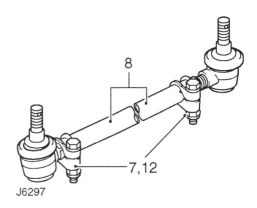

J6297

9. Push vehicle rearwards turning steering wheel from side to side to settle ball joints. With road wheels set in straight ahead position, push vehicle forward a short distance.
10. Recheck track and adjust if necessary.
11. When alignment is correct, tap ball joints in direction of arrows to maximum of travel, to ensure full unrestricted movement of track rod.
12. Tighten clamp bolts to **14 Nm (10 lbf/ft).**

## POWER STEERING PUMP DRIVE BELT

**Service repair no - 57.20.01**

**Adjust**

⚠️ NOTE: For details of drive belt adjust procedure *See ELECTRICAL, Repair, Drive Belt.*

# Notes

## STEERING COLUMN

**Service repair no - 57.40.01**

**Remove**

1. Remove bonnet.
2. Set road wheels and steering wheel in straight ahead position.

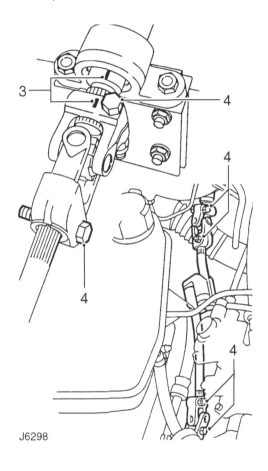

J6298

3. Mark relationship of steering column inner shaft to top universal joint.

⚠ **NOTE: collapsible shaft can be disconnected from steering column only, if required, by removing bolts from top universal joint and slackening top bolt of lower universal joint.**

4. Remove 2 bolts from top universal joint and lower bolt of bottom universal joint. Slacken top bolt of lower universal joint and withdraw shaft.

5. Prise centre cap from steering wheel.
6. Remove steering wheel retaining nut and withdraw wheel from column spline.
7. Disconnect battery.
8. Remove 4 screws securing instrument panel and pull panel away from facia to enable speedometer cable to be disconnected.

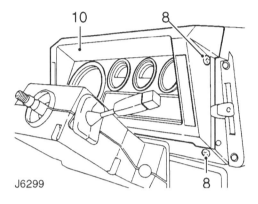

J6299

9. Disconnect multi-plugs, electrical leads and connections to vehicle alarm system, if fitted. *See ELECTRICAL, Repair, Vehicle immobilisation and alarm system.*
10. Withdraw panel complete with instruments.

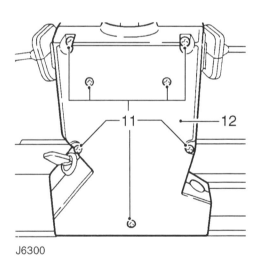

J6300

11. Remove 5 screws and 2 self-tapping screws to remove top half of nacelle.
12. Ease bottom half of nacelle from switch gaiters/grommets and remove.

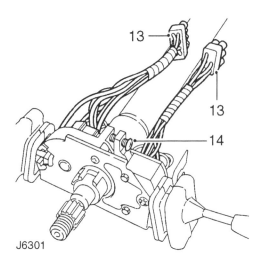

J6301

13. Disconnect 3 switch multi-plugs.
14. Slacken clamp screw on top of switch cluster and withdraw switch assembly.

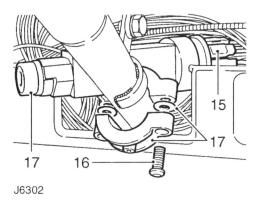

J6302

15. Note position of harness leads on back of starter switch and disconnect lucars. If fitted, remove alarm system passive coil from switch *See ELECTRICAL, Repair, Vehicle immobilisation and alarm system* .
16. Using a punch or stud extractor remove 2 shear bolts securing switch to column.
17. Remove switch and collect 2 plain washers between switch and clamp.
18. Remove brake pedal box *See BRAKES, Repair, Brake pedal box.*
19. Remove bolt securing tie-bar to steering column, behind instrument panel.
20. Remove 2 bolts securing column lower support to mounting bracket.
21. Remove bolts securing two halves of top clamp and bolts that secure top half of clamp to bulkhead.

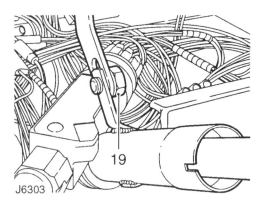

J6303

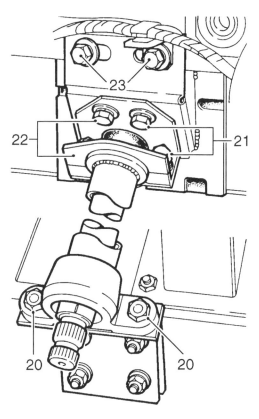

J6304

22. Remove clamp and rubber packing.
23. Remove 2 bolts securing column main support bracket to bulkhead.
24. Remove steering column and main support bracket from vehicle.

 **NOTE: The steering column is a non serviceable component and can only be serviced as a complete assembly.**

25. Fit main support bracket and padding to steering column and manoeuvre column into position in vehicle.
26. Loosely secure main support bracket and harness bracket to bulkhead.
27. Loosely fit clamp and rubber packing strip to column.
28. Loosely secure lower end of column to lower support bracket.
29. Loosely secure clamp bracket to main support bracket.
30. Working inside vehicle cab, fit tie-bar to column bracket and secure with single bolt to **22 Nm (16 lbf/ft)**.
31. Finally, tighten main support bracket, clamp bracket, upper clamp, and lower support bracket nuts and bolts. (M6 bolts **9 Nm (6 lbf/ft)** , M8 bolts **22 Nm (16 lbf/ft)**.
32. Fit brake pedal box **See BRAKES, Repair, Brake pedal** .
33. Fit steering lock/switch in position and rotate steering column inner shaft to line up slot with switch plunger.
34. Secure lock to column with clamp and shear bolts. Evenly tighten bolts but do not shear them.
35. Temporarily fit steering wheel and operate switch and lock mechanism several times to ensure it functions correctly.
36. Fully tighten switch retaining bolts until heads shear.
37. Connect electrical leads to rear of switch. Fit alarm system passive coil, if applicable. **See ELECTRICAL, Repair, Vehicle immobilisation and alarm system** .
38. Fit switch assembly on steering column and tighten clamping screw.
39. Connect switch assembly multi-plugs and electrical leads to main harness.
40. Offer up instrument panel, connect speedometer cable, multi-plugs and electrical leads to main harness. If applicable, fit vehicle alarm system connections. **See ELECTRICAL, Repair, Vehicle immobilisation and alarm system** .
41. Secure panel with 4 screws.
42. Locate top half of nacelle in position and fit to switch gaiters/grommets.

43. Fit lower half of nacelle and loosely tighten fixing screws.
44. Ensure switch gaiters/grommets are correctly located and fully tighten fixings.
45. Turn indicator cancelling ring so that slots are vertical and lug with arrow points to the left, in direction of indicator switch.
46. Fit steering wheel with finisher attachment lug at bottom, ensuring that indicator cancelling forks locate in cancelling ring slots.
47. Secure wheel with nut and new shake-proof washer. Tighten to **43 Nm (32 lbf/ft)**.
48. Fit steering wheel decal.
49. If necessary, fit new universal joints to support. Note that long joint is fitted to short length of shaft and short joint to long end. Joints can only be fitted one way to shaft.
50. With steering lock engaged and road wheels in straight ahead position, align reassembly marks, and fit collapsible shaft assembly with long leg of shaft to steering box. Fit pinch bolts and tighten to **25 Nm (18 lbf/ft)**.

## POWER STEERING BOX

**Service repair no - 57.10.01**

 NOTE: A chassis undertray may be fitted on some vehicle derivatives to conform to legal requirements. When under chassis remove and refit procedures are required, it may be necessary to remove the undertray *See CHASSIS AND BODY, Repair, Front undertray* .

### General precautions

- Whenever any part of system, is removed or disconnected, utmost cleanliness must be observed.
- Disconnected ports and hoses must be plugged to prevent ingress of dirt. If metal sediment is found in system, establish cause, rectify and flush system.
- Do not start engine until reservoir is full as pump will be damaged.
- Metric pipe fittings are used with 'O' ring pipe ends on fittings to steering box.
- Follow normal 'O' ring replacement procedure whenever pipes are disconnected.
- Ensure compatible metric components when fitting replacement pipes.

 CAUTION: After refitting steering linkage parts follow correct procedure to ensure that road wheels, steering box and steering wheel are correctly positioned relative to each other when in straight ahead condition.

 NOTE: When drag link is disconnected from steering box, travel available at steering wheel to each full lock is not equal.

### Remove

1. Site vehicle on level surface.
2. Apply park brake, chock rear wheels, raise vehicle and locate axle stands. Alternatively, raise vehicle on a hoist.
3. Remove road wheel.
4. Remove panhard rod *See FRONT SUSPENSION, Repair, Panhard rod* .
5. Disconnect steering damper from drag link.
6. Disconnect drag link from drop arm, see J6305 on opposite page, using a suitable extractor.
7. Slacken, but do not remove nut securing tie bar to mounting arm.

8. Remove 2 bolts securing tie bar to steering box and move aside.
9. Remove filler cap from power steering fluid reservoir.
10. Position suitable container under steering box.
11. Disconnect feed and return pipes from steering box and drain fluid.

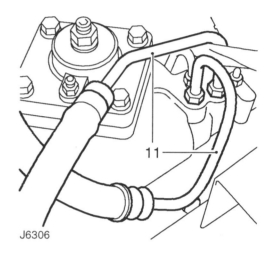
J6306

12. Plug open pipes and steering box ports to prevent ingress of dirt. Refit fluid reservoir filler cap.
13. Centralise steering *See Centralise steering box* .
14. Remove pinch bolt securing lower shaft universal joint to power steering box.
15. Remove 4 bolts and 2 tab washers securing steering box to chassis side member.
16. Withdraw steering box.
17. Clean all mounting faces, unions etc. prior to refitting.

### Refit

18. Position steering box to chassis side member, ensuring locating peg is engaged. Fit tab washers and tighten bolts to *81 Nm (60 lbf/ft).*
19. Fit pinch bolt and nut securing universal joint to power steering box spline. Tighten to *25 Nm (18 lbf/ft).*
20. Secure tie bar to mounting arm and steering box. Tighten fixings to *81 Nm (60 lbf/ft),* starting with tie bar to mounting nut, then loosen fixings by one complete turn.
21. Check steering box and adjust if necessary *See Adjustment, Power steering box - adjust* .
22. Refit drag link to drop arm and tighten nut to *40 Nm (30 lbf/ft).* Fit new split pin to retaining nut.

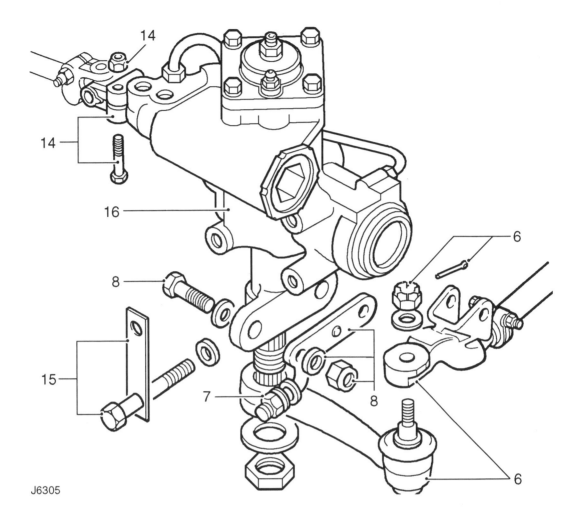

J6305

23. Fit panhard rod *See FRONT SUSPENSION, Repair, Panhard rod* .

24. Fit road wheels. Lower vehicle to ground and tighten wheel nuts to correct torque:
Alloy wheels - 130 Nm (96 lbf/ft)
Steel wheels - 100 Nm (80 lbf/ft)
Heavy duty wheels - 170 Nm (125 lbf/ft)

25. Remove plugs and refit feed and return pipes to steering box. Tighten 16mm thread to *20 Nm (15 lbf/ft),* 14mm thread to *15 Nm (11 lbf/ft).*

26. Remove filler cap. Fill reservoir to oil level mark on dipstick, using recommended fluid *See LUBRICANTS, FLUIDS AND CAPACITIES, Information, Recommended lubricants and fluids* .

27. Bleed power steering system *See Power steering system - bleed* .

28. Recheck fluid level and replace cap.

29. With engine running, test steering system for leaks by holding steering in both full lock directions.

 **CAUTION: Do not maintain this pressure for more than 30 seconds in any one minute, to avoid oil overheating and possible seal damage.**

30. Test drive vehicle: using both full lock directions, to settle steering components. If possible, drive vehicle over uneven ground and include harsh braking.

 **WARNING: Do not test drive vehicle on public highway.**

31. Drive vehicle in a straight line on level ground and stop.

32. Tighten tie bar to mounting nut to *110 Nm (81 lbf/ft).*

33. Tighten tie bar to steering box fixings to *81 Nm (60 lbf/ft).*

34. Ensure steering wheel is correctly aligned when wheels are positioned straight ahead.

35. If necessary, reposition steering wheel *See Steering wheel* .

36. Road test vehicle.

## POWER STEERING SYSTEM - BLEED

**Service repair no - 57.15.02**

1. Check that fluid level is at maximum level *See MAINTENANCE , Under bonnet maintenance.*
2. Run engine to normal operating temperature.
3. Recheck reservoir fluid level, top up if necessary

 **NOTE: During operations 4 to 6, maintain maximum fluid level in reservoir. Do not increase engine speed or move steering wheel.**

4. With engine at idle speed, slacken bleed screw. When fluid seeps past bleed screw retighten screw.

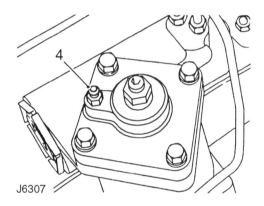

J6307

5. Check fluid level.
6. Clean away fluid around bleed screw.
7. Check hose connections, pump and steering box for fluid leaks by holding steering on full lock in both directions.

 **CAUTION: Do not maintain this pressure for more than 30 seconds in any one minute to avoid overheating fluid and possibly damaging seals.**

8. Carry out road test.

## POWER STEERING FLUID RESERVOIR

**Service repair no - 57.15.08**

**Remove**

1. Position drain tin beneath reservoir.
2. Slacken mounting bracket clamp bolt and raise reservoir to gain access to feed and return hose retaining clips.
3. Slacken clips, disconnect hoses from reservoir, allow fluid to drain.
4. Remove reservoir.

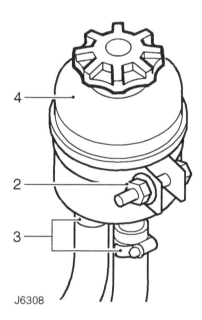

J6308

 **CAUTION: Plug connections to prevent ingress of dirt.**

 **CAUTION: Discard fluid drained from system. Do not allow fluid to contact paintwork, if spilled, remove fluid and clean area with warm water.**

**Refit**

5. Position reservoir, connect feed and return hoses and tighten clips to *3 Nm (2 lbf/ft).*
6. Fit reservoir in clamp, tighten clamp bolt.
7. Fill reservoir between upper mark and end of dipstick with power steering fluid *See MAINTENANCE , Under bonnet maintenance*

8. Bleed power steering system *See Power steering system - bleed* .

## POWER STEERING PUMP

**Service repair no - 57.20.14**

**Remove**

⚠ NOTE: A chassis undertray may be fitted on some vehicle derivatives to conform to legal requirements. When under chassis remove and refit procedures are required, it may be necessary to remove the undertray *See CHASSIS AND BODY, Repair, Front undertray* .

1. Disconnect battery.
2. Remove viscous fan unit *See COOLING SYSTEM, Repair, Viscous coupling and fan* .
3. Restrain steering pump pulley, slacken but do not remove 3 bolts securing pulley.
4. Remove drive belt *See ELECTRICAL, Repair, Auxiliary drive belt* .
5. Remove bolts and remove pulley.
6. Position suitable container beneath steering pump.

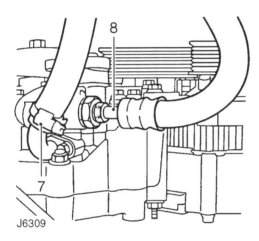

J6309

7. Slacken retaining clip and disconnect return hose from steering pump.
8. Disconnect high pressure pipe from steering pump.
9. Allow steering fluid to drain into container.

⚠ CAUTION: Plug all connections to prevent ingress of dirt.

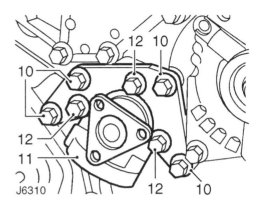

J6310

10. Remove 4 bolts securing steering pump bracket to engine auxiliary mounting bracket.
11. Remove pump and bracket assembly.
12. Remove 3 bolts and detach mounting bracket from pump.

**Refit**

13. Fit mounting bracket to replacement steering pump. Tighten bolts to *9 Nm (7 lbf/ft).*
14. Fit pump and bracket to auxiliary mounting bracket. Tighten bolts to *35 Nm (26 lbf/ft).*
15. Connect high pressure feed pipe to steering pump and tighten to *20 Nm (15 lbf/ft).*
16. Connect return hose to steering pump. Tighten retaining clip to *3 Nm (2 lbf/ft).*
17. Position pulley to steering pump, coat threads of bolts with Loctite 242; fit but do not fully tighten bolts.
18. Fit drive belt *See ELECTRICAL, Repair, Auxiliary drive belt* .
19. Restrain steering pump pulley, tighten bolts to *10 Nm (7lbf/ft).*
20. Fit viscous fan unit *See COOLING SYSTEM, Repair, Viscous coupling and fan* .
21. Bleed power steering system *See Power steering system - bleed* .

## POWER STEERING PUMP DRIVE BELT

**Service repair no - 57.20.02**

⚠ NOTE: For details of drive belt remove and refit *See ELECTRICAL, Repair, Auxiliary drive belt* .

## LOWER STEERING SHAFT AND UNIVERSAL JOINTS

**Service repair no - 57.40.16**

### Remove

1. Remove vehicle bonnet.
2. Set road wheels and steering wheel in straight ahead position.

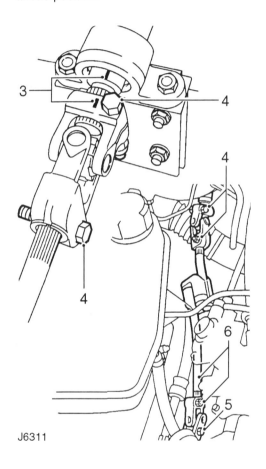

J6311

3. Mark relationship of steering column inner shaft to top universal joint.
4. Remove 2 bolts from top universal joint.
5. Remove lower bolt from bottom universal joint.
6. Slacken upper bolt of lower universal joint and withdraw shaft.
7. Inspect upper and lower universal joints for wear and excessive play, renew if necessary.
8. Inspect universal joints for stiffness, lubricate if necessary.

### Refit

9. Fit universal joints so pinch bolt holes line up with flat on shaft. Note that the long joint is fitted to short length of shaft and short joint to long end.
10. With steering lock engaged and road wheels in straight ahead position, line up assembly marks.
11. Position shaft assembly onto steering column. Move assembly up spline to enable lower universal joint to fit onto steering box splines.
12. Align bolt holes with grooves in splines. Fit pinch bolts and tighten to *25 Nm (18 lbf/ft)*.

## STEERING WHEEL

**Service repair no - 57.60.01**

### Remove

1. Set road wheels and steering wheel in straight ahead position.
2. Prise decal from steering wheel pad.
3. Remove retaining nut and shakeproof washer. Make alignment marks on column and wheel pad.
4. Withdraw steering wheel from column spline.

### Refit

5. Turn indicator cancelling ring so that slots are vertical and lug with arrow points to the left, in direction of indicator switch.
6. Ensure front road wheels are in straight ahead position.
7. Fit steering wheel with finisher attachment lug at the bottom, ensuring indicator cancelling forks locate in cancelling ring slots. Align assembly marks.
8. Secure wheel with retaining nut and new shakeproof washer. Tighten to *43 Nm (32 lbf/ft)*.

## STEERING COLUMN LOCK

**Service repair no - 57.40.28**

**Remove**

1. Disconnect battery.
2. Set road wheels in straight ahead position.
3. Remove steering wheel *See Steering wheel* .
4. Remove instrument panel *See INSTRUMENTS, Repair, Instrument panel* .
5. Remove steering column nacelle *See Steering column nacelle* .

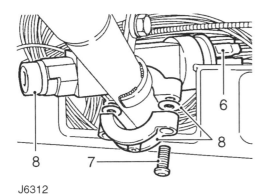

J6312

6. Note position of harness leads on back of starter switch and disconnect lucars. If fitted, remove alarm system passive coil from switch *See ELECTRICAL, Repair, Vehicle immobilisation and alarm system* .
7. Using a punch or stud extractor remove 2 shear bolts securing steering lock/starter switch to column.
8. Remove steering lock and collect 2 washers between lock and clamp.

**Refit**

9. Fit steering lock/switch in position and line up with switch plunger.
10. Secure lock to column with clamp and new shear bolts. Evenly tighten bolts but do not shear them.
11. Temporarily fit steering wheel and operate lock and switch mechanism to ensure it functions correctly.
12. Fully tighten retaining bolts until heads shear.
13. Connect harness leads to rear of starter switch. If applicable, fit alarm system passive coil *See ELECTRICAL, Repair, Vehicle immobilisation and alarm system* .

14. Fit steering column nacelle *See Steering column nacelle* .
15. Fit instrument panel *See INSTRUMENTS, Repair, Instrument panel* .
16. Fit steering wheel *See Steering wheel* .
17. Reconnect battery.

## STEERING COLUMN NACELLE

**Service repair no - 57.40.29**

**Remove**

1. Disconnect battery.
2. Remove steering wheel *See Steering wheel* .

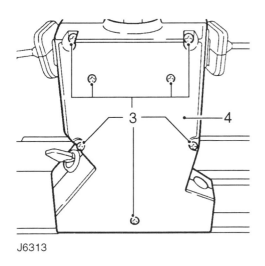

J6313

3. Remove 5 screws and 2 self tapping screws and lift top half of nacelle from steeering column switch assembly.
4. Ease bottom half of nacelle from switch gaiters/grommets. Remove lower nacelle.

**Refit**

5. Locate top half of nacelle in position and fit to switch assembly gaiters/grommets.
6. Locate lower half of nacelle and loosely fit retaining screws.
7. Ensure switch gaiters/grommets are correctly located and nacelle is aligned with switch assembly brackets.
8. Fully tighten screws.
9. Fit steering wheel *See Steering wheel* .
10. Reconnect battery.

## DROP ARM

**Service repair no - 57.50.14**

**Remove**

1. Park vehicle on level surface and chock rear wheels.
2. Raise vehicle and locate axle stands or use a ramp.
3. Disconnect steering damper from drag link *See Steering damper* .

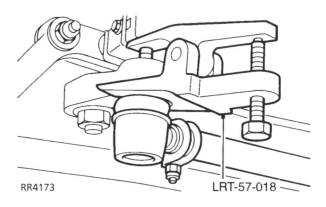

RR4173                    LRT-57-018

4. Disconnect drag link ball joint from drop arm using extractor **LRT-57-018**.
5. Mark drop arm and steering box for reassembly.

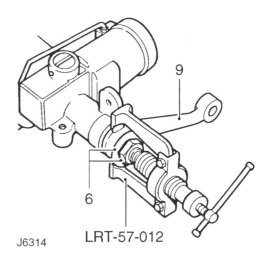

J6314          LRT-57-012

6. Bend back tabs on locking washer, slacken retaining nut, but do not remove.
7. Fit extractor **LRT-57-012** and release drop arm from steering box spline.

**8.** Remove nut and discard locking washer.
**9.** Remove drop arm.

**Refit**

**10.** Centralise steering box *See Adjustment, Centralise steering box.*
**11.** Align reassembly marks and fit drop arm onto steering box splines.
**12.** Fit new tab washer and retaining nut. Tighten to *176 Nm (130 lbf/ft)* and bend over tab washer.
**13.** Fit drag link to drop arm. Tighten ball joint nut to *40 Nm (30 lbf/ft).*
**14.** Remove axle stands or vehicle from ramp.

## STEERING DAMPER

**Service repair no - 57.55.21**

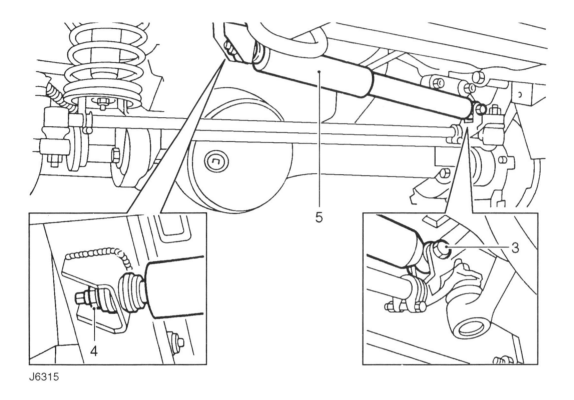

J6315

### Remove

1. Park vehicle on level ground and chock rear wheels.
2. Raise vehicle and locate axle stands or use a ramp.
3. Remove bolt securing steering damper to drag link bracket.
4. Remove retaining nuts, washers and rubber bush securing damper to chassis mounting.
5. Withdraw damper.
6. Check rubber bushes and washers, renew if necessary.

### Refit

7. Ensuring rubber bushes and washers are correctly positioned, fit steering damper to chassis mounting.
8. Fit damper to drag link bracket.
9. Remove axle stands or vehicle from ramp.

## TRACK ROD AND LINKAGE

**Service repair no - 57.55.09**

**Remove**

1. Park vehicle on level ground and chock rear wheels.
2. Raise vehicle and locate axle stands or use a ramp.
3. Centralise steering *See Adjustment, Centralise steering box* .

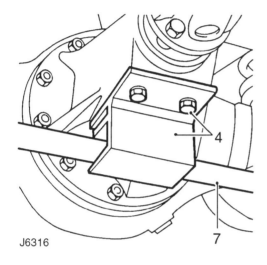

J6316

4. Unscrew 2 bolts and remove track rod protection bracket from axle differential housing.
5. Remove split pin and castellated nut securing track rod to swivel housing arms.

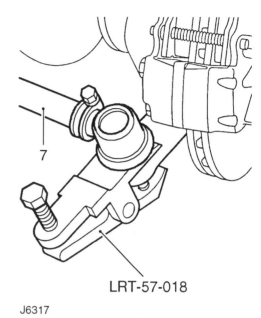

LRT-57-018

J6317

6. Disconnect track rod ball joints using **LRT-57-018**.
7. Remove track rod.

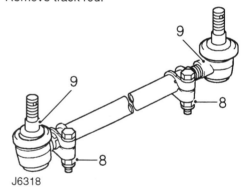

J6318

8. Slacken clamp bolts.
9. Unscrew ball joints.

**Refit**

10. Fit new ball joints to track rod and loosely tighten clamp bolts.
11. Screw in ball joints to full extent of threads and fully tighten clamp bolts.

 **CAUTION: A track rod that is damaged or bent must be renewed. DO NOT attempt to repair or straighten it.**

12. Fit track rod to swivel housing arms and tighten ball joint nuts to **40 Nm (30 lbf/ft).** Fit new split pin.
13. Fit track rod protection bracket to axle differential housing.
14. Check wheel alignment **See Adjustment, Front wheel alignment** .
15. Remove axle stands or vehicle from ramp.

## DRAG LINK AND DRAG LINK ENDS

**Service repair no - 57.55.17**

**Remove**

1. Park vehicle on level ground and chock rear wheels.
2. Set road wheels in straight ahead position.
3. Raise vehicle and fit axle stands or use a ramp.

4. Remove front road wheel.
5. Disconnect steering damper at drag link bracket.
6. Remove split pin and castellated nut securing drag link ball joint to swivel housing arm.
7. Disconnect drag link ball joints using **LRT-57-018**.
8. Remove drag link.
9. Slacken clamp bolts.
10. Unscrew ball joints and remove from drag link.
11. Clean internal threads of drag link.

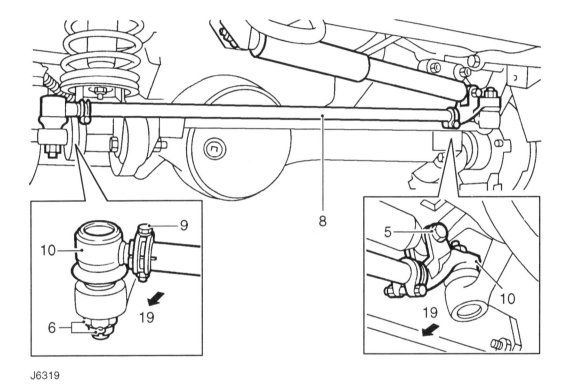

J6319

12. Fit new ends to drag link and loosely fit clamp bolts.
13. Set ball joints to drag link measurement to 28,5 mm.
14. Adjust ball pin centres to nominal length of 924 mm, this length is adjusted during refit.

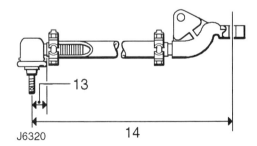

J6320

15. Centralise steering box **See Adjustment, Centralise steering box** .
16. Align steering wheel, if necessary.

 **CAUTION: A drag link that is damaged or bent must be renewed. DO NOT attempt repair.**

17. Fit drag link to swivel housing arms and tighten nuts to **40 Nm (30 lbf/ft).** Fit new split pins.
18. Ensure full steering travel is obtained between lock stops **See Adjustment, Steering lock stops** . Adjust drag link length to suit.
19. Tap ball joints in direction shown so both pins are in same angular plane.
20. Tighten clamp bolts to **14 Nm (10 lbf/ft).**
21. Refit road wheel and remove axle stands or vehicle from ramp.
22. Road test vehicle.
23. If driving straight ahead and steering wheel is offset by 0° ±5° in either direction, correct by adjusting drag link length.

 **WARNING: To correct steering wheel deviations greater than ±5 ° remove and reposition steering wheel See Steering wheel** .

## POWER STEERING BOX - ADWEST

Service repair no - 57.10.07

Overhaul

 NOTE: Overhaul of steering box should not be carried out during the warranty period.

 WARNING: Wear safety glasses while removing and refitting circlips and retaining ring.

 CAUTION: Absolute cleanliness is essential when overhauling power steering box.

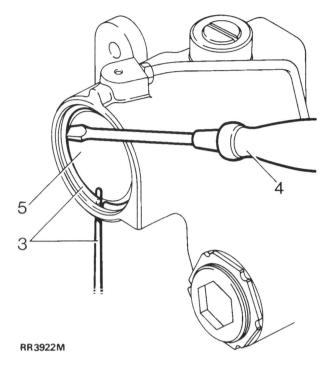

RR3922M

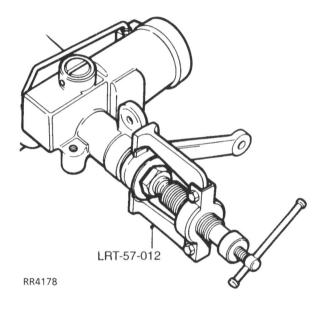

LRT-57-012

RR4178

1. Remove steering box from vehicle *See Repair, Power Steering Box.* Mark drop arm and steering box for realignment on assembly. Remove drop arm using extractor **LRT-57-012**. Loosen drop arm securing nut, but do not remove before using extractor. Remove dirt excluder from output shaft.
2. Drain oil, remove blanking plugs and bleed screw. Hold steering box over suitable container, turn input shaft from lock to lock, until oil is drained. Refit bleed screw.
3. Rotate retainer ring until one end is 12 mm from extractor hole. Using a drift through hole in cylinder, lift retaining ring from groove in cylinder bore.
4. Remove retainer ring, using a screwdriver.
5. Turn input shaft (left lock on left hand drive, right lock on right hand drive) until piston pushes out cover. Turn input shaft fully in opposite direction, applying pressure to piston.

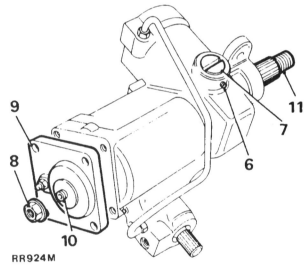

RR924M

6. Remove set screw retaining rack pad adjuster.
7. Remove rack adjuster and pad.
8. Remove sector shaft adjuster locknut.
9. Remove four bolts from sector shaft cover.
10. Screw in sector shaft adjuster until cover is removed.

 NOTE: Sealant is applied to hexagon socket to 'tamperproof' sector shaft adjuster.

11. Slide out sector shaft.

**12.** Remove piston, a bolt screwed into piston will
assist removal.

**13.** Remove input shaft dirt excluder.

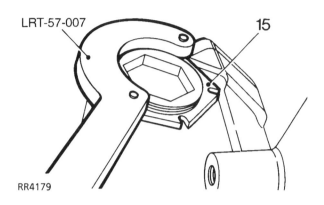

LRT-57-007

15

RR4179

**14.** Remove worm adjuster locknut using 'C' wrench
**LRT-57-007**.

**15.** Remove worm adjuster using wrench
**LRT-57-006**.

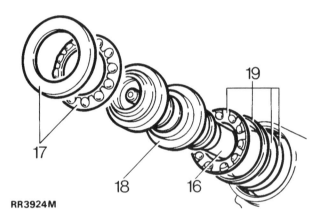

19

17

18    16

RR3924M

**16.** Tap splined end of shaft to free bearing.

**17.** Remove bearing cup and caged ball bearing
assembly.

**18.** Remove valve and worm assembly.

**19.** Remove inner bearing cage, cup and shim
washers. Retain shims for reassembly.

⚠ **NOTE: Should difficulty be experienced
warm casing and bearing assembly. Cool
bearing cup using a mandrel and tap
steering box on a bench.**

**Steering box seals**

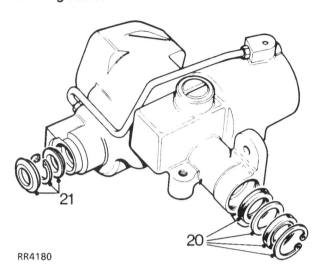

21

20

RR4180

**20.** Remove circlip and seal from sector shaft
housing bore.

⚠ **CAUTION: Do not remove sector shaft
bearings from casing. Replacement parts
are not available. If sector shaft bearings
are worn fit a new steering box.**

**21.** Remove dirt excluder, circlip and seal from input
shaft housing bore.

⚠ **CAUTION: The use of a seal puller is
recommended to prevent damage to
casing, and possible oil leaks.**

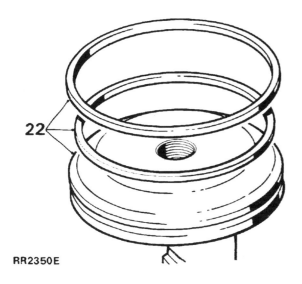

RR2350E

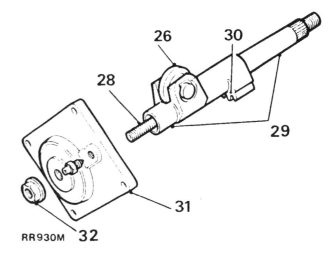

RR930M

## INSPECTING

### Piston

22. Discard all rubber seals and obtain replacements.

 **NOTE: A rubber seal is fitted behind plastic ring on rack piston. Discard seal and plastic ring.**

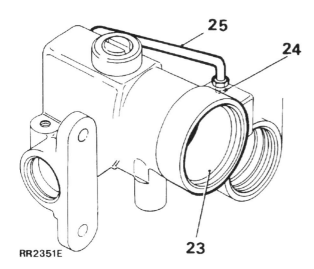

RR2351E

### Steering box casing

23. Examine piston bore for scoring and wear.
24. Examine feed tube.
25. Fit a new feed tube if damaged. Tighten union to **22 Nm (16 lbf/ft).**

### Sector shaft assembly

26. Check there is no side play on roller.
27. If side play on roller exists fit a new sector shaft.
28. Check condition of adjuster screw threads. Check adjuster end float. Fit new adjuster if end float exceeds 0.15 mm.
29. Examine bearing areas on shaft for excessive wear.
30. Examine gear teeth for uneven or excessive wear.

### Sector shaft cover assembly

31. Inspect cover and bearing. If worn or damaged, fit a new steering box.

### Sector shaft adjuster locknut

32. The locknut is also a fluid seal. Fit new nut at overhaul.

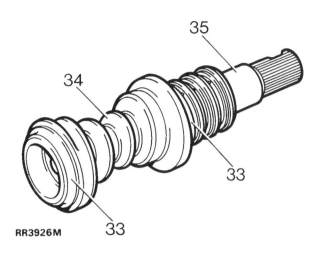

RR3926M

## Valve and worm assembly

33. Examine bearing areas for wear. The areas must be smooth and not indented.
34. Examine worm track which must be smooth and not indented.
35. Check for wear on torsion bar assembly pin. No free movement should exist between input shaft and torsion bar or between torsion bar and worm.

 **NOTE: Any sign of wear makes it essential to fit new valve and worm assembly.**

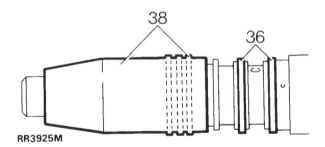

RR3925M

36. Examine valve rings for cuts, scratches and grooves. The valve rings should be free to rotate in grooves.

37. If required, replace all three rings, using ring expander **LRT-57-019**. The expander will not pass over rings already fitted. Remove rings to allow access without damaging seal grooves.
38. Warm rings and expander tool to aid assembly. Fit rings to expander, slide expander over valve and worm assembly. In turn fit rings to their grooves. Remove expander, slide valve and worm assembly into ring compressor **LRT-57-020** and allow to cool.

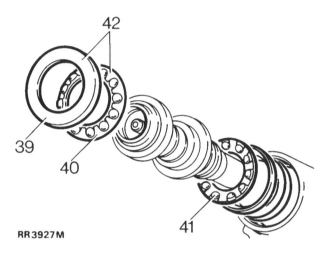

RR3927M

## Ball bearing and cage assemblies

39. Examine ball races and cups for wear and general condition.
40. If ball cage has worn against bearing cup, fit replacements.
41. Bearing balls must be retained by cage.
42. Bearing and cage repair is carried out by complete replacement of assembly.

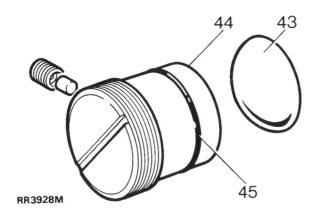

RR3928M

## Rack thrust pad and adjuster

43. Examine thrust pad for scores.
44. Examine adjuster for wear in pad seat.
45. Fit new sealing ring to rack adjuster.

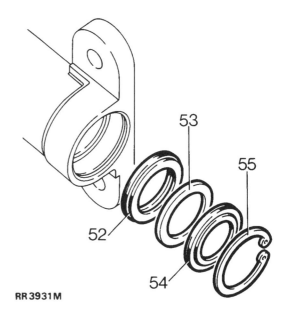

RR3931M

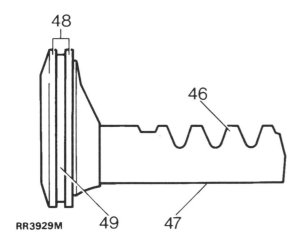

RR3929M

## Rack and piston

46. Examine for excessive wear on rack teeth.
47. Ensure thrust pad bearing surface is free from scores and wear.
48. Ensure piston outer diameters are free from burrs and damage.
49. Examine seal and ring groove for scores and damage.
50. Fit new ring to piston. Warm nylon seal and fit to piston.
51. Slide piston assembly into cylinder with rack tube outwards.

## Reassemble

 NOTE: When fitting replacement oil seals lubricate with recommended fluid and ensure absolute cleanliness.

### Sector shaft oil seal

52. Fit oil seal, lip side first.
53. Fit extrusion washer.
54. Fit dust seal, lipped side last.
55. Fit circlip.

### Fitting valve and worm assembly

56. Refit original shims and inner bearing cup. Use Petroleum Jelly to aid assembly.

 NOTE: If original shims are not used, fit shims of 0.76 mm thickness.

57. Fit inner cage and bearings assembly.
58. Fit valve and worm assembly.
59. Fit outer cage and bearings assembly.
60. Fit outer bearing cup.

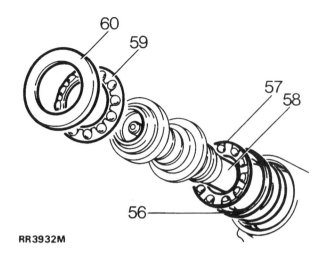

RR3932M

**61.** Fit new worm adjuster sealing ring.

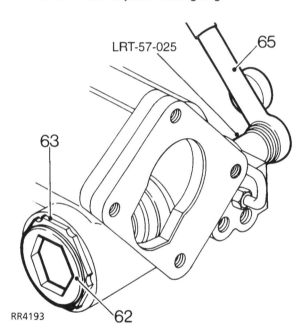

LRT-57-025

65

63

62

RR4193

**62.** Loosely screw adjuster into casing.
**63.** Fit locknut, do not tighten.
**64.** Turn in worm adjuster until end float is almost eliminated. Ensure bearing cages are seated correctly.
**65.** Measure maximum rolling torque of valve and worm assembly, using a torque wrench and spline socket **LRT-57-025**.
**66.** Turn in worm adjuster while rotating shaft to increase figure measured to 0.56 Nm.

**67.** Back off worm adjuster 1/4 turn. Turn in worm adjuster to increase reading by 0.21 - 0.34 Nm with locknut tight, **100 Nm (74 lbf/ft).** Use worm adjusting wrench **LRT-57-006** and locknut wrench **LRT-57-028**.

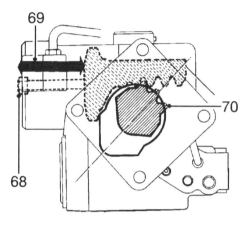

69

70

68

57M0660

## Fitting rack and piston

**68.** Screw slave bolt into piston to aid assembly.
**69.** Fit piston and rack so piston is 70 mm (2.75 in) from outer end of bore.

## Fitting sector shaft

**70.** Fit sector shaft using seal saver **LRT-57-021**. Align roller with cut out in casing as shown. Push in sector shaft while rotating input shaft to allow sector roller to engage worm.

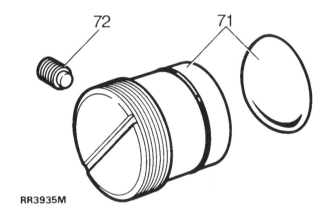

72

71

RR3935M

## Fitting rack adjuster

**71.** Fit rack adjuster and thrust pad to engage rack. Back off half turn on adjuster.
**72.** Loosely fit new nylon pad and adjuster set screw assembly.

## Fitting sector shaft cover

**73.** Fit new sealing ring to cover.

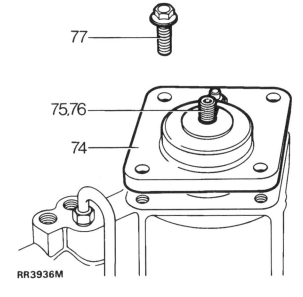

RR3936M

**74.** Align cover with casing.
**75.** Screw cover assembly fully on to sector shaft adjuster screw.
**76.** If necessary back off sector shaft adjuster screw. Tap cover in place to allow cover to joint fully with casing.

 **NOTE: Before tightening fixings, rotate input shaft to ensure sector shaft roller is free to move in valve worm. If initial resistance is left, turn adjuster screw approximately two turns in a clockwise direction.**

**77.** Fit cover bolts. Tighten to **75 Nm (55 lbf/ft).**

## Fitting cylinder cover

**78.** Fit new square section seal to cover.
**79.** Remove slave bolt fitted at instruction 68. Press cover into cylinder just to clear retainer ring groove.
**80.** Fit retaining ring to groove with one end of ring positioned 12 mm from extractor hole.

## Adjusting sector shaft

△ **NOTE: Refit drop arm and tighten nut sufficiently to ensure that no backlash exists between drop arm and sector shaft.**

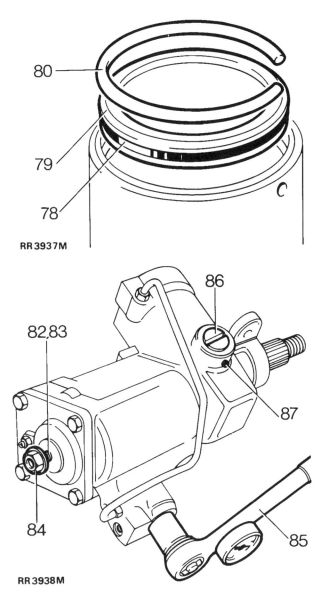

RR3937M

RR3938M

**81.** To set worm on centre, rotate input shaft to full inner-lock (full right lock for a left hand drive vehicle, full left lock for a right hand drive vehicle). Rotate input shaft back towards centre two full turns.
**82.** The box is now on centre and can be adjusted.
**83.** Hold input shaft and rock drop arm to establish backlash is present. Continue rocking and slowly turn sector shaft adjusting screw clockwise. Continue rotating adjuster screw until backlash has almost been eliminated.

**84.** Refit locknut and tighten.

⚠️ **NOTE: It is important steering box is centralised before any adjustments are made.**

**85.** Check maximum rolling torque one and a quarter turns either side of centre position, using a torque wrench and spline socket **LRT-57-025**. Rotate adjuster screw to obtain across centre torque of 0.34 Nm plus torque figure at one and a quarter turns. Tighten adjuster locknut to **60 Nm (44 lbf/ft).**

**Adjusting rack adjuster.**

**86.** Turn in rack adjuster to increase figure measured in instruction 85. by 0.23 - 0.34 Nm. **The final figure may be less, but must not exceed 1.35 Nm.**
**87.** Lock rack adjuster in position with grub screw. Tighten to **5 Nm (4 lbf/ft).**

**Torque peak check**

With input shaft rotated from lock to lock, rolling torque figures should be greatest across centre position and equally disposed about centre position.

The condition depends on value of shimming fitted between valve and worm assembly inner bearing cup and casing. The original shim washer value will give correct torque peak position unless major components have been replaced.

**Procedure**

**88.** With input coupling shaft toward the operator, turn shaft fully counter-clockwise.
**89.** Check torque figures obtained from lock to lock using torque wrench and spline socket **LRT-57-025**.
**90.** Check also for equal engagement either side of centre.

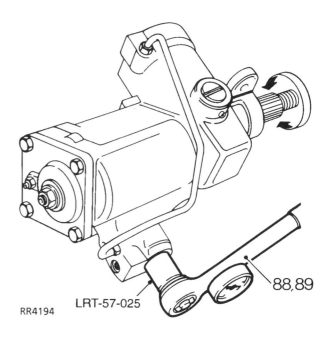

RR4194    LRT-57-025     88,89

**Adjustments**

**91.** Note where greatest figures are recorded relative to steering position. If greatest figures are not recorded across centre of travel (steering straight-ahead), adjust as follows:

If torque peak occurs **before** centre position, **add** to shim washer value; if torque peak occurs **after** centre position, **subtract** from shim washer value, *refer to fitting valve and worm assembly* .

Shim washers are available as follows:
0.03mm, 0.07mm, 0.12mm and 0.24mm.

⚠️ **NOTE: Adjustment of 0.07mm to shim value will move torque peak area by 1/4 turn on the shaft.**

⚠️ **CAUTION: When reshimming valve and worm, extreme caution must be exercised to prevent seal damage during reassembly.**

**Input shaft oil seal**

92. Fit seal, lip side first, into housing. Use seal saver **LRT-57-016** and seal installer **LRT-57-026**. Note that seal is fitted to a depth of 4.75 - 5.00 mm from face of box.
93. Secure seal with circlip.
94. Smear inner lip of dirt excluder with PTFE grease. Fit dirt excluder using **LRT-57-027**. When fitted correctly outer shoulder of excluder is 4.00 - 4.50 mm from face of box, dimension X.

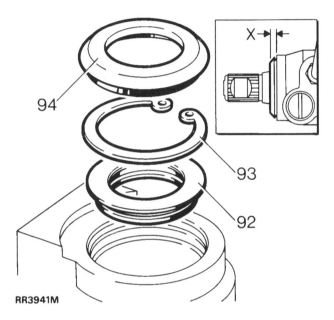

RR3941M

95. Remove drop arm. Smear inner lip of dirt excluder with PTFE grease and refit, ensuring outer lip is flush with casing.
96. With input shaft on centre, align assembly marks on drop arm and steering box. Fit drop arm to steering box using a new tab washer. Tighten to **176 Nm (130 lbf/ft),** bend over tab.
97. Fit steering box *See Repair, Power Steering Box.*

# Notes

## TORQUE VALUES

 **NOTE: Torque wrenches should be regularly checked for accuracy to ensure that all fixings are tightened to the correct torque.**

|  | Nm |
|---|---|
| Ball joint nuts | 40 |
| Clamp bolt nuts | 9 |
| Steering column bracket nuts | 22 |
| Steering wheel nut | 43 |
| Tie bar to mounting nut | 110 |
| Universal joint pinch bolt | 25 |
| PAS box | |
|     Adjuster locknut | 60 |
|     Drop arm nut | 176 |
|     Sector shaft cover to steering box | 75 |
|     Steering box to chassis | 81 |
|     Steering box fluid pipes 14mm thread | 15 |
|     Steering box fluid pipes 16mm thread | 20 |
|     Tie bar | 81 |
| PAS pump | |
|     High pressure fluid pipe | 20 |
|     Power steering pump mounting | 35 |
|     Pulley bolts, power steering pump | 10 |
|     Hose clamp | 3 |
|     Front mounting plate bolts | 9 |
| PAS reservoir | |
|     Hose clamp | 3 |

**\* Torque values below are for all screws and bolts used except for those that are specified otherwise.**

| METRIC | Nm |
|---|---|
| M5 | 6 |
| M6 | 9 |
| M8 | 25 |
| M10 | 45 |
| M12 | 90 |
| M14 | 105 |
| M16 | 180 |

| UNC / UNF | |
|---|---|
| 1/4 | 9 |
| 5/16 | 24 |
| 3/8 | 39 |
| 7/16 | 78 |
| 1/2 | 90 |
| 5/8 | 136 |

# Notes

# 60 - FRONT SUSPENSION

## CONTENTS

Page

# Notes

## DESCRIPTION

The front suspension design allows maximum wheel travel and axle articulation providing good ground clearance without loss of traction or directional stability.

Long radius arms are fitted to the front axle and provide maximum axle articulation which is vital for off road performance. The radius arms are secured to fabricated mounting brackets welded to the front axle. Flexible rubber bushes are used on a stem end joint to secure the rear of the radius arms to mountings on the chassis cross member.

A panhard rod, which ensures that the front axle remains centrally located, is fitted transversely and also uses ferrule rubber bush mountings at both axle and chassis locations.

Two rubber bearing bushes, with retaining straps, secure the rear of the anti-roll bar to the chassis mountings, while bushed links support the front of the bar to the front axle.

Conventional long travel coil springs and hydraulic shock absorbers are used to control body movement in all conditions. The shock absorbers are secured to fabricated towers which are bolted to the chassis. The upper and lower fixings use a single location stud with flexible rubber bushes, support washers and securing nuts. Retaining plates are used to secure the coil springs to the fabricated towers and axle mountings.

Rubber bump stops are fitted underneath the chassis, adjacent to the front road springs, and prevent possible damage that could occur should there be excessive axle to chassis movement.

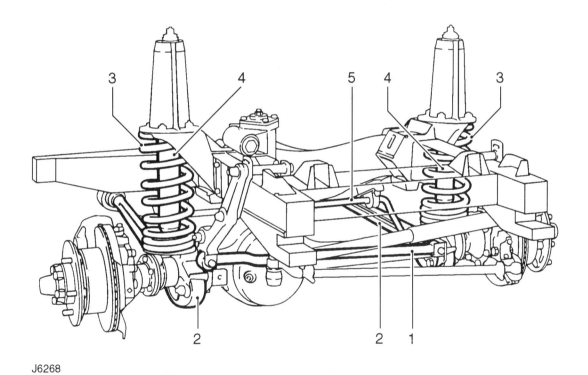

J6268

**Front suspension**

1. Panhard rod
2. Radius arms
3. Coil springs
4. Shock absorber
5. Anti-roll bar

# Notes

## SELF LOCKING NUTS

 **WARNING: Where self locking nuts are removed, they must be replaced with new nuts of same specification.**

## PANHARD ROD

**Service repair no - 60.10.07.**

### Remove

1. Remove fixings at mounting arm.
2. Remove fixings at axle bracket.
3. Remove panhard rod.
4. Using a suitable length of steel tubing, press out flexible bushes. Ensure tubing locates on outer edge of bush and not on rubber inner.

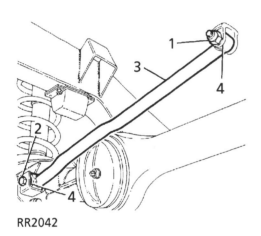

RR2042

### Refit

5. Fit replacement bushes.

 **CAUTION: Apply pressure to outer edge of bush, and not rubber inner.**

6. Fit panhard rod to axle bracket and mounting arm. Tighten fixings to *88 Nm (65 lbf/ft).*

## RADIUS ARM

**Service repair no - 60.10.16.**

### Remove

1. Loosen road wheel retaining nuts.
2. Raise front of vehicle. Support chassis on stands and remove wheel.

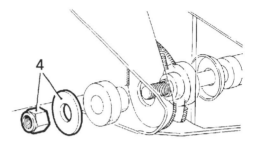

RR983

3. Support front axle weight with jack.
4. Remove radius arm to chassis side member fixings.

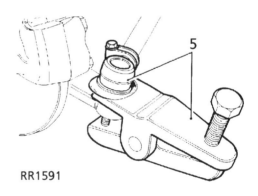

RR1591

5. Disconnect track rod at ball joint.

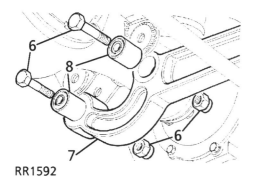

RR1592

6. Remove fixings, radius arm to axle.
7. Lower radius arm front end to clear axle and remove from vehicle.
8. Using suitable length of steel tubing, press out flexible bushes.

**Refit**

9. Press in replacement bushes.

 **CAUTION: When pressing in new bushes press on outer edge of bush and not rubber inner.**

10. Fit radius arm to axle mounting.
11. Fit track rod at ball joint.
12. Fit radius arm to chassis. Tighten bolts to *176 Nm (130 lbf/ft)*.
13. Fully tighten radius arm to axle fixings to *197 Nm (145 lbf/ft)*.
14. Fit road wheel, remove chassis stands and jack. Tighten wheel nuts to correct torque:
    Alloy wheels - *130 Nm (96 lbf/ft)*
    Steel wheels - *100 Nm (80 lbf/ft)*
    Heavy duty wheels - *170 Nm (125 lbf/ft)*

## FRONT SHOCK ABSORBER

**Service repair no - 60.30.02.**

**Remove**

1. Loosen road wheel retaining nuts.
2. Support chassis on stands and remove road wheel.
3. Support axle weight with jack.

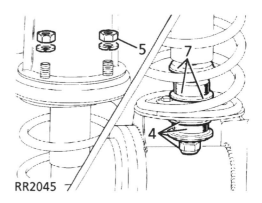

RR2045

4. Remove shock absorber lower fixing and withdraw cupwasher, rubber bush and seating washer.
5. Remove four shock absorber bracket fixings.

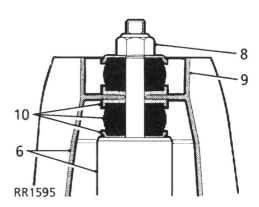

RR1595

6. Withdraw shock absorber and bracket assembly.
7. Withdraw lower seating washer, rubber bush and cupwasher.
8. Remove fixings, shock absorber to mounting bracket.
9. Withdraw mounting bracket.
10. Lift off top seating washer, rubber bush and cupwasher.

## Refit

11. Assemble shock absorber components.
12. Position shock absorber, complete with bracket and secure with 4 fixings.
13. Secure shock absorber lower fixing.
14. Fit road wheel, remove chassis stands and jack. Tighten wheel nuts to correct torque:
    Alloy wheels - *130 Nm (96 lbf/ft)*
    Steel wheels - *100 Nm (80 lbf/ft)*
    Heavy duty wheels - *170 Nm (125 lbf/ft)*

## FRONT ROAD SPRING

**Service repair no - 60.20.11.**

**Remove**

1. Remove front shock absorber *See Front shock absorber*.

⚠ **CAUTION: Avoid over stretching brake hoses. If necessary, loosen hose connector locknuts to allow hoses to follow axle.**

2. Lower axle sufficient to free road spring.

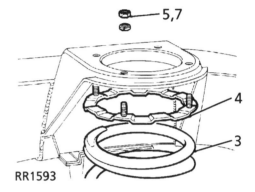

RR1593

3. Withdraw road spring.
4. Withdraw shock absorber bracket securing ring.

**Refit**

5. Fit shock absorber bracket retaining ring. Retain in position with a nut.
6. Position road spring and raise axle.
7. Remove nut retaining securing ring.
8. Fit front shock absorber *See Front shock absorber*.

## BUMP STOP

**Service repair no - 60.30.10.**

**Remove**

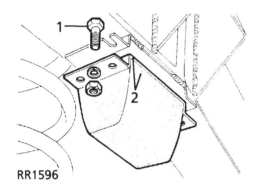

RR1596

1. Remove fixings.
2. Remove bump stop.

⚠️ **NOTE: A chassis undertray may be fitted on some vehicle derivatives to conform to legal requirements. When under chassis remove and refit procedures are required, it may be necessary to remove the undertray** *See CHASSIS AND BODY, Repair, Front undertray* .

**Refit**

3. Position bolts in slots in chassis brackets.
4. Fit bump stop, secure with washers and nuts.

## ANTI-ROLL BAR

**Service repair no - 60.10.01**

**Remove**

1. Mark for reassembly position of rubber bushes on anti-roll bar.
2. Remove 4 nuts, bolts and washers securing both anti-roll bar bush straps to chassis mounting brackets.

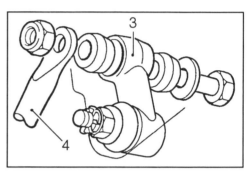

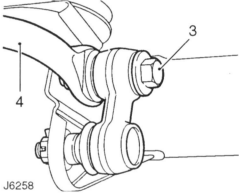

J6258

3. Remove nuts, bolts, washers and rubber bushes securing anti-roll bar to both links
4. Remove anti-roll bar.

**Refit**

5. Position bushes on anti-roll bar. Ensure split points towards axle on RH bush and away from axle on LH bush.
6. Fit anti-roll bar with two straps. To ensure correct fit angled sides of bar should point down. Loosely fit the bolts, washers and nyloc nuts.
7. Fit bolt, washers and rubber bushes. Using new nuts fit anti-roll bar to links and tighten to *68Nm (50 lbf/ft).*
8. Tighten nuts securing straps to *30Nm (22lbf/ft).*

## ANTI-ROLL BAR LINKS

**Service repair no - 60.10.04.**

**Remove**

1. Remove 2 nuts, bolts, washers and rubber bushes from ball joint links.
2. Remove cotter pin and loosen castellated nut a few turns.
3. Release link joint using special tool **18G 1063A** as shown.
4. Remove castellated nut and link.

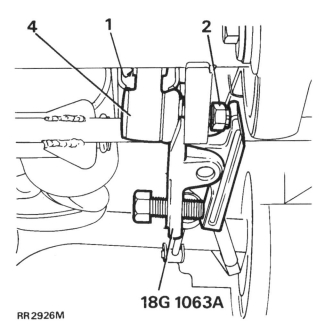

RR 2926M

**18G 1063A**

**Refit**

5. Fit link and castellated nut. Ensure ball joint link arm points up. Tighten nut to **40 Nm (30 lbf/ft)** and fit new cotter pin.
6. Align anti-roll bar to links.
7. Fit bolts, washers and rubber bushes using new self locking nuts and secure anti-roll bar to links. Tighten fixings to **68 Nm (50 lbf/ft).**

# Notes

## TORQUE VALUES

 **NOTE: Torque wrenches should be regularly checked for accuracy to ensure that all fixings are tightened to the correct torque.**

|  | **Nm** |
|---|---|
| **Anti-roll bar** | |
| - Strap nyloc nuts | 30 |
| - Ball link self lock nut | 68 |
| - Castellated nut | 40 |
| Drag link to axle | 40 |
| Securing ring for mounting turret | 14 |
| Radius arm to chassis | 176 |
| Panhard rod mounting arm to chassis | 88 |
| Panhard rod to axle | 88 |
| Panhard rod to mounting bracket | 88 |
| Tie bar to Panhard rod | 110 |
| Radius arm to axle | 197 |

# Notes

# 64 - REAR SUSPENSION

## CONTENTS

# Notes

## DESCRIPTION

The rear suspension design locates the rear axle with two round section steel lower link arms and a forged 'A' frame, upper link assembly. This system allows maximum axle articulation and wheel travel while maintaining roll stiffness and directional stability.

The link arm is secured by a single retaining nut to the chassis mounting, comprising a rubber bushed bracket, which is retained by three fixings. A ferrule rubber bush with a single retaining bolt is used to secure the link arm to its axle mounting.

The upper link assembly is located on the rear differential housing by a pivot ball-pin assembly. Two brackets bolted to the chassis crossmember support both sides of the 'A' frame of the link assembly, secured by single retaining bolts.

A Boge Hydromat self levelling unit can be fitted, as an option, on 110/130 models to give additional support when the vehicle is used to carry heavier loads.

Two rubber bearing bushes, with retaining straps, secure the rear of the anti-roll bar, if fitted, to the chassis mountings, while bushed links support the front of the anti-roll bar to the axle.

Conventional long travel coil springs and hydraulic shock absorbers are used to control body movement. The shock absorbers are secured to chassis mounting brackets and fabricated lower mountings welded to to the rear axle. Retaining plates are used to secure the coil springs to the axle mounting while fabricated brackets, welded to the chassis, are used for the upper spring location.

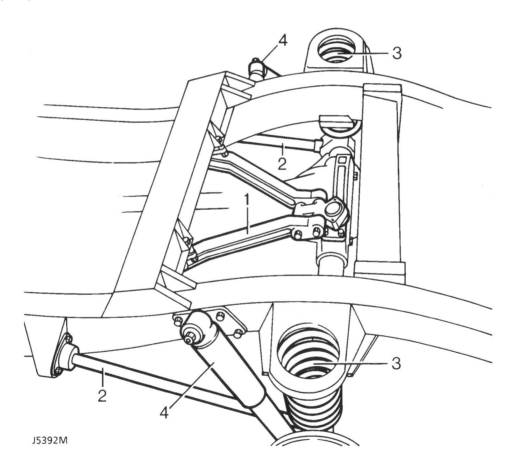

J5392M

**Rear axle suspension**

1. 'A' frame, upper link assembly
2. Lower link
3. Coil springs
4. Shock absorber

# Notes

## REAR ROAD SPRING

**Service repair no - 64.20.01.**

**Remove**

1. Loosen rear road wheel retaining nuts.
2. Support chassis on stands and remove wheels.

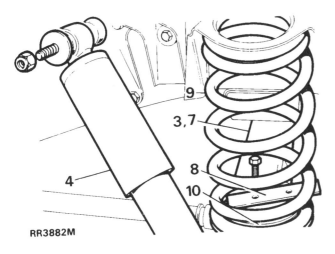

RR3882M

3. Support rear axle weight with jack.
4. Disconnect shock absorbers at one end.
5. Position coil spring compressor correctly on road spring.
6. Compress spring evenly to facilitate removal.
7. Lower axle to free road spring from upper seat.

 **CAUTION: Avoid lowering axle further than rear brake flexible hose will allow.**

8. Remove spring retainer plate.
9. Withdraw road spring.
10. Collect spring seat.

**Refit**

11. Position spring seat on axle location.
12. Fit road spring into chassis location and, using a turning motion, fit to spring seat.
13. Fit spring retainer plate. Tighten bolts to *14 Nm (10 lbf/ft).*
14. Secure shock absorber. Tighten fixing to *37 Nm (27 lbf/ft).*
15. Fit road wheels, remove chassis stands and jack. Tighten wheel nuts to correct torque:
    Alloy wheels - *130 Nm (96 lbf/ft)*
    Steel wheels - *100 Nm (80 lbf/ft)*
    Heavy duty wheels - *170 Nm (125 lbf/ft)*

## REAR SHOCK ABSORBER

**Service repair no - 64.30.02.**

**Remove**

1. Loosen road wheel retaining nuts.
2. Support chassis on stands. Remove road wheel and support rear axle weight with jack.

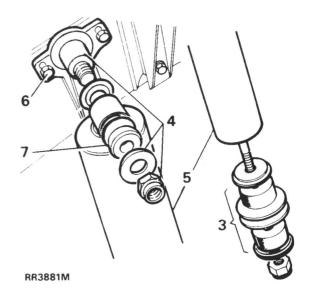

RR3881M

3. Remove fixings and withdraw shock absorber from axle bracket.
4. Remove upper fixings.
5. Withdraw shock absorber.
6. If required, remove mounting bracket
7. If required, remove mounting rubbers.

**Refit**

8. Position shock absorber and fit upper fixings.
9. Secure shock absorber with lower fixings to axle bracket. Tighten upper and lower fixings to *37 Nm (27 lbf/ft).*
10. Fit road wheels, remove chassis stands and jack. Tighten wheel nuts to correct torque:
    Alloy wheels - *130 Nm (96 lbf/ft)*
    Steel wheels - *100 Nm (80 lbf/ft)*
    Heavy duty wheels - *170 Nm (125 lbf/ft)*

## BUMP STOP

**Service repair no - 64.30.15.**

### Remove

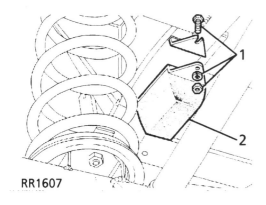

RR1607

1. Remove fixings.
2. Remove bump stop.

### Refit

3. Position bolts in slots in bracket.
4. Fit bump stop, secure with washers and nuts.

## SUSPENSION LINK - UPPER

**Service repair no - 64.35.44.**

### Remove

1. Support rear of chassis on stands, allow axle to hang freely.

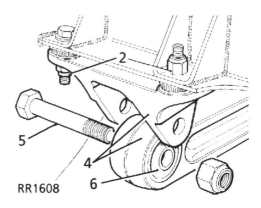

RR1608

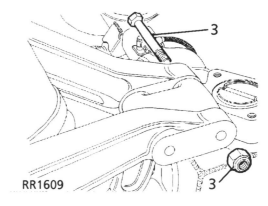

RR1609

2. Remove fixings, upper link bracket to frame.
3. Remove fixings, upper links to pivot bracket.
4. Remove upper link, complete with frame bracket.
5. Remove bolt.
6. Separate link from bracket.

### Renew bush

7. Press out rubber bushes.
8. Fit bush centrally in housing.

 **CAUTION: Apply pressure to outer edge of bush, and not rubber inner.**

## Refit

 **NOTE: Do no fully tighten fixings until all components are in position.**

9. Secure link to frame bracket.
10. Fit upper link to pivot bracket.
11. Fit frame bracket to chassis mounting.
12. Fully tighten fixings to *176 Nm (130 lbf/ft)*.

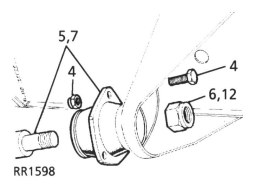

RR1598

## SUSPENSION LINK - LOWER

**Service repair no - 64.35.02.**

### Remove

1. Site vehicle on a ramp .
2. Alternatively, support vehicle on stands under rear axle.

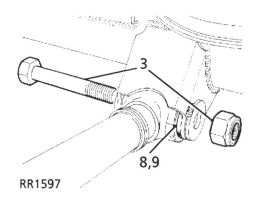

RR1597

3. Remove lower link rear fixings.
4. Remove mounting bracket fixings at side member bracket.
5. Remove lower link complete.
6. Remove locknut.
7. Remove mounting bracket from lower link.

### Renew bush

8. Press out rubber bushes.
9. Fit bush centrally in housing.

 **CAUTION: Apply pressure to outer edge of bush, and not rubber inner.**

### Refit

10. Fit mounting rubber to lowerlink.
11. Secure mounting rubber to chassis bracket, but do not fully tighten locknut.
12. Fit lower link to axle mounting and secure fixing to *176 Nm (130 lbf/ft)*.
13. Lower vehicle, allow axle to take up static laden position, and fully tighten link chassis fixing to *176 Nm (130 lbf/ft)*.

## ANTI-ROLL BAR

**Service repair no - 64.35.08**

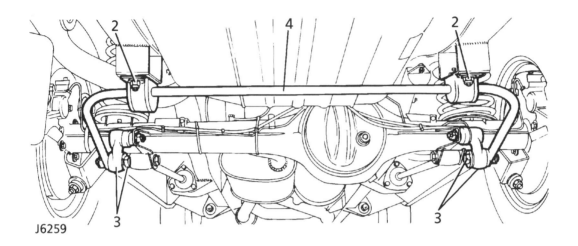

J6259

### Remove

1. Note for reassembly, position of rubber bushes on anti-roll bar.
2. Remove 4 nuts, bolts and washers securing both anti-roll bar bush straps to chassis mounting brackets.
3. Remove nuts, bolts, washers and rubber bushes securing anti-roll bar to links.
4. Remove anti-roll bar.

### Refit

5. Position rubber bushes on anti-roll bar. Fit joint towards axle.
6. Fit anti-roll bar with two straps. Ensure link arms point down as shown. Loosely fit, bolts, washers and new nyloc nuts.
7. Fit bolt, washers and rubber bushes. Fit anti-roll bar to links and tighten to **68Nm (50 lbf/ft).**
8. Tighten nuts securing straps to **30Nm (22 lbf/ft).**

## ANTI-ROLL BAR LINKS

**Service repair no - 64.35.24.**

**Remove**

1. Remove 2 nuts, bolts, washers and rubber bushes from links and lower anti-roll bar to clear links.
2. Remove cotter pin and loosen castellated nut a few turns.
3. Release link using special tool **18G 1063A** as shown.
4. Remove castellated nut and remove link.

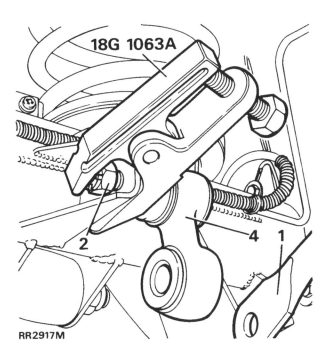

RR2917M

**Refit**

5. Fit anti-roll bar link arm and castellated nut. Point link arm down as shown. Tighten fixing to **40 Nm (30 lbf/ft)** and fit new cotter pin.
6. Align anti-roll bar to links.
7. Fit bolts, washers and rubber bushes using new self locking nuts and secure anti-roll bar to links. Tighten to **68Nm (50 lbf/ft).**

## SELF LEVELLING UNIT

**Service repair no - 64.30.09**

**Remove**

⚠️ **WARNING: The levelling unit contains pressurised gas and MUST NOT be dismantled. Repair is by replacement of complete unit only.**

1. Raise and support the vehicle under chassis and use a jack to support weight of the axle.
2. Disconnect upper links at pivot bracket.
3. Ease up levelling unit lower gaiter and unscrew lower ball joint at push rod using thin jawed spanners.
4. Release webbing strap from the chassis.
5. Remove 4 nuts securing top bracket to chassis and withdraw levelling unit complete with bracket.

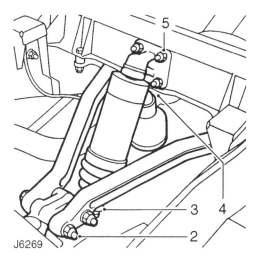

J6269

**Renew levelling unit ball joints**

The ball joints for the levelling unit may be dismantled for cleaning and examination.

6. Unscrew lower ball joint from pivot bracket.
7. Unscrew ball joint from top bracket.
8. Reassemble ball joints, packing with Dextagrease G.P. or equivalent. Renew joints if worn.
9. Check condition of gaiters and renew if necessary.

**Refit**

10. Ensure ball pin threads are clean and smear Loctite grade CVX on ball pin threads.
11. Fit upper ball joint to levelling unit and secure gaiter.
12. Fit top bracket complete with levelling unit to chassis and secure with 4 nuts and tighten to *47 Nm (35 lbf/ft)*.
13. Fit levelling unit to lower ball joint and secure gaiter.
14. Attach webbing strap to chassis cross member.
15. Fit upper links to the pivot bracket and retain with 2 bolts and nuts but do not tighten at this stage.
16. Remove jack in support of axle and support from under chassis.
17. Allow suspension to settle and then tighten 2 bolts and nuts retaining upper links to pivot bracket to *176 Nm (130 lbf/ft)*.

---

## TORQUE VALUES

 **NOTE: Torque wrenches should be regularly checked for accuracy to ensure that all fixings are tightened to the correct torque.**

|  | Nm |
|---|---|
| **Anti-roll bar** | |
| - Strap nyloc nuts | 30 |
| - Ball link self lock nut | 68 |
| - Castellated nut | 40 |
| Top link to mounting bracket | 176 |
| Bottom link to axle | 176 |
| Bottom link to chassis | 176 |
| Top link bracket to rear cross member | 47 |
| Shock absorber to axle | 37 |

# Notes

# 70 - BRAKES

## CONTENTS

Page

**DESCRIPTION AND OPERATION**

**REPAIR**

**OVERHAUL**

# Notes

## DESCRIPTION

The mechanical components of the hydraulic braking system consists of four piston caliper disc brakes at the front and two piston caliper disc brakes at the rear.

Vented front brake discs are fitted as standard on 110/130 models, while 90 models have solid discs. However, on 90 models with a heavy duty chassis, vented front discs may also be fitted.

A cable controlled parking brake operates a single drum brake mounted on the output shaft of the transfer gearbox and is completely independent of the main braking system.

The basic hydraulic system involves 2 separate and independent primary and secondary circuits which permits a degree of braking should a fault occur in one of the circuits. The primary circuit operates the rear brake calipers and the secondary circuit the front brake calipers.

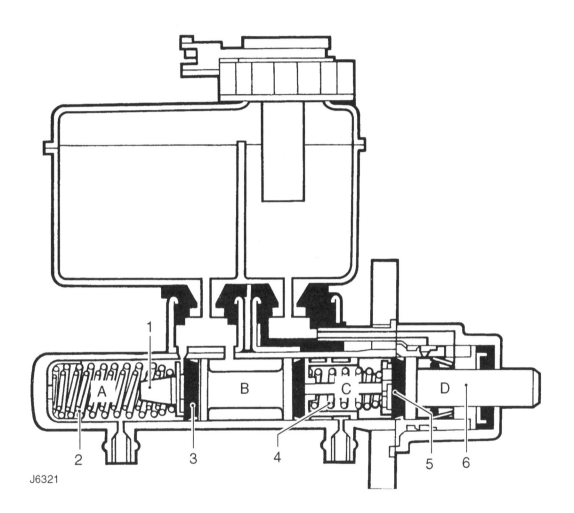

J6321

**Master cylinder components**

1. Secondary plunger
2. Secondary spring
3. Recuperation seal
4. Primary spring
5. Recuperation seal
6. Primary plunger

## OPERATION

### Master cylinder

A tandem master cylinder, which is assisted by a light weight, short, compact servo, is fed by a divided fluid reservoir. The rear section supplies fluid for the primary circuit and the front section the secondary circuit.

When the brakes are off, the fluid can move unrestricted between the dual line system and the separate reservoirs in the fluid supply tank.

When the footbrake is applied, the primary plunger assembly moves up the cylinder bore and the pressure created acts in conjunction with the primary spring to overcome the secondary springs, thus moving the secondary plunger assembly up the bore. At the same time initial movement of both plungers takes the recuperating seals past the cut-off holes in the cylinder chambers 'A' and 'C',see J6321, and applies pressure to the fliud in those chambers, which is directed to the respective circuits.

The fluid in chambers 'B' and 'D'is unaffected by movement of the plungers and can move unrestricted between the separate chambers and respective reservoirs in the fluid supply tank, both before and during brake application. When the brakes are released, the plunger assemblies, aided by the return springs are retracted faster than the fluid; this creates a depression between the fluid in chambers 'A' and 'C'and the recuperation seals.

The recuperation seals momentarily collapse allowing fluid in chambers 'B' and 'D'to flow through the holes in the plungers, over the collapsed seals and into chambers 'A' and 'C'respectively. The movement of fluid from one set of chambers to the other, is compensated for by fluid from the separate reservoirs in the supply tank moving through the feed holes in the cylinder. Conversely, the final return movement of the plunger assemblies causes the extra fluid in chambers 'A' and 'C'to move through the cut off holes into the fluid reservoir.

The servo unit provides controlled power assistance to to the brake pedal when pressure is applied. Power is obtained from a vacuum pump located on the RH side of the engine cylinder block. The vacuum is applied to both sides of a flexing diaphragm, and by admitting atmosheric pressure to the rear diaphragm, assistance is obtained. The servo unit is mounted between the brake pedal and master cylinder and is linked to these by push rods. Should a vacuum failure occur, the two push rods will act as a single rod allowing the brakes to function in the normal way, although more effort will be required to operate the brake pedal.

### Hydraulic system

A brake fluid loss switch is fitted to the master cylinder reservoir filler cap. The switch is wired to a warning light on the vehicle fascia and will illuminate as a bulb check when the ignition is switched on and extinguishes when the engine is running and the handbrake is released. A hydraulic failure in the system will result in fluid loss, causing the warning light to illuminate.

On 90 models a pressure reducing valve (PRV), fitted to the RH bulkhead in the engine compartment, maintains the braking balance, see J6322. Pressure to the rear calipers is regulated by the PRV, this valve is of the failure by-pass type, allowing full system pressure to the rear brake calipers in the event of a front (secondary) circuit failure.

 **NOTE: In some countries, a pressure reducing valve may be fitted to 110 models to conform to legal requirements.**

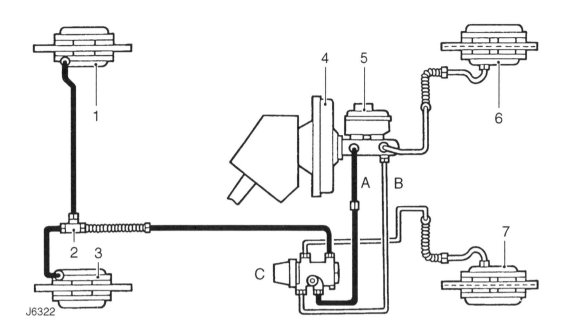

J6322

**90 Models**

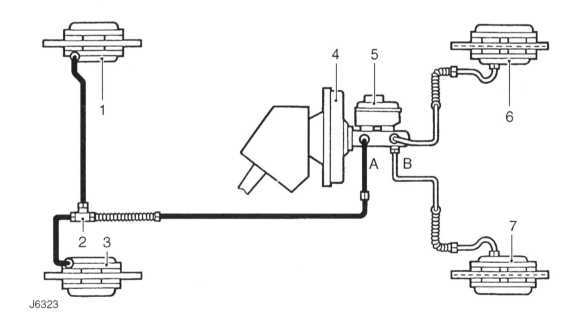

J6323

**110/130 Models**

**Hydraulic system**

A- Primary circuit
B- Secondary circuit
C- Pressure reducing valve (PRV)

1. LH rear brake caliper
2. T-connector
3. RH rear brake caliper
4. Brake servo
5. Master cylinder and reservoir
6. LH front brake caliper
7. RH front brake caliper

# Notes

## GENERAL BRAKE SERVICE PRACTICE

**Brake fluid precautions**

 **WARNING: Do not allow brake fluid to come into contact with eyes or skin.**

 **CAUTION: Brake fluid can damage paintwork, if spilled wash off immediately with plenty of clean water.**

 **CAUTION: Use only correct grade of brake fluid. If an assembly fluid is required use ONLY brake fluid. Do NOT use mineral oil, i.e. engine oil etc.**

 **CAUTION: Thoroughly clean all brake calipers, pipes and fittings before commencing work on any part of the brake system. Failure to do so could cause foreign matter to enter the system and cause damage to seals and pistons which will seriously impair the efficiency of the brake system. To ensure the brake system efficiency is not impaired the following warnings must be adhered to :-**

- **DO NOT use any petroleum based cleaning fluids or any proprietary fluids containing petrol.**
- **DO NOT use brake fluid previously bled from the system.**
- **DO NOT flush the brake system with any fluid other than the recommended brake fluid.**

**The brake system should be drained and flushed at the recommended service intervals.**

**Cover all electrical terminals carefully to make absolutely certain that no fluid enters the terminals and plugs.**

## FLUID LEVEL CHECK / TOP UP

 **WARNING: Clean reservoir body and filler cap before removing cap. Use only fluid from a sealed container.**

1. Park vehicle on level ground.
2. Check level is between 'MIN' and 'MAX' marks.
3. If level is below 'MIN' mark top up fluid level to 'MAX' mark on reservoir, using correct fluid *See LUBRICANTS, FLUIDS AND CAPACITIES, Information, Recommended lubricants and fluids.*

 **CAUTION: Do not fill reservoir above maximum line.**

## BRAKE SYSTEM BLEED

**Service repair no - 70.25.02**

### Preparation

 **WARNING: Before bleeding the brake system refer to general brake service practice.** *See General Brake Service Practice.*

- **During bleed procedure, brake fluid level must not be allowed to fall below the MIN level.**
- **To bleed the hydraulic circuits, four bleed nipples are provided, one at each caliper.**
- **There are two methods by which air can be removed from the braking system:-**

1. **MANUAL BLEED PROCEDURE.**
2. **PRESSURE BLEED PROCEDURE.**

### Pressure bleed procedure

Purpose designed equipment for pressure filling and bleeding of hydraulic systems may be used on Land Rover vehicles. The equipment manufacturer's instructions must be followed and the pressure must not exceed 4.5 bar, 65 lb/in$^2$.

### Manual bleed procedure

Equipment required

- Clean glass receptacle
- Bleed hose
- Wrench
- Approx 2 litres (3 pints) brake fluid *See LUBRICANTS, FLUIDS AND CAPACITIES, Information, Recommended lubricants and fluids.*

### Master cylinder bleed

1. Disconnect battery.
2. Depress brake pedal fully and slowly 5 times.
3. Release the pedal and wait for ten seconds.
4. Air bubbles will rise into the reservoir during these instructions.
5. Repeat instructions until a firm resistance is felt at the pedal.

### Complete circuit bleed

1. Disconnect battery.
2. Bleed front calipers, driver's side first. Fit bleed hose to bleed screw.
3. Dip free end of bleed hose into brake fluid in bleed bottle.
4. Open bleed screw of caliper.
5. Depress brake pedal fully several times until fluid is clear of air bubbles.
6. Keeping pedal fully depressed, tighten bleed screw, then release pedal.
7. Repeat procedure on other front caliper followed by rear calipers.
8. Fit all bleed screw protection caps.
9. Check/top-up fluid level when bleeding is complete *See Fluid Level Check/Top-Up.*

## MASTER CYLINDER

**Service repair no - 70.30.08**

Before starting repair refer to general brake service practice *See  General Brake Service Practice.*

**Remove**

1. Disconnect battery.
2. Place a container under the master cylinder to catch escaping brake fluid.
3. Clean area round master cylinder ports.

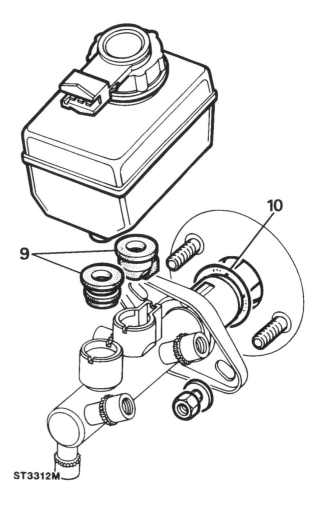

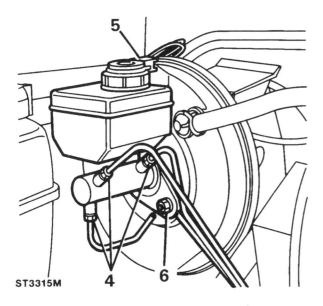

4. Disconnect pipes from master cylinder ports. Cover, not plug, the pipe ends to prevent entry of dirt.
5. Disconnect electrical leads from reservoir cap.
6. Remove two nuts securing master cylinder to servo and withdraw cylinder.
7. Remove reservoir cap and drain fluid into suitable container for disposal.
8. The reservoir is a push fit in the master cylinder and secured by seals. Carefully ease the reservoir from the master cylinder by rolling it from the seals. Note that the two seals are different sizes.

**Refit**

9. Insert new reservoir seals in the master cylinder ports and fit reservoir to master cylinder.
10. Ensuring that water ingress seal is in position, fit master cylinder to servo. Tighten fixings to *26 Nm (19 lbf/ft).*
11. Connect brake pipes to master cylinder ports and tighten to *15 Nm (11 lbf/ft).*
12. Fit electrical leads to reservoir cap
13. Fill reservoir with recommended brake fluid *See LUBRICANTS, FLUIDS AND CAPACITIES, Information,  Recommended lubricants and fluids.*
14. Bleed the brake system *See  Brake system bleed.*
15. Reconnect battery and road test vehicle.

## PRESSURE REDUCING VALVE (PRV)

**Service repair no - 70.25.21**

**Remove**

1. Disconnect battery.
2. Clean area around reducing valve ports.
3. Place a container under valve to catch escaping brake fluid.

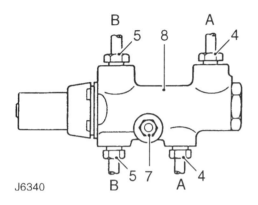

J6340

4. Disconnect primary circuit pipe unions æAæ from valve.
5. Disconnect secondary circuit pipe unions æBæ from valve.
6. Cover pipes to prevent ingress of dirt.
7. Remove single retaining nut and bolt securing valve to engine bulkhead.
8. Remove valve.

**Refit**

9. Fit valve to engine bulkhead. Tighten bolt to *15 Nm (11 lbf/ft).*
10. Connect primary and secondary circuit pipes to valve. Tighten to *16 Nm (12 lbf/ft).*
11. Fill brake reservoir with recommended brake fluid *See LUBRICANTS, FLUIDS AND CAPACITIES, Information, Recommended lubricants and fluids.*
12. Bleed the brake system *See Brake system bleed.*
13. Reconnect battery and road test vehicle.

## SERVO NON RETURN VALVE

**Service repair no - 70.50.15**

**Remove**

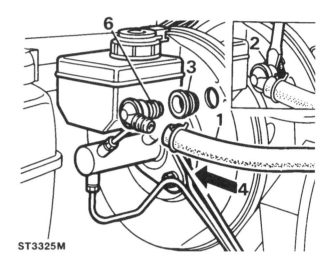

ST3325M

1. Disconnect brake vacuum hose from servo non return valve.
2. Carefully prise valve out with a screwdriver blade between valve and grommet. Take care not to exert too much pressure on the vacuum chamber.
3. Remove rubber grommet but be careful not to allow it to fall into the vacuum chamber.
4. Check the valve for correct operation; it should not be possible to pass air through into the servo in direction of arrow. Do not use compressed air.

**Refit**

5. Fit rubber grommet.
6. Smear ribs of the valve with Lucas Girling rubber grease to assist assembly, and push valve fully home.
7. Connect vacuum hose to the valve.
8. Road test vehicle.

## SERVO ASSEMBLY

**Service repair no - 70.50.01**

**Remove**

Before starting repair refer to general brake service practice *See  General Brake Service Practice.*

 **NOTE: The non-return valve and grommet, are the only serviceable components. In event of failure or damage, fit a new unit.**

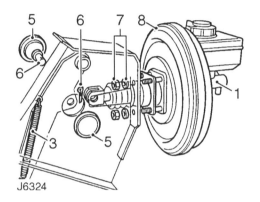

J6324

1. Remove master cylinder *See  Master cylinder.*
2. Disconnect vacuum supply hose from servo unit.
3. At footwell, release 2 brake pedal return springs.
4. Disconnect leads from brake light switch at rear of pedal box.
5. Remove blanking grommets from each side of pedal box.
6. Remove split pin and clevis pin securing servo push rod to brake pedal.
7. Remove 4 nuts and plain washers securing servo to pedal box.
8. Remove servo assembly and rubber washer from bulkhead.

**Refit**

9. Locate servo assembly and rubber washer to engine bulkhead and secure to pedal box. Tighten fixings to *14 Nm (10 lbf/ft).*
10. Fit brake pedal to servo push rod with clevis pin and new split pin.
11. Fit blanking grommets to each side of pedal box.
12. At footwell, attach pedal return springs.
13. Connect vacuum hose to servo non-return valve.
14. Fit brake master cylinder to servo unit *See Brake master cylinder.*

## BRAKE PEDAL

**Service repair no - 70.35.01 - Brake pedal**
**Service repair no - 70.35.03 - Pedal box**

### Remove

1. Remove brake servo assembly. *See Brake servo assembly.*

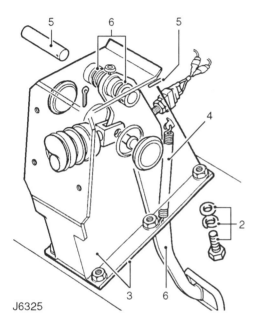

J6325

2. Remove 6 bolts securing pedal box to engine bulkhead.
3. Taking care not damage brake fluid pipes, remove pedal box assembly and gasket.
4. Release return springs from pedal and pedal box bosses.
5. Using a suitable punch, drift out retaining pin and withdraw pedal pivot shaft.
6. Remove brake pedal complete with pivot bushes.
7. Examine components for wear or damage, renew as necessary.
8. If it is necessary to fit new pivot bushes, they must be reamed out to 15,87 mm ± 0,02 mm (0.625 ± 0.001 in.) after fitment.

### Refit

9. Lubricate pedal pivot shaft and bushes with general purpose grease.
10. Fit pedal to pedal box, insert pivot shaft and secure with new split pin.
11. Attach return springs to pedal and pedal box bosses.
12. Fit pedal box and gasket to engine bulkhead. Tighten fixings to *25 Nm (18 lbf/ft).*
13. Fit brake servo assembly. *See Brake servo assembly.*

## FRONT BRAKE PADS - ALL MODELS

**Service repair no - 70.40.02**

**Remove**

1. Remove front road wheels .
2. Clean exterior of calipers.

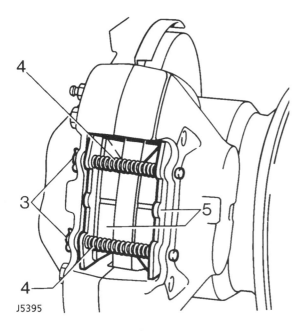

J5395

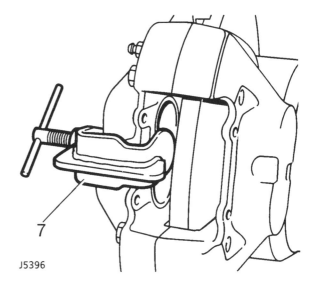

J5396

3. Remove split pin from retaining pins.
4. Remove pad retaining pins and anti-rattle springs.
5. Remove brake pads.
6. Clean exposed parts of pistons, using new brake fluid. Wipe away excess with a lint free cloth.
7. Using piston clamp **LRT-70-500** press each piston back into its bore. Ensure that displaced brake fluid does not overflow from reservoir.

**Refit**

8. Fit brake pads.
9. Fit pad retaining pins and anti-rattle springs. Secure with new split pins.
10. Apply service brake pedal several times to locate pads.
11. Fit road wheels. Tighten wheel nuts to correct torque:
    Alloy wheels - *130 Nm (96 lbf/ft)*
    Steel wheels - *100 Nm (80 lbf/ft)*
    Heavy duty wheels - *170 Nm (125 lbf/ft)*
12. Check fluid reservoir. Top up if necessary, using correct grade of fluid *See LUBRICANTS, FLUIDS AND CAPACITIES, Information, Recommended lubricants and fluids* .

## REAR BRAKE PADS

**Service repair no - 70.40.03**

**Service tool:**

**Remove**

1. Remove rear road wheels.
2. Clean exterior of calipers.
3. Remove pad retaining pins and anti-rattle springs. Note differences between 90 and 110/130 models.
4. Remove brake pads.
5. Clean exposed parts of pistons, using new brake fluid. Wipe away excess with a lint free cloth.
6. Using piston clamp **LRT-70-500** press each piston back into its bore. Ensure that displaced brake fluid does not overflow from reservoir.

**Refit**

7. Insert brake pads.
8. Fit anti-rattle springs and secure with retaining pins.
9. Apply service brake pedal several times to locate pads.
10. Fit road wheels, remove chassis stands and jack. Tighten wheel nuts to correct torque:
    Alloy wheels - ***130 Nm (96 lbf/ft)***
    Steel wheels - ***100 Nm (80 lbf/ft)***
    Heavy duty wheels - ***170 Nm (125 lbf/ft)***
11. Check fluid reservoir, top up if necessary, using correct grade of fluid ***See LUBRICANTS, FLUIDS AND CAPACITIES, Information, Recommended lubricants and fluids*** .

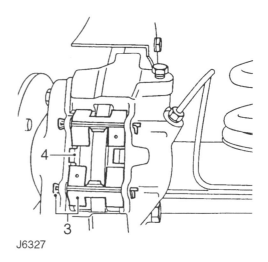

J6327

**90 Models**

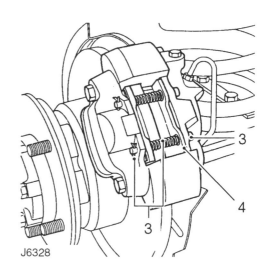

J6328

**110/130 Models**

## FRONT BRAKE CALIPER ASSEMBLY

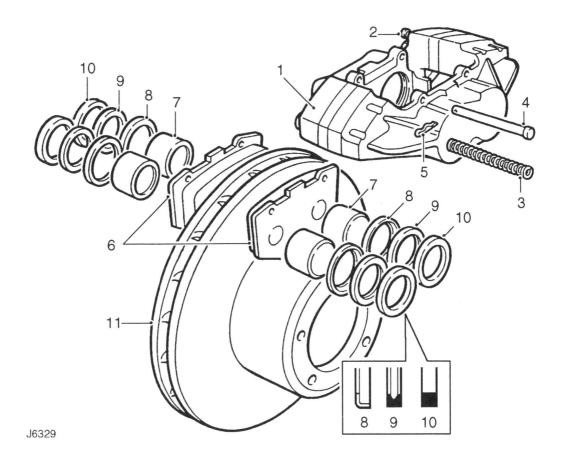

J6329

**Key to caliper**

1. Caliper
2. Bleedscrew
3. Anti-rattle springs
4. Pad retaining pins
5. Split pin
6. Friction pads

7. Piston
8. Wiper seal retainer
9. Wiper seal
10. Fluid seal
11. Brake disc

## FRONT BRAKE CALIPERS

**Service repair no - 70.55.05**
**Service repair no - 70.55.16**

Before starting repair refer to general brake service practice *See General Brake Service Practice.*

**Remove**

1. Remove front road wheels.

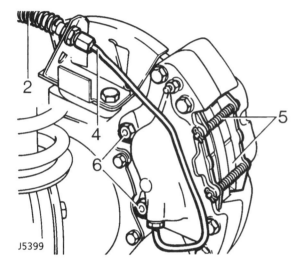

2. Expose flexible brake hose by moving coiled protective covering.
3. Using a recognised hose clamp, clamp hose to prevent loss of brake fluid.
4. Disconnect rigid brake pipe from flexible hose, seal exposed ends to prevent ingress of dirt.
5. Remove split pin, retaining pins and springs, withdraw pads. If refitting pads, identify them for assembly to original locations.
6. Remove 2 bolts and withdraw caliper from swivel housing.

 **WARNING: Do not separate caliper halves**

7. Clean outer surfaces of caliper using aerosol brake cleaner.

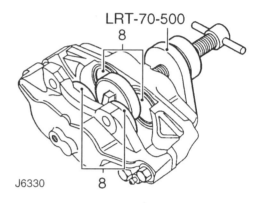

8. Using special tool **LRT-70-500**, clamp pistons in inboard half of caliper. Gently, keeping fingers clear, and with **CAUTION**, apply air pressure to fluid inlet port to expel pistons. It is unlikely that pistons will expel at same time, regulate rate with a suitable piece of wood between appropriate piston and caliper.
9. Finally remove pistons, identifying them with their respective bores.
10. Remove wiper seal retainer by inserting a blunt screwdriver between retainer and seal. Pry retainer carefully from mouth of bore.
11. Taking care not to damage seal grooves, extract wiper seal and fluid seal.
12. Clean bores, pistons and seal grooves using clean brake fluid only. If caliper or pistons are corroded, or their condition is not perfect, new parts must be fitted.

BRAKES

## Assemble outboard pistons

13. Coat new fluid seal with brake fluid. Ease seal into groove in bore using only fingers, ensuring it is properly seated. Fluid seal and groove are not same in section, so when seal is seated it feels raised to touch at edge furthest away from mouth of bore.
14. Coat appropriate piston with brake fluid. Insert it squarely into bore by hand only. Do not tilt piston during insertion, leave approximately 8mm projecting from bore.
15. Coat new wiper seal with brake fluid and fit to new seal retainer. Slide assembly, seal first, over protruding piston and into bore recess. Use piston clamp to press home seal retainer and piston.

## Mounting inboard pistons

16. Clamp outboard pistons and carry out same procedure for removing and fitting outboard pistons and seals, instructions 8 to 15.

## Fit calipers and pads

17. Fit caliper, tighten bolts evenly to **82 Nm (60 lbf/ft).**
18. Connect brake flexible hoses to caliper. Tighten to **15 Nm (11 lbf/ft).**
19. Remove hose clamps.
20. Insert pads. Fit pins and springs, secure using new split pin.
21. Bleed brake system **See Brake System Bleed**

22. Press brake pedal firmly several times to locate friction pads.
23. Fit road wheels, remove axle stands. Finally tighten road wheel nuts to correct torque:
    Alloy wheels - **130 Nm (96 lbf/ft)**
    Steel wheels - **100 Nm (80 lbf/ft)**
    Heavy duty wheels - **170 Nm (125 lbf/ft)**
24. Road test vehicle. Note that new friction pads require 'bedding-in', this may take several hundred miles before brakes are at maximum efficiency.

## FRONT BRAKE DISCS

**Service repair no - 70.10.10.**

### Remove

1. Remove hub assembly **See FRONT AXLE AND FINAL DRIVE, Repair, Front hub assembly** .

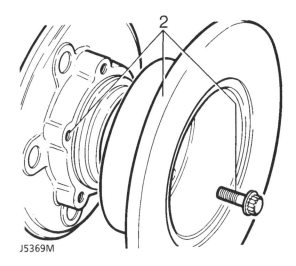

J5369M

2. Remove 5 hub to disc bolts.
3. Tap disc to separate from hub.

 **NOTE: On 110/130 vehicles ventilated discs are fitted as standard.**

### Refit

4. Locate disc to hub.
5. Apply Loctite 270 to disc bolts and tighten to **73 Nm (54 lbf/ft).**
6. Check total disc runout with a dial indicator, this must not exceed 0,15 mm, 0.006 in. If necessary reposition disc.
7. Fit hub assembly **See FRONT AXLE AND FINAL DRIVE, Repair, Front hub assembly** .

### Disc reclamation

8. Check disc thickness. This dimension may be machined to minimum thickness of 12 mm (0.47 in.) - solid discs, 22 mm (0.90 in) - ventilated discs. Machine equal amount off each face.

 **NOTE: The disc MUST BE renewed if the minimum running thickness stamped on the disc is recorded.**

## REAR BRAKE CALIPER ASSEMBLY

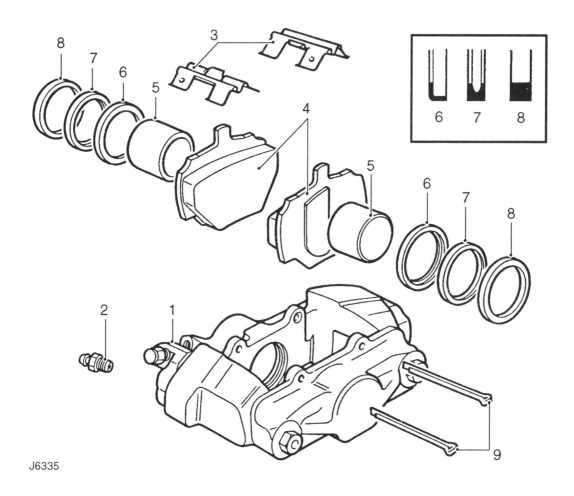

J6335

**Key to rear caliper**

1. Caliper
2. Bleed screw
3. Pad retaining springs
4. Brake pads
5. Piston

6. Wiper seal retainer
7. Wiper seal
8. Fluid seal
9. Retaining pins

## REAR BRAKE CALIPERS

**Service repair no - 70.55.06**
**Service repair no - 70.55.17**

Before starting repair refer to General brake service practice *See General Brake Service Practice.*

### Remove caliper

1. Remove rear road wheels.
2. Using a recognised hose clamp, clamp flexible brake hose above rear axle.

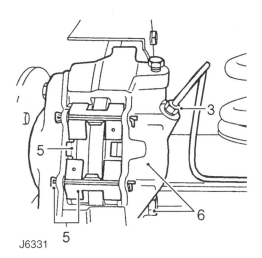

J6331

**90 Models**

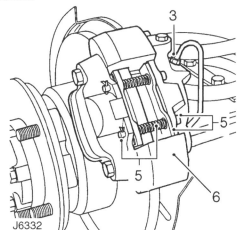

J6332

**110/130 Models**

3. Remove brake pipe from rear brake caliper.

4. Seal pipe ends to prevent ingress of dirt.
5. Remove retaining pins and springs and withdraw pads. If same pads are to be refitted, identify them for assembly in original positions.
6. Remove 2 bolts and withdraw caliper from rear axle.

### Repair

> ⚠ **WARNING: Do not separate caliper halves.**

7. Clean outer surfaces of caliper with aerosol brake cleaner.

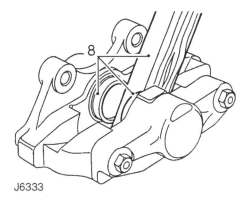

J6333

8. **WITH CAUTION** expel pistons from their bores by applying air pressure to fluid inlet port. It is unlikely both pistons will expel at same time, regulate rate with a suitable piece of wood inserted between two pistons.
9. Finally, remove pistons keeping them identified with their respective bores.
10. Remove wiper seal retainer by inserting a blunt screwdriver between retainer and seal and pry retainer carefully from mouth of bore.
11. Taking care not to damage seal grooves, extract wiper seal and fluid seal.
12. Clean bores, pistons and particularly seal grooves using clean brake fluid only. If caliper or pistons are corroded or their condition is not perfect new parts must be fitted.
13. Apply brake fluid to new seal. Fit seal into groove in bore. When seal is seated it feels raised to touch at edge furthest away from mouth of bore.
14. Coat piston with brake fluid. Insert it squarely into bore. Do not tilt piston during insertion and leave 8mm projecting from bore.

**15.** Coat a new wiper seal with brake fluid and fit to new seal retainer. Slide assembly, seal first, over protruding piston into bore recess.

**16.** Using special tool **LRT-70-500** - piston clamp, press home seal retainer and piston.

### Mounting inboard piston

**17.** Carry out same procedure as for removing and fitting outboard piston and seals, instructions 8 to 16.

### Fit calipers and pads to vehicle

**18.** Fit caliper to axle, tighten 2 bolts evenly to *82 Nm (60 lbf/ft).*

**19.** Connect brake pipe to caliper. Tighten to *15 Nm (11 lbf/ft).*

**20.** Remove clamp from flexible brake hose.

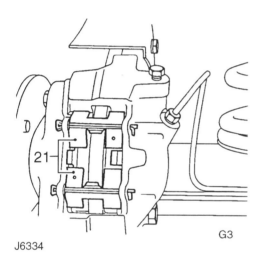

J6334

G3

**21.** Insert pads and retaining springs, secure in position with new retaining pins and spread ends or fit new split pins, depending on vehicle model. Note correct position of retaining springs on 90 models.

**22.** Bleed brake system *See Brake System Bleed .*

**23.** Press brake pedal firmly several times to locate pads.

**24.** Fit road wheels, remove axle stands. Finally tighten road wheel nuts to correct torque:
Alloy wheels - *130 Nm (96 lbf/ft)*
Steel wheels - *100 Nm (80 lbf/ft)*
Heavy duty wheels - *170 Nm (125 lbf/ft)*

**25.** Road test vehicle. Note new brake pads require 'bedding-in', for several hundred miles before brakes are at maximum efficiency.

## REAR BRAKE DISC

**Service repair no - 70.10.11.**

### Remove

**1.** Remove rear hub assembly *See REAR AXLE AND FINAL DRIVE, Repair, Rear hub assembly .*

**2.** Remove disc bolts.

**3.** Remove disc from rear hub.

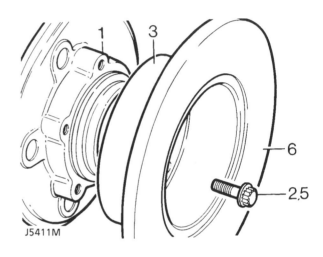

J5411M

### Refit

**4.** Fit disc to rear hub.

**5.** Fit disc bolts. Tighten to *73 Nm (54 lbf/ft).*

**6.** Check total disc run out, this must not exceed 0,15 mm (0.006 in). If necessary reposition disc.

**7.** Fit rear hub assembly *See REAR AXLE AND FINAL DRIVE, Repair, Rear Hub Assembly .*

### Disc reclamation

**8.** Check disc thickness. This dimension may be machined to minimum thickness of 12 mm. Machine equal amounts off each face.

 **NOTE: The brake disc MUST BE renewed if the minimum running thickness stamped on the disc is recorded.**

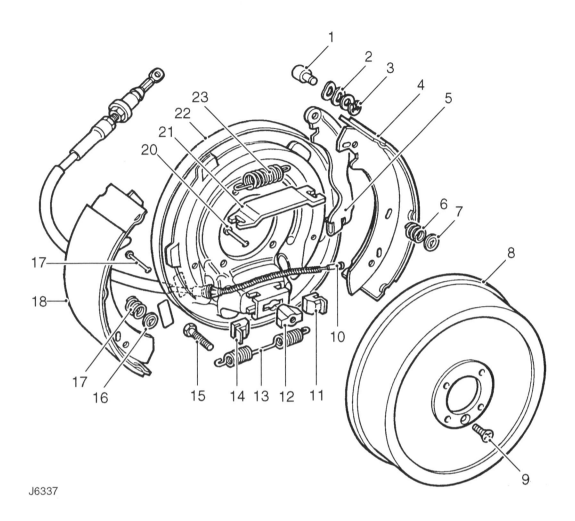

J6337

## TRANSMISSION BRAKE

1. Pin
2. Washer
3. 'C' clip
4. Brake shoe
5. Cable lever
6. Hold down spring
7. Dished washer
8. Brake drum
9. Screw
10. Brake cable
11. Adjuster slide
12. Aadjuster nut

13. Spring
14. Adjuster slide
15. Adjuster bolt
16. Dished washer
17. Hold down spring
18. Brake shoe
19. Hold down pin
20. Hold down pin
21. Abutment plate
22. Back plate
23. Spring

## TRANSMISSION BRAKE SHOES

**Service repair no - 70.45.18**

**Remove**

1. Park vehicle on level ground, chock road wheels and release handbrake. Alternatively, raise vehicle on a ramp.
2. Disconnect rear propeller shaft from transmission output flange at brake drum.

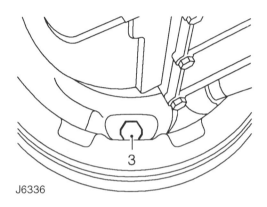

J6336

3. Slacken off transmission brake drum adjustment bolt.
4. Remove single screw securing brake drum to output flange.
5. Withdraw drum to expose brake assembly.
6. Release top and bottom springs from brake shoes, see J6337.
7. Grip dished washer with a pair of pliers, depress washer and turn through 90°.
8. Remove dished washer, complete with hold down spring and pin from both shoes.
9. Move brake shoes out from adjuster slides, release from abutment plate and remove from backplate.
10. Check that springs are satisfactory for continued use. If new brake shoes are to be fitted, the srings should also be renewed.

**Refit**

11. Locate RH brake shoe in slide and secure brake shoe and lever assembly to backplate with hold down pin, spring and dished washer.
12. Locate LH brake shoe in slide and fit abutment plate between both brake shoes. Secure LH shoe with hold down pin, spring and dished washer.
13. Fit pull-off springs to brake shoes.
14. Fit brake drum. Tighten screw to **25 Nm (18 lbf/ft).**
15. Check that hand brake lever is released.
16. Screw in and tighten adjuster bolt until brake drum will not rotate by hand.
17. Tighten adjuster bolt to **25 Nm (18 lbf/ft)** to ensure brake drum is locked.
18. Slacken off adjuster bolt by 1.5 turns to give shoes a running clearance. Check that the drum is free to rotate.
19. Fit propeller shaft to output flange. Tighten fixings to **46 Nm (34 lbf/ft).**
20. Remove wheel chocks and check operation of handbrake.

## HANDBRAKE CABLE

**Service repair no - 70.35.25**

**Remove**

1. Park vehicle on level ground, chock road wheels and release handbrake. Alternatively, raise vehicle on ramp.

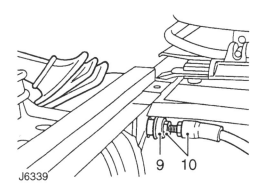

J6339

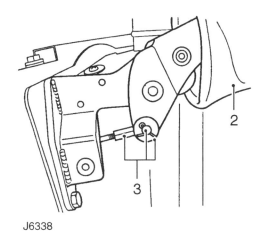

J6338

2. Remove 3 trim studs and lift up handbrake gaiter.
3. Remove split pin, clevis pin, washer and disconnect cable from handbrake lever.
4. Slacken off transmission brake drum adjusting screw.
5. Disconnect propeller shaft from output flange.
6. Remove retaining screw and withdraw brake drum.
7. Release handbrake cable clevis from abutment on cable lever, see J6337, and pull through aperture in back plate.
8. Pull cable from heelboard and remove from vehicle.

**Refit**

9. Feed new cable through heelboard ensuring rubber grommet is correctly located.
10. Position cable over guide plate, insert through backplate and connect to cable lever.
11. Fit cable to handbrake lever and secure with clevis pin and split pin.
12. Fit handbrake gaiter.
13. Fit brake drum. Tighten screw to **25 Nm (18 lbf/ft).**
14. Screw in and tighten adjuster bolt until brake drum will not rotate by hand.
15. Tighten adjuster bolt further to **25 Nm (18 lbf/ft)** to ensure brake drum is locked.
16. Slacken off adjuster bolt by 1.5 turns to give brake shoes running clearance. Check that the drum is free to rotate.
17. Slacken locknut and adjust cable to give the handbrake pawl two notches free movement on the rachet before being fully operational on third notch (brake shoes are fully expanded against drum).

 **NOTE: Cable adjustment is for a new cable or to compensate for cable stretch. Cable adjustment must not be used to take up brake shoe wear.**

18. Fit propeller shaft to output flange. Tighten fixings to **46 Nm (34 lbf/ft).**
19. Remove wheel chocks and check operation of handbrake.

## VACUUM PUMP

**Service repair no - 70.50.19**

**Remove**

> **NOTE: To ease pump removal set engine to T.D.C. on No.1 cylinder.**

1. Disconnect battery.
2. Remove air cleaner **See FUEL SYSTEM, Repair, Air cleaner.**

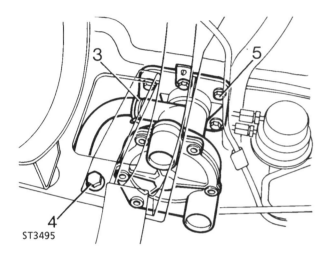

ST3495

3. Detach servo hose from vacuum pump.
4. Remove bolt securing air cleaner support bracket strut.
5. Remove 6 bolts securing vacuum pump.
6. Detach pump complete with strut and harness bracket. Note location of strut and bracket for Refit.

**Refit**

7. Clean mating faces of pump and block.
8. Loosely assemble pump to block with a new gasket and with air cleaner strut and harness bracket located under heads of bolts noted during Remove.
9. Evenly tighten bolts, to depress pump plunger, finally tightening to **25 Nm (18 lbf/ft).**
10. Secure strut to air cleaner bracket.
11. Connect vacuum hose and secure with clip.
12. Refit air cleaner **See FUEL SYSTEM, Repair, Air cleaner.**

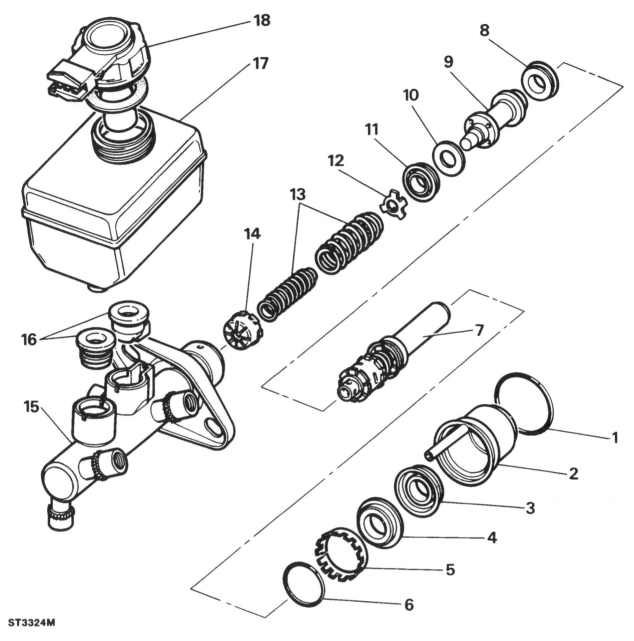

ST3324M

**Key to master cylinder**

1. Water ingress seal
2. Transfer housing
3. Vacuum seal
4. Guide ring
5. Retaining ring
6. 'O' ring seal
7. Primary plunger assembly
8. 'L' seal
9. Secondary plunger

10. Washer
11. Recuperating seal (primary cup)
12. Seal retainer
13. Springs
14. Swirl tube
15. Master cylinder body
16. Reservoir seals
17. Reservoir
18. Low fluid level switch and cap

## MASTER CYLINDER

**Service repair no - 70.30.09**

Before starting overhaul procedure refer to general brake service practice *See Repair, General brake service practice* .

### Dismantling master cylinder

1.  Disconnect battery and remove master cylinder from servo *See Repair, Master cylinder* .
2.  Before commencing overhaul procedure thoroughly clean master cylinder and inspect outer surfaces for damage and condition, renew complete assembly if necessary.

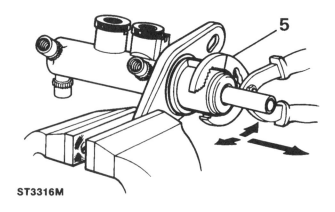

ST3316M

5.  Hold outside of transfer housing with a suitable pair of grips, carefully pull, while working pliers in a backwards and forwards rocking motion to ease housing off master cylinder, discard housing and vacuum seal.

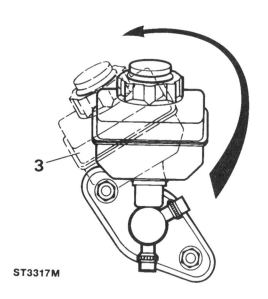

ST3317M

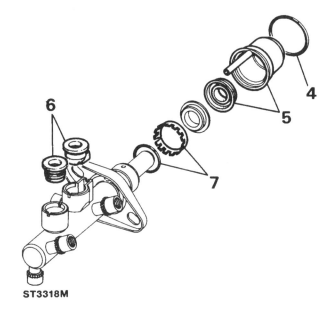

ST3318M

3.  The reservoir is a push fit in master cylinder and secured by seals. Carefully ease reservoir from master cylinder by rolling it from seals as illustrated.
4.  Using soft jaws, one either side of master cylinder flange and clamp flange in a suitable vice. Remove water ingress 'O' ring seal from master cylinder to servo flange and discard.

6.  Withdraw 2 reservoir seals from master cylinder and note their positions in inlet ports for reassembly. Discard both seals.
7.  Remove retaining ring and 'O' ring seal from machined outer surface of master cylinder, discard both seal and retaining ring.

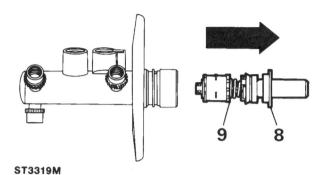

ST3319M

8. Remove guide ring from mouth of master cylinder which supports primary plunger assembly and place to one side, this component is not part of master cylinder service kit and is to be refitted on assembly of unit.
9. Pull primary plunger assembly out of master cylinder.

⚠ NOTE: The primary plunger assembly cannot be broken down any further and is serviced as a complete unit. Discard assembly.

10. The secondary plunger assembly will remain at bottom of master cylinder bore, plunger can be easily expelled by tapping assembly on a piece of timber until plunger appears at cylinder mouth, carefully pull plunger from master cylinder.

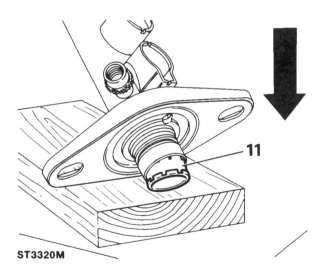

ST3320M

11. If swirl tube was not expelled at same time as secondary plunger, repeat above operation to expel it from bottom of master cylinder bore and discard.

12. Clean all parts with Girling cleaning fluid or unused brake fluid and place cleaned parts on to a clean sheet of paper. Inspect cylinder bore and plungers for signs of corrosion, ridges and score marks. Provided working surfaces are in perfect condition, new seals from a Girling Service repair kit may be used.

**Renewing secondary plunger seals**

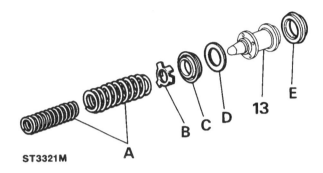

ST3321M

A. Springs
B. Seal retainer
C. Recuperating seal (primary cup)
D. Washer
E. 'L' seal

13. Remove components above from secondary plunger and discard:

⚠ NOTE: A small screwdriver with end rounded and polished is required to remove 'L' seal. DO NOT damage secondary plunger.

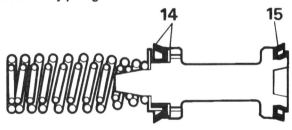

ST3322M

14. Coat new seals in unused brake fluid and firstly fit 'L' seal to plunger.
15. Fit washer followed by recuperating seal. Fit seal retainer and springs, ensure springs are correctly seated.

**Assembling master cylinder**

⚠️ **CAUTION: It is important that the following instructions are carried out precisely, otherwise damage could be caused to new seals when inserting plungers into cylinder bore. Generous amounts of new brake fluid should be used to lubricate parts during assembly.**

⚠️ **NOTE: Thoroughly check that no debris is lodged in fluid passageways and drillings. If debris is found, carefully remove, re-clean cylinder and re-check.**

16. Fit new swirl tube to bottom of cylinder bore.

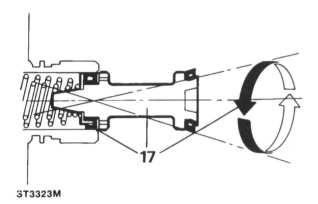

ST3323M

17. Lubricate secondary plunger and cylinder bore. Offer plunger assembly to cylinder until recuperation seal is resting centrally in mouth of bore. Gently introduce plunger with a circular rocking motion, as illustrated. Ensuring that seal does not become trapped, ease seal into bore and slowly push plunger down bore in one continuous movement.
18. Fit primary plunger assembly using same method as for secondary plunger, push plunger down bore.
19. Fit original guide ring to support primary plunger.
20. Coat a new 'O' ring with brake fluid and fit to its respective groove on outer location surface of master cylinder.

⚠️ **CAUTION: 'O' ring should not be rolled down outer location surface of master cylinder but should be slightly stretched and eased down cylinder and into its groove. Do not over stretch seal.**

21. Fit a new retaining ring on outer surface of master cylinder ensuring that serrations of ring are facing mounting flange.
22. Fit two new reservoir seals in their respective ports.
23. Fit a new vacuum seal to either primary plunger or to bottom of transfer housing bore, open face of seal towards primary plunger guide ring.
24. Lubricate vacuum seal with brake fluid, fit transfer housing to master cylinder, push housing fully up to cylinder mounting flange. Do not adjust transfer housing after fitting.
25. Lubricate a new water ingress seal with brake fluid, slightly stretch seal and ease it down housing until seal is in correct position between housing and flange.
26. Roll reservoir into top of master cylinder, reversing procedure described in instruction 3.
27. Fit master cylinder to servo *See Repair, Master cylinder.*
28. Reconnect battery, and road test vehicle.

# 74 - WHEELS AND TYRES

## CONTENTS

# Notes

## TYPES OF WHEEL RIMS AND TYRES

### Description

Dependent on specification and model type, the vehicle is equipped with pressed steel or alloy wheel rims, both using tubeless radial ply tyres.

### Tyre codes

The text, codes and numbers moulded into the tyre wall vary between tyre manufacturers, however most tyres are marked with the information shown in the illustrated example.

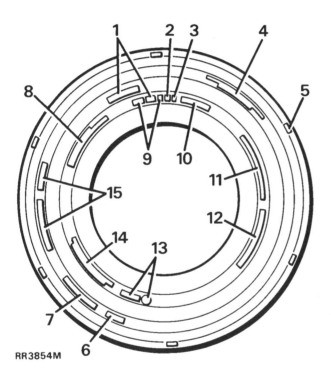

RR3854M

1. Type of tyre construction - **Radial Ply**
2. Load index - **104**
3. Speed symbol - **S or T**
4. USA Tyre quality grading - **Tread wear 160 Traction A temperature B**
5. Tread wear indicators moulded into tread pattern are located at intervals around the tyre and marked by a code - **E66 103S6**
6. Tyres with 'Mud Snow' type tread pattern are marked - **M&S**
7. Tyre reinforcing mark - **Reinforced**
8. USA Load and pressure secification - **(900Kg(1984LBS) at 340KA (50PSI) MACS PRESS**
9. Tyre size - **205 16 ot 235/70 R16**
10. Type of tyre - **TUBELESS**
11. Country of manufacture - **MADE IN GREAT BRITAIN**
12. USA Compliance symbol and identification - **DOT AB7C DOFF 267**
13. European type approval identification - **E11 01234**
14. Tyre construction - **SIDE WALL 2 PLIES RAYON. TREAD 2 RAYON 2 STEEL**
15. Manufacturers brand name/type - **TRACTION PLUS mzx M**

⚠ **NOTE: The illustration is an example of the type of markings moulded into tyres and is for guidance only. For specific tyre specifications** *See GENERAL SPECIFICATION DATA, Information, Tyre size and pressures.*

# Notes

## TYRE WEAR CHART

| FAULT | CAUSE | REMEDY |
|---|---|---|
| Rapid wear at shoulders | Tyres under-inflated<br>Worn suspension components i.e. ball joints, panhard rod bushes, steering damper<br><br>Excessive cornering speeds | Inflate to correct pressure<br>Replace worn components |
| Rapid wear at centre of tread | Tyres over-inflated | Inflate to correct pressure |
| Wear at one shoulder | Track out of adjustment<br><br>Bent panhard rod | Adjust track to correct figure<br><br>Check and replace worn or damaged components |
| Bald spots or tyre cupping | Wheel out of balance<br><br>Excessive radial runout<br><br>Shock absorber worn<br><br>Excessive braking | Balance wheel and tyre assembly<br><br>Check runout and replace tyre if necessary<br>Replace shock absorber |
| Tyre scalloped | Track out of adjustment<br>Worn suspension components<br><br>Excessive cornering speeds | Adjust toe to correct figure<br>Replace tyre as necessary |

RR2136E

 **CAUTION: This diagnosis chart is for general guidance only and does not necessarily include every cause of abnormal tyre wear.**

## FAULT - SYMPTOMS

**Vibration through steering wheel**

1. Check tyre pressures *See Repair, Tyre Pressures.*
2. Check condition of tyres *See Tyre Wear Chart.*
3. Check front wheel alignment *See STEERING, Adjustment, Front Wheel Alignment.*
4. Check wheel balance *See Repair, Wheel Balancing.*

 **NOTE: In the event that any apparent vibration is not eliminated at this stage** *See PROPELLER SHAFTS, Fault diagnosis, Vibration Harshness.*

 **NOTE: In the event that any apparent vibration is not eliminated at this stage, go to steering Fault Diagnosis, Fault - Symptom (Steering vibration, road wheel shimmy/wobble)** *See STEERING, Fault diagnosis, Steering Faults.*

 **NOTE: Radial ply tyres have a flexible sidewall, which produces a sidewall bulge making the tyre appear under-inflated. This is a normal condition for radial ply tyres. Do not attempt to reduce this bulge by over-inflating the tyre.**

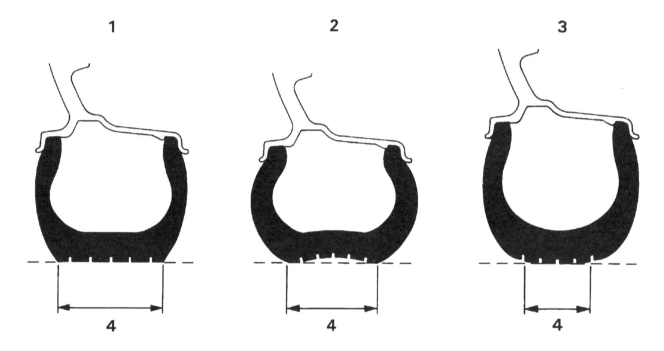

RR2133E

**Key to illustration**

1. Correct inflation.
2. Under-inflation.
3. Over-inflation.
4. Tread contact with road.

## GENERAL INFORMATION

 **WARNING: This is a multi-purpose vehicle with wheels and tyres designed for both on and off road usage. Only use wheels and tyres specified for use on the vehicle.**

The vehicle is equipped with tubeless 'S','T' or 'H' rated radial ply tyres as standard equipment. The tyres are of European metric size and must not be confused with the "P" size metric tyres available in North America.

Vehicle wheel sets, including spare wheel, must be fitted with the same make and type of tyre to the correct specification and tread pattern. Under no circumstances must cross-ply or bias-belted tyres be used.

For tyre specification and pressures *See GENERAL SPECIFICATION DATA, Information, Wheels and Tyres* .

### Steel wheels

Tubeless tyres are mounted on 7.0 inch wide by 16 inch diameter steel wheels.

### Alloy Wheels

Tubeless tyres are mounted on 7.0 inch wide by 16 inch diameter cast aluminium alloy wheels. The surface has a paint finish covered with a clear polyurethane lacquer. Care must be taken when handling the wheel to avoid scratching or chipping the finish.

**The alloy wheel rim is of the asymmetric hump type incorporating a safety hump to improve location of the tyre bead in its seat. If difficulty is experienced in fitting tyres to this type of rim** *See Tyre Fitting* .

 **WARNING: DO NOT fit an inner tube to an alloy wheel.**

## TYRE INSPECTION

Inspect tyres at weekly intervals to obtain maximum tyre life and performance and to ensure compliance with legal requirements. Check for signs of incorrect inflation and uneven wear, which may indicate a need for balancing or front wheel alignment, *See Fault diagnosis, Tyre Wear Chart* , if the tyres have abnormal or uneven wear patterns.

Check tyres at least weekly for cuts, abrasions, bulges and for objects embedded in the tread. More frequent inspections are recommended when the vehicle is regularly used in off road conditions.

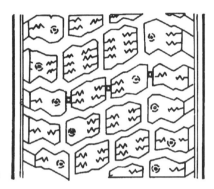
RR2145E

To assist tyre inspection, tread wear indicators are moulded into the bottom of the tread grooves, as shown in the illustration above.

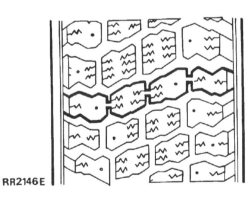
RR2146E

When the tread has worn to a depth of 1.6 mm the indicators appear at the surface as bars which connect the tread pattern across the width of the tread as shown in the illustration above.

When the indicators appear in two or more adjacent grooves, at three locations around the tyre, a new tyre must be fitted.

 **NOTE: DO NOT attempt to interchange tyres, e.g. from front to rear, as tyre wear produces characteristic patterns depending on their position. If tyre position is changed after wear has occured, the performance of the tyre will be adversely affected.**

 **NOTE: Territorial vehicle regulations governing tyre wear MUST be adhered to.**

## WHEELS INSPECTION

Regularly check the condition of the wheels. Replace any wheel that is bent, cracked, dented or has excessive runout.

## VALVES INSPECTION

Check condition of inflation valve. Replace any valve that is worn, cracked, loose, or leaking air.

## TYRE PRESSURES

**Maximum tyre life and performance will be obtained only if tyres are maintained at the correct pressures .**

Tyre pressures must be checked at least once a week and preferably daily, if the vehicle is used off road.

The tyre inflation pressure is calculated to give the vehicle satisfactory ride and steering characteristics without compromising tyre tread life. For recommended tyre pressures in all conditions *See GENERAL SPECIFICATION DATA, Information, Wheels and Tyres* .

**Always check tyre inflation pressures using an accurate gauge and inflate tyres to the recommended pressures only .**

Check and adjust tyre pressures **ONLY** when the tyres are cold, vehicle parked for three hours or more, or driven for less than 3.2 km (2 miles) at speeds below 64 km/h (40 mph). Do not reduce inflation pressures if the tyres are hot or the vehicle has been driven for more than 3.2 km (2 miles) at speeds over 64 km/h (40 mph), as pressures can increase by 0.41 bars (6 lb/in$^2$) over cold inflation pressures.

Check **ALL** tyre pressures including the spare. Refit the valve caps as they form a positive seal and keep dust out of the valve.

## WHEEL BALANCING

⚠️ CAUTION: It is essential that all wheel balancing is carried out off the vehicle. The use of on the vehicle balancing could cause component damage or personal injury and MUST NOT be attempted.

⚠️ NOTE: Before attempting to balance a wheel and tyre assembly clean all mud and dirt deposits from both inside and outside rims and remove existing balance weights.

Remove stones from the tyre tread in order to avoid operator injury during dynamic balancing and to obtain the correct balance.

Inspect tyres for damage and correct tyre pressures and balance according to the equipment manufacturer's instructions.

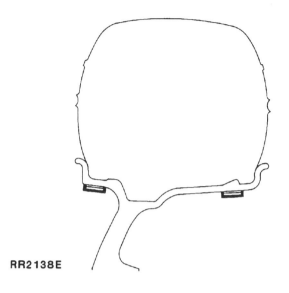

RR2138E

**Alloy wheels**

Clean area of wheel rim and attach adhesive balance weights in position shown. Cut through rear face of weight strip to detach required weights.

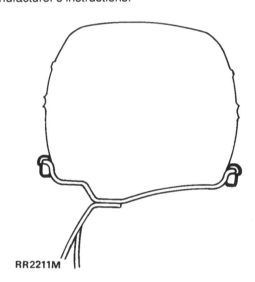

RR2211M

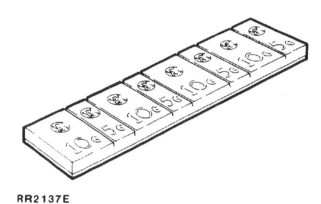

RR2137E

**Steel wheels**

Clean area of wheel rim and attach balance weights in position shown.

⚠️ CAUTION: Use only correct adhesive balance weights to avoid damage to aluminium wheel rim. DO NOT attempt to use a steel wheel weight on an aluminium wheel.

## Static balance

Wheel tramp

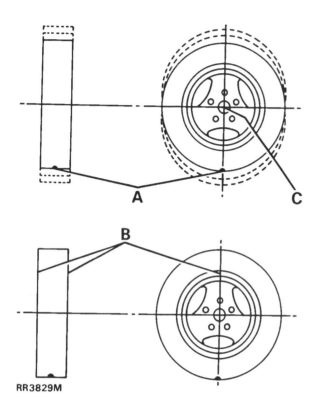

RR3829M

## Dynamic balance

Wheel shimmy

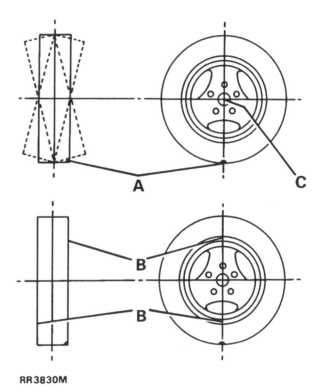

RR3830M

**A** - Heavy spot.
**B** - Add balance weights here.
**C** - Centre line of spindle.

Static balance is the equal distribution of weight around the wheel. A statically unbalanced wheel will cause a bouncing action called wheel tramp. This condition will eventually cause uneven tyre wear.

**A** - Heavy spot.
**B** - Add balance weights here.
**C** - Centre line of spindle.

Dynamic balance is the equal distribution of weight on each side of the centre line so that when the wheel spins there is no tendency for side to side movement. A dynamically unbalanced wheel will cause wheel shimmy.

## Off Vehicle Balancing

Balance wheel assembly referring to equipment manufacturer's instructions.

It is essential that the wheel is located by the centre hole **NOT** the stud holes. To ensure positive wheel location the diameter of the locating collar on the machine shaft must be 112,80 to 112,85 mm (4.441 to 4.443 in). This diameter will ensure that the collar fits correctly within the centre hole of the wheel.

Where possible, always use the vehicle wheel retaining nuts to locate the wheel on the balancer, to avoid damaging the wheel. If this is not possible, the locating nuts must be of a similar pattern to the original wheel nuts. The use of conical type wheel nuts for this purpose may damage the surface on alloy wheels.

## Cleaning

Wash the aluminium wheels using a suitable wash and wax concentrate, correctly diluted and rinse with cold clear water. **DO NOT** use abrasives or aluminium wheel cleaners containing acid, as they will destroy the lacquer finish.

## Tyre changing

Use only tyre changing equipment to mount or demount tyres, following the equipment manufacturer's instructions. **DO NOT** use hand tools or tyre levers, as they may damage tyre beads or the wheel rim.

## Puncture repair

Remove punctured tyre from wheel and repair using a combination service plug and vulcanising patch. Always follow manufacturer's instructions when using a puncture repair kit.

Only punctures in tread area are reparable, **DO NOT** attempt to repair punctures in tyre shoulders or sidewalls.

Do not attempt to repair a tyre that has sustained the following: bulges or blisters, ply separation, broken or cracked beads, wear indicators visible and punctures larger than 6 mm diameter.

⚠ **CAUTION: Do not use tyre sealants that are injected through valve stem to repair punctured tyres, they may produce wheel corrosion and tyre imbalance.**

Aluminium wheel rim bead seats should be cleaned using a non-abrasive cleaner to remove the mounting lubricants and old rubber. Before mounting or demounting a tyre, bead area should be well lubricated with a suitable tyre lubricant.

## TYRE FITTING

Alloy wheels

1. Install a new valve assembly.
2. Ensure wheel and tyre is adequately lubricated.
3. Mount tyre in normal manner. Inflate tyre and at same time apply hand pressure to area around valve to aid seating over valve first.

⚠ **NOTE: Stop inflation immediately if tyre seats opposite valve, as this will result in valve being blocked by tyre beading, making further inflation impossible, and carry out following procedure.**

4. Deflate tyre, unseat and rotate it around the rim until valve is in line with that part of tyre which seated initially. This part of beading having seated over hump previously will automatically seat first when tyre is re-inflated.
5. Inflate tyre to seat beads correctly, finally inflate to correct pressure.

## WHEELS

### Remove

**WARNING: The parking brake acts on transmission, not rear wheels, and may not hold vehicle when jacking unless following procedure is used. If one front wheel and one rear wheel is raised no vehicle holding or braking effect is possible. Wheels MUST be chocked in all circumstances.**

**Apply parking brake, select a gear in main gearbox and engage low gear in transfer box.**

1. Loosen 5 wheel nuts.
2. Using a suitable trolley jack, raise vehicle and place on axle stands *See INTRODUCTION, Information, Jacking* .
3. Remove wheel nuts and carefully withdraw wheel over studs.

### Refit

4. Ensure that retaining studs and nuts are clean.
5. Alloy wheels: Lightly coat wheel mounting spigot face with a suitable anti-seize compound to minimise possibility of adhesion between wheel and spigot face.
6. Refit wheel taking care not to damage stud threads. (Do not apply oil).
7. Fit wheel nuts and turn by hand for at least three full threads before using any form of wheel wrench.

8. Tighten nuts as much as possible using a suitable wrench.
9. Lower vehicle and finally tighten nuts to correct torque sequence shown.
   Alloy wheels - *130 Nm (96 lbf/ft)*
   Steel wheels - *100 Nm (80 lbf/ft)*
   Heavy duty wheels - *170 Nm (125 lbf/ft)*

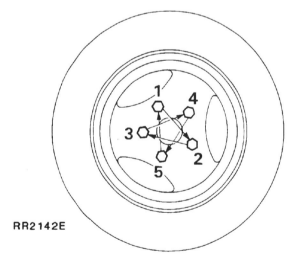

RR2142E

## WHEEL STUD

**Remove**

1. Remove wheel *See  Wheels* .

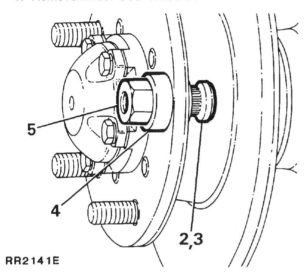

**RR2141E**

2. Drive stud out of driveshaft flange.

**Refit**

3. Position stud in flange.
4. Install a suitable spacer over stud.
5. Using a M16 x 1.5 nut, a slave wheel nut is suitable, pull stud into flange until shoulder of stud abuts flange.
6. Refit wheel. *See  Wheels*

# Notes

# 76 - CHASSIS AND BODY

## CONTENTS

Page

**DESCRIPTION AND OPERATION**

**REPAIR**

# 76 - CHASSIS AND BODY

## CONTENTS

Page

## CHASSIS AND BODY

### Chassis

The chassis on all Defender variants are of the box section, ladder type construction, manufactured from 2 mm (14swg) steel and treated with zinc phosphate, cathodic electro coated, followed by waxing in the rear crossmember.

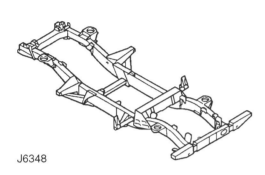

J6348

Outriggers and angled brackets welded to the chassis support suspension and axle components and are also used as body mounting points. A detachable box section crossmember, located between the two chassis longitudinals is fitted to facilitate main gearbox and tranfer box assembly removal.

Should chassis damage occur, a comprehensive range of components are available, including body support outriggers, cross members and radius arm mounting brackets. ALWAYS fit genuine parts that are fully guaranteed and to original equipment specification, fitted with Land Rover's BS 5135 welding standard.

J6349

### Body

All body panels, with the exception of the fascia bulkhead, are manufactured from aluminium alloy. Galvanized steel is used for the front wheel arches to give optimum protection. Most panels are also treated with zinc phosphate and cathodic electro coated with polyester surfacer, and are bolted to the welded chassis.

**LAND ROVER 90**

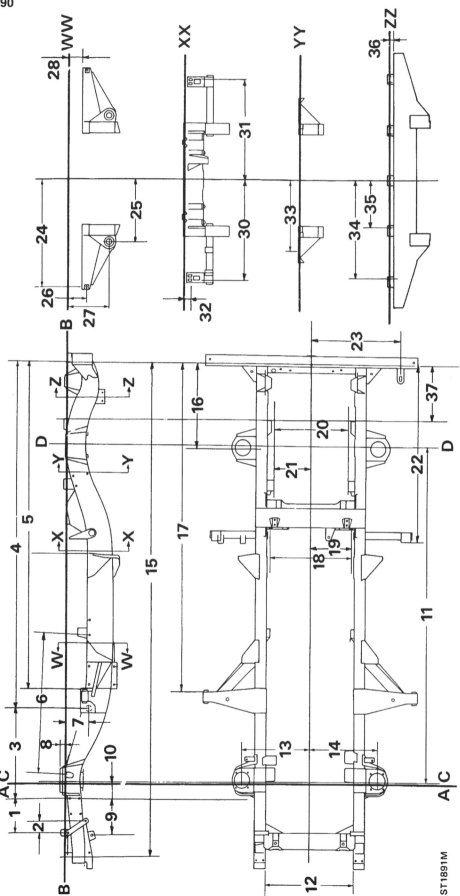

ST1891M

## LAND ROVER 90

## CHASSIS ALIGNMENT DIMENSIONS

**A - Front Datum**
**B - Chassis Datum**
**C - Front axle centre line**
**D - Rear axle centre line**

1. 239,0 - 236,5 mm
2. 82,0 - 79,5 mm
3. 633 mm
4. 2420,6 - 2418,6 mm
5. 2306,4 - 2305,4 mm
6. 981,2 - 978,7 mm
7. 182,7 mm
8. 41,5 - 37,0 mm
9. 252 - 250 mm

10. 110 mm
11. 2360mm - Wheelbase
12. 636 - 634 mm
13. 488 - 483 mm
14. 488 - 483 mm
15. 3431,1 - 3426,1 mm
16. 588,3 - 586,3 mm
17. 2313,8 - 2311,8 mm
18. 590,5 mm
19. 295,25 mm
20. 519,60 - 517,00 mm
21. 259,80 - 258,50 mm
22. 1242,6 - 1240,6 mm
23. 642,5 - 639,5 mm

24. 750,9 mm
25. 439,5 - 436,5 mm
26. 136,5 mm
27. 299,5 - 295,5 mm
28. 103 - 100 mm
29. 131,5 - 126,5 mm
30. 705,5 - 704,5 mm
31. 705,5 - 704,5 mm
32. 42,2 - 40,2 mm
33. 491 - 486 mm
34. 594,2 - 593,4 mm
35. 283,0 - 282,2 mm
36. 32,25 - 31,25 mm
37. 397 - 395 mm

**LAND ROVER 110**

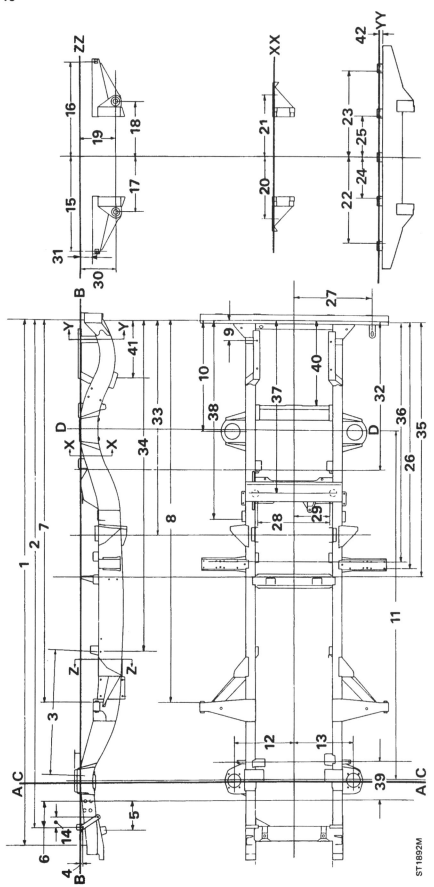

ST 1892M

**LAND ROVER 110**

**CHASSIS ALIGNMENT DIMENSIONS**

**A - Front Datum**
**B - Chassis Datum**
**C - Front axle centre line**
**D - Rear axle centre line**

| | | |
|---|---|---|
| **1.** 4148 - 4143 mm | **13.** 488 - 483 mm | **29.** 290,5 mm |
| **2.** 4009,5 - 4005 mm | **14.** 82 - 79,5 mm | **30.** 295,5 mm |
| **3.** 978,7 - 981,2 mm | **15.** 750,9 mm | **31.** 299,5 - 295,5 mm |
| **4.** 22 - 20 mm | **16.** 750,9 mm | **32.** 103 - 100 mm |
| **5.** 252 - 250 mm | **17.** 439,5 - 436,5 mm | **33.** 1177,5 - 1175,5 mm |
| **6.** 239 - 236,5 mm | **18.** 439,5 - 436,5 mm | **34.** 1692,5 - 1689,5 mm |
| **7.** 3023,3 - 3022,3 mm | **19.** 299,5 - 295,5 mm | **35.** 2610 - 2606 mm |
| **8.** 3030,7 - 3028,7 mm | **20.** 500 - 495 mm | **36.** 2040,5 - 2037,5 mm |
| **9.** 155 - 153 mm | **21.** 500 - 495 mm | **37.** 1912,5 - 1909,5 mm |
| **10.** 871,2 - 869,2 mm | **22.** 594,2 - 593,4 mm | **38.** 1359 - 1357 mm |
| **11.** 2794 mm - Wheelbase | **23.** 594,2 - 593,4 mm | **39.** 1573 - 1571 mm |
| **12.** 488 - 483 mm | **24.** 283 - 282,2 mm | **40.** 270 - 268 mm |
| | **25.** 283 - 282,2 mm | **41.** 665,5 - 663,5 mm |
| | **26.** 1970 - 1968 mm | **42.** 440 - 438 mm |
| | **27.** 642,9 - 639,5 mm | **43.** 32,25 - 31,25 mm |
| | **28.** 750,9 mm | |

**LAND ROVER 130**

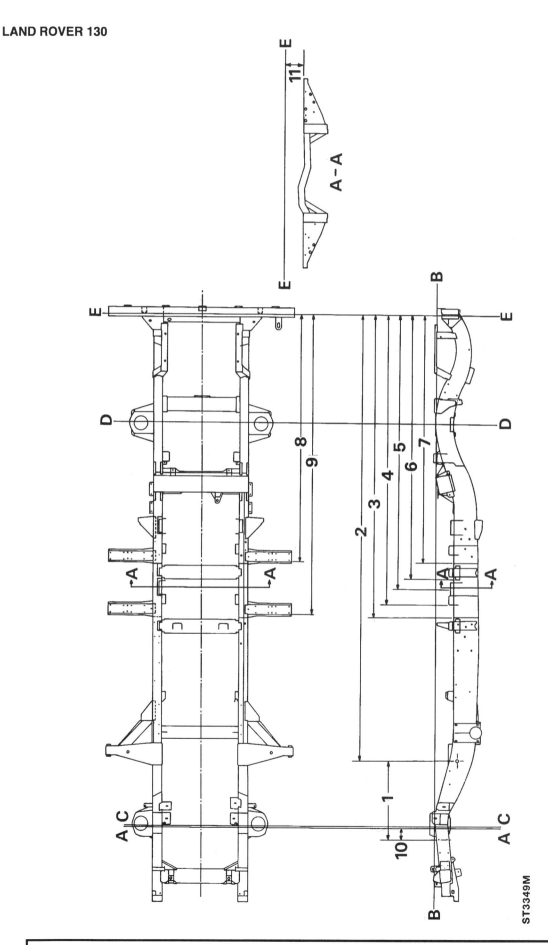

ST3349M

## LAND ROVER 130

### CHASSIS ALIGNMENT DIMENSIONS

A - Front Datum
B - Chassis Datum
C - Front axle centre line
D - Rear axle centre line
E - Chassis Datum, section A - A

1. 633,0 mm reference only
2. 3569,3 - 3567,3 mm
3. 2421,8 - 2419,8 mm
4. 2317,5 - 2314,5 mm
5. 2188,3 - 2185,3 mm
6. 2119,5 - 2117,3 mm

7. 1990 - 1988 mm
8. 1970 - 1968 mm
9. 2401,8 - 2399,8 mm
10. 110,0 mm reference
11. 149,7 - 146,7 mm reference dimension

 NOTE: The above dimensions are for the Land Rover 130 chassis frame. For additional measurements, refer to the Land Rover 110 chassis frame drawing and aligment dimensions.

## CHASSIS FRAME ALIGNMENT

With the vehicle assembled, a check for chassis squareness can be made as follows:

1. Place the vehicle on a level floor.
2. Mark measuring points at approximately the locations shown in LR4412M ensuring that the marks are exactly opposite on each side of the chassis frame.

3. Hold a plumb line against each of the measuring points in turn and mark the floor directly beneath the plumb-bob.
4. Move the vehicle and measure diagonally between the marks made on the floor, if the chassis is square the diagonals between the related measuring points should agree within 9,50 mm.
5. Chassis frame dimensional checks can be made, with the vehicle upper structure removed, referring to the applicable illustration and associated key.

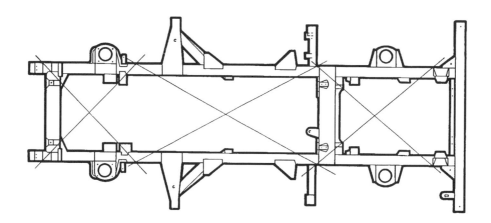

LAND ROVER 90

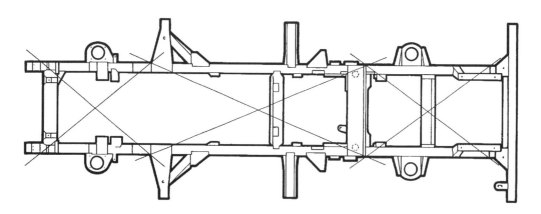

LAND ROVER 110

LR4412M

**DOORS**

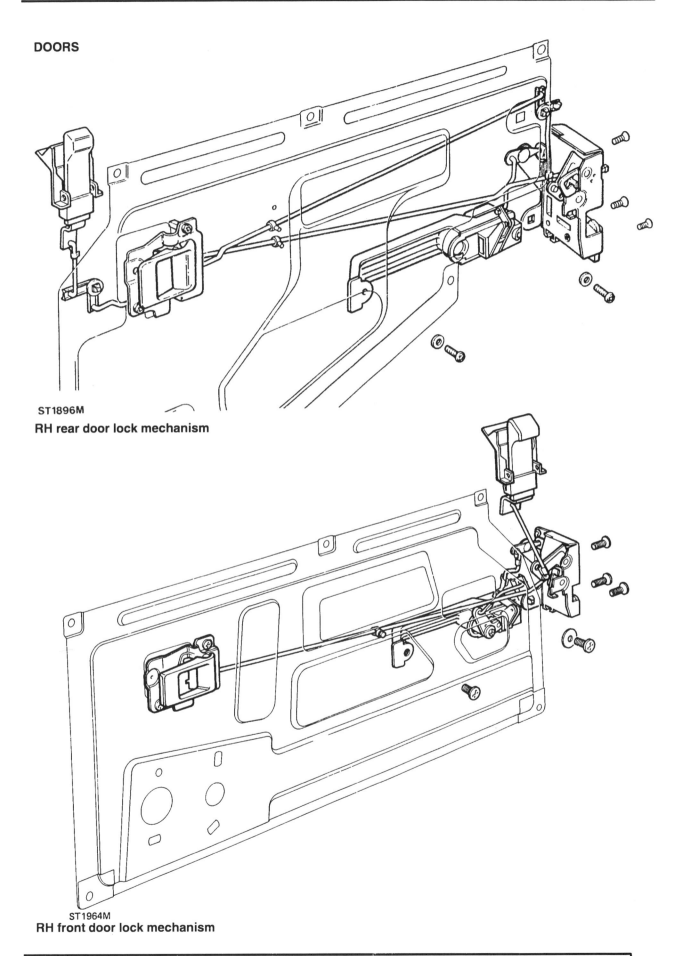

ST1896M

**RH rear door lock mechanism**

ST1964M

**RH front door lock mechanism**

## DOOR TRIM CASING

**Service repair no - 76.34.01 - Front doors**
**Service repair no - 76.34.04 - Rear doors**

**Remove**

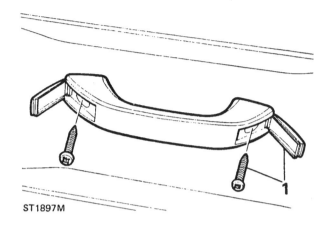

ST1897M

1. Prise open finisher caps, remove 2 screws, and detach door pull.

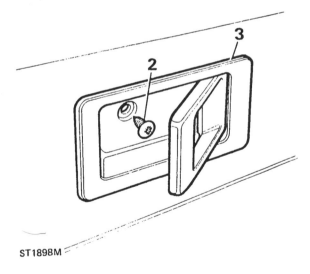

ST1898M

2. Remove single screw behind remote control lever.
3. Prise off remote control lever bezel.
4. Prise off door locking button bezel.

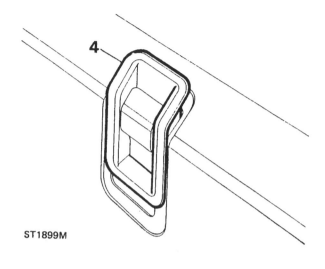

ST1899M

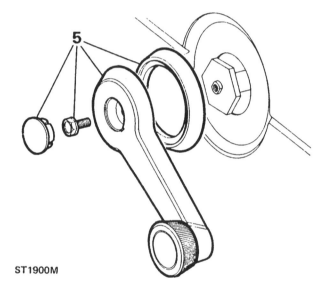

ST1900M

5. Prise out window regulator handle centre finisher, remove retaining screw, and withdraw handle and bezel.
6. Using a screwdriver to release trim fasteners, carefully ease trim casing from door.

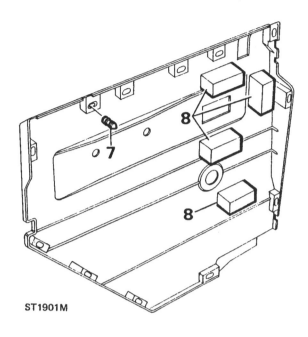

ST1901M

### Refit

7. Remove any trim fasteners held in door panel. Refit or insert new clips to trim panel.
8. Ensure that anti-vibration pads are in position and offer-up trim casing to door. Align fasteners with holes in door and firmly push trim into position.
9. Fit bezels to locking button and remote control lever.
10. Fit single screw behind remote control lever.
11. Fit door pull and secure with 2 screws and finisher caps.
12. Fit window regulator handle and retain with single screw and finisher.

### WINDOW REGULATOR - REAR SIDE DOOR

**Service repair no - 76.31.45**

#### Remove

1. Remove door trim casing *See Door trim casing.*
2. Remove plastic sheet.
3. Temporarily fit handle, wind window up to its fullest extent and support glass with a length of timber, to prevent it falling when removing regulator.

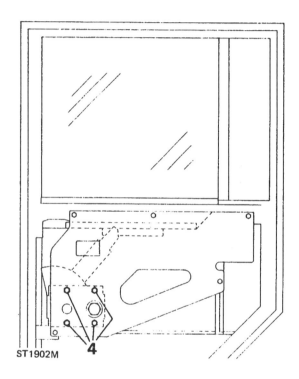

ST1902M

4. Remove 4 screws retaining regulator to mounting panel and withdraw regulator whilst sliding lifting arm button from lifting channel. To assist this operation, remove timber and lower glass.

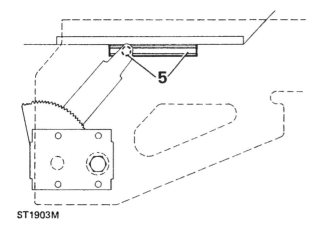

ST1903M

## Refit

5. Insert lifting arm button into lifting channel.
6. Position regulator so that fixing holes line-up with holes in mounting panel.
7. Secure with 4 screws and tighten evenly.
8. Temporarily fit handle and check that glass can be raised and lowered smoothly without tight spots.
9. Fit plastic sheet.
10. Fit door trim **See Door trim casing.**

## EXTERIOR HANDLE - REAR SIDE DOOR

**Service repair no - 76.58.02**

### Remove

1. Remove door trim casing **See Door trim casing.**
2. Peel back sufficient of plastic sheet to gain access to handle mechanism.

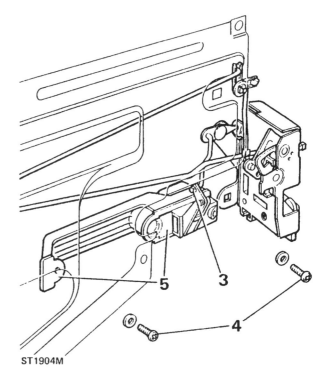

ST1904M

3. Disconnect actuating rod from handle operating lever.
4. Remove 2 screws and withdraw handle and bezels.

### Refit

5. Fit handle to door ensuring that both bezels are in position - flat faces towards door and secure with 2 screws.
6. Connect actuating rod to handle operating lever and secure with spring clip.
7. Re-seal plastic sheet.
8. Fit door trim casing **See Door trim casing.**

## SILL LOCKING BUTTON - REAR SIDE DOOR

**Service repair no - 76.37.30**

**Remove**

1. Remove door trim casing **See Door trim casing.**
2. Peel back sufficient of plastic sheet to reveal mechanism.

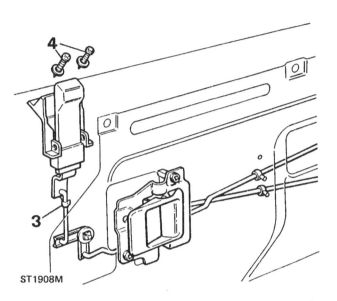

ST1908M

3. Release spring clip securing button to operating rod and withdraw rod from button.
4. Remove 2 screws securing button to door panel and remove button.

**Refit**

5. Secure locking button assembly to door panel with 2 screws.
6. Fit operating rod to button assembly and secure with spring clip.
7. Re-seal plastic sheet and fit door trim casing **See Door trim casing.**

## REMOTE CONTROL LEVER - REAR SIDE DOOR

**Service repair no - 76.37.32**

**Remove**

1. Remove door trim casing **See Door trim casing.**
2. Peel-back sufficient of plastic sheet to gain access to remote lever.

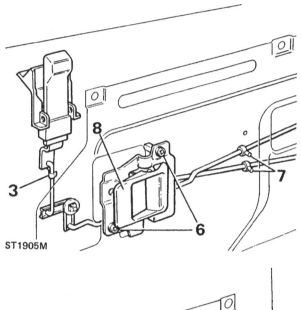

ST1905M

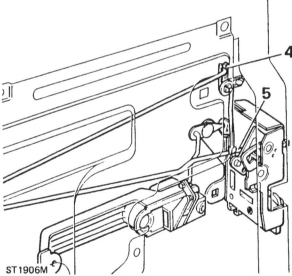

ST1906M

3. Remove spring clip and disconnect control rod from locking button.
4. Release spring clip and disconnect short locking button control rod from latch mechanism.
5. Disconnect long remote control rod from latch assembly.

6. Remove 2 screws securing remote control lever to mounting panel.
7. Release control rods from plastic retaining clips located in mounting panel.
8. Withdraw remote control lever and rods from door.

**Refit**

9. Fit plastic retaining clips to rod assembly into position and secure with 2 screws.
10. Connect control rods to latch assembly and secure with clips.
11. Fit plastic retaining rod clips to mounting panel.
12. Connect control rod to locking button and secure with clip.
13. Re-seal plastic sheet and fit door trim casing *See Door trim casing.*

## DOOR LATCH - REAR SIDE DOOR

**Service repair no - 76.37.13.**

**Remove**

1. Remove door trim casing *See Door trim casing.*
2. Peel-back sufficient of plastic sheet to reveal latch.

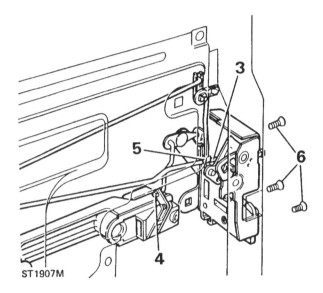

ST1907M

3. Release remote control lever rod from latch assembly.
4. Disconnect door outer handle control rod from latch assembly.
5. Disconnect door locking button remote control rod from latch mechanism.
6. Remove 3 retaining screws and withdraw latch assembly from door.

**Refit**

7. Fit latch assembly to door and secure with 3 screws, noting that uppermost screw is longer.
8. Connect remote control levers to latch mechanism reversing instructions 3, 4 and 5.
9. Re-seal plastic sheet and fit door trim casing *See Door trim casing.*

## DOOR GLASS - REAR SIDE DOOR

**Service repair no - 76.31.02**

**Remove**

1. Disconnect door check rod from door post.
2. Remove door trim casing *See Door trim casing.*
3. Remove plastic sheet.
4. Remove window regulator assembly *See Window regulator - rear side door.*
5. Disconnect and remove door sill locking button *See Sill locking button.*

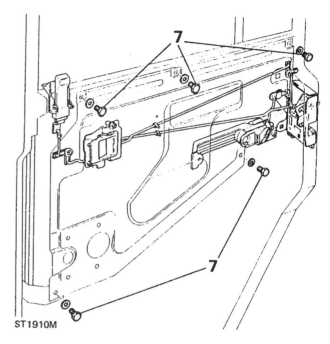

ST1910M

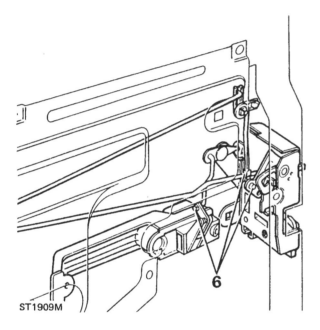

ST1909M

6. Disconnect control rods from latch 'and door outer handle mechanism.
7. Remove 4 screws retaining mounting panel to door and remove panel, complete with rods and control lever.
8. Remove single self tapping screw to remove water channel.
9. Remove 2 screws and remove door check torsion bar.
10. Remove door check rod by bending back end stop to enable rod to be withdrawn.

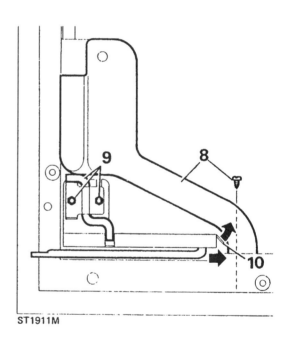

ST1911M

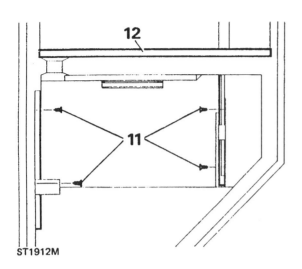

ST1912M

11. Remove 2 self-tapping screws from each side and remove glass lower channels.
12. Remove inner and outer weather strips from door sill.

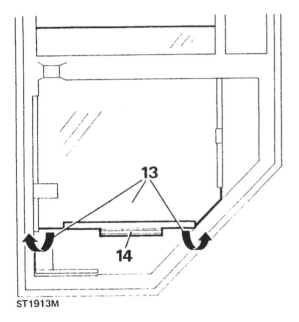

ST1913M

13. Lower glass down to bottom of door, lift glass over lower edge and withdraw from door.
14. Remove lift channel from glass, if necessary.

**Refit**

15. Fit lift channel to new glass, if necessary.
16. Insert glass into lower channels and carefully push glass up to top of frame.
17. Secure lower channels with 4 self-tapping screws. Ensure that screw heads are screwed down firmly below bottom of channels to prevent damage to glass.
18. Fit door check rod and bend end stop back to closed position.
19. Fit check stop torsion bar and secure with 2 nuts and bolts.
20. Fit water channel and secure with single self-tapping screw.
21. Fit mounting panel complete with rods and remote control lever.
22. Connect control rods to latch and door outer handle mechanism.
23. Fit door sill locking button and connect control rod *See* *Sill locking button.*
24. Fit window regulator *See* *Window regulator.*
25. Fit door inner and outer sill wear strips.
26. Fit and re-seal plastic sheet.
27. Fit door trim casing *See* *Door trim casing.*
28. Connect door check rod to door post.

## MOUNTING PANEL - FRONT DOOR

**Service repair no - 76.11.28**

**Remove**

1. Remove door trim casing *See Door trim casing* and plastic sheet.

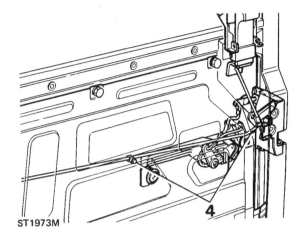

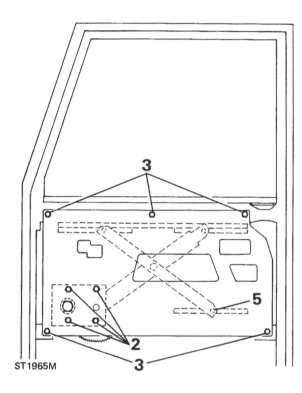

ST1965M

2. Remove 4 screws securing window regulator to mounting panel.
3. Remove 5 screws securing mounting panel to door frame.
4. Release remote control lever rod from latch mechanism and from plastic clip in mounting panel.
5. Slide window regulator arm from mounting panel channel and remove panel with remote control lever and rod.

**Refit**

6. Engage window regulator arm in mounting panel channel.
7. Connect remote control rod to latch mechanism and secure with clip.
8. Fit mounting panel and retain with 5 screws.
9. Secure window regulator to mounting panel with 4 screws.
10. Raise and lower window to check for free movement.
11. Fit plastic sheet, and door trim casing *See Door trim casing.*

## SILL LOCKING BUTTON - FRONT DOOR

**Service repair no - 76.37.29**

**Remove**

1. Remove door trim casing *See Door trim casing.*
2. Peel back sufficient of plastic sheet to expose mechanism.

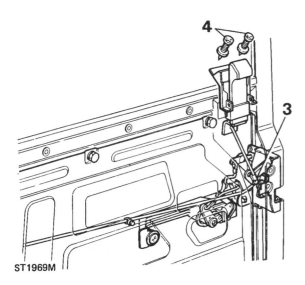

ST1969M

3. Release spring clip and disconnect operating rod from latch mechanism.
4. Remove 2 screws and withdraw locking button assembly.

**Refit**

5. Secure locking button assembly to door with 2 screws.
6. Connect operating rod to latch mechanism and secure with spring clip.
7. Re-seal plastic sheet and fit door trim casing *See Door trim casing.*

## WINDOW REGULATOR - FRONT DOOR

**Service repair no - 76.31.45**

**Remove**

1. Remove door trim casing *See Door trim casing.*
2. Remove plastic sheet.
3. Temporarily fit handle, position window half open and support with a length of timber.

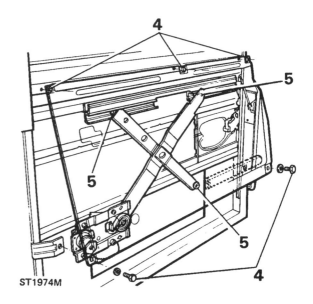

ST1974M

4. Remove 2 lower screws securing mounting panel to door and slacken 3 upper screws.
5. Remove 4 screws retaining window regulator to mounting panel and slide operating arms from channels attached to glass and mounting panel and remove regulator.

**Refit**

6. Insert regulator operating arms into channels.
7. Fit and tighten mounting panel lower screws and tighten upper screws.
8. Position holes in regulator to line-up with holes in mounting panel and secure with 4 screws.
9. Temporarily fit regulator handle and check that glass can be raised and lowered without tight spots.
10. Secure plastic sheet.
11. Fit door trim casing *See Door trim casing.*

## REMOTE CONTROL LEVER - FRONT DOOR

**Service repair no - 76.37.31**

**Remove**

1. Remove door trim casing *See Door trim casing.*
2. Peel back sufficient of plastic sheet to gain access to remote lever.

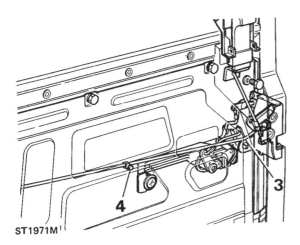

ST1971M

3. Release spring clip and disconnect control rod from latch mechanism.
4. Release control rod from plastic clip in mounting panel.

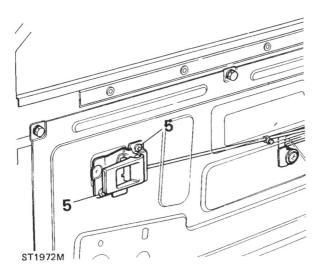

ST1972M

5. Remove 2 screws securing remote control lever to mounting panel and withdraw lever and control rod.

**Refit**

6. Feed control rod into position and loosely secure lever to mounting panel with 2 screws.
7. Connect control rod to latch mechanism and secure with spring clip.
8. Tighten control lever retaining screws.
9. Secure control rod to plastic clip in mounting panel.
10. Secure plastic sheet.
11. Fit door trim casing *See Door trim casing.*

## EXTERIOR HANDLE - FRONT DOOR

**Service repair no - 76.58.01**

### Remove

1. Remove door trim casing *See Door trim casing.*
2. Remove mounting panel *See Mounting panel - front door* and support glass with timber.

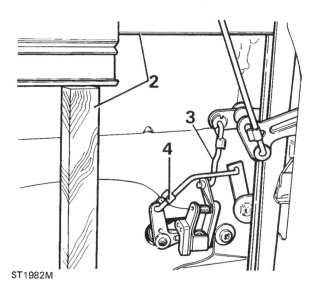

ST1982M

3. Disconnect operating rod from handle mechanism.
4. Disconnect rod from locking barrel lever.

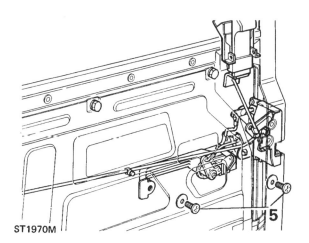

ST1970M

5. Remove 2 screws and withdraw handle assembly.

### Refit

6. Fit handle to door ensuring that two bezels are in position - flat faces towards door, and secure with 2 screws.
7. Connect rod to handle operating lever and secure with spring clip.
8. Connect rod to locking barrel lever and retain with spring clip.
9. Fit mounting panel *See Mounting panel - front door.*

## LATCH ASSEMBLY - FRONT DOOR

Service repair no - 76.37.12

**Remove**

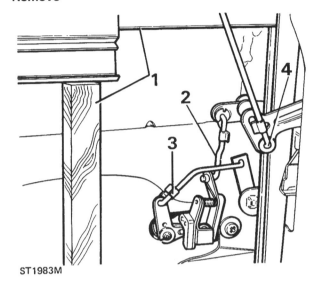

ST1983M

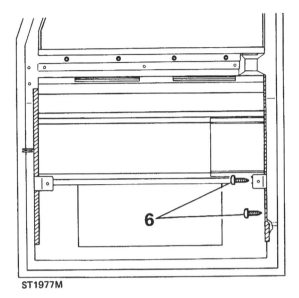

ST1977M

1. Remove mounting panel *See Mounting panel* and support glass with timber.
2. Disconnect control rod from handle operating lever.
3. Disconnect control rod from locking lever on handle.
4. Disconnect locking button control rod from latch mechanism.
5. Remove 2 screws and remove handle assembly from door.
6. Remove 2 self-tapping screws retaining lower end of window glass runner.
7. Remove 3 screws securing latch assembly to door.
8. Whilst taking care not to damage runner, ease runner away from latch and manoeuvre latch assembly from door.

**Refit**

9. Carefully ease window runner away, sufficiently to enable latch to be located into position.
10. Secure latch to door with 3 screws.
11. Secure window runner with 2 screws ensuring that packing strip is in position and that screw heads are below bottom of runner to prevent damage to glass.

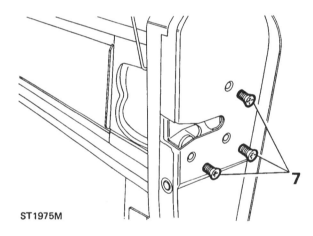

ST1975M

12. Fit handle with 2 screws, ensuring that bezels are in position.
13. Connect control rod to handle operating lever and secure with spring clip.
14. Connect control rod to locking lever and retain with spring clip.
15. Connect locking button control rod to latch lever and secure with spring clip.
16. Fit mounting panel *See Mounting panel.*

## DOOR GLASS - FRONT DOOR

**Service repair no - 76.31.01**

**Remove**

1. Remove mounting panel *See Mounting panel - front door.*
2. Remove window regulator.
3. Push glass up to top of its travel and support with a suitable length of timber.

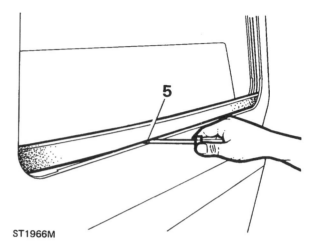

ST1966M

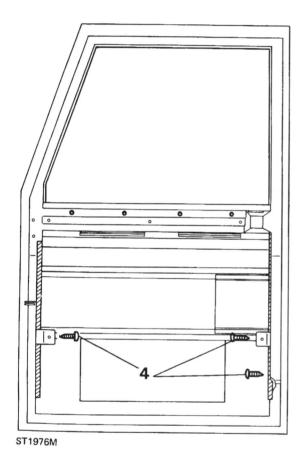

ST1976M

4. Remove 2 self tapping screws securing window glass runner on latch side of door and single screw from hinge side.

5. Taking care not to damage paint, prise exterior waist weather strip from door.
6. Remove timber support and lower glass to bottom of door.

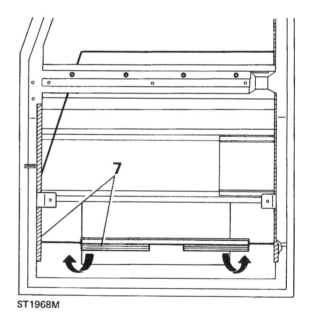

ST1968M

7. Ease runner from glass at hinge side of door, lift glass over bottom edge of door and withdraw.

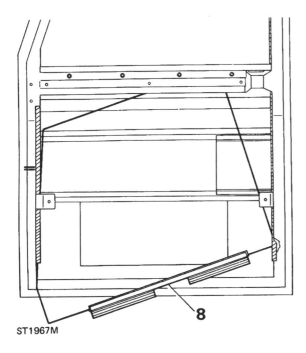

ST1967M

**Refit**

8. Insert glass into runners at an angle as illustrated.
9. Whilst lifting glass, position it squarely in runners, raise to top of travel and insert timber support.
10. Secure hinge side runner with single screw ensuring that packing strip is in position.
11. Locate packing strip and secure opposite runner with 2 screws. Ensure that all 3 screw heads are well below bottom of runners to prevent damage to glass.
12. Locate regulator in window lift channels.
13. Fit mounting panel *See Mounting panel - front door.*

**LOCKING BARREL - FRONT DOOR**

**Service repair no - 76.37.39**

**Remove**

1. Remove door trim casing *See Door trim casing - front door* and plastic sheet.
2. Remove mounting panel *See Mounting panel - front panel.*

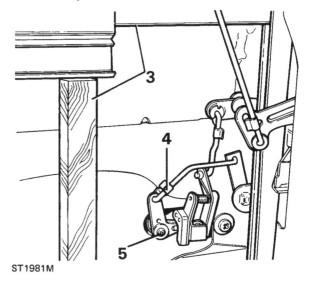

ST1981M

3. Raise and support glass to gain access to latch mechanism.
4. Release spring clip and disconnect rod from lock operating lever.
5. Remove single screw and withdraw lock lever assembly.

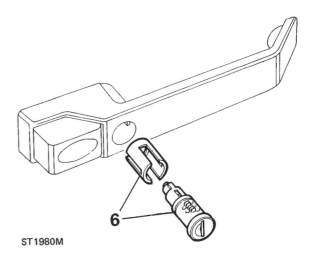

ST1980M

6. Withdraw lock barrel from exterior door handle complete with locking sleeve.

**7.** To remove barrel from plastic retaining sleeve, depess spring loaded button and withdraw sleeve.

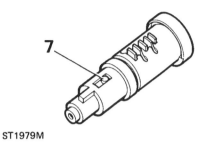

ST1979M

**Refit**

 **NOTE: If a new barrel is being fitted, check that number on barrel coincides with number on accompanying key.**

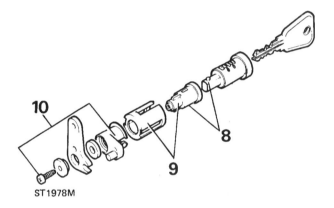

ST1978M

**8.** Push plastic retaining sleeve over barrel until spring loaded peg locks it into position.
**9.** Fit barrel and plastic sleeve assembly to locking sleeve and insert into exterior handle reversing instruction 6.
**10.** Assemble lock lever components as illustrated and from inside of door panel, fit them to barrel assembly with single screw.
**11.** Connect operating rod to lock lever and secure with spring clip, reversing instruction 4.
**12.** Fit mounting panel *See Mounting panel - front door.*

## DOOR STRIKER - ADJUST

**Service repair no - 76.37.23 - front door**
**Service repair no - 76.37.24 - rear door, 110/130**

**Adjust**

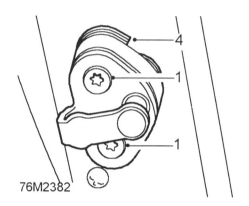

76M2382

**1.** Loosen 2 Torq bolts securing striker to body.
**2.** Adjust alignment of striker vertically and horizontally, lightly tighten bolts.
**3.** Close door, check for correct latching with door lock and for centering on striker.
**4.** Add or remove packing shims as necessary behind striker and fully tighten bolts.
**5.** Carry out further adjustment as necessary. If full adjustment is not achieved carry out the following:
**6.** Remove striker and nut plate.
**7.** Elongate striker bolt holes in 'B' or 'C' post in direction required.
**8.** Refit striker and adjust as necessary.

## REAR SEAT CUSHION - 90

**Service repair no - 78.10.18/99**

**Remove**

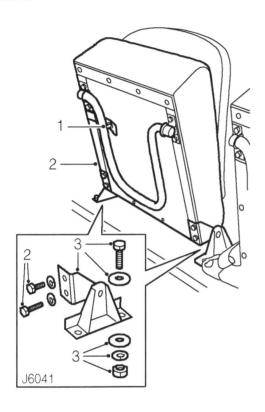

J6041

1. Release seat cushion stowage strap.
2. Remove 4 bolts and spring washers and lift seat cushion from pivot brackets.
3. Remove 4 bolts, plain washers, spring washers and nuts. Detach both pivot brackets from wheel arch.

**Refit**

4. Secure pivot brackets to wheel arch and tighten bolts to *10 Nm (7 lbf/ft).*
5. Position seat cushion in pivot brackets and secure with 4 bolts and spring washers.
6. Fit stowage strap.

## REAR SEAT SQUAB - 90

**Service repair no - 78.10.58/99**

**Remove**

1. Release seat cushion stowage strap and lower seat cushion.

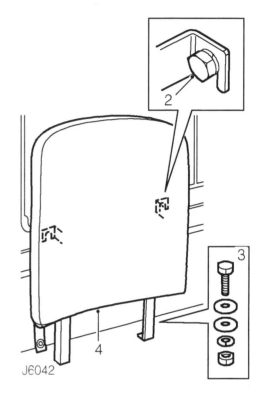

J6042

2. Slacken 2 bolts securing seat squab brackets to body side.
3. Remove 2 bolts, plain washers, spring washers and nuts securing seat squab to wheel arch.
4. Lift seat squab and release brackets from retaining bolts.

**Refit**

5. Lower seat squab brackets over retaining bolts, tighten bolts to *10 Nm (7 lbf/ft).*
6. Secure seat squab to wheel arch, tighten bolts to *10 Nm (7 lbf/ft).*
7. Raise seat cushion and fit stowage strap.

## REAR BENCH SEAT

**Service repair no - 78.10.57/99**

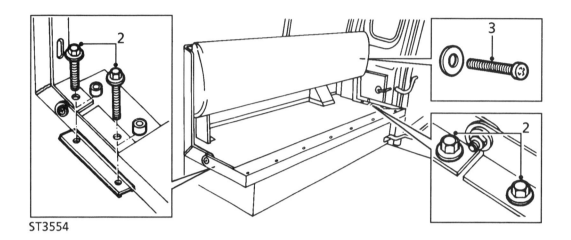

ST3554

### Remove

1. Remove rear bench seat cushion.
2. Remove 4 bolts securing seat frame to body and collect spacers and brackets containing captive nuts.
3. Remove screw securing rear end of squab to body.
4. Remove rear bench seat.

### Refit

5. Position rear bench seat to body.
6. Position bracket and spacers, and loosely fit bolts securing front end of cushion frame to body.
7. Loosely fit bolts securing rear end of cushion frame to body while second person holds bracket in position from under vehicle.
8. Fit screw securing squab to body.Tighten to *10 Nm (7 lbf/ft).*
9. Tighten cushion frame to body bolts to *10 Nm (7 lbf/ft).*
10. Fit bench seatcushion.

## FRONT SEAT BELTS

**Service repair no - 76.73.13**

**Remove**

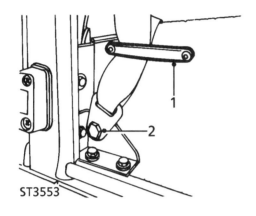

ST3553

1. Remove plastic seat belt guide from side of front seat base.
2. Remove seat belt lower anchorage bolt.

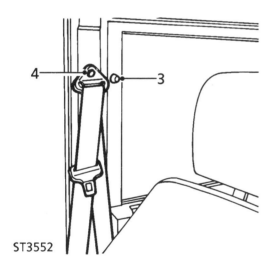

ST3552

3. Remove plastic cap from upper belt guide bolt.
4. Remove bolt securing belt guide to 'B' post.

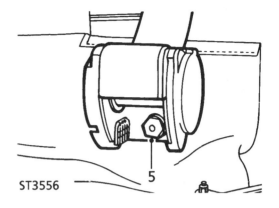

ST3556

5. Move rear carpet aside and remove bolt securing inertia reel to base of 'B' post.

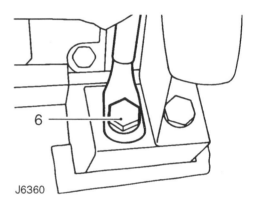

J6360

6. Remove seat buckle stalk anchorage bolt at inside rear of front seat.

**Refit**

 **NOTE: Tighten all seat belt anchorage bolts to *32 Nm (24 lbf/ft)*.**

7. Fit seat buckle stalk to mounting at rear of front seat.
8. Position inertia reel to base of 'B' post and secure with bolt.
9. Reposition carpet.
10. Fit upper guide to 'B' post.
11. Fit plastic cap to guide bolt.
12. Fit seat belt to seat base lower anchorage bracket.
13. Fit plastic seat belt guide to seat base.

## REAR SEAT BELTS - 90/110 STATION WAGON, INWARD FACING SEATS

**Service repair no - 76.73.18**

**Remove**

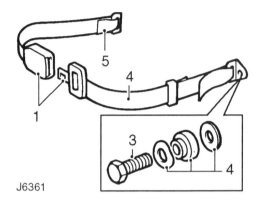

J6361

1. Release belt straps from buckles.
2. Release stowage straps and lower both seat cushions.
3. Unscrew bolt securing lap strap to body mounting.
4. Remove lap strap, wavy washer, spacer and plain washer.
5. Repeat operation for buckle strap.

**Refit**

6. Secure lap strap and buckle straps to body. Tighten bolts to *32 Nm (24 lbf/ft).*
7. If required, secure seat cushions and belts in stowed position.

## REAR SEAT BELTS - 110

**Service repair no - 76.73.18**

**Remove**

1. Remove rear inward facing seats *See Rear seat squab or Rear bench seat.*
2. Remove side trim panel *See Side trim panel.*

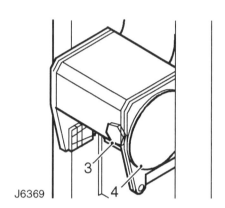

J6369

3. Remove bolt securing seat belt inertia reel to 'C' post.
4. Remove seat belt assembly.

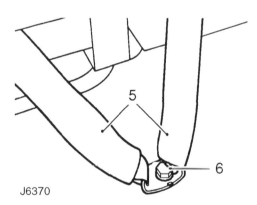

J6370

5. Pull seat belt straps between seat cushion and squab into rear of vehicle.
6. Remove finisher cap and bolt securing seat belt anchorage to floor.
7. Remove seat belt assembly.

**Refit**

8. Secure seat belt straps to floor mounting. Tighten bolt to *32 Nm (24 lbf/ft)* and fit finisher cap.
9. Feed belt straps between seat cushion and squab.
10. Fit inertia reel to 'C' post. Tighten bolt to *32 Nm (24 lbf/ft).*
11. Fit side trim panel *See Side trim panel* .
12. Fit rear inward facing seats *See Rear seat squab - 90* or *See Rear bench seat* .

## SIDE TRIM PANEL - 90 STATION WAGON

**Service repair no - 76.13.70**

**Remove**

1. Remove rear seat squabs *See Rear seat squab* .
2. Remove rear end trim panel *See Rear end trim panel* .

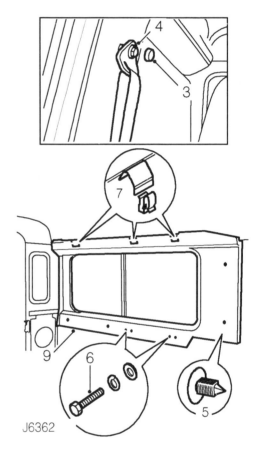

J6362

3. Prise cap from front seat belt upper guide retaining bolt.
4. Unscrew retaining bolt and remove seat belt from 'B' post.
5. Carefully prise trim stud from 'B' post.
6. Remove 4 bolts securing side trim panel to body side.
7. Release top edge of side trim panel by striking upwards with the hand to disengage 3 spring clips.
8. Lift trim panel from window surround and remove from vehicle.

**Refit**

9. Fit new spring clips to the 3 brackets on top edge of side trim panel.
10. Align trim panel, ensuring it is correctly positioned around side window.
11. Locate trim panel spring clips on inner cant rail and press firmly down to secure top edge of trim panel.
12. Align bosses of trim panel with body side fixing holes and secure with 4 bolts and washers. Do not fully tighten at this stage.
13. Fit trim stud to secure bottom edge of trim panel to 'B' post.
14. Secure seat belt guide to 'B' post, tighten bolt to *32 Nm (24 lbf/ft)* and fit cap.
15. Fit rear end trim panel *See Rear end trim panel* .
16. Fit rear seat squab *See Rear seat squab* .

## SIDE TRIM PANEL - 110 STATION WAGON

**Service repair no - 76.13.70**

**Remove**

1. Remove rear inward facing seats *See Rear seat squab - 90* , or *See Rear bench seat* .
2. Remove rear end trim panel *See Rear end trim panel* .

J6366

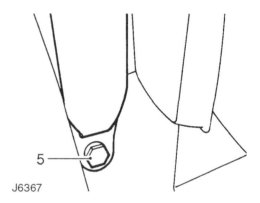

J6367

3. Prise finisher cap from rear seat belt upper guide bracket retaining bolt.
4. Unscrew bolt and remove guide bracket from 'C' post.
5. Remove bolt securing seat belt to wheel arch mounting.
6. Prise trim panel cap fastener from 'C' post.
7. Remove seat belt aperture finisher from side trim panel.
8. Remove screw and release seat belt clip from 'C' post.

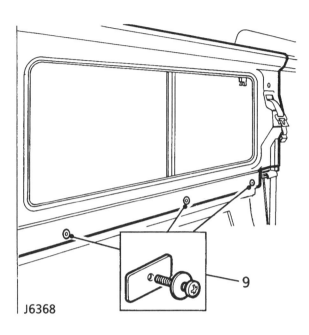

J6368

9. Remove fixings securing bottom edge of trim panel to body side.
10. Release top edge of trim panel by striking upwards with the hand to disengage 3 spring clips.
11. Lift trim panel from window surround and feed seat belt through panel aperture.
12. Remove trim panel from vehicle.

**Refit**

13. Fit new spring clips to the 3 brackets on top edge of side trim panel.
14. Feed seat belt through aperture in trim panel and fit finisher.
15. Align trim panel, ensuring it is correctly positioned around side window.
16. Locate trim panel spring clips on inner cant rail and press firmly down to secure top edge of trim panel.
17. Align bosses of trim panel with body side fixing holes and secure with bolts or screws. If individual type seats are fitted do not fully tighten fixings at this stage.
18. Fit seat belt clip to 'C' post.
19. Fit trim panel cap fastener to 'C' post.
20. Fit seat belt to wheel arch. Tighten bolt to **32 Nm (24 lbf/ft)**.
21. Fit seat belt guide bracket to 'C' post. Tighten bolt to **32 Nm (24 lbf/ft)** and fit finisher cap.
22. Fit rear end trim panel **See Rear end trim panel.**
23. Fit inward facing seats **See Rear seat squab, or Rear bench seat.**

## REAR END TRIM PANEL - 90/110 STATION WAGON

**Service repair no - 76.13.71**

**Remove**

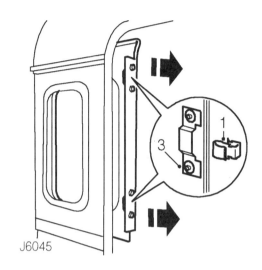

J6045

1. Pull edge of rear end trim panel firmly to release 2 spring retaining clips from vertical rail at door aperture.
2. Remove rear end trim panel.

**Refit**

3. Fit new spring clips to the two brackets on side of trim panel.
4. Position outboard edge of trim panel in corner to abut side trim panel and locate spring clips on vertical rail.
5. Press edge of trim panel firmly to secure in position.

## CUBBY BOX - 90/110 STATION WAGON

**Service repair no - 76.25.04**

**Remove**

1. Remove radio/cassette player, if fitted.

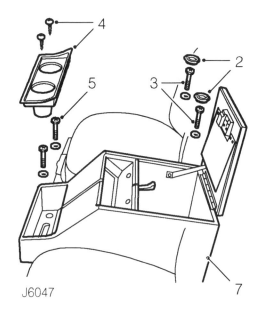

J6047

2. Open cubby box lid and remove two caps concealing fixing bolts.
3. Remove fixing bolts and washers.
4. Remove 2 screws and lift cup holder from cubby box.
5. Unscrew 2 bolts securing front of cubby box to floor mounting.
6. Lift cubby box and, if applicable, release radio/cassette player leads.
7. If fitted, disconnect multi-plug from EGR control unit, located on base of cubby box.
8. Remove cubby box.

**Refit**

9. Position cubby box to mounting and, if applicable, insert radio/ cassette player leads.
10. Secure front of cubby box to floor and fit cup holder.
11. Open cubby box lid, secure in position, and fit bolt caps.
12. Fit radio/cassette player, if fitted.

## REAR GRAB HANDLE - 90/110 STATION WAGON

**Service repair no - 76.58.35**

**Remove**

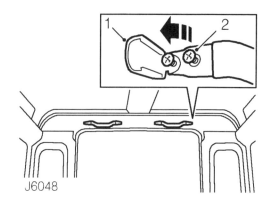

J6048

1. Carefully prise top and bottom edges of finisher caps from grab handle and then hinge outwards to gain access to fixing screws.
2. Remove 4 fixing screws and detach grab handle from rear end trim panel.

**Refit**

3. Position grab handle on rear end trim panel and secure with 4 fixing screws.
4. Press finisher caps over screws.

## REAR END LINING - 90/110 STATION WAGON

**Service repair no - 76.64.12**

**Remove**

1. Remove rear end trim panel *See Rear end trim panel.*
2. Remove rear grab handles *See Rear grab handle.*

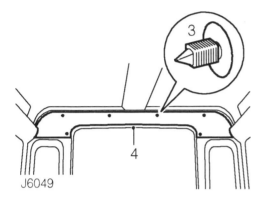

3. Carefully prise out 6 trim studs securing rear end lining to mounting brackets.
4. Remove rear end lining.

**Refit**

5. Position rear end lining on mounting brackets and secure with 6 trim studs.
6. Fit rear grab handles *See rear grab handle.*
7. Fit rear end trim panel *See rear end trim.*

## FRONT HEADLINING - 90 STATION WAGON

**Service repair no - 76.64.10**

**Remove**

1. Remove sun roof headlining finisher.
2. Remove sun visors *See Sun visors.*
3. Remove interior lamp *See ELECTRICAL, Repair, Interior lamp.*
4. Remove interior mirror and mounting plate *See Interior mirror.*
5. Remove 4 retaining screws and detach both 'A' post trims.
6. Remove caps and unscrew front seat belt fixing bolts from 'B' posts.

7. Carefully prise side trim panel cap fastener from 'B' posts.
8. Carefully prise 2 cap fasteners, from both sides, securing headlining to body at door aperture.
9. Carefully prise out 5 cap fasteners securing front and rear headlinings to roof.
10. From both sides, pull side trim panel inwards enough to release rear corners of front headlining.
11. Lower headlining and remove from vehicle.

 **NOTE: Take care not to bend the headlining on removal and refitting.**

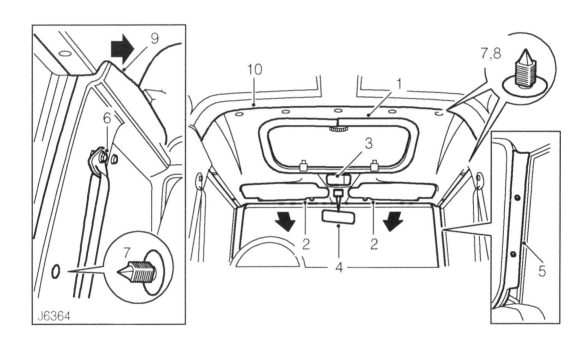

J6364

**Refit**

12. With assistance, raise headlining to roof.
13. Carefully pull side trim panel inwards, on both sides, and slide headlining behind trim panel.
14. Position front headlining into recess of rear headlining and secure both to roof mounting brackets with 5 cap fasteners.
15. Secure both sides of front headlining to body at door apertures with cap fasteners.

16. Fit side cap fasteners at 'B' posts.
17. Secure seat belts to 'B' posts and tighten bolts to *32 Nm (24 lbf/ft).* Fit caps to bolts.
18. Fit 'A' post trims.
19. Fit interior mirror *See Interior mirror.*
20. Fit interior lamp *See ELECTRICAL, Repair, Interior lamp.*
21. Fit sun visors *See Sun visors.*
22. Fit sun roof headlining finisher.

### REAR HEADLINING - 90 STATION WAGON

**Service repair no - 76.64.11**

**Remove**

1. Remove side trim panels *See Side trim panel.*
2. Remove rear end lining *See Rear end lining.*
3. Remove rear interior lamp *See ELECTRICAL, Repair, Rear interior lamp.*
4. Carefully prise out 5 trim studs securing rear and front headlining to roof mounting brackets.

5. Release front corners of headlining from cant rail, on both sides.
6. Pull headlining forwards sufficiently to clear rear end lining mounting brackets.
7. Release rear corners of headlining from cant rail, on both sides.
8. Lower rear headlining from roof and remove from vehicle.

 **NOTE: Take care not to bend headlining on removal and refitting.**

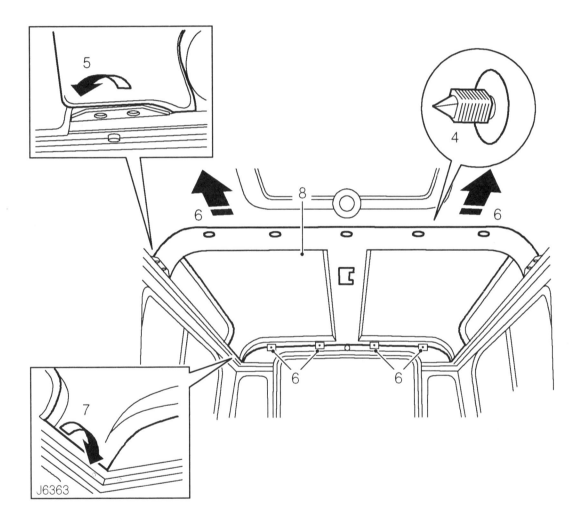

**Refit**

9. With assistance, position rear headlining to roof and locate rear corners in cant rail.
10. Push headlining rearwards and position over rear end lining mounting brackets.
11. Locate front corners of headlining in cant rail.

12. Position front edge of rear headlining over front headlining and secure with trim studs.
13. Adjust rear headlining to achieve good fit at all corners.
14. Fit rear interior lamp *See ELECTRICAL, Repair, Interior lamp.*
15. Fit rear end lining *See Rear end lining.*
16. Fit side trim panels *See Side trim panel.*

## TAIL DOOR TRIM CASING

**Service repair no - 76.34.09**

### Remove

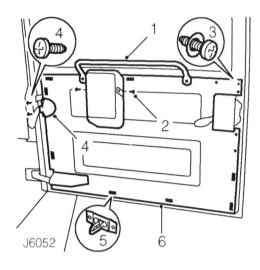

J6052

1. Unscrew 2 bolts and remove grab handle from rear door.
2. Remove 2 screws and detach wiper motor cover.
3. Remove 7 screws securing trim casing to door.
4. Remove 2 screws and lift wiper motor harness cover from harness support bracket.
5. Carefully release 8 clips securing trim casing to door.
6. Remove trim casing and collect door lock cover.

### Refit

7. Position door lock cover, fit trim casing and secure with clips.
8. Fit harness cover and secure with two screws.
9. Secure door panel with retaining screws.
10. Position wiper motor cover and secure with 2 screws.
11. Position grab handle and secure with 2 bolts.

## TAIL DOOR LOCK

**Service repair no - 76.37.16**

### Remove

1. Remove door casing *See Tail door trim casing.*

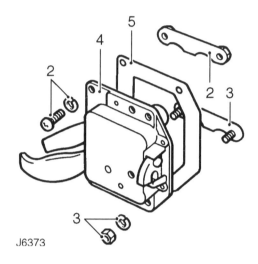

J6373

2. Remove screws, washers and nut retainer plate securing top of lock to door.
3. Remove nuts, washers and stud retainer plate securing bottom of lock to door.
4. Withdraw lock assembly.
5. Remove door lock gasket.
6. Clean sealant from retainer plates.
7. Insert key into barrel.
8. Depress lock barrel plunger and withdraw barrel from lock.

### Refit

9. Fit new barrel into lock.
10. Apply sealant to lock retainer plates.
11. Fit lock to door with a new gasket.
12. Secure with retainer plates, screws, washers and nuts.
13. Close door and check for correct latching with striker. Adjust striker as necessary *See Tail door striker - adjust.*
14. Fit door casing *See Tail door trim casing.*

## TAIL DOOR STRIKER - ADJUST

**Service repair no - 76.37.25**

**Adjust**

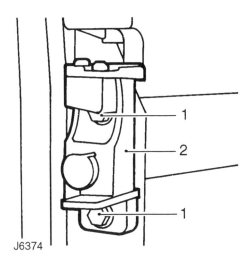

J6374

1. Loosen striker securing screws.
2. Adjust striker and retighten screws.
3. Close door and check for correct latching with door lock.
4. Carry out further adjustment as necessary. If full adjustment cannot be achieved carry out following:
5. Remove striker and nut plate.
6. Elongate holes in body metal which is sandwiched between striker and nut plate.
7. Refit striker and adjust as necessary.

## SUN ROOF

**Service repair no - 76.83.01**

**Remove**

1. Open sun roof fully.
2. Disengage spring lock from operating handle catch.
3. Holding sun roof at both sides, release hinges from locating brackets at front of outer frame.

4. Remove sun roof.
5. Starting from centre rear, peel headlining finisher from inner frame.
6. Remove 18 screws securing inner frame to outer frame and detach inner frame.
7. Lift outer frame from roof.

 **NOTE: Assistance may be required to remove the sun roof assembly.**

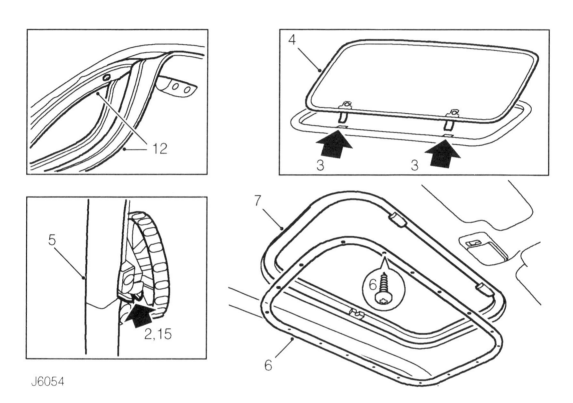

J6054

**Refit**

8. Clean roof area around outer frame seating.
9. Position outer frame on roof.
10. Fit inner frame to headlining and secure to outer frame with 18 screws but do not fully tighten.
11. Check alignment of inner and outer frames with roof mounting and headlining, adjust as necessary, and fully tighten fixing screws to *10 Nm (7 lbf/ft)*.

12. Starting from centre rear, fit headlining finisher lip into locating channel of inner frame.
13. Press finisher firmly over inner frame and continue around complete frame, ensuring finisher lies flat on headlining.
14. Fit sun roof hinges fully into locating brackets on outer frame, and lower the glass panel.
15. Engage operating handle catch with spring lock of outer frame and close sunroof.

## INTERIOR MIRROR

**Service repair no - 76.10.51**

**Remove**

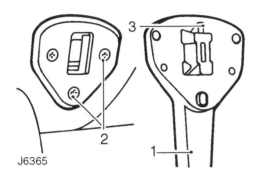

J6365

1. Prise interior mirror arm from mounting plate.
2. Remove 3 screws and remove mounting plate from headlining.

**Refit**

3. Fit mounting plate to headlining.
4. Locate lower lug of mirror arm in mounting plate aperture.
5. Press mirror arm firmly to engage spring clip in mounting plate aperture.

## SUN VISORS

**Service repair no - 76.10.47**

**Remove**

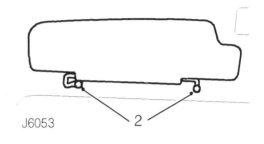

J6053

1. Raise sun visor.
2. Remove 2 screws and collect sun visor.

**Refit**

3. Position sun visor and secure with 2 screws.

## BONNET LOCK

**Service repair no - 76.16.21**

### Remove

1. Open bonnet.

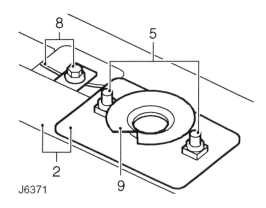

J6371

2. Mark position of guide plate and lock to bonnet platform.
3. Remove 8 screws securing grille.
4. Remove grille.
5. Remove 2 bolts securing guide plate and lock.
6. Remove guide plate.
7. Release spring securing lock to bonnet platform.
8. Slacken clamping bolt securing bonnet release cable.
9. Remove lock.

### Refit

10. Fit spring between lock and bonnet platform.
11. Position lock and guide plate to bonnet platform and nip up bolts.
12. Position guide plate and lock to position marks and tighten bolts to **10 Nm (7 lbf/ft).**
13. Fit cable to lock and tighten clamping bolt.
14. Check operation of release cable and adjust if necessary.
15. Fit grille and tighten securing screws.
16. Close bonnet.

## BONNET RELEASE CABLE

**Service repair no - 76.16.29**

### Remove

1. Open bonnet.
2. Remove 8 screws securing grille.
3. Remove grille.

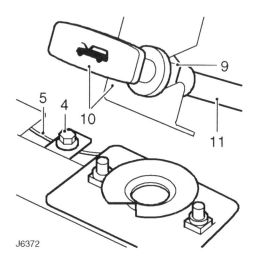

J6372

4. Slacken clamping bolt securing bonnet release cable.
5. Remove cable from lock.
6. Release cable from clip on underside of bonnet platform.
7. Feed cable through valance and collect grommet.
8. Release cable from clip fixed to wheelarch under expansion tank.
9. Loosen clamping nut securing bonnet release handle to mounting bracket.
10. Remove bonnet release handle from mounting bracket.
11. Withdraw cable through bulkhead.

### Refit

12. Feed cable through bulkhead and fit bonnet release handle to mounting bracket. Tighten clamping nut.
13. Route cable behind expansion tank and fit to securing clip.
14. Feed cable through valance.
15. Fit grommet between cable and valance.
16. Fit cable to securing clip on underside of bonnet platform.

17. Fit cable to lock and tighten clamping bolt.
18. Check operation of release cable and bonnet
    lock and adjust if necessary.
19. Fit grille and tighten screws.
20. Close bonnet.

## LOWER FASCIA PANEL (HEATER DUCT) ASSEMBLY

**Service repair no - 76.46.05**

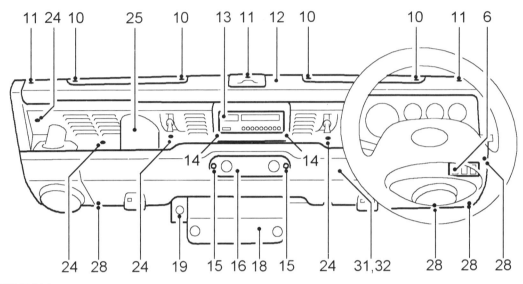

76M2414

### Remove

1. Disconnect battery.
2. Remove steering wheel **See STEERING, Repair, Steering wheel**.
3. Remove steering column nacelle **See STEERING, Repair, Steering column nacelle**.
4. Remove instrument panel **See INSTRUMENTS, Repair, instrument panel**.
5. Release heater cable at control lever **See HEATING AND VENTILATION, Repair, Heater control cable - air distribution**.
6. Remove 2 screws, withdraw switch panel from lower fascia and disconnect switch multi-plugs.
7. Prise out Land Rover decal and remove screw securing grab handle to crash pad.
8. Remove lower screw and lift grab handle from lower fascia panel.
9. On RH drive vehicles only, remove screw securing LH side of finisher to wiper motor cover.
10. Remove 4 screws and remove both demister vents from crash pad.
11. Remove 3 screws securing crash pad to fascia bulkhead.
12. Remove crash pad.
13. Remove radio, if fitted.
14. Remove 2 trim studs securing radio housing to trim panel. Remove radio housing.

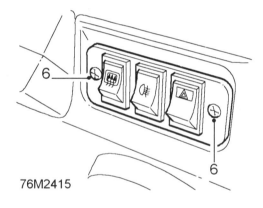

76M2415

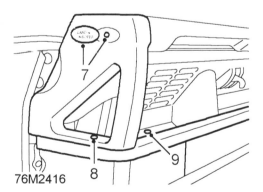

76M2416

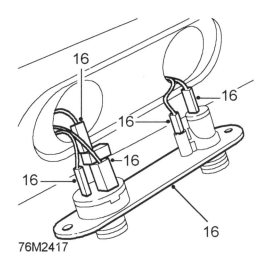

76M2417

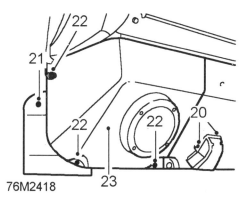

76M2418

**15.** If fitted, remove 2 screws, washers and nuts securing auxiliary switch panel to lower fascia panel and switch cover.

**16.** Withdraw switch panel and disconnect switch leads.

**17.** Remove 2 screws securing switch cover to parcel tray.

**18.** Remove fuse box cover.

**19. Models with hand throttle:**
Remove fuse box LH retaining screw.
Pivot fuse box down to gain access to lower inner hand throttle cover fixing screw.
Remove 4 screws and lift up hand throttle cover from lower fascia panel.

**20.** Remove 2 screws and remove both footwell vents from lower fascia panel.

**21.** Remove single screw and detach door check strap cover from LH and RH doors.

**22.** Remove 3 screws securing wiper motor cover to fascia bulkhead.

**23.** Release locating pins from fascia panel, lower wiper motor cover and, if applicable, disconnect radio speaker leads. Retain wiper motor rack cover. On LH drive vehicles, disconnect multi-plugs from rear of switch panel.

**24.** Prise out 2 large and 5 small cap fasteners securing trim panel to parcel shelf and fascia bulkhead.

**25.** Carefully fold back trim panel to clear fresh air vent operating levers and remove panel from parcel shelf.

26. Release demist hose and lift parcel shelf from lower fascia panel (heater duct). Feed main harness leads and plugs through aperture in parcel shelf.
27. Remove parcel shelf.

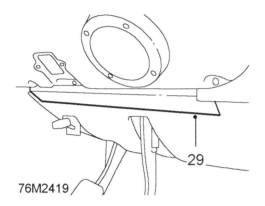

76M2419

28. Remove 7 screws securing bottom edge of lower fascia panel to fascia bulkhead, noting position of both footwell cover retaining plates.
29. Remove both retaining plates and lower footwell covers.
30. Unscrew 2 retaining bolts securing top edge of lower fascia panel to bulkhead.
31. With assistance, lower fascia panel and, if applicable, disconnect RH radio speaker leads.
32. Remove fascia panel from vehicle.

**Refit**

33. Position lower fascia panel to bulkhead, reconnect RH speaker leads, if applicable, and secure top edge with 2 bolts.
34. Locate RH footwell cover retaining plate under bottom edge of fascia panel and secure with 3 screws.
35. Repeat operation for LH footwell cover retaining plate.
36. Fit remaining lower fascia panel fixing screws.
37. Locate parcel shelf. Ensure all radio and auxiliary switch panel harness leads and plugs are fed through aperture in parcel shelf.
38. Fit demist hoses into heater duct of lower fascia panel. Ensure flanges of hose grommets are correctly seated.
39. Fit trim panel and secure with cap fasteners.
40. Reconnect LH speaker leads, if applicable, locate wiper motor cover pins in lower fascia panel and secure wth 3 screws. Ensure wiper rack cover is correctly seated. On LH drive vehicles, reconnect multi-plugs to rear of switch panel.
41. Secure finisher to wiper motor cover.
42. Fit door check strap covers on both sides.
43. Fit footwell vents to lower fascia panel.
44. **Models fitted with hand throttle:**
    Fit hand throttle cover.
    Secure LH side of fuse box.
45. Fit fuse box cover.
46. Fit auxiliary switch cover to parcel tray, if applicable.

47. Connect leads and plugs to auxiliary switches and clock.
48. Secure switch panel to lower fascia panel and switch cover.
49. Position radio housing, if applicable, and feed radio multi- plug, aerial and speaker leads from switch cover to radio housing.
50. Secure radio housing to trim panel.
51. Fit radio connections and secure radio in housing.
52. Fit crash pad to fascia bulkhead.
53. Fit demister vents in crash pad.
54. Fit grab handle to lower fascia panel and secure to crash pad. Refit Land Rover decal.
55. Connect multi-plugs to rear screen, hazard and interior lamp switches and fit switch panel to fascia panel.
56. Fit heater control cable **See HEATING AND VENTILATION, Repair, Heater control cable - air distribution** .
57. Fit instrument panel **See INSTRUMENTS, Repair, instrument panel** .
58. Fit steering column nacelle **See STEERING, Repair, Steering column nacelle** .
59. Fit steering wheel **See STEERING, Repair, Steering wheel** .
60. Reconnect battery.

## FRONT UNDERTRAY

**Service repair no - 76.11.81 - Front undertray**
**Service repair no - 76.11.85 - Acoustic pad**

### Remove

1. Raise vehicle on ramp.
2. Position support under chassis front crossmember.
3. Lower ramp to give clearance between axle and undertray.

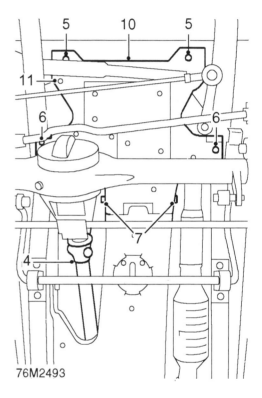

76M2493

4. Remove 4 nuts, disconnect propeller shaft from front axle, and move aside.
5. Remove 2 bolts securing undertray to chassis front crossmember.
6. Remove nut securing undertray to bump stop front fixing bolt on both sides.
7. Remove 2 bolts securing sides of undertray to rear undertray.
8. Pull front undertray forwards to release flanges from rear undertray.
9. Lower undertray to clear steering box etc. and manouvre rearwards over axle.
10. Remove front undertray.
11. If necessary, remove 8 fasteners to release acoustic pad from undertray.

**Refit**

12. If applicable, fit acoustic pad to undertray.
13. Fit undertray in position, ensuring flanges are correctly located in rear undertray.
14. Secure undertray to chassis front crossmember, bump stops and rear undertray. Tighten fixings to *14 Nm (10 lbf/ft)*.
15. Fit propeller shaft to front axle and tighten nuts to 47 Nm (35 lbf/ft).
16. Raise ramp to remove chassis support.
17. Lower ramp.

## REAR UNDERTRAY

**Service repair no - 76.11.80 - Rear undertray**
**Service repair no - 76.11.82 - Acoustic pad**

**Remove**

1. Raise vehicle on ramp.

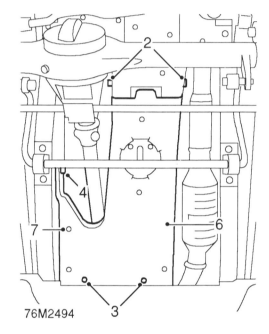

76M2494

2. Remove 2 bolts securing sides of undertray to front undertray.
3. Remove 2 bolts securing rear undertray to chassis crossmember brackets.
4. Remove bolt securing undertray to RH side of chassis.
5. Pull undertray rearwards to release from flanges of front undertray.
6. Remove rear undertray.
7. If necessary, remove 7 fasteners and release acoustic pad from undertray.

**Refit**

8. If applicable, fit acoustic pad to undertray.
9. Fit undertray in position, ensuring flanges of front undertray are correctly located.
10. Secure undertray to chassis crossmember, RH chassis side, and front undertray. Tighten fixings to *14 Nm (10 lbf/ft)*.
11. Lower ramp.

## ACCESS PANEL - FRONT UNDERTRAY

**Service repair no - 76.11.85 - Access panel**
**Service repair no - 76.11.83 - Acoustic pad**

The access panel is provided in the front undertray to enable fitment of the wading plug into the engine timing cover.

### Remove

1. Raise vehicle on ramp.

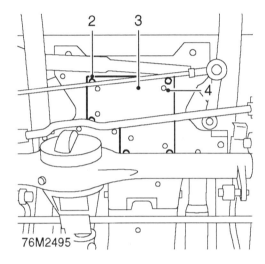

76M2495

2. Remove 5 bolts securing access panel to front undertray.
3. Remove access panel.
4. If necessary, remove 5 fasteners and release acoustic pad from access panel.

### Refit

5. If applicable, fit acoustic pad to access panel.
6. Fit access panel to front undertray, Tighten fixings to *14 Nm (10 lbf/ft).*
7. Lower ramp.

## ACCESS PANEL - REAR UNDERTRAY

**Service repair no - 76.11.84**

The access panel is provided in the rear undertray to enable fitment of the wading plug or timing tool **LRT-12-044** in the flywheel housing, and access to the engine oil sump drain plug.

### Remove

1. Raise vehicle on ramp.

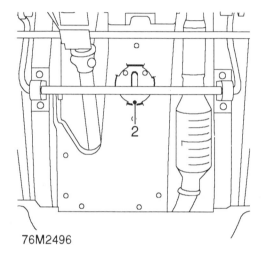

76M2496

2. Rotate access panel anti-clockwise to release locking flanges.
3. Remove access panel from undertray.

### Refit

4. Locate access panel flanges in undertray apertures.
5. Rotate panel clockwise to secure in undertray.
6. Lower ramp.

# Notes

## CONTENTS

# Notes

## HEATING AND VENTILATION SYSTEM

### Description

The heating and ventilation system is standard on all models. Air conditioning is an optional system which provides fully integrated climate control for the vehicle interior.

The heater assembly, comprising a matrix housed in a distribution unit and a variable speed blower motor, is located on one side of the engine compartment and attached directly to the fascia bulkhead.

The heating controls are positioned on the outside of the instrument binnacle and cable linked to mechanical flaps in the distribution unit.

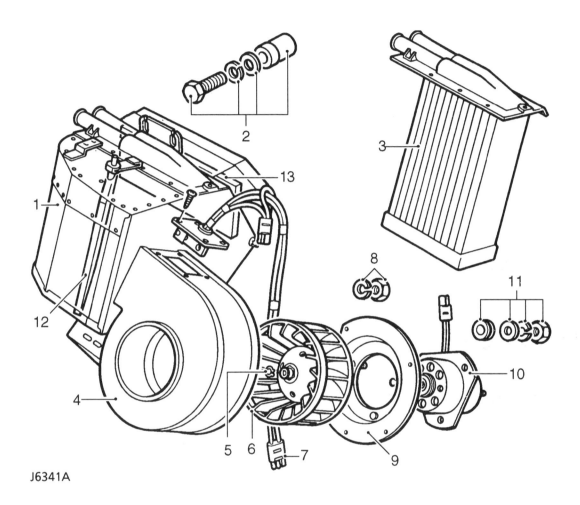

J6341A

### Heater assembly

1. Heater distribution unit
2. Fixings, heater to fascia bulkhead
3. Heater matrix
4. Blower motor housing
5. Circlip, impeller to blower motor
6. Impeller
7. Resistor unit and harness connector
8. Fixings, blower motor mounting plate
9. Mounting plate, blower motor
10. Blower motor
11. Fixings, blower motor to mounting bracket
12. Temperature flap, air flow to heater matrix
13. Air flap, air supply to plenum chamber (heater duct)

## HEATER OPERATION

The heater matrix (3), located in the distribution unit (1), see J6341, is connected to the engine cooling system. As water is circulated continuously through the matrix, a selection of heated or ambient air is controlled by two flaps within the distribution unit. The temperature flap (12) controls the amount of ambient air to the heater matrix, air being supplied

through a ducted vent on top of the vehicle front wing to the blower motor (volute) housing (4). The blower motor (10) can be used to boost the air flow into the distribution unit. The air flap (13) controls the supply of heated or ambient air from the heater unit into a plenum chamber integeral with the vehicle fascia. Two flaps in the plenum chamber (heater duct) distribute the air flow to either the footwell vents or windscreen demister vents as shown.

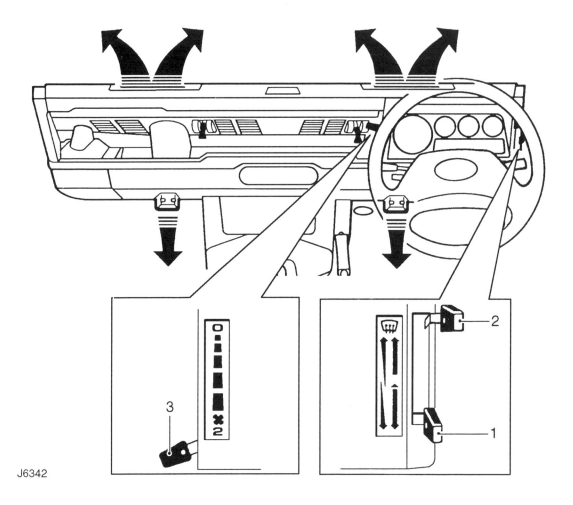

J6342

## HEATER CONTROLS

### 1. Temperature control

Move the lever downwards to increase air temperature or up to decrease air temperature.

### 2. Air distribution control

Lever fully up - windscreen vents only.
Lever midway - footwell and windscreen vents.
Lever fully down - footwell vents.

### 3. Blower motor fan speed control

Move the lever progressively downwards to increase fan speed. With the control at '0' the fan is switched off and the volume of air entering the passenger compartment is solely dependent on ram air when the vehicle is moving.

**Fresh air vents**

Two fresh air vents are fitted in the windscreen frame
and are controlled independently of the vehicle
heating system. Each vent is operated separately.

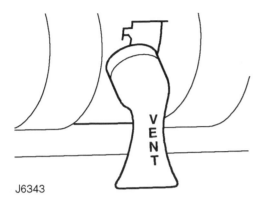

J6343

To open the vents, push the lever to the right and then
down to the required position.

# Notes

## HEATER UNIT

**Service repair no - 80.20.01**

### Remove

1. Remove bonnet and disconnect battery.
2. Remove radiator bottom hose at radiator union and drain cooling system *See COOLING SYSTEM, Repair, Drain and refill cooling system.*

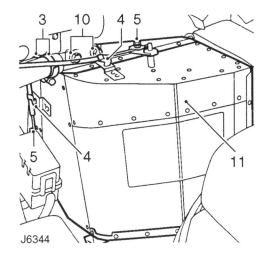

J6344

3. Slacken clips and remove heater hoses at heater box unions.
4. Remove outer cable securing clips.
5. Slacken trunnions and remove control cables from heater vent flap levers.
6. Remove heater wiring harness securing loop.
7. Disconnect harness multi-plug.
8. Remove interior bulkhead trim.
9. Remove lower nuts and bolts securing the heater unit to the bulkhead.
10. Slacken heater unit upper retaining bolts.
11. Manoeuvre heater unit, complete with blower motor, clear of air inlet duct and remove from engine compartment.
12. If existing heater unit is to be refitted, remove sealing rubber.
   For heater matrix removal *See Heater matrix.*
   For blower motor removal *See Blower motor.*

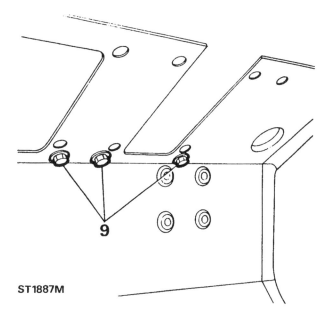

ST1887M

### Refit

13. Smear a new heater unit sealing rubber with a suitable impact adhesive and fit to heater.
14. Manoevre heater unit into position in engine compartment, fit blower motor to air inlet duct and locate upper fixing bolts.
15. Loosely fit heater unit lower fixing bolts.
16. Fully tighten upper fixing bolts.
17. Fully tighten lower fixings and refit interior bulkhead trim.
18. Secure wiring harness and reconnect multi-plug.
19. Fit control cables to vent flap trunnions and secure with outer cable clips.
20. Connect heater hoses.
21. Fit radiator bottom hose and refill cooling system *See COOLING SYSTEM, Repair, Drain and refill cooling system.*
22. Fit bonnet and reconnect battery.

## BLOWER MOTOR

**Service repair no - 80.20.15**

### Remove

1. Remove heater unit *See Heater unit.*
2. Remove 3 nuts securing angled bracket to heater unit. Pivot bracket to remove from studs.

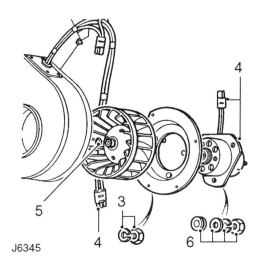

J6345

3. Remove 5 nuts securing blower motor assembly to volute housing.
4. Disconnect harness connector and remove blower motor from volute housing.
5. Release circlip and withdraw impeller from motor shaft.
6. Remove 3 nuts securing blower motor to mounting plate.
7. Remove blower motor.
8. Examine components for signs of wear and renew as necessary.

### Refit

9. Apply Bostik 1261 adhesive to mating faces of mounting plate and blower motor.
10. Fit blower motor to mounting plate and secure with 3 nuts. Ensure rubber mountings are correctly fitted.
11. Fit impeller to motor shaft and secure with circlip.
12. Position blower motor assembly in volute housing and secure with 5 nuts. Fit angled bracket to lower fixing.
13. Reconnect harness plug to resistor harness and fit angled bracket to heater unit.
14. Fit heater unit *See Heater unit.*

## HEATER MATRIX

**Service repair no - 80.20.29**

### Remove

1. Remove heater unit *See Heater unit.*
2. Remove 2 nuts securing angled bracket to heater unit. Pivot bracket to remove from studs.

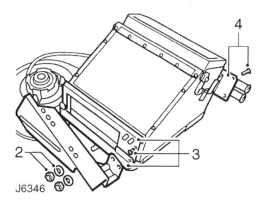

J6346

3. Remove 14 screws and detach two matrix retaining plates from heater unit base.

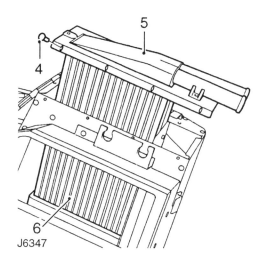

J6347

4. Remove 9 screws securing matrix top retaining plate.
5. Withdraw heater matrix through top of heater unit casing.

**Refit**

6. Fit foam rubber to heater matrix casing.
7. Position matrix in heater unit casing.
8. Check that both vent flaps operate correctly without sticking.
9. Secure matrix top retaining plate.
10. Secure matrix bottom retaining plates.
11. Fit heater unit **See Heater unit.**

## RESISTOR UNIT

**Service repair no - 80.20.17**

**Remove**

1. Remove heater unit **See Heater unit.**

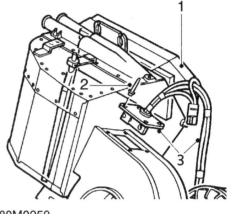

80M0259

2. Drill out 4 rivets securing resistor mounting plate to top of volute housing.
3. Remove resistor and disconnect blower motor plug from harness.

**Refit**

4. Apply Bostik adhesive to resistor mounting plate and rivet to volute housing.
5. Reconnect blower harness motor plug.
6. Fit heater unit **See Heater unit.**

## HEATER CONTROL CABLE - TEMPERATURE CONTROL

**Service repair no - 80.10.05**

**Remove**

1. Disconnect battery.

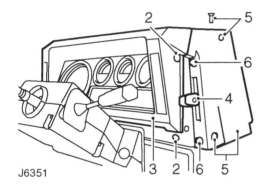

J6351

2. Remove 4 screws securing instrument panel to fascia cowl.
3. Pull instrument panel away from fascia and disconnect speedometer cable to give easier access to control cable at bulkhead.
4. Remove retaining screws and pull off air distribution and temperature control lever knobs.
5. Remove 3 screws and detach side cover, complete with control lever assembly.
6. Remove 2 screws securing control lever assembly to side cover and remove cover. Note plastic screw spacers fitted between cover and control lever assembly and retain.
7. Remove small bolt and release outer cable retaining clip.
8. Slacken grub screw and release inner cable from clevis.
9. From inside engine compartment, release outer cable retaining clip at heater unit.
10. Slacken trunnion fixing and release inner cable from heater unit flap lever.
11. Release 2 retaining clips securing control cables to engine bulkhead and heater hoses.
12. Pull control cable through bulkhead grommet and remove from vehicle.

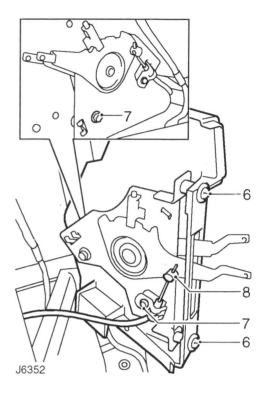

J6352

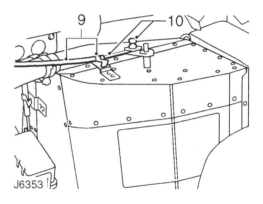

J6353

**Refit**

13. Fit new control cable to heater flap lever trunnion with approximately 10 mm of inner cable protruding from trunnion. Fully tighten trunnion.
14. Secure outer cable with retaining clip.
15. Route control cable through sealing grommet and along inside of engine bulkhead to fascia panel.

16. Secure control cables to engine bulkhead and heater hoses with retaining clips.
17. With control lever in closed position, fit inner cable to lever clevis and fully tighten clevis grub screw.
18. Fit outer cable retaining clip and fully tighten securing bolt.
19. Fit side cover to control lever assembly. Ensure fixing screw spacers are positioned between cover and lever assembly.
20. Fit side cover to fascia.
21. Fit control lever knobs.
22. Reconnect speedometer cable and fit instrument panel.
23. Reconnect battery.

## HEATER CONTROL CABLE - AIR DISTRIBUTION

**Service repair no - 80.10.12**

**Remove**

1. Disconnect battery.
2. Remove steering wheel *See STEERING, Repair, Steering wheel.*

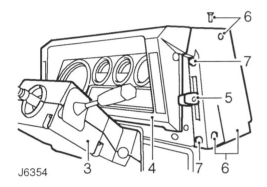

J6354

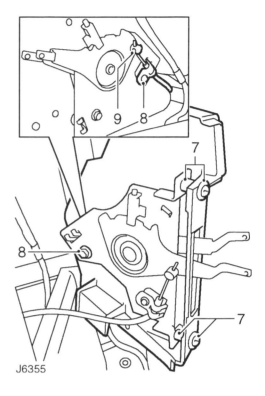

J6355

3. Remove steering column nacelle *See STEERING, Repair, Steering column nacelle.*
4. Remove instrument panel *See INSTRUMENTS, Repair, Instrument panel.*
5. Remove retaining screws and pull off air distribution and temperature control lever knobs.
6. Remove 3 screws and detach side cover, complete with control lever assembly.
7. Remove 2 screws securing control lever assembly to side cover and remove cover. Note plastic screw spacers fitted between cover and control lever assembly and retain.
8. Remove small bolt and release outer cable retaining clip.
9. Slacken grub screw and release inner cable from clevis.
10. Remove lower fascia panel assembly *See CHASSIS AND BODY, Repair, Lower fascia panel (heater duct) assembly.*

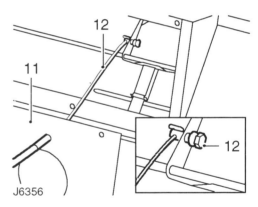

J6356

11. Remove 19 screws and lift off heater duct cover.
12. Slacken vent flap trunnion fixing, release air distribution control cable and remove from heater duct.
13. Check condition of foam sealant on heater duct cover and renew if necessary.

**Refit**

14. Fit new control cable through heater duct cover and secure to vent flap trunnion. Bend over cable end to fully secure.
15. Fit heater duct cover.
16. Fit lower fascia panel assembly to fascia bulkhead *See CHASSIS AND BODY, Repair, lower fascia panel (heater duct) assembly.*
17. Route control cable along fascia bulkhead to contol lever assembly.
18. With control lever in closed position, secure cable to clevis.
19. Fit outer cable retaining clip to lever assembly.
20. Fit lever assembly to side cover. Ensure screw spacers are fitted between cover and lever assembly.
21. Fit side cover to fascia cowl.
22. Fit control lever knobs.
23. Fit instrument panel *See INSTRUMENTS, Repair, Instrument panel.*
24. Fit steering column nacelle *See STEERING, Repair, Steering column nacelle.*

**CONTROL CABLE AND BLOWER MOTOR SWITCH**

**Service repair no - 80.10.17 - Control cable**
**Service repair no - 80.10.22 - Blower motor switch**

**Remove**

1. Disconnect battery.

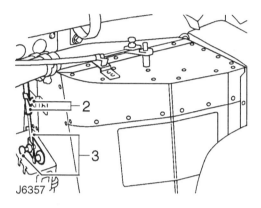

2. From inside engine compartment, release outer cable retaining clip at heater unit.
3. Slacken trunnion fixing and release inner cable from heater unit flap lever.
4. Release 2 retaining clips securing control cables to engine bulkhead and heater hoses.

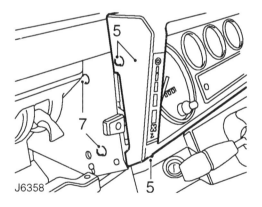

5. Remove 4 screws securing instrument panel to fascia cowl.
6. Pull instrument panel away from fascia and disconnect speedometer cable to ease access to control cable.
7. Remove 2 screws securing control lever assembly to side of fascia panel cowl. Note plastic screw spacers fitted between cowl and lever assembly and retain.

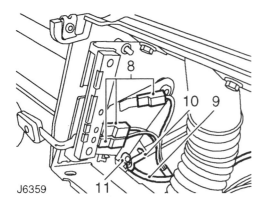

J6359

8. Release lever assembly and disconnect 3 blower motor leads, noting their positions.
9. Pull control cable through bulkhead grommet and out from instrument panel cowl.
10. Release retaining clip securing outer cable to lever assembly.
11. Release inner cable from lever peg.

 **NOTE: If the blower motor switch is faulty the complete lever assembly will have to be renewed.**

**Refit**

12. Fit new control cable to lever assembly peg.
13. Fit retaining clip to secure outer cable.
14. Reconnect blower motor leads.
15. Route cable to rear of instrument panel cowl, along bulkhead and out through grommet into engine compartment.
16. Fit lever assembly to panel cowl. Ensure screw spacers are fitted between cowl and lever assembly.
17. Fit instrument panel to fascia cowl.
18. With lever in closed position, fit control cable to heater unit flap lever trunnion.
19. Secure outer cable with retaining clip.
20. Secure control cables to engine bulkhead and heater hoses with retaining clips.
21. Reconnect battery.

# 82 - AIR CONDITIONING

## CONTENTS

Page

# Notes

## AIR CONDITIONING SYSTEM

### Description

Air conditioning is an optional system which provides fully integrated climate control for the vehicle interior. The air conditioning system comprises four major units as follows:- An evaporator matrix and expansion valve (1), housed in the heater/ cooler unit (3), an engine mounted compressor (4), a condenser (5),

mounted in front of the radiator, and a receiver/drier (7) located to the right of the condenser.
Ancillary components in the system comprise a blower motor (2), also housed in the heater/cooler unit, and condenser cooling fan motors (6), mounted on a support frame. The four major units are interconnectd by preformed metal and flexible refrigerant pipes as illustrated below (RH drive installation shown). Coolant flow to a heater matrix, housed in the heater cooler unit, is controlled by a water valve (8) from a combined air conditioning panel on the vehicle fascia.

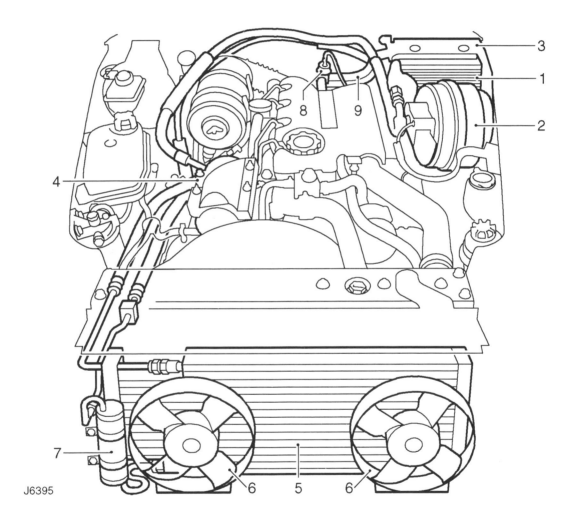

J6395

1. Evaporator matrix and expansion valve
2. Blower motor
3. Heater/cooler unit
4. Compressor
5. Condenser

6. Condenser fan motors
7. Receiver/drier
8. Water valve
9. Heater matrix feed and return hoses

## Operation

### Evaporator unit and expansion valve

High pressure liquid refrigerant is delivered to the expansion valve which is the controlling device for the air conditioning system. A severe pressure drop occurs across the valve and as the refrigerant flows through the evaporator it picks up heat from the ambient air, boils and vaporizes. As this change of state occurs, a large amount of latent heat is absorbed. The evaporator is therefore cooled and as a result heat is extracted from the air flowing across the evaporator. The refrigerant leaves the evaporator, on its way to the compressor, as a low pressure gas. An evaporator sensor measures the air temperature at the evaporator and engages or disengages the compressor clutch to prevent icing of the air ways.

### Compressor

The compressor, a pump specially designed to raise the pressure of the refrigerant, is mounted on the front of the engine and is driven by an independent drive belt from the crankshaft pulley. The compressor draws vaporized refrigerant from the evaporator. It is compressed with a resulting rise in temperature and passed on to the condenser as a hot, high pressure vapour.

### Condenser

The condenser is mounted directly in front of the radiator and consists of a refrigerant coil mounted in a series of thin cooling fins to provide the maximum heat transfer. Air flow across the condenser is induced by vehicle movement and assisted by two electric fans attached to the frame of the condenser. The refrigerant high pressure vapour enters the condenser inlet on the RH side. As the vapour passes through the condenser coils the air flow, assisted by the two fans, carries the latent heat away from the condenser. This induces a change of state resulting in the refrigerant condensing into a high pressure warm liquid. From the condenser, the refrigerant continues to the receiver/ drier.

### Receiver/drier

This component acts as a reservoir and is used to hold extra refrigerant until it is needed by the evaporator. The drier within the receiver unit contains a filter and dessicant (drying material) which absorb moisture and prevent dessicant dust from being carried with the refrigerant into the system.

## AIR CONDITIONING AND HEATER CONTROLS - LH DRIVE

### 1. Temperature control

Move the lever upwards (RED) to increase air temperature, or downwards (BLUE) to reduce air temperature.

### 2. Air conditioning switch

Press the switch (indicator lamp illuminates) to activate the air conditioning. Press again to switch off.

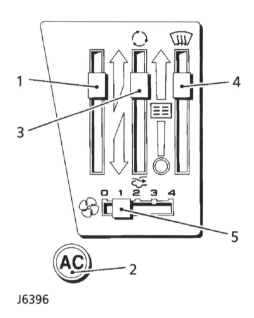

J6396

### 3. Air recirculation control

Move the lever fully upwards to activate air recirculation. Move the lever fully downwards to cancel recirculation.

 NOTE: Prolonged recirculation may cause the windows to mist up.

### 4. Air distribution control

Lever fully up - air to windscreen vents (also provides some air to the footwell).
Lever midway - air to fascia vents (also provides some air to the footwell).
Lever fully down - air to footwell vents (also provides some air to the windscreen).

**5. Blower motor fan speed control**

Move the lever to the right to progressively increase fan speed.

**Location of air vents - LH drive**

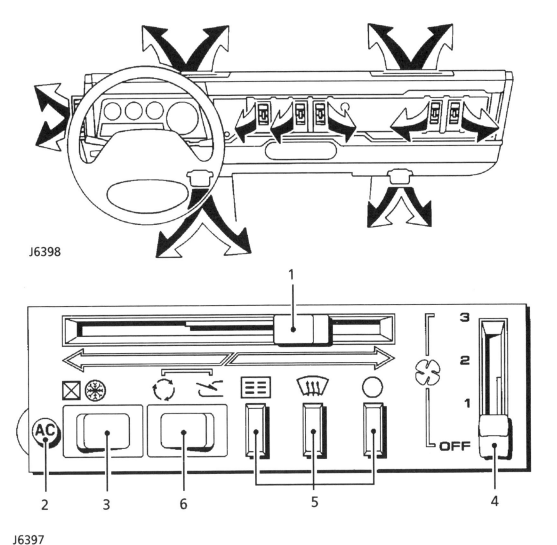

J6398

J6397

## AIR CONDITIONING AND HEATER CONTROLS - RH DRIVE

### 1. Temperature control

Move the lever to the right (RED) to increase air temperature, or to the left (BLUE) to reduce air temperature.

### 2. Air conditioning indicator lamp

Illuminates when the air conditioning system is operating.

### 3. Air conditioning switch

Press the RH portion of the switch to activate the air conditioning (indicator lamp illuminates). Press the LH portion to switch off.

⚠ **NOTE: Air conditioning should only be activated when the engine is running.**

### 4. Blower motor fan speed control

Move the lever upwards to progressively increase fan speed.

### 5. Air distribution control

Push LH button - air to windscreen vents (also provides some air to the footwell).
Push middle button - air to fascia vents (also provides some air to the footwell).
Push RH button - air to footwell vents (also provides some air to the windscreen).

### 6. Air recirculation switch

Press the LH portion of the switch to activate air recirculation. Press the RH portion for fresh air.

 **NOTE: Prolonged recirculation may cause the windows to mist up.**

## GENERAL PRECAUTIONS

The refrigerant used in the air conditioning system is HFC (Hydrofluorocarbon) R134a.

⚠️ **WARNING: R134a is a hazardous liquid and when handled incorrectly can cause serious injury. Suitable protective clothing must be worn when carrying out servicing operations on the air conditioning system.**

⚠️ **WARNING: R134a is odourless and colourless. Do not handle or discharge in an enclosed area, or in any area where the vapour or liquid can come in contact with naked flame or hot metal. R134a is not flammable, but can form a highly toxic gas.**

⚠️ **WARNING: Do not smoke or weld in areas where R134a is in use. Inhalation of concentrations of the vapour can cause dizziness, disorientation. uncoordination, narcosis, nausea or vomiting.**

⚠️ **WARNING: Do not allow fluids other than R134a or compressor lubricant to enter the air conditioning system. Spontaneous combustion may occur.**

⚠️ **WARNING: R134a splashed on any part of the body will cause immediate freezing of that area. Also refrigerant cylinders and replenishment trolleys when discharging will freeze skin to them if contact is made.**

⚠️ **WARNING: The refrigerant used in an air conditioning system must be reclaimed in accordance with the recommendations given with a Refrigerant Recovery Recycling Recharging Station.**

△ **NOTE: Suitable protective clothing comprises: Wrap around safety glasses or helmet, heatproof gloves, rubber apron or waterproof overalls and rubber boots.**

## REMEDIAL ACTIONS

1. If liquid R134a strikes the eye, do not rub it. Gently run large quantities of eyewash over the eye to raise the temperature. If eyewash is not available cool, clean water may be used. Cover eye with clean pad and seek immediate medical attention.
2. If liquid R134a is splashed on the skin run large quantities of water over the area as soon as possible to raise the temperature. Carry out the same actions if skin comes into contact with discharging cylinders. Wrap affected parts in blankets or similar material and seek immediate medical attention.
3. If suspected of being overcome by inhalation of R134a vapour seek fresh air. If unconscious remove to fresh air. Apply artificial respiration and/or oxygen and seek immediate medical attention.

△ **NOTE: Due to its low evaporating temperature of -30° C, R134a should be handled with care.**

⚠️ **WARNING: Do not allow a refrigerant container to be heated by a direct flame or to be placed near any heating appliance. A refrigerant container must not be heated above 50° C.**

⚠️ **WARNING: Do not leave a container of refrigerant without its cap fitted. Do not transport a container of refrigerant that is unrestrained, especially in the boot of a car.**

## SERVICING PRECAUTIONS

Care must be taken when handling refrigeration system components. Units must not be lifted by their hoses, pipes or capillary lines. Hoses and lines must not be subjected to any twist or stress. Ensure that hoses are positioned in their correct run before fully tightening the couplings, and ensure that all clips and supports are used. Torque wrenches of the correct type must be used when tightening refrigerant connections to the stated value. An additional spanner must be used to hold the union to prevent twisting of the pipe.

Before connecting any hose or pipe ensure that refrigerant oil is applied to the seat of the new '0' ring but not to the threads.

Check the oil trap for the amount of oil lost.

All protective plugs on components must be left in place until immediately prior to connection.

The receiver/drier contains desiccant which absorbs moisture. It must be positively sealed at all times.

 **CAUTION: Whenever the refrigerant system is opened, the receiver/drier must be renewed immediately before evacuating and recharging the system.**

Use alcohol and a clean cloth to clean dirty connections.
Ensure that all new parts fitted are marked for use with **R134a.**

### Refrigerant oil

Use the approved refrigerant lubricating oil - Nippon Denso ND-OIL 8.

 **CAUTION: Do not use any other type of refrigerant oil.**

Refrigerant oil easily absorbs water and must not be stored for long periods. Do not pour unused oil back into the container.
When renewing system components, add the following quantities of refrigerant oil:

| | |
|---|---|
| Condenser | 40ml |
| Evaporator | 80ml |
| Pipe or hose | 20ml |
| Receiver/drier | 20ml |

Total quantity of refrigerant oil in system = 140ml

A new compressor is sealed and pressurised with Nitrogen gas, slowly release the sealing cap, gas pressure should be heard to release as the seal is broken.

 **NOTE: A new compressor should always have its sealing caps in place and these must not be removed until immediately prior to fitting**

A new compressor is supplied with an oil fill of 140ml.

A calculated quantity of oil must be drained from a new compressor before fitting.

To calculate the quantity of oil to be drained:

1. Remove sealing plugs from the OLD compressor.
2. Invert compressor and gravity drain oil into measuring cylinder. Rotating the compressor clutch plate will assist complete draining.
3. Note the quantity of oil drained (Yml).
4. Calculate the quantity (Qml) of oil to be drained from the NEW compressor using the following formula:

**Xml - (Yml + 20ml) = Qml**

### Rapid refrigerant discharge

When the air conditioning system is involved in accident damage and the circuit is punctured, the refrigerant is discharged rapidly. The rapid discharge of refrigerant will also result in the loss of most of the oil from the system. The compressor must be removed and all the remaining oil in the compressor drained and refilled as follows:

1. Gravity drain all the oil, assist by rotating the clutch plate (not the pulley).
2. Refill the compressor with 90ml of new refrigerant oil.
3. Plug the inlet and outlet ports.

### Servicing Equipment

The following equipment is required for full servicing of the air conditioning system.

Recovery, recycling and charging station
Leak detector
Thermometer +20° C to -60° C
Safety goggles and gloves

## REFRIGERANT RECOVERY, RECYCLING, RECHARGING

 **WARNING: The air conditioning system is charged with a high pressure, potentially toxic refrigerant. Repairs or servicing must only be carried out by an operator familiar with both the vehicle system and the charging and testing equipment.**

**All operations must be carried out in a well-ventilated area away from open flame and heat sources.**
**Always wear safety goggles and gloves when opening refrigerant connections.**

 **WARNING: Wear eye and hand safety protection. Open connections slowly in case liquid or pressure is present. Allow to bleed off slowly.**

 **CAUTION: Overcharging air conditioning system will cause excessive head pressure.**

An air conditioning portable Refrigerant Recovery Recycling Recharging Station for use with R134a refrigerant incorporates all the features necessary to recover refrigerant R134a from the air conditioning system, to filter and remove moisture, to evacuate and recharge with the reclaimed refrigerant. The unit can also be used for performance testing and air conditioning system analysis.

The operator must adhere to the equipment manufacturers' instructions.

### Recovery and recycling

1. Connect a Refrigerant Station to the high and low pressure servicing connections.
2. Operate the refrigerant recovery system according to the manufacturers instructions.
3. Measure the amount of oil discharged from the system. Add an equal amount of new refrigerant oil to compressor before evacuation sequence.

 **WARNING: Refrigerant must always be recycled before reuse, to ensure that the purity of the refrigerant is high enough for safe use in the air conditioning system. Recycling should always be carried out with equipment which is design certified by Underwriter Laboratory Inc. for compliance with SAE-J1991. Other equipment may not recycle refrigerant to the required level of purity.**

**A R134a Refrigerant Recovery Recycling Recharging Station must not be used with any other type of refrigerant.**

**Refrigerant R134a from domestic and commercial sources must not be used in motor vehicle air conditioning systems.**

### Evacuation and recharging

1. Add refrigerant oil to compressor if necessary.
2. Renew the receiver/drier.

**CAUTION: When a major repair has been carried out, a leak test should be carried out using inert gas.**

3. Connect a Refrigerant Station to the high and low pressure servicing connections.

**CAUTION: Whenever the refrigerant system is opened, the receiver/drier must be renewed immediately before evacuating and recharging the system.**

4. Operate the refrigerant evacuation system according to the manufactures instructions.

**NOTE: If the vacuum reading is below 700mmHg after 15 minutes, suspect a leak in the system. Partially recharge the system and check for leaks using an electronic leak tester. Check suction lines first, then run the compressor for 5 minutes and then check the high pressure lines.**

**CAUTION: The system must be Evacuated immediately before recharging commences. Delay between Evacuation and Recharging is not permitted.**

5. Operate the refrigerant recharging system according to the manufactures instructions. Refrigerant to charge system is 1.1 kg.
6. If the full charge has not been accepted by the system, start the engine and run it at 1500 rev/min for a minimum of 2 minutes.
   Switch on the air conditioning system, open the vehicle windows, set the temperature control to cold and switch the blower to maximum speed.
7. Consult Refrigerant Station Manual for correct procedure to complete the charge.
8. Carry out the air conditioning system performance test.

## LEAK TEST SYSTEM

The following instructions refer to an electronic type Refrigerant Leak Detector for use with R134a, which is the safest and most sensitive.

 **CAUTION: When a major repair has been carried out, a leak test should be carried out using an inert gas (see below).**

1. Place the vehicle in a well ventilated area but free from draughts, as leakage from the system could be dissipated without detection.
2. Follow the instructions issued by the manufacturer of the particular leak detector being used.
3. Commence searching for leaks by passing the detector probe around all joints and components, refrigerant gas is heavier than air.
4. Insert the probe into an air outlet of the evaporator or into the evaporator drain tube. Switch the air conditioning blower on and off at intervals of ten seconds. Any leaking refrigerant will be gathered in by the blower and detected.
5. Insert the probe between the magnetic clutch and compressor to check the shaft seal for leaks.
6. Check all service valve connections, valve plate, head and base plate joints and back seal plate.
7. Check the condenser for leaks at the pipe unions.
8. If any leaks are found, the system must be discharged before rectification.
9. Rectify any leaks and recheck for leaks during evacuation prior to charging.

### Leak test using inert gas

Use Nitrogen or Helium gas.

1. Connect gas line to recharging station.
2. Pressurise system to 3 bar.
3. Carry out leak test as above.

## AIR CONDITIONING SYSTEM - PERFORMANCE TEST

 **WARNING: R134a is hazardous** *See Repair, General Precautions.*

Carry out this test with bonnet and doors or windows open, air conditioning switched on, temperature control set to cold and blower at maximum speed. Set the air supply control to supply fresh air.

1. Close low pressure valve on refrigerant station.
2. Close high pressure valve on refrigerant station.
3. Connect a Refrigerant Station to the high and low pressure servicing connections.

4. Insert dry bulb thermometer into cold air outlet and position dry and wet bulb thermometer close to outside air inlet.
   Do not spill water from the wet thermometer (psychrometer).
5. Start engine and run it at 1500 rev/min for 10 minutes with air conditioning switched on.
6. Read both pressure gauges and thermometers. Check readings against table below with humidity between 60% and 80%.
7. Switch off air conditioning, stop engine, disconnect test equipment.

### Performance range

| Intake temperature | Outlet temperature | Low pressure | High pressure |
|---|---|---|---|
| 20 - 24° C | 4 - 10° C | 18 - 28 lbf/in² | 213 - 299 lbf/in² |
| | | 1.2 - 1.9 bar | 14.7 - 20.6 bar |
| 25 - 29° C | 9 - 19° C | 27 - 37 lbf/in² | 256 - 341 lbf/in² |
| | | 1.9 - 2.6 bar | 17.6 - 23.5 bar |
| 30 - 35° C | 20 - 27° C | 33 - 47 lbf/in² | 299 - 384 lbf/in² |
| | | 2.3 - 3.2 bar | 20.6 - 26.5 bar |

### Table 1

| Ambient Temperature | | Compound Gauge Readings | | High Pressure Gauge Readings | |
|---|---|---|---|---|---|
| °C | °F | bar | lbf/in² | bar | lbf/in² |
| 16 | 60 | 1,03-1,4 | 15-20 | 6,9-10,3 | 100-150 |
| 26,7 | 80 | 1,4-1,72 | 20-25 | 9,6-13,1 | 140-190 |
| 38 | 100 | 1,72-2,1 | 25-30 | 12,4-15,5 | 180-225 |
| 43,5 | 110 | 2,1-2,4 | 30-35 | 14,8-17,2 | 215-250 |

## SYSTEM TEST

1. Place the vehicle in a ventilated, shaded area free from excessive draught, with the doors and windows open.
2. Check that the surface of the condenser is not restricted with dirt, leaves, flies, etc. Do not neglect to check the surface between the condenser and the radiator. Clean as necessary.
3. Switch on the ignition and the air conditioner air flow control. Check that the blower is operating efficiently at low, medium and high speeds. Switch off the blower and the ignition.
4. Check that the evaporator condensate drain tubes are open and clear.
5. Check the tension of the compressor driving belt, and adjust if necessary.
6. Inspect all connections for the presence of refrigerant oil. If oil is evident, check for leaks, and repair as necessary.

 **NOTE: The compressor oil is soluble in Refrigerant R134a and is deposited when the refrigerant evaporates from a leak.**

7. Start the engine.
8. Set the temperature controls to cold and switch the air conditioner blower control on and off several times, checking that the magnetic clutch on the compressor engages and releases each time.
9. With the temperature control at maximum cooling and the blower control at high speed, warm up the engine and fast idle at 1000 rev/min.
10. Repeat at 1800 rev/min.
11. Gradually increase the engine speed to the high range and check the sight glass at intervals.
12. Check for frosting on the service valves.
13. Check the high pressure hoses and connections by hand for varying temperature. Low temperature indicates a restriction or blockage at that point.
14. Switch off the air conditioning blower and stop the engine.
15. If the air conditioning equipment is still not satisfactory, carry out a pressure test as previously described in this section.

## PRECAUTIONS IN HANDLING REFRIGERANT LINES

 **WARNING: Wear eye and hand protection when disconnecting components containing refrigerant. Plug all exposed connections immediately.**

1. When disconnecting any hose or pipe connection the system must be discharged of all pressure. Proceed cautiously, regardless of gauge readings. Open connections slowly, keeping hands and face well clear, so that no injury occurs if there is liquid in the line. If pressure is noticed, allow it to bleed off slowly.
2. Lines, flexible end connections and components must be capped immediately they are opened to prevent the entrance of moisture and dirt.
3. Any dirt or grease on fittings must be wiped off with a clean alcohol dampened cloth. Do not use chlorinated solvents such as trichloroethylene. If dirt, grease or moisture cannot be removed from inside the hoses, they must be replaced with new hoses.
4. All replacement components and flexible end connections must be sealed, and only opened immediately prior to making the connection.
5. Ensure the components are at room temperature before uncapping, to prevent condensation of moisture from the air that enters.
6. Components must not remain uncapped for longer than 15 minutes. In the event of delay, the caps must be fitted.
7. Receiver/driers must never be left uncapped as they contain Silica Gel crystals which will absorb moisture from the atmosphere. A receiver/drier left uncapped must not be used, fit a new unit.
8. The compressor shaft must not be rotated until the system is entirely assembled and contains a charge of refrigerant.
9. A new compressor contains an initial charge of refrigerant oil. The compressor also contains a holding charge of gas when received which should be retained by leaving the seals in place until the pipes are re-connected.
10. The receiver/drier should be the last component connected to the system to ensure optimum dehydration and maximum moisture protection of the system.

11. All precautions must be taken to prevent damage to fittings and connections. Slight damage could cause a leak with the high pressures used in the system.
12. Always use two wrenches of the correct size, one on each fitting when releasing and tightening refrigeration unions.
13. Joints and 'O' rings should be coated with refrigeration oil to aid correct seating. Fittings which are not lubricated with refrigerant oil are almost certain to leak.
14. All lines must be free of kinks. The efficiency of the system is reduced by a single kink or restriction.
15. Flexible hoses should not be bent to a radius less than 90mm radius.
16. Flexible hoses should not be within 100mm of the exhaust manifold.
17. Completed assemblies must be checked for refrigeration lines touching metal panels. Any direct contact of lines and panels transmits noise and must be eliminated.

## PERIODIC MAINTENANCE

Routine servicing, apart from visual checks, is not necessary. The visual inspections are as follows:

### Condenser

With a water hose or air line, clean the fins of the condenser to remove flies, leaves, etc. Check the pipe connections for signs of oil leakage.

### Compressor

Check pipe connections for signs of oil leakage. Check flexible hoses for swelling. Examine the compressor belt for tightness and condition.

### Sight glass

Examine the sight glass for bubbles with the system operating. Check connections for leakage.

### Evaporator

Examine the refrigeration connections at the unit.

# Notes

## COMPRESSOR

**Service repair no - 82.10.20**

### Remove

1. Disconnect battery.
2. Recover refrigerant from air conditioning system *See Adjustment, Refrigerant recovery, recycling, recharging.*
3. Remove compressor drive belt *See Compressor drive belt.*

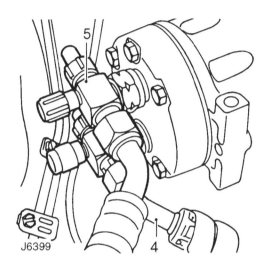

J6399

4. Disconnect high pressure pipe from compressor.
5. Disconnect low pressure pipe from compressor.
6. Remove 'O' ring from each flange.
7. Disconnect compressor clutch harness multi-plug.
8. Remove compressor from mounting bracket studs.

### Refit

9. If a new compressor is to be fitted first drain oil from new compressor. Drain and measure oil from old compressor. Measure new oil equal to amount from old compressor, add 30 ml extra to this amount and refill new compressor through outlet port.
10. Locate compressor over mounting bracket studs.
11. Reconnect compressor clutch harness multi-plug.
12. Fit new 'O' rings to high and low pressure hose flanges, lubricate with refrigerant oil.
13. Fit high and low pressure hoses.
14. Fit compressor drive belt *See Compressor drive belt.*
15. Evacuate and recharge air conditioning system *See Adjustment, Refrigerant recovery, recycling, recharging.*
16. Reconnect battery.
17. Perform a leak test on disturbed joints.
18. Carry out a functional check.

## COMPRESSOR DRIVE BELT

**Service repair no - 82.10.02**

**Remove**

1. Disconnect battery.
2. Remove auxiliary drive belt *See ELECTRICAL, Repair, Auxiliary drive belt.*

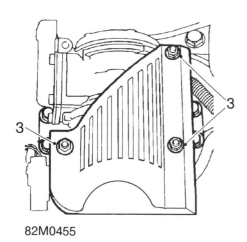

82M0455

3. Remove 3 nuts securing drive belt guard to compressor retaining studs.

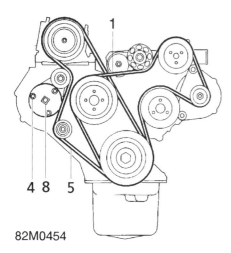

82M0454

4. Slacken 3 belt tensioner retaining bolts.
5. Remove compressor drive belt. Mark direction on belt if refitting.

**Refit**

6. Fit compressor drive belt.
7. Fit drive belt guard.
8. Fit torque meter to centre of tensioner, apply and hold a torque of *35 Nm (26 lbf/ft).*
9. Tighten tensioner retaining bolts.
10. Rotate crankshaft 2 full turns.
11. Reapply and hold a torque of *35 Nm (26 lbf/ft)* to tensioner, then fully slacken and retighten tensioner retaining bolts to *25 Nm (18 lbf/ft).*
12. Fit auxiliary drive belt *See ELECTRICAL, Repair, Auxiliary drive belt.*
13. Reconnect battery.

## CONDENSER FAN AND MOTORS

**Service repair no - 82.15.08**

### Remove

1. Disconnect battery.
2. Remove 6 screws and lift grille panel from vehicle.

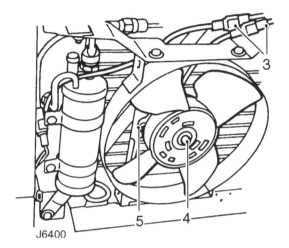

J6400

3. Disconnect fan motor multi-plugs and release harness retaining clips.
4. Remove nut and washers and withdraw fan blade from motor drive shaft.
5. Remove 2 retaining screws, release motor fan from shroud support brackets and feed motor multi-plug lead through appropriate aperture.

### Refit

6. Feed motor lead through fan shroud.
7. Fit motor to fan shroud support brackets.
8. Reconnect fan lead multi-plug and secure with retaining clips.
9. Fit fan blade to motor drive shaft.
10. Fit grille panel.
11. Reconnect battery.

## CONDENSER

**Service repair no - 82.15.07**

### Remove

1. Disconnect battery.
2. Recover refrigerant from air conditioning system *See Adjustment, Refrigerant recovery, recycling, recharging.*
3. Remove 6 screws and lift grille panel from vehicle .

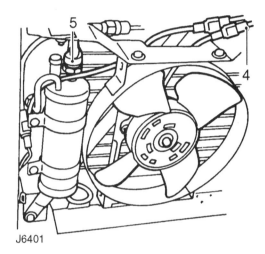

J6401

4. Disconnect condenser fan motor lead multi-plugs.
5. Disconnect receiver/drier dual pressure switch multi-plug.

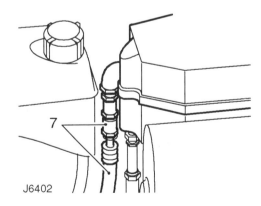

J6402

6. Disconnect condenser low pressure pipe at compressor.
7. Disconnect high pressure hose/pipe at evaporator.

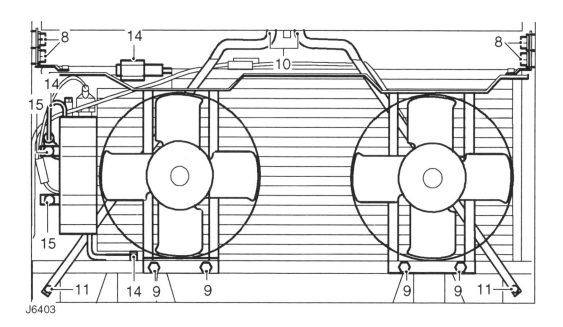

J6403

**8.** Remove 4 bolts and large packing washers securing fan cowling brackets to wing sides.
**9.** Remove 4 nuts securing fan cowling to lower mounting bracket and lift complete assembly from condenser.
**10.** Remove 2 bolts securing bonnet striker support plate and cross braces to grille top panel.
**11.** Remove 2 bolts securing cross braces to front wings.
**12.** Lift condenser, from bottom mounting lugs and carefully ease forwards to clear top grille panel.
**13.** Lift condenser, complete with receiver/drier, from vehicle taking care to clear high and low pressure hose/pipes at side of radiator.
**14.** Disconnect condenser and receiver/drier pipes.
**15.** Remove clamp bolts and release receiver/drier if a new condenser is to be fitted.
**16.** Discard all pipe connection 'O' rings. Cap or plug all connections to prevent ingress of dirt and moisture.

**Refit**

**17.** Coat unions, threads and new 'O' rings with refrigerant oil prior to reassembly.
**18.** Secure receiver/drier to mounting clamps.
**19.** Fit condenser and receiver/drier pipes.
**20.** Lower condenser into position ensuring high and low pressure pipes are located between radiator and front wing.
**21.** Secure cross braces and bonnet striker support plate to top grille.
**22.** Secure cross braces to front wings.
**23.** Secure fan cowl assembly to lower mounting bracket and front wings.
**24.** Fit high pressure pipe at evaporator.
**25.** Fit condenser low pressure pipe at compressor.
**26.** Connect multi-plug at receiver/drier dual pressure switch.
**27.** Connect fan motor lead multi-plug.
**28.** Evacuate and recharge air conditioning system *See Adjustment, Refrigerant recovery, recycling, recharging.*
**29.** Reconnect battery.
**30.** Fit grille panel.

## RECEIVER/DRIER

**Service repair no - 82.17.01**

**Remove**

1. Disconnect battery.
2. Recover refrigerant from air conditioning system *See Adjustment, Refrigerant recovery, recycling, recharging.*
3. Remove 6 screws and lift grille panel from vehicle.

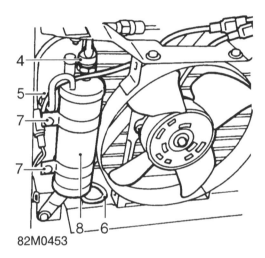
82M0453

4. Disconnect receiver/drier dual pressure switch multi-plug.
5. Disconnect high pressure pipe at receiver/drier.
6. Disconnect bottom union at condenser.
7. Remove retaining bolts and open clamps.
8. Release receiver/drier from condenser and discard. It is NOT recommended to refit old unit.
9. Discard all pipe connection 'O' rings. Cap or plug all connections to prevent ingress of dirt and moisture.

**Refit**

10. Coat unions, threads and new 'O' rings with refrigerant oil prior to reassembly.
11. Secure new receiver/drier in retaining clamp.
12. Fit receiver/drier bottom union connector at condenser.
13. Fit high pressure pipe to receiver/drier.
14. Fit pressure switch multi-plug.
15. Evacuate and recharge air conditioning system *See Adjustment, Refrigerant recovery, recycling, recharging.*
16. Reconnect battery.
17. Fit grille panel assembly.

## HEATER/COOLER UNIT - LH DRIVE

**Service repair no - 82.25.21**

**Remove**

1. Disconnect battery.
2. Recover refrigerant from air conditioning system *See Adjustment, Refrigerant recovery, recycling, recharging.*

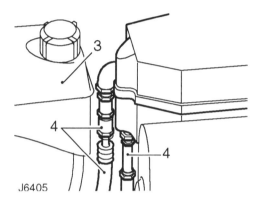
J6405

3. Remove expansion tank *See COOLING SYSTEM, Repair, Expansion tank* to gain access to air conditioning high and low pressure pipes.
4. Disconnect high and low pressure pipes. Discard pipe connection 'O' rings. Cap or plug connections to prevent ingress of dirt and moisture.
5. Disconnect compressor clutch switch multi-plug.
6. Remove pipe connector from vacuum switch.

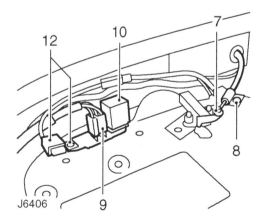
J6406

7. Remove retaining clip and disconnect control cable from evaporator flap operating rod.
8. Remove screw and release outer cable retaining bracket.

9. Remove plug connector from resistor.
10. Remove relay from connecting block to gain access to fixing screw.
11. Remove screw and release relay connector block. Retain relay in connector block.
12. Remove screw and detach air conditioning 30 amp fuse bracket from resistor. Refit both resistor retaining screws.

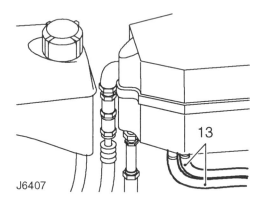

J6407

13. Using suitable pipe clamps, clamp heater matrix feed and return hoses at base of heater/cooler unit. Release retaining clips and remove hoses.
14. From inside vehicle remove front passenger carpet, if fitted.
15. Remove retaining screws and fold back footwell insulation.

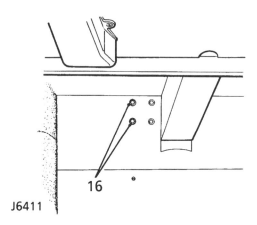

J6411

16. Remove 2 bolts securing heater/cooler unit lower mounting bracket to bulkhead.
17. From inside engine compartment remove 2 bolts securing top heater/cooler unit mounting bracket to engine bulkhead. This also releases earthing leads.
18. Remove bolt securing support bracket to front of heater/cooler casing.

19. Lift heater/cooler unit clear of air duct seal and remove from vehicle.
20. Discard all pipe connection 'O' rings.

**Refit**

21. Coat unions, threads and new 'O' rings with refrigerant oil prior to reassembly.
22. Position heater/cooler unit in engine compartment and locate with air duct seal.
23. Secure unit top and bottom mounting brackets to bulkhead and support bracket to front of unit casing. Fully tighten fixing bolts when unit is correctly positioned.
24. Fit footwell insulation.
25. Reconnect heater matrix hoses.
26. Fit air conditioning fuse bracket, relay connector block, relay and resistor plug connector.
27. Fit control cable to evaporator air flap operating rod, using a new clip.
28. Fit pipe connector to vacuum switch.
29. Connect compressor clutch switch multi-plug.
30. Connect high and low pressure pipes to evaporator.
31. Fit expansuion tank *See COOLING SYSTEM, Repair, Expansion tank.*
32. Evacuate and recharge air conditioning system *See Adjustment, Refrigerant recovery, recycling, recharging.*
33. Reconnect battery.

## EVAPORATOR - LH DRIVE

**Service repair no - 82.25.20**

**Remove**

1. Remove heater/cooler unit *See Heater/cooler unit.*
2. Suitably support unit on a bench to prevent damage to heater matrix pipes.

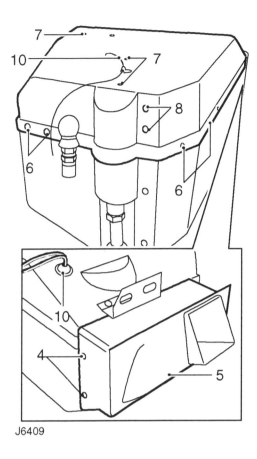

J6409

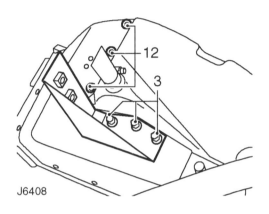

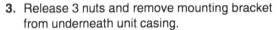

J6408

3. Release 3 nuts and remove mounting bracket from underneath unit casing.
4. Remove 7 screws securing outlet duct to heater/cooler unit.
5. Carefully break sealing compound around edge of duct and pull ducting from unit.
6. Remove 15 screws located around cover seam. Break sealing compound from unit body and top cover.
7. Remove 4 screws and 4 nuts from top of cover.
8. From front of unit remove 2 screws adjacent to low pressure pipe moulding.
9. At side of unit remove 2 screws adjacent to air intake aperture.
10. Lift off top cover, release grommet and feed blower motor wiring and air control flap rod through respective apertures. Note thermostat temperature probe which is inserted in evaporator matrix through top cover.
11. Lift support plate and insulation pad from heater matrix.
12. From bottom of unit casing, remove 3 screws adjacent to dump valve outlet, and screws next to heater matrix pipes.

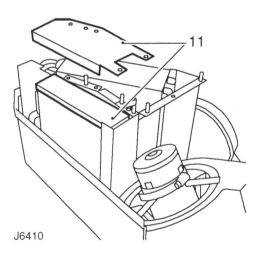

J6410

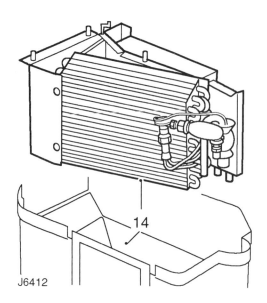

J6412

13. Remove all other fixings securing evaporator and heater matrix support frame to unit casing.
14. Lift evaporator and heater matrices, complete with support frame assembly, clear of casing. Retain heater matrix pipe seal pad.
15. Remove 4 screws securing evaporator matrix to support frame.
16. Withdraw evaporator matrix, complete with expansion valve, from support frame.
17. Clean sealing compound from all joints of main casing, top cover and outlet duct.

⚠ **NOTE: The evaporator matrix is supplied complete with the expansion valve. However, a faulty expansion valve can be serviced separately, *See Expansion valve.***

**Refit**

18. Fit evaporator matrix in support frame.
19. Fit evaporator, heater matrix and support frame assembly in casing. Ensure studs for lower mounting bracket are located through bottom of casing.
20. Apply mastic sealant around heater matrix pipes to seal pipe apertures in casing. Fit seal pad over pipes.
21. Fit 3 bottom fixings to secure to secure base of support frame.
22. Fit all other fixings to secure support frame assembly.
23. Locate heater matrix insulation pad and cover plate.
24. Apply sealng compound around top edge of main casing.
25. Feed blower motor wiring through top cover and fit grommet.
26. Fit top cover to casing. Ensure thermostat temperature probe is inserted in top of evaporator. Apply mastic sealant to air flap operating rod aperture.
27. Apply sealing compound to joint face of blower motor outlet duct.
28. Locate duct over blower motor outlet and secure to casing.
29. Secure lower mounting bracket to retaining studs on base of main casing.
30. Fit heater/cooler unit assembly in engine compartment *See Heater/cooler unit.*

## EXPANSION VALVE - LH DRIVE

**Service repair no - 82.25.01**

**Remove**

1. Remove heater/cooler unit *See Heater/cooler unit.*
2. Suitably support unit on a bench to prevent damage to heater matrix pipes.

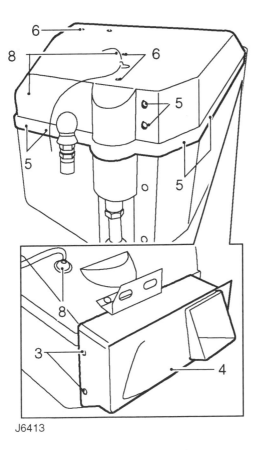

J6413

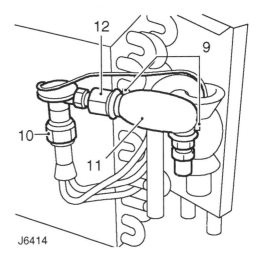

J6414

3. Remove 7 screws securing outlet duct to heater/cooler unit.
4. Break sealing compound around edge of duct and pull duct from unit.
5. Remove all fixing screws securing top cover seam and cover sides to main casing.
6. Remove 4 screws and 4 nuts from top of cover.
7. Break sealing compound from unit casing and top cover.
8. Lift off top cover, release grommet and feed blower motor wiring and air flap operating rod through respective apertures. Note thermostat temperature probe which is inserted in top of evaporator.

9. Release 2 clips securing expansion valve sensor and lagging to low pressure pipe.
10. Unscrew union securing expansion valve to evaporator high pressure pipe.
11. Remove expansion valve, complete with high pressure pipe.
12. Disconnect high pressure pipe from expansion valve.
13. Discard all pipe connection 'O' rings.
14. Clean sealing compound from all joints of main casing, top cover and outlet duct.

**Refit**

15. Coat unions, threads and new 'O' rings with refrigerant oil prior to reassembly.
16. Fit high pressure pipe to new expansion valve.
17. Fit expansion valve to evaporator pipe connector.
18. Position valve sensor at low pressure pipe and secure with lagging and clips.
19. Apply sealing compound around top edge of main casing.
20. Feed blower motor wiring through top cover and fit grommet.
21. Fit top cover to casing. Ensure thermostat temperature probe is inserted in top of evaporator. Apply mastic sealant to air flap operating rod aperture.
22. Apply sealing compound to joint face of blower motor outlet duct.
23. Locate duct over blower motor outlet and secure to casing.
24. Fit heater/cooler unit *See Heater/cooler unit.*

## HEATER MATRIX - LH DRIVE

**Service repair no - 82.25.19**

**Remove**

1. Remove evaporator *See Evaporator.*

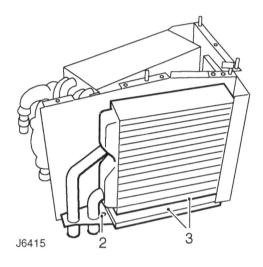

J6415

2. Leaving evaporator in place, remove single screw securing heater matrix pipe plate to base of support frame.
3. Remove heater matrix and insulation pad.

**Refit**

4. Position insulation pad and fit heater matrix to support frame.
5. Fit heater matrix and evaporator assembly *See Evaporator .*

## BLOWER MOTOR ASSEMBLY- LH DRIVE

**Service repair no - 82.25.14**

**Remove**

1. Remove heater/cooler unit *See Heater/cooler unit.*

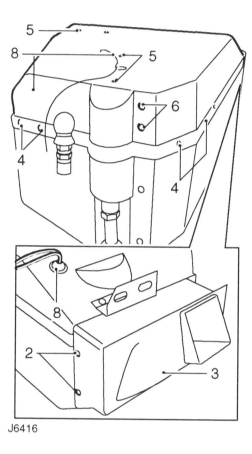

J6416

2. Remove 7 screws securing outlet duct to heater/cooler unit.
3. Carefully break sealing compound around edge of duct and pull ducting from unit.
4. Remove 15 screws located around cover seam. Break sealing compound from unit body and top cover.
5. Remove 4 screws and 4 nuts from top of cover.
6. From front of unit remove 2 screws adjacent to low pressure pipe moulding.
7. At side of unit remove 2 screws adjacent to air intake aperture.
8. Lift off top cover, release grommet and feed blower motor wiring and air control flap rod through respective apertures. Note thermostat probe which is inserted in evaporator matrix through top cover.

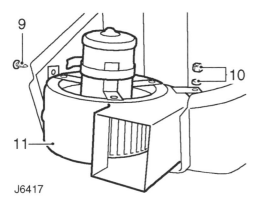

J6417

9. Remove screw securing blower motor mounting bracket to side of casing.
10. Remove nut and washer securing blower motor housing to pedestal mounting bracket.
11. Lift blower motor assembly from casing.

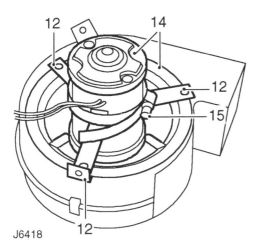

J6418

12. Remove 3 screws and withdraw blower motor and impellor from housing. Note position of side mounting bracket and spacing washers between motor mounting and housing.
13. Remove star washer and withdraw impeller from blower motor.
14. Lift motor from plastic mounting.
15. Slacken retaining clip and remove 3 support brackets.

**Refit**

16. Secure support brackets to new blower motor. Do not fully tighten clip at this stage.
17. Insert motor into plastic mounting and fit impeller.
18. Locate spacing washers, side mounting bracket, and fit motor and mounting into motor housing.
19. Secure assembly to motor housing and fully tighten support bracket retaining clip.
20. Fit blower motor assembly in main casing.
21. Apply sealing compound around top edge of main casing.
22. Feed blower motor wiring through top cover and fit grommet.
23. Fit top cover to casing. Ensure thermostat temperature probe is inserted in top of evaporator. Apply mastic sealant to air flap operating rod aperture.
24. Apply sealing compound to joint face of blower motor outlet duct.
25. Locate duct over blower motor outlet and secure to casing.
26. Fit heater/cooler unit *See  Heater/cooler unit.*

## BLOWER MOTOR ASSEMBLY - RH DRIVE

**Service repair no - 82.25.14**

**Remove**

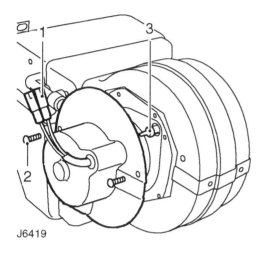

J6419

1. Disconnect blower motor wiring plugs.
2. Remove 2 screws securing blower motor cover to main casing.
3. Withdraw cover sufficiently to release motor Lucar connector and earth eylet. Remove cover.

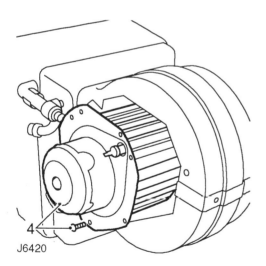

J6420

4. Remove 6 screws and withdraw blower motor and impeller.
5. Remove retaining nut and washer and withdraw impeller from blower motor shaft.

**Refit**

6. Secure impeller on new blower motor.
7. Fit blower motor assembly in main casing.
8. Fit Lucar connector and earth eyelet to blower motor.
9. Fit blower motor cover and connect wiring plugs.

## HEATER/COOLER UNIT - RH DRIVE

**Service repair no - 82.25.21**

**Remove**

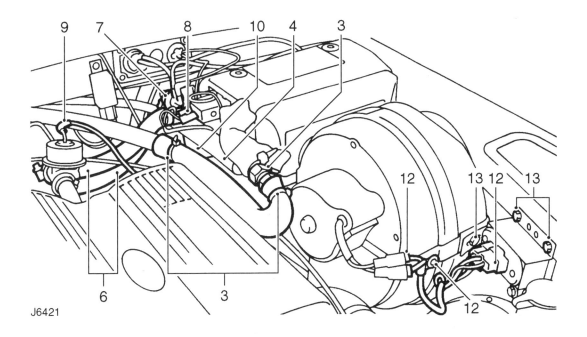

J6421

1. Disconnect battery.
2. Recover refrigerant from air conditioning system *See Refrigerant recovery, recycling, recharging.*
3. Release ties, remove insulation cover and disconnect evaporator low pressure pipe.
4. Disconnect evaporator high pressure pipe.
5. Discard all pipe connection 'O' rings. Cap or plug all connections to prevent ingress of dirt and moisture.
6. Using suitable pipe clamps, clamp heater matrix feed and return pipes at heater/cooler unit.
7. Remove screw securing air control flap solenoid.
8. Disconnect 2 leads from thermostat.
9. Remove pipe from water valve vacuum switch.
10. Remove retaining clip and disconnect control cable from evaporator flap operating rod.
11. Remove screw and release outer cable retaining bracket.

12. Disconnect blower motor wiring plugs and release harness retaining clip from housing.
13. Remove bolt securing front support bracket to blower motor housing. If necessary, remove blower motor resistor block to facilitate operation.
14. From inside vehicle remove front passenger carpet, if fitted.
15. Remove fixing screws and fold back footwell insulation.
16. Remove 4 bolts securing heater/cooler unit lower mounting bracket to bulkhead. Ensure spacing washers from two innermost bolts are retrieved from engine bulkhead side.
17. From inside engine compartment remove 2 bolts securing top heater/cooler unit mounting bracket to engine bulkhead.
18. Lift heater/cooler unit clear of air duct seal and remove from vehicle.

**Refit**

19. Coat unions, threads and new 'O' rings with refrigerant oil prior to reassembly.
20. Position heater/cooler unit in engine compartment and locate with air duct seal.
21. Secure unit top and bottom mounting brackets to bulkhead and support bracket to front of unit casing. Fully tighten fixing bolts when unit is correctly positioned.
22. If applicable, fit blower motor resistor block to vehicle wing.
23. Connect blower motor wiring plugs.
24. Fit footwell insulation and carpet.
25. Fit control cable to evaporator flap operating rod using new clip. Secure outer cable.
26. Connect water valve vacuum switch pipe and thermostat leads.
27. Fit air control flap solenoid to side of heater/cooler unit.
28. Reconnect heater matrix hoses.
29. Connect high pressure pipe to evaporator.
30. Connect low pressure pipe and fit insulation cover.
31. Evacuate and recharge air conditioning system
    ***See Adjustment, Refrigerant recovery, recycling, recharging.***
32. Reconnect battery.

## EVAPORATOR - RH DRIVE

**Service repair no - 82.25.20**

**Remove**

1. Remove heater/cooler unit *See Heater/cooler unit - RH drive.*
2. Suitably support unit on a bench.
3. Remove sealant and release thermostat probe from low pressure pipe.

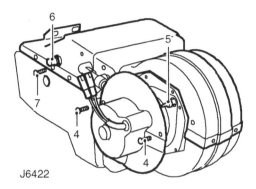

J6422

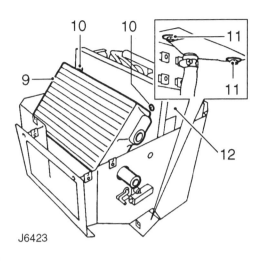

J6423

4. Remove 2 screws securing blower motor cover to main casing.
5. Withdraw cover sufficiently to release motor Lucar connector and earth eyelet. Remove cover.
6. Unscrew top adaptor pipe from heater matrix.
7. Remove 18 fixings securing top cover to main casing and heater/cooler support frame.
8. Carefully break sealing compound around edge of joint seam and remove top cover from main casing.
9. Lift out heater matrix.
10. Remove 2 screws securing back of evaporator to support frame.
11. From underneath, remove 2 nuts and washers securing evaporator matrix to base of casing.
12. Lift evaporator matrix from casing, complete with side plates.
13. Remove side plates
14. Clean sealing compound from all joint seams of main casing and top cover.

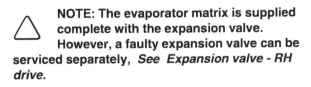

NOTE: The evaporator matrix is supplied complete with the expansion valve. However, a faulty expansion valve can be serviced separately, *See Expansion valve - RH drive.*

**Refit**

15. Locate side panels to new evaporator lower fixing studs.
16. Fit evaporator, with side plates, into main casing. Ensure both studs are located through bottom of casing and secure.
17. Apply sealing compound around joint seam of main casing.
18. Fit top cover to main casing.
19. Fit thermostat probe to to low pressure pipe and apply sealant.
20. Fit top adaptor pipe to heater matrix.
21. Fit Lucar connector and eath eyelet to blower motor.
22. Fit blower motor cover.
23. Fit heater/cooler unit assembly into engine compartment *See Heater/cooler unit.*

## EXPANSION VALVE - RH DRIVE

**Service repair no - 82.25.01**

**Remove**

1. Remove evaporator *See Evaporator - RH drive.*

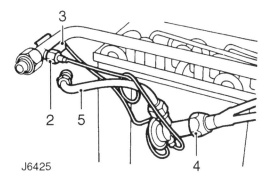

J6425

2. Unscrew union securing pressure sensor to low pressure pipe.
3. Release spring clip securing temperature sensor to low pressure pipe.
4. Unscrew union and remove expansion valve from evaporator high pressure pipe.
5. Remove high pressure pipe from expansion valve.
6. Discard all pipe connection 'O' rings.

**Refit**

7. Coat unions, threads and new 'O' rings with refrigerant oil prior to reassembly.
8. Fit high presssure pipe to new expansion valve.
9. Fit expansion valve to evaporator high pressure pipe.
10. Secure temperature and pressure sensors to low pressure pipe.
11. Fit evaporator *See Evaporator - RH drive.*

## HEATER MATRIX - RH DRIVE

**Service repair no - 82.25.19**

**Remove**

1. Remove heater/cooler unit *See Heater/cooler unit - RH drive.*
2. Suitably support unit on a bench.
3. Remove sealant and release thermostat probe from low pressure pipe.

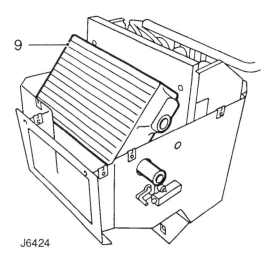

J6424

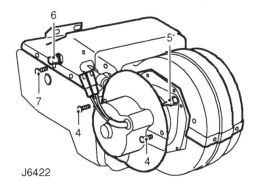

J6422

4. Remove 2 screws securing blower motor cover to main casing.
5. Withdraw cover sufficiently to release motor Lucar connector and earth eyelet. Remove cover.
6. Unscrew top adaptor pipe from heater matrix.
7. Remove 18 fixings securing top cover to main casing and heater/cooler support frame.
8. Carefully break sealing compound around edge of joint seam and remove top cover from main casing.
9. Lift out heater matrix.
10. Clean sealing compound from all joint seams of main casing and top cover.

**Refit**

11. Locate heater matrix in main casing.
12. Apply sealing compound around joint seam of main casing.
13. Fit top cover to main casing.
14. Fit adaptor pipe to heater matrix.
15. Fit thermostat probe to to low pressure pipe and apply sealant.
16. Fit Lucar connector and eath eyelet to blower motor.
17. Fit blower motor cover.
18. Fit heater/cooler unit assembly into engine compartment *See Heater/cooler unit.*

## RESISTOR, BLOWER MOTOR - LH DRIVE

**Service repair no - 82.20.26**

**Remove**

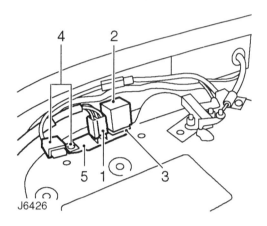

1. Remove multi-plug from resistor.
2. Remove blower motor relay from connecting block to gain access to fixing screw.
3. Remove screw and release relay connector block. Retain relay in connector block.
4. Remove screw and detach air conditioning 30 amp fuse bracket from resistor.
5. Lift resistor unit from top cover.

**Refit**

6. Locate resistor unit in top cover.
7. Fit fuse bracket.
8. Fit blower motor relay connector block and relay.
9. Fit resistor multi-plug.

## RESISTOR, BLOWER MOTOR - RH DRIVE

**Service repair no - 82.20.26**

**Remove**

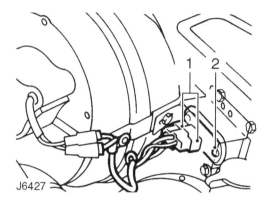

1. Remove multi-plugs from resistor.
2. Remove 2 screws securing resistor to wing mounted block.
3. Withdraw resistor unit.

**Refit**

4. Secure resistor to mounting block.
5. Fit resistor multi-plugs.

# 84 - WIPERS AND WASHERS

## CONTENTS

Page

# Notes

## WIPER MOTOR AND DRIVE RACK

**Service repair no - 84.15.09**

**Remove**

1. Disconnect battery.
2. Remove wiper arms.

 **NOTE: Operations 3 - 5 are for RH drive vehicles only.**

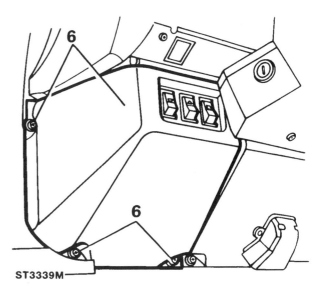

ST3339M

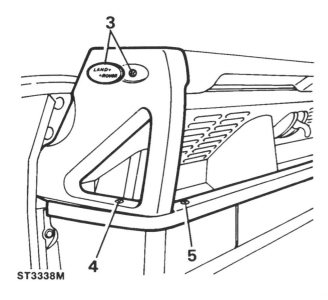

ST3338M

3. Prise Land Rover decal from grab handle and remove screw.
4. Remove lower screw and lift handle from fascia.
5. Remove screw fixing finisher to wiper motor cover.
6. Remove door check strap cover, remove 3 screws and withdraw wiper motor cover. If applicable, disconnect switch multi-plugs and/or radio speaker leads.
7. Disconnect multi-plug from wiper motor.
8. Disconnect wiper motor earth lead. (Not applicable on later models)
9. Lift rubber sleeve and slacken wiper motor to drive tube nut.
10. Remove 2 screws and release wiper motor retaining strap.
11. Fully unscrew tube nut.
12. Pull wiper motor and drive rack clear of tube and retrieve mounting pad and earth tag.

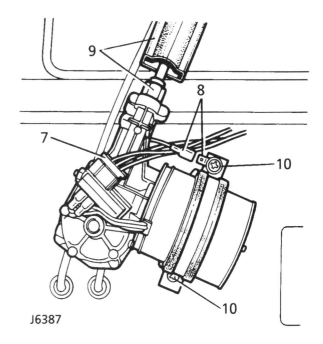

J6387

**Refit**

13. Feed wiper motor drive rack into tube until fully seated.
14. Loosely fit drive tube securing nut.
15. Fit wiper motor securing strap, earth tag and mounting pad. Align motor and tighten fixing screws.

16. Fully tighten tube nut and fit rubber sleeve.
17. Reconnect earth lead and multi-plug.
18. Before fitting cover and grab handle, fit wiper blades. Reconnect battery and test operation of wiper motor and drive assembly. If necessary, adjust position of wiper blades.
19. Fit wiper motor cover and door check strap cover.
20. On RH drive vehicles, fit finisher and grab handle.

## WIPER MOTOR AND DRIVE RACK - VEHICLE WITH AIR CONDITIONING, LH DRIVE

**Service repair no - 84.15.20**

**Remove**

1. Disconnect battery.
2. Remove wiper arms.

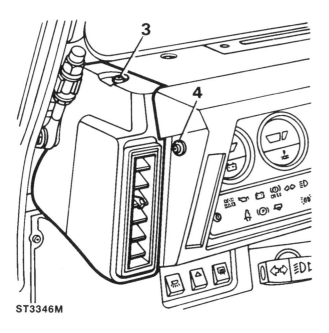

ST3346M

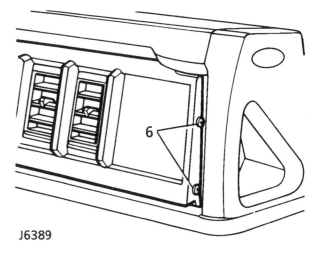

J6389

3. Remove single screw and remove fascia side panel.
4. Remove 5 screws and withdraw instrument panel as far as possible without straining wires and cables.
5. Remove steering wheel *See STEERING, Repair, Steering wheel.*
6. Remove 2 screws at RH side and single screw at LH side, inside instrument cowel, and withdraw air conditioning panel and controls.
7. Release fascia panel LH support bracket.
8. Remove wiper motor cover finisher.

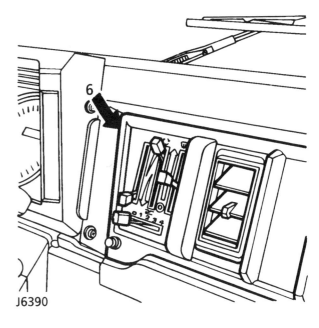

J6390

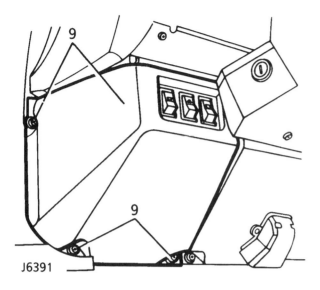

J6391

9. Remove door check strap cover and 3 screws and withdraw wiper motor cover. If applicable, disconnect switch multi-plugs and/or radio speaker leads.

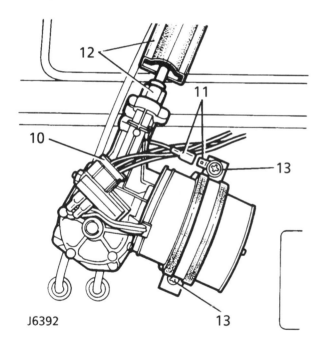

J6392

10. Disconnect wiper motor multi-plug.
11. Disconnect earth lead. (Not applicable on later models)
12. Lift rubber sleeve from wiper motor and slacken wiper motor to drive tube nut.
13. Remove 2 screws and release wiper motor retaining strap, complete with mounting pad and earth tag.
14. Pull wiper motor and drive rack clear of drive tubes.

**Refit**

15. Feed drive rack into drive tube until fully located in wheel boxes.
16. Finger tighten drive tube nut.
17. Position motor mounting pad, fit retaining strap, including earth tag and secure wiper motor assembly.
18. Fully tighten drive tube nut and fit rubber sleeve.
19. Fit wiper motor multi-plug and earth lead to tag on motor retaining strap.
20. Before fitting fascia panels, fit wiper blades, reconnect battery and test wiper operation.
21. Refit fascia panels, noting that air conditioning panel must be located and secured, on LH side, with single screw, before instrument panel is fitted.
22. Fit steering wheel **See STEERING, Repair, Steering wheel.**

## WINDSCREEN WIPER ARMS

**Service repair no - 84.15.01**

### Remove

1. Pull wiper arm away from windscreen.
2. Using a small screwdriver, hold back spring clip which retains arm to spindle adaptor.
3. Pull wiper arm from splined adaptor.

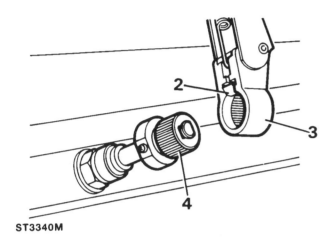

ST3340M

### Refit

4. Switch wiper motor to 'park' position, with grub screw retaining adaptor, uppermost.
5. Push arm on to adaptor so that wiper blade is just clear of windscreen surround rubber.
6. Operate wipers and, if necessary, adjust position of arms.

## WINDSCREEN WIPER/WASHER SWITCH

**Service repair no - 84.15.34**

For remove and refit procedure *See ELECTRICAL, Repair, Windscreen wiper/washer switch.*

## REAR SCREEN WIPER/WASHER SWITCH

**Service repair no - 84.35.34**

For remove and refit procedure *See ELECTRICAL, Repair, Rear screen wiper/washer switch.*

**WINDSCREEN WIPER WHEEL BOXES - NON AIR CONDITIONED VEHICLES**

**Service repair no - 84.15.25**

**Remove**

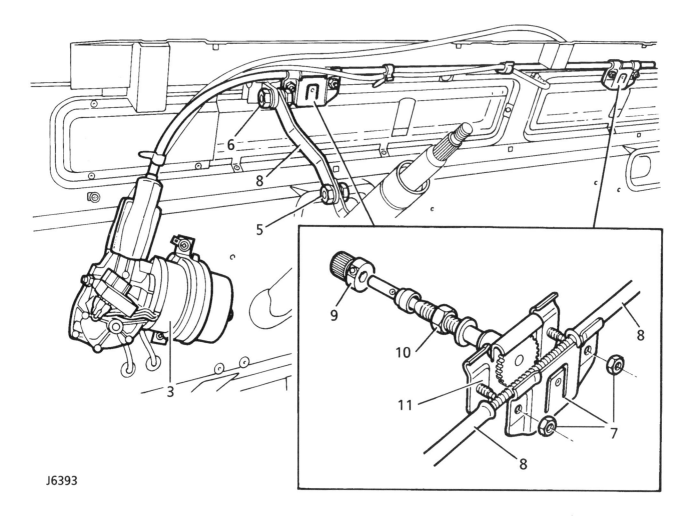

J6393

1. Disconnect battery.
2. Remove wiper arms *See Windscreen wiper arms.*
3. Remove wiper motor *See Wiper motor and drive.*
4. Remove instrument housing, fascia crash pad, and ventilator grille panel.
5. Slacken steering column support rod lower fixing.

6. Remove steering column upper support fixing.
7. Slacken nuts to release back plates from LH and RH wheel boxes.
8. Remove drive rack tubes.
9. Slacken grub screws and remove wiper arm adaptors.
10. Remove LH and RH wheelbox spindle nuts.
11. Remove wheel box assemblies from vehicle.

**Refit**

⚠ NOTE: During reassembly all fixings related to wiper motor and wheelboxes are finger tightened only, until all components are correctly aligned.

12. Fit wheelboxes to bulkhead and secure with retaining nuts and washers.
13. Fit drive rack tubes to wheelboxes.
14. Apply grease to drive rack and wheelboxes.
15. Align wiper motor and mounting pad, secure with retaining strap and tighten drive tube nut.
16. Fully tighten wheelbox back plate nuts.
17. Fully tighten both wheelbox spindle nuts.
18. Fit wiper arm adaptors and secure with grub screw.
19. Before refitting panels fit wiper blades, connect multi-plug and earth lead, reconnect battery and check wiper operation.
20. If satisfactory, secure steering column upper and lower fixings and tighten to correct torque.
21. Fit ventilator grille panel, fascia crash pad, instrument housing and all other components removed to gain access to wiper motor and wheelboxes.

## WINDSCREEN WIPER WHEELBOXES - AIR CONDITIONED VEHICLES

Service repair no - 84.15.25/20

**Remove**

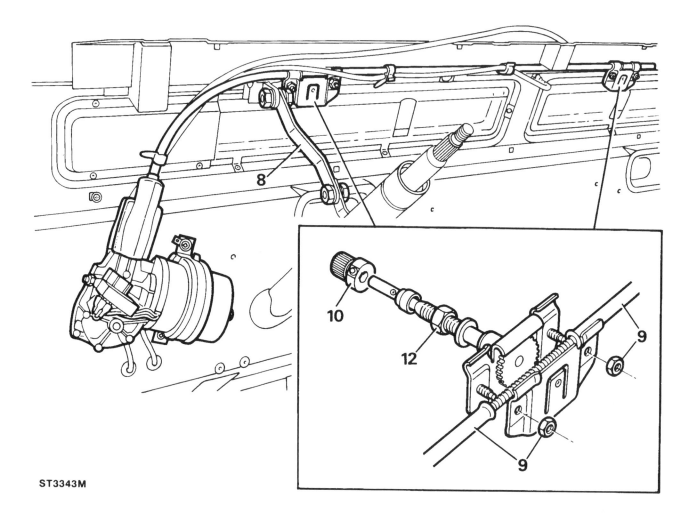

ST3343M

1. Disconnect battery.
2. Remove wiper motor and drive rack *See Wiper motor and drive rack - air conditioned vehicles*
3. Remove centre and LH fascia top crash rail support bracket fixings.
4. Remove both demister vents from ducts.
5. Remove RH demister vent hose from duct.
6. Remove RH vent demister vent fixing and pivot vent and hose aside.
7. Remove demister vent top duct.

8. Release steering column upper and lower support rods.
9. Slacken LH and RH wheelbox nuts and remove drive tubes from wheelboxes.
10. Remove wiper arm splined adaptor.
11. Remove spacer, where fitted, early vehicles only.
12. Remove nuts securing left and RH wheel boxes and withdraw wheelboxes from bulkhead.

△ **NOTE: During assembly all fixings related to wiper motor and wheelboxes are finger tightened only until all components are correctly aligned.**

13. Fit wheelboxes to bulkhead.
14. Fit drive tubes to wheelboxes.
15. Feed drive rack through tubes until fully seated in both wheelboxes.
16. Secure drive tube nut to wiper motor.
17. Fit wiper motor strap and earth lead.
18. When all components are correctly aligned, fully tighten wheelboxes nuts to secure drive tubes. Tighten wheelbox to bulkhead nuts.
19. Fully tighten drive tube nut to wiper motor and motor strap screws.
20. Connect multiplug to wiper motor and earth lead to strap tag.
21. Fit spacer, where used, early vehicles only.
22. Fit wiper arm adaptors.
23. Reconnect battery and check operation of wiper motor and drive assembly and wheelboxes.
24. Disconnect battery.
25. Fit steering column upper and lower supports. Tighten fixings to correct torque.
26. Fit demister vent top duct.
27. Secure RH demister vent and hose.
28. Fit LH and RH demister vents to ducts.
29. Fit centre and LH fascia top crash rail support brackets.
30. Fit all other components removed to gain access to wiper motor and wheelboxes.
31. Reconnect battery, check wiper motor operation again and adjust wiper arms, if necessary.

## REAR WIPER MOTOR

**Service repair no - 84.35.12**

**Remove**

1. With assistance, unscrew 3 retaining nuts and remove spare wheel from rear door mounting studs.

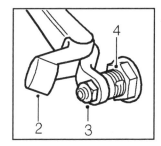

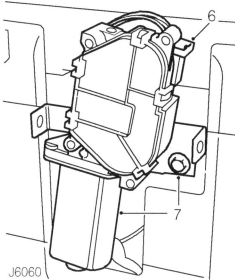

J6060

2. Lift wiper arm end cap to gain access to securing nut.
3. Remove nut and withdraw wiper arm from drive spindle.
4. Remove retaining nut, plain washer and rubber washer securing wiper motor drive spindle to door.
5. Remove 2 screws and remove cover from wiper motor mounting bracket.
6. Disconnect wiper motor harness multi-plug.
7. Remove bolt, with rubber washer, and detach wiper motor, complete with mounting bracket, from rear door.

**Refit**

8. Locate wiper motor drive spindle through aperture in rear door.
9. Position wiper motor mounting bracket and secure to rear door. Tighten bolt to *23 Nm (17 lbf/ft)*.
10. Reconnect harness multi-plug.
11. Secure drive spindle to door.
12. Fit wiper motor cover.
13. Fit rear wiper arm.
14. Fit spare wheel. Tighten retaining nuts to *130Nm (96 lbf/ft)*.

## WIPER MOTOR

**Service repair no - 84.15.18.**

**Dismantle**

1. Remove wiper motor from vehicle *See Repair, Wiper motor and drive rack.*
2. Remove wiper motor gearbox cover.
3. Remove circlip and plain washer securing connecting rod.
4. Withdraw connecting rod.
5. Withdraw flat washer.
6. Remove circlip and washer securing shaft and gear.
7. Clean any burrs from gear shaft and withdraw gear.
8. Withdraw dished washer.
9. Add alignment marks to yoke and gearbox for reassembly.
10. Remove yoke securing bolts.

11. Withdraw yoke and armature.
12. Remove brush gear assembly.
13. Remove limit switch.

**Inspection and test**

14. Check brushes for excessive wear, if they are worn to 4,8 mm in length, fit a new brush gear assembly.
15. Using a push type gauge, check that brush spring pressure is 140 to 200 g when bottom of brush is level with bottom of slot in brush box. Fit a new brush gear assembly if springs are not satisfactory.
16. Test armature for insulation and open- or short-circuits. Use a 110 V 15 W test lamp. Fit a new armature if faulty.
17. Examine gear wheel for damage or excessive wear.

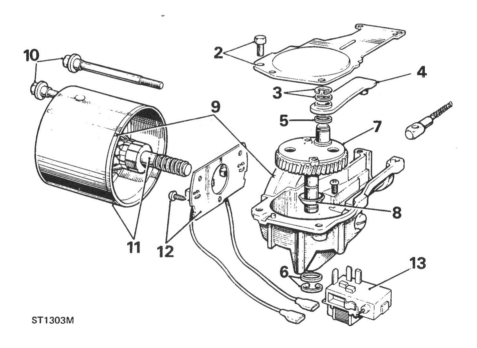

ST1303M

**Key to wiper motor components**

1. Flexible drive
2. Gearbox cover
3. Connecting-rod retaining washer and circlip
4. Connecting-rod
5. Flat washer
6. Gear shaft retaining washer and circlip
7. Drive gear
8. Dished washer
9. Alignment marks - yoke to body
10. Yoke securing bolts
11. Armature and yoke
12. Brush gear assembly
13. Limit switch

**Assemble**

Use Ragosine Listate Grease to lubricate gear wheel teeth, armature shaft worm gear, connecting rod and pin, cable rack and wheelbox gear wheels.

Use Shell Turbo 41 oil sparingly to lubricate bearing bushes, armature shaft bearing journals, gear wheel shaft and wheelbox spindles. Thoroughly soak felt washer in yoke bearing with oil.

18. Fit limit switch.
19. Fit brush gear assembly.

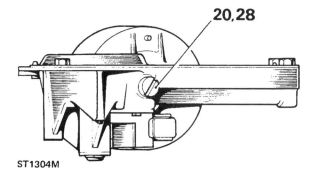

ST1304M

20. Fit armature and yoke to gearbox using alignment marks, secure with yoke retaining bolts tightening to **23 Nm (17 lbf/ft).** If a replacement armature is being fitted slacken thrust screw to provide end-float for fitting yoke.
21. Fit dished washer beneath gear wheel with concave side towards gear wheel.
22. Fit gear wheel to gearbox.
23. Secure gear wheel shaft with plain washer and circlip.
24. Fit larger flat washer over crankpin.
25. Fit connecting rod and secure with smaller plain washer and circlip.
26. Fit gearbox cover and secure with retaining screws.
27. Connect electrical leads between wiper motor and limit switch.
28. To adjust armature shaft end-float, hold yoke vertically with adjuster screw uppermost. Carefully screw in adjuster until resistance is felt, then back-off one quarter turn.

# 86 - ELECTRICAL

## CONTENTS

# 86 - ELECTRICAL

## CONTENTS

## ELECTRICAL EQUIPMENT

### Description

The electrical system is Negative ground, and it is most important to ensure correct polarity of electrical connections at all times. Any incorrect connections made when reconnecting cables may cause irreparable damage to semi-conductor devices used in generator and regulator. Incorrect polarity would also seriously damage any transistorized equipment such as a radio.

⚠ **WARNING: During battery removal or before carrying out any repairs or maintenance to electrical components always disconnect battery negative lead first. If positive lead is disconnected with negative lead in place, accidental contact of wrench to any grounded metal part could cause a severe spark, possibly resulting in personal injury. Upon installation of battery positive lead should be connected first.**

## GENERATOR

The generator is a three phase, field sensed unit. The rotor and stator windings produce three phase alternating current, AC, which is rectified to direct current, DC. The electronic voltage regulator unit controls generator output voltage by high frequency switching of the rotor field circuit. Use only correct replacement drive belt. Occasionally check that engine and generator pulleys are accurately aligned.

It is essential that good electrical connections are maintained at all times. Of particular importance are those in the charging circuit (including those at battery) which should be occasionally inspected to see that they are clean and tight. In this way any significant increase in circuit resistance can be prevented.

Do not disconnect battery cables while engine is running or damage to semi-conductor devices may occur. It is also inadvisable to break or make any connections in the generator charging and control circuits while engine is running.

The electronic voltage regulator employs micro-circuit techniques resulting in improved performance under difficult service conditions. The whole assembly is encapsulated in silicone rubber and housed in an aluminium heat sink, ensuring complete protection against adverse effects of temperature, dust, and moisture etc.

The regulating voltage is set during manufacture to give required regulating voltage range of 14.2 ± 0.2 volts, and no adjustment is necessary. The only maintenance needed is occasional check on terminal connections and wiping with a clean dry cloth.

The generator system provides for direct connection of a charge (ignition) indicator warning lamp, and eliminates the need for a field switching relay or warning light control unit. In the event of bulb failure, an 'exciter' voltage is supplied through a resistor, wired in parallel to the bulbs, ensuring that generator output is maintained. The lamp should be checked regularly.

When using rapid charge equipment to re-charge battery, the battery must be disconnected from the vehicle.

## VEHICLE IMMOBILISATION AND ALARM SYSTEM

A sophisticated engine immobilisation and anti-theft alarm system is offered on the Land Rover Defender 300 Tdi vehicle range, which incorporates the following features:

### Perimeter protection

This part of the alarm system protects side doors, bonnet and rear door against unauthorised entry - alarm sounding if any one of these apertures is opened without alarm first being disarmed.

### Interior protection

Also known as volumetric protection, this part of the system protects space inside the vehicle. Once armed, the alarm will sound if a door is opened, or if movement is detected inside the vehicle.

### Engine immobilisation

The engine is immobilised electronically whenever the alarm system is armed. Even if the alarm has not been armed, engine immobilisation will occur automatically thirty seconds after the driver's door is opened, or five minutes after the starter switch is turned to position '0'.

## ALARM SYSTEM COMPONENTS

### Electronic control unit (ECU)

The ECU is the alarm system brain and controls all vehicle immobilisation and alarm functions. It responds to the inputs received, by supplying suitable outputs to indicate status of the alarm system or activating relevant warning devices. unit is located under fascia behind instrument binnacle.

### Handset and key

The handset is the primary source of control for the alarm system i.e. it arms and disarms the alarm components. The key can be used to override engine immoblisation if the handset is lost or fails to operate, see **Engine immobilisation override.**

The handset battery should last for approximately three years dependent upon use. The following symptoms will be noticed when the battery requires replacement:

1. The handset will only work every other operation while disarming.
2. The direction indicator lamps will not flash when the alarm is disarmed.

For battery replacement procedure, see **Handset Battery.**

### Passive coil

The passive coil is fitted on the starter switch and activates a receiving coil in the handset, causing it to automatically transmit a remobilisation signal to the ECU.

### Aerial

The aerial is integral within the alarm system harness and supplies the ECU with the signal received from handset.

### Immobilisation spider

The immobilisation spider provides an interface between ECU and immobilised areas of the vehicle. This is installed in a sealed (safe) box inside the vehicle battery box.

### Digital diesel shut-off valve - 97 MY

When fitted, the digital diesel shut-off valve immobilises the fuel injection pump by preventing power reaching the fuel shut-off solenoid, **See Immobilisation and alarm system circuit diagram - with DDS.**

## Door and bonnet switches

Perimetric protection for the vehicle is provided by ECU inputs connected to the starter switch, bonnet switch and door switches.

## Ultrasonic sensor

The ultrasonic sensor operates by emitting an air pressure carrier wave which is subsequently received by the sensor as it bounces back from objects inside the vehicle. Once armed, the alarm will sound if wave is disturbed by a door opening, or if movement is detected inside the vehicle.

When the volumetric sensor is activated it monitors movement within the vehicle for 15 seconds before detecting and responding to intrusions. If the sensor detects movement it delays arming until a quiet period has lapsed; if continuous movement is detected, the alarm will not arm volumetrically.

 **NOTE: Interior protection will not operate until 15 seconds after alarm is set.**

The ultrasonic sensor is positioned in a different location, according to vehicle type, as follows:

- 90/110 Station Wagon - RH cantrail trim

- 90/110 Pick-up - On headlining, between interior lamp and rear view mirror

- 130 Crewcab - On headlining above RH door

## Alarm sounder

Two types of alarm sounder can be fitted, one with a battery back-up facility and or without battery back-up, both providing an audible warning whenever the alarm is triggered. The vehicle horn will also operate if the alarm sounds.

The alarm sounder is fitted to LH inner front wing in the engine compartment.

**NOTE: Disconnecting the battery on vehicles fitted with the battery backed-up facility will result in the alarm sounding, if correct procedure has not been followed.**

## Engine immobilisation warning light

The engine immobilisation warning light is located on the instrument panel, and provides a visual indication that the engine is immobilised.

## Anti-theft alarm indicator light

The anti-theft alarm indicator light is located on the instrument panel, between the fuel and coolant temperature indicators, and provides a visual indication of the alarm/ immobiliser status.

## ALARM SYSTEM COMPONENT LOCATION

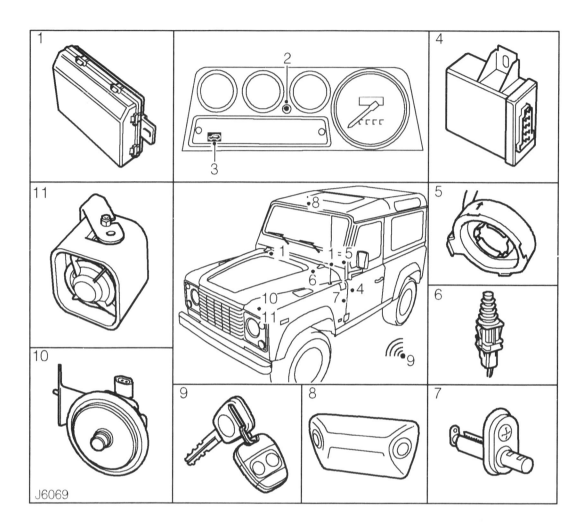

J6069

| COMPONENT | LOCATION |
|-----------|----------|
| 1. Electronic control unit (ECU) | Under dash, LH and RH drive |
| 2. Anti-theft alarm indicator light | Instrument panel |
| 3. Engine immobilisation warning light | Instrument panel |
| 4. Immobilisation spider* | Inside vehicle battery box |
| 5. Passive coil | Over starter switch barrel |
| 6. Bonnet switch | Engine compartment, LH and RH drive |
| 7. Door switches | |
| 8. Ultrasonic sensor | Varies according to vehicle type |
| 9. Handset and key | |
| 10. Alarm sounder (without battery back-up) | LH inner front wing |
| 11. Alarm sounder (with battery back-up) | LH inner front wing |

* Replaced in some markets by a digital diesel shut-off valve (DDS), secured directly to fuel shut-off solenoid on injection pump.

## ALARM SYSTEM OPERATION

### Arming alarm

To arm the alarm, aim handset at vehicle and press the RH button (Padlock symbol). Provided all doors and or apertures are closed, the direction indicator lamps will flash three times to confirm that the alarm is armed. All security features previously described will be active.

Once armed, the alarm will sound if a door or the bonnet is opened, or if movement is detected inside the vehicle.

### Disarming alarm

Within range of the vehicle, briefly press the LH (Plain) button on the handset; the direction indicator lamps will flash once to indicate that the alarm has been disarmed and the engine re-mobilised.

 **NOTE: In some territories, the interior lamps will illuminate when the alarm is disarmed.**

**If the direction indicators fail to flash when the alarm is armed:**

This indicates that a door or the bonnet is not fully closed, in which case the alarm will be partially armed and engine immobilised, but interior protection will not be active.

Once the open door or bonnet is closed, the direction indicators will flash three times and the alarm will fully arm as described previously.

**If the alarm sounds:**
**The vehicle horn and alarm sounder will operate continuously for 30 seconds when the alarm is triggered. The horn and alarm sounder can be triggered up to three times.**

To silence the alarm, press either handset button. If the handset is inoperative, the alarm can only be disarmed by entering the emergency key access code, see **Engine immobilisation override.**

### Anti-theft alarm indicator light

A RED indicator light on the instrument panel indicates the status of the alarm system. When the alarm is armed successfully, the light flashes rapidly. After 10 seconds, the light adjusts to a slower frequency and continues flashing as an anti-theft deterrent.

If the light fails to illuminate during the rapid flash phase, this indicates a 'mislock' (door or the bonnet not fully closed or key in starter switch). If this occurs, the indicator light will still flash at slower frequency as an anti-theft deterrent.

The indicator light will illuminate continuously under the following conditions:

1. Alarm system armed and immobilised with ignition 'on' or driver's door open.
2. Engine immobilised with ignition 'on' or driver's door open.

### Interior protection

Interior protection is activated automatically when the alarm system is armed; twin sensors inside the vehicle monitor interior space and will activate the alarm if an intrusion is detected.

However, if passengers or animals are to be left inside the vehicle, or if a window or sunroof is to be left open, the alarm must be armed with the interior protection DISABLED as follows:

**To disable interior protection:**

1. Open the driver's door.
2. Use the handset to arm the alarm in normal way.
3. Close the driver's door (the direction indicator lamps will flash three times and the anti-theft indicator light commences flashing rapidly). The alarm system is now armed with the interior protection disabled.

 **NOTE: Interior protection will not operate until 15 seconds after the alarm is set.**

## ENGINE IMMOBILISATION

Engine immobilisation is an important aspect of the vehicle's security system, and occurs automatically whenever the alarm system is armed.

The system also includes a feature known as 'passive immobilisation', which is designed to safeguard the vehicle from theft should the driver forget to arm the alarm.

Passive immobilisation occurs automatically as follows:

- Thirty seconds after the starter switch has been turned off and the driver's door opened.

- Five minutes after the starter switch is turned off or the alarm system is disarmed.

If the engine has immobilised passively, re-mobilisation will occur when the starter switch is turned to position 'II', provided the handset is on the same ring as key and in close proximity to the switch.

ALWAYS keep the handset on the same ring as the key.

NEVER attach both handsets to the same key ring.

Any attempt to start the engine while it is immobilised will cause the engine immobilisation warning light to flash.

### Engine immobilisation override

If the handset is lost or fails to operate, the engine immobilisation can be overridden by using the starter key to enter the four digit emergency access code. The procedure for entering the code is described after the following note:

⚠ **NOTE: If the handset is lost or inoperative, it is impossible to disarm the alarm. As soon as the door is opened, the alarm will sound (continuously for up to three 30 second periods), and continue while the code is being entered.**

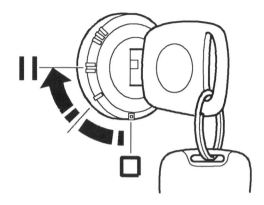

J6076

1. With the driver's door closed, insert the key into the starter switch.
2. Turn the switch to position 'II' the required number of times to enter first digit of code (if first digit is 4, turn key to position 'II' and then back to '0' four times.
3. Open the driver's door (to enter first digit) and then close the door again.
4. Turn the starter switch to position 'II' and back to '0' the required number of times to enter SECOND digit of code.
5. Open the driver's door (to enter second digit) and then close the door again.
6. Turn the starter switch to position 'II' and back to '0' the required number of times to enter THIRD digit of code.
7. Open the driver's door (to enter third digit) and then close door again.
8. Turn the starter switch to position 'II' and back to '0' the required number of times to enter FOURTH digit of code.
9. Finally, open and close the driver's door. If the code has been entered correctly, the anti-theft indicator light will extinguish, the engine can be started and the alarm will disarm.

**If an incorrect code has been entered:**

If the code is entered incorrectly, the anti-theft indicator light will continue to illuminate and the engine will fail to start. Before entering the code again, turn the starter switch to position 'II', hold in this position for 5 seconds and then switch off.

After three failed attempts, the security system invokes a delay period of thirty minutes during which the system will not accept any further codes.

## ALARM SYSTEM FUSES

When the vehicle immobilisation and alarm system is fitted, three fuses are used to protect the circuit:

- Alarm system 15 amp fuse, main harness, located behind instrument binnacle.

- Alarm sounder 20 amp fuse No.10, located in main fuse box.

- Alarm system 5 amp fuse No.20, located in main fuse box.

The main fuse box is positioned in the centre of the fascia, in front of the main gear lever. A label in the fuse box cover shows the circuits protected, the fuse rating and their locations. They are also listed below.

**MAIN FUSE BOX**

| Fuse No. | Value (amps) | Electrical circuit |
|---|---|---|
| 1 | 15 | Hazard warning lights |
| 2 | 20 | Interior lamp, horn |
| 3 | 15 | Wipers & washers - rear |
| 4 | 10 | Wipers & washers - front |
| 5 | 15 | Heater |
| 6 | 7.5 | Rear fog guard lamps |
| 7 | 5 | Radio/cassette player |
| 8 | 15 | Heated rear window |
| 9 | 10 | Cigar lighter |
| 10 | 20 | Alarm sounder |
| 11 | 7.5 | Headlamp - RH, dipped beam |
| 12 | 7.5 | Headlamp - LH, dipped beam |
| 13 | 7.5 | Headlamp - RH, main beam |
| 14 | 7.5 | Headlamp - LH, main beam |
| 15 | 5 | Side lamps - LH |
| 16 | 5 | Side lamps - RH |
| 17 | 15 | Stop & reverse lamps |
| 18 | 20 | Air conditioning |
| 19 | 5 | Air conditioning |
| 20 | 5 | Alarm system |

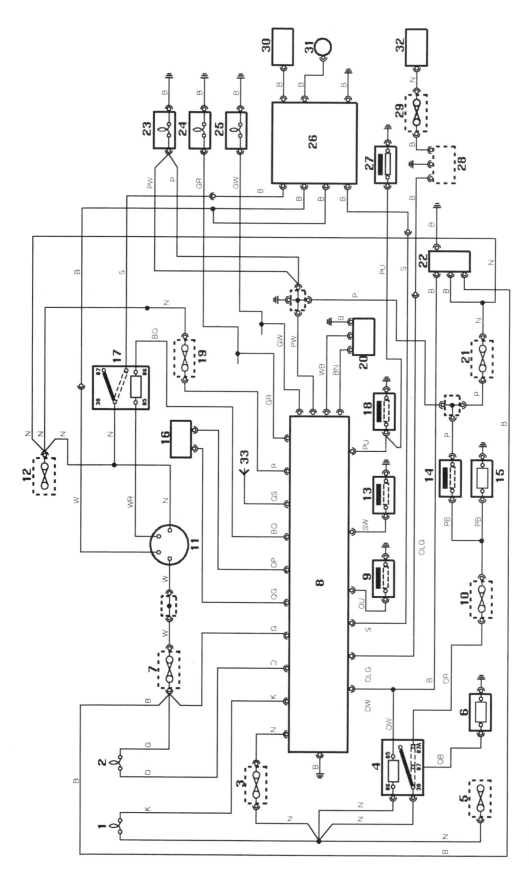

J6082

## IMMOBILISATION AND ALARM SYSTEM CIRCUIT DIAGRAM

1. Anti-theft alarm indicator light (LED)
2. Engine immobilisation warning light
3. Alarm system fuse - 15 amp
4. Alarm sounder relay
5. Under bonnet lighting fuse
6. Alarm sounder (without battery back-up)
7. Alarm system fuse - 5 amp (position 20)
8. Electronic control unit (ECU)
9. Bonnet switch
10. Alarm sounder protection fuse - 20 amp (position 10)
11. Starter switch
12. Under bonnet ignition fuse
13. Driver's door switch
14. Vehicle horn switch
15. Vehicle horn
16. Passive coil
17. Starter switch relay
18. Front passenger door switch
19. Hazard warning light fuse - 15 amp (position 1)
20. Ultrasonic sensor
21. Interior lamp and horn fuse - 20 amp (position 3)
22. Alarm sounder (with battery back-up)
23. LH direction indicator lamps
24. RH direction indicator lamps
25. Interior lamp
26. Immobilisation spider
27. Rear side doors and rear door switches
28. Diagnostic connector
29. Diagnostic fuse - 7.5 amp
30. Starter solenoid
31. Fuel switch-off solenoid (injection pump)
32. Generator
33. Aerial

### Key to cable colours

B-Black
G-Green
K-Pink
LG-Light Green
N-Brown
O-Orange
P-Purple
R-Red
S-Slate
U-Blue
W-White
Y-Yellow

The last letter of a colour code denotes the tracer colour

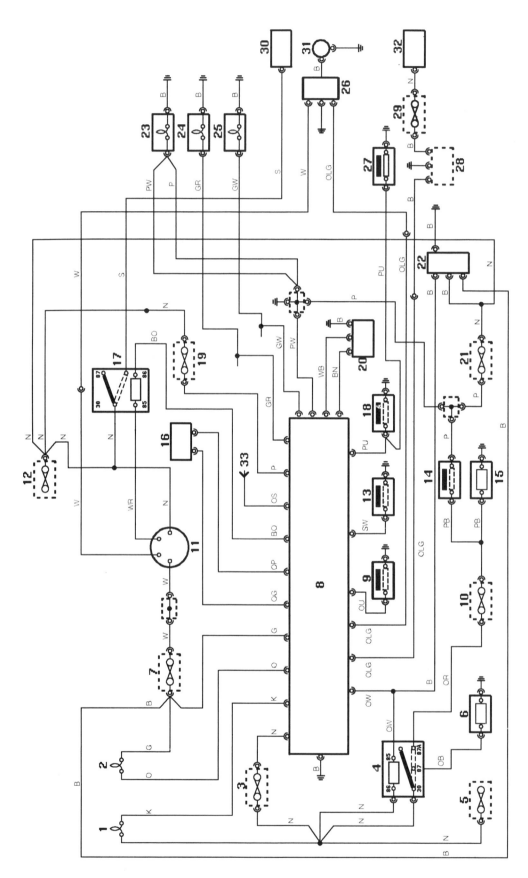

J6445

**IMMOBILISATION AND ALARM SYSTEM CIRCUIT
DIAGRAM - WITH DDS**

1. Anti-theft alarm indicator light (LED)
2. Engine immobilisation warning light
3. Alarm system fuse - 15 amp
4. Alarm sounder relay
5. Under bonnet lighting fuse
6. Alarm sounder (without battery back-up)
7. Alarm system fuse - 5 amp (position 20)
8. Electronic control unit (ECU)
9. Bonnet switch
10. Alarm sounder protection fuse - 20 amp
    (position 10)
11. Starter switch
12. Under bonnet ignition fuse
13. Driver's door switch
14. Vehicle horn switch
15. Vehicle horn
16. Passive coil
17. Starter switch relay
18. Front passenger door switch
19. Hazard warning light fuse - 15 amp (position 1)
20. Ultrasonic sensor
21. Interior lamp and horn fuse - 20 amp (position 3)
22. Alarm sounder (with battery back-up)
23. LH direction indicator lamps
24. RH direction indicator lamps
25. Interior lamp
26. Digital diesel shut-off valve (DDS)
27. Rear side doors and rear door switches
28. Diagnostic connector
29. Diagnostic fuse - 7.5 amp
30. Starter solenoid
31. Fuel shut-off solenoid (injection pump)
32. Generator
33. Aerial

**Key to cable colours**

B-Black
G-Green
K-Pink
LG-Light Green
N-Brown
O-Orange
P-Purple
R-Red
S-Slate
U-Blue
W-White
Y-Yellow

The last letter of a colour code denotes the tracer
colour

## VEHICLE ALARM SYSTEM BUILT-IN TEST

 **NOTE: The handset should be detached from the key to allow perimetric testing of the alarm system. The system will automatically switch to volumetric testing if the handset is in close proximity to the starter switch.**

The built-in test procedure can be accessed providing the following conditions exist:

**Alarm disarmed.**
**Ignition 'off'.**
**Doors unlocked.**
**Bonnet closed.**

With assistance, the test mode can be entered by completing the following instructions within 5 seconds:

1. Open bonnet.
2. Turn starter switch 'on'.
3. Open driver's door (far enough to activate door switch).
4. Turn starter switch 'off'.
5. Turn starter switch 'on'.

If the test mode has been correctly accessed, the alarm sounder/horn will operate briefly and the anti-theft alarm indicator and direction indicator lamps will flash.

### Perimetric tests

The anti-theft alarm indicator light and direction indicator lamps will flash when:

1. Door switches are activated.
2. The bonnet is opened.
3. Key switches are activated.

### Volumetric tests

Press the LH (unlock) button or move the handset close to the starter switch to disable perimetric testing and enable volumetric testing. If movement is detected within the vehicle by the ultrasonic sensor the anti-theft alarm indicator and direction indicator lamps will illuminate.

 **NOTE: Exit the anti-theft alarm built-in test by turning the starter switch to the 'off' position.**

If the previously described conditions are not achieved during the built-in test procedure, this would indicate a fault in the alarm system. Before undertaking detailed fault diagnosis procedures, first make visual checks of components such as a faulty door switch or blown alarm system fuse.

## GENERAL INFORMATION

Detailed information of electrical systems, component locations and circuit diagrams are covered in the Defender Electrical Troubleshooting Manual.

This section covers checks of the charging system.

## GENERATOR TESTING

**Service repair no - 86.10.01**

**Charging system check**

1. Check battery is in good condition, with an open circuit voltage of at least 12.6 V. Recharge or substitute battery to carry out test.
2. Check drive belt condition *See SECTION 10, Maintenance, Under bonnet maintenance.*
3. Check battery connections are clean and tight.
4. Check generator connections are clean and tight.
5. Ensure there is no drain on battery from, for example, interior or exteriorlamps.

**Generator test**

Following instructions refer to use of suitable test equipment using a carbon pile rheostat.

6. Connect test equipment referring to manufacturer's instructions.
7. Start engine and run at 3000 rev/min without accessory load.
8. Rotate carbon pile load control to achieve greatest output (amps) without allowing voltage to fall below 12.0 V. A reading in amps, of generator output should be obtained.
9. Run engine at 3000 rev/min, switch selector to regulator test, read voltmeter. A reading of 13.6 to 14.4 V should be obtained.
10. Switch selector to diode/stator test, switch on headlamps to load generator. Raise engine speed to 3000 rev/min, read voltmeter, needle must be within 'OK' range.

## TESTING IN POSITION

**Charging circuit resistance test.**

1. Connect a low range voltmeter between generator terminal marked B+ and positive terminal of battery.

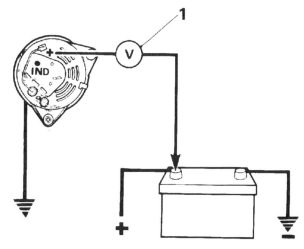

RR 2317E

2. Switch on headlamps, start engine. Run engine at approximately 3000 rev/min. Note voltmeter reading.
3. Transfer voltmeter connections to frame of generator and negative terminal of battery, and again note voltmeter reading.

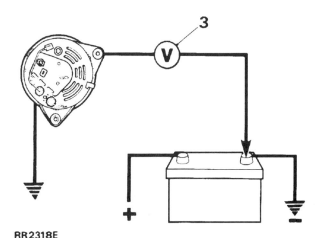

RR 2318E

4. If reading exceeds 0.5 volt on positive side or 0.25 volt on negative side, there is a high resistance in charging circuit which must be traced and remedied.

# Notes

## ELECTRICAL PRECAUTIONS

The following guidelines are intended to ensure the safety of the operator whilst preventing damage to electrical and electronic components fitted to the vehicle.

### Polarity

Never reverse connect the vehicle battery and always observe the correct polarity when connecting test equipment.

### High voltage circuits

 **WARNING: Before commencing work on an ignition system, all high tension terminals, adaptors and diagnostic equipment for testing should be inspected to ensure that they are adequately insulated and shielded to prevent accidental personal contacts and minimize the risk of shock. Wearers of surgically implanted pacemaker devices should not be in close proximity to ignition circuits or diagnostic equipment.**

Whenever disconnecting live high tension circuits always use insulated pliers and never allow the open end of a high tension lead to come into contact with other components particularly electronic control units. Exercise caution when measuring the voltage on the coil terminals while the engine is running, since, high voltage spikes can occur on these terminals.

### Connectors and harness

Always ensure that these items are dry and oil free before disconnecting and connecting test equipment. Never force connectors apart either by using tools or by pulling on the wiring harness. Always ensure locking tabs are disengaged before removal and note orientation to enable correct reconnection. Ensure that any protective covers and substances are replaced if disturbed. Having confirmed a component to be faulty switch-off the ignition and disconnect the battery. Remove the component and support the disconnected harness. When replacing the component keep oily hands away from electrical connection areas and push connectors home until any locking tabs fully engage.

### Battery disconnecting

Before disconnecting the battery, switch off all electrical equipment.

### Battery charging

Recharge the battery out of the vehicle and keep the top well ventilated. While being charged or discharged, and for approximately 15 minutes afterwards, batteries emit hydrogen gas which is flammable. Always ensure any battery charging area is well ventilated and that every precaution is taken to avoid naked flames and sparks.

## GENERAL PRECAUTIONS

Switch-off ignition prior to making any connection or disconnection in the system as electrical surge caused by disconnecting 'live' connections can damage electronic components.

Ensure hands and work surfaces are clean and free of grease, swarf, etc. as grease collects dirt which can cause tracking or high-resistance contacts.

When handling printed circuit boards, treat them as you would a disc - hold by the edges only.

Prior to commencing a test, and periodically during a test, touch a good earth, for instance, a cigar lighter socket, to discharge body static as some electronic components are vulnerable to static electricity.

## BATTERY

**Service repair no - 86.15.01**

 NOTE: If the vehicle is fitted with a battery backed-up alarm sounder, disconnecting the vehicle battery will cause the alarm to sound unless the following procedure is followed:

1. Remove LH front seat cushion.
2. Release retaining clip and remove battery access cover.
3. Slacken battery negative lead clamp bolt.
4. Turn starter switch 'on'.
5. Turn starter switch 'off' and remove key.
6. Disconnect battery WITHIN 15 SECONDS.

If alarm is accidentally activated, ensure sounder is connected and silence by turning the starter switch to position 'II'.

## Remove

⚠ WARNING: During battery removal or before carrying out any repairs or maintenance to electrical components always disconnect negative lead first. If positive lead is disconnected with negative lead in place, accidental contact of a wrench to any grounded metal part could cause a severe spark, possibly resulting in personal injury. Upon installation of battery always connect positive lead first.

1. Remove LH front seat cushion.
2. Release retaining clip and remove battery access cover.

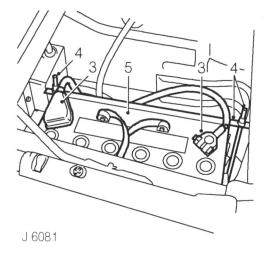

J 6081

3. Disconnect both battery leads, negative first.
4. Slacken securing nuts and move battery clamp, with 'J' bolts aside.
5. Remove battery.

 NOTE: Coat battery clamps and terminals with petroleum jelly before refitting.

## Refit

6. Position battery and secure with clamp. Ensure 'J' bolts are hooked correctly under retaining brackets on base of battery box.
7. Reconnect battery leads, positive lead first.
8. Fit battery access cover.
9. Fit seat cushion.

## ELECTRONIC CONTROL UNIT (ECU)

**Service repair no - 86.55.85**

**Remove**

1. Remove LH front seat cushion.
2. Release retaining clip and remove battery access cover.
3. Slacken battery negative lead clamp bolt.
4. Turn starter switch 'on'.
5. Turn starter switch 'off' and remove key.
6. Disconnect battery negative lead.

 **NOTE: Operation 6 needs to be carried out within 15 seconds to avoid activating battery backed-up alarm sounder, if fitted.**

7. Remove steering wheel *See STEERING, Repair, Steering wheel.*
8. Remove 4 screws securing instrument panel to fascia cowl *See INSTRUMENTS, Repair, Instrument panel.*
9. Pull instrument panel away from fascia cowl and disconnect speedometer cable, multi-plugs, alarm LED plug lead, heated rear screen lead, gearbox oil temperature lead and immobiliser warning light leads.
10. Remove instrument panel.
11. Remove 2 screws securing ECU to fascia cowl (LH drive shown). On RH drive vehicles ECU is positioned lower down, on vertical face of fascia panel.
12. Release ECU from fascia cowl and disconnect both multi-plugs.
13. Remove ECU.

 **NOTE: A new ECU must be initialised using TestBook.**

**Refit**

14. Position ECU at fascia cowl and reconnect both multi-plugs.
15. Locate ECU on mounting face of fascia cowl and secure with 2 screws.
16. Position instrument panel to fascia cowl and reconnect immobiliser warning light leads, gearbox oil temperature lead, heated rear screen lead, alarm LED plug lead, multi-plugs and speedometer cable.

J6070

17. Secure instrument panel to fascia cowl with 4 screws *See INSTRUMENTS, Repair, Instrument panel.*
18. Fit steering wheel *See STEERING, Repair, Steering wheel.*
19. Reconnect battery negative lead.
20. Fit battery access cover.
21. Fit LH seat cushion.

## HANDSET BATTERY

**Service repair no - 86.77.13**

### Remove

1. Unlock vehicle and disarm alarm system.
2. Turn starter switch to position 'II'.
3. Turn starter switch back to position '0' and remove key.

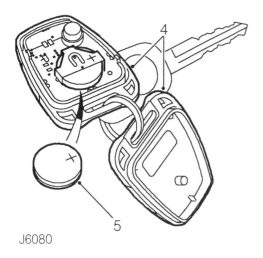

J6080

4. Carefully prise handset apart, starting from keyring end, using a coin or small screwdriver.
5. Slide battery out from retaining clip.
6. Press and hold one of the handset buttons for at least five seconds to drain any residual power from handset.

△ **NOTE: The engine will immobilise five minutes after key is removed from starter switch.**

### Refit

7. Fit new battery into handset retaining clip with positive side uppermost. Finger marks will adversely affect battery life; if possible, avoid touching flat surfaces of battery and wipe clean before fitting.
8. Reassemble two halves of handset.
9. Press RH (Padlock) button at least four times within range of vehicle to resynchronise handset.
10. Check operation of alarm system.

⚠ **WARNING: The handset contains delicate electronic circuits and must be protected from impact and water damage, high temperatures and humidity, direct sunlight and effects of solvents, waxes and abrasive cleaners.**

△ **NOTE: New handsets must be be initialised using TestBook.**

## PASSIVE COIL

**Service repair no - 86.77.35**

**Remove**

1. Remove LH front seat cushion.
2. Release retaining clip and remove battery access cover.
3. Slacken battery negative lead clamp bolt.
4. Turn starter switch 'on'.
5. Turn starter switch 'off' and remove key.
6. Disconnect battery negative lead.

 **NOTE: Operation 6 needs to be carried out within 15 seconds to avoid activating battery backed-up alarm sounder, if fitted.**

7. Remove steering wheel **See STEERING, Repair, Steering wheel.**
8. Remove 4 screws securing instrument panel to fascia cowl **See INSTRUMENTS, Repair, Instrument panel.**
9. Pull instrument panel away from fascia and disconnect speedometer cable, multi-plugs, alarm LED plug lead, heated rear screen lead, gearbox oil temperature lead and immobiliser warning light leads.
10. Remove instrument panel.
11. Remove 7 screws securing upper and lower halves of nacelle to steering column mounting bracket **See STEERING, Repair, Steering column nacelle .**
12. Release multi-switch gaiters from both sides of nacelle.
13. Remove nacelle upper and lower halves from steering column; collect blanking grommet from RH side.
14. Disconnect multi-plug and remove passive coil from starter switch.

**Refit**

15. Feed passive coil plug lead into fascia cowl area and reconnect multi-plug .
16. Fit coil on starter switch.
17. Position nacelle upper and lower halves to steering column mounting bracket and secure with 7 screws. Do not fully tighten screws at this stage **See STEERING, Repair, Steering column nacelle.**
18. Check that passive coil is still fitted correctly on starter switch.

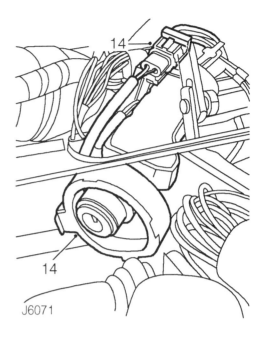

J6071

19. Check fit of nacelle at starter switch and steering column and fully tighten fixing screws.
20. Fit multi-switch gaiters to both sides of nacelle and check that blanking grommet is located.
21. Position instrument panel to fascia cowl area and reconnect immobiliser warning light leads, gearbox oil temperature lead, heated rear screen lead, alarm LED plug lead, main harness multi-plugs and speedometer.
22. Secure instrument panel to fascia cowl with 4 screws **See INSTRUMENTS, Repair, Instrument panel.**
23. Fit steering wheel **See STEERING, Repair, Steering wheel.**
24. Reconnect battery negative lead.
25. Fit battery access cover.
26. Fit LH seat cushion.
27. Test immobilisation and alarm system.

## IMMOBILISATION SPIDER

**Service repair no - 86.77.03**

**Remove**

1. Remove LH front seat cushion.
2. Release retaining clip and remove battery access cover.
3. Slacken battery lead clamp bolts.
4. Turn starter switch 'on'.
5. Turn starter switch 'off' and remove key.
6. Disconnect battery leads.

 **NOTE: Operation 6 needs to be carried out within 15 seconds to avoid activating battery backed-up alarm sounder, if fitted.**

7. Remove battery clamp and 'J' bolts.
8. Remove 4 nuts securing immobilisation spider housing box to fixing studs on front face of battery box.
9. Remove grommet securing spider harness to corner face of battery box.
10. Carefully pull harness into battery box, lift spider housing box and place on front edge of seat base.
11. Using a suitable sheet to protect inside of vehicle, grind heads off 6 monobolts securing lid to spider box housing.
12. Detach lid from housing and disconnect spider harness plug.
13. Unscrew two nuts and remove immobilisation spider from lid studs.

 **NOTE: If spider box lid and/or sealing gasket is damaged during operation 11 a new lid will need to be fitted.**

 **NOTE: A new immobilisation spider must be initialised using TestBook.**

**Refit**

14. Fit immobilisation spider onto lid studs and secure with retaining nuts.
15. Reconnect harness plug to spider and ensure it fully 'clicks' home.
16. Position lid and spider assembly into box housing so that harness plug is furst away from harness entry.

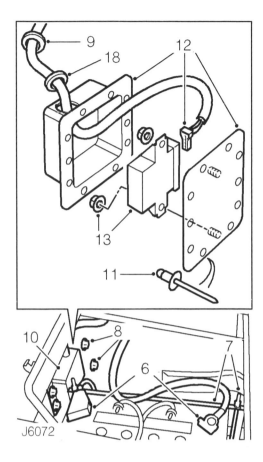

J6072

17. Secure lid to spider box housing with monobolts.
18. Refit harness grommet into spider box, if disturbed on removal procedures, and ensure harness covering is fully inserted through grommet to make water tight seal.
19. Push excess harnes cable through corner face of battery box and fit grommet.
20. Fit spider housing box to fixing studs and secure with four nuts.
21. Fit 'J' bolts and clamp to secure battery,
22. Reconnect battery leads.
23. Fit battery access cover.
24. Fit LH seat cushion.
25. Test immobilisation and alarm system.

## BONNET SWITCH

**Service repair no - 86.55.89**

**Remove**

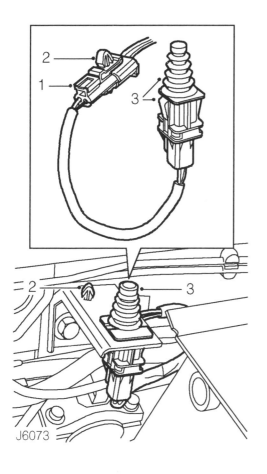

J6073

1. Disconnect bonnet switch harness multi-plug.
2. Release harness retaining clip from switch mounting bracket.
3. Press in retaining clips and remove switch from mounting bracket.

**Refit**

4. Insert harness multi-plug and bonnet switch into mounting bracket. Push switch firmly down to secure in position.
5. Connect harness multi-plug.
6. Fit harness retaining clip in mounting bracket.

## ULTRASONIC SENSOR

**Service repair no - 86.77.32**

**Remove**

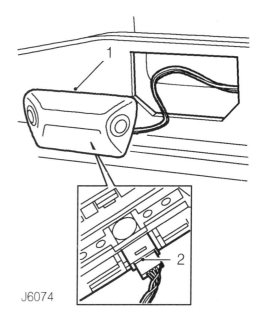

J6074

1. Carefully prise ultrasonic sensor from cantrail trim.
2. Disconnect harness plug and remove sensor.

 **NOTE: Position of sensor will change according to vehicle type.**

**Refit**

3. Connect harness plug to sensor.
4. Fit sensor to cantrail trim.

## ALARM SOUNDER

**Service repair no - 86.55.87**

**Remove**

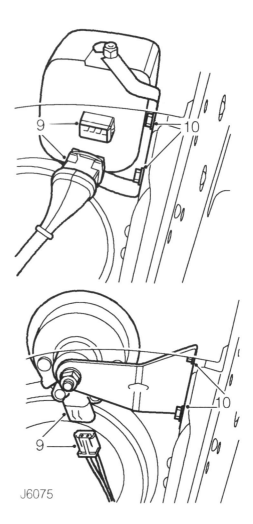

1. Remove LH front seat cushion.
2. Release retaining clip and remove battery access cover.
3. Slacken battery negative lead clamp bolt.
4. Turn starter switch 'on'.
5. Turn starter switch 'off' and remove key.
6. Disconnect battery negative lead.

 **NOTE: Operation 6 needs to be carried out within 15 seconds to avoid activating battery backed-up alarm sounder, if fitted.**

 **NOTE: If an alarm sounder without battery back-up is fitted, it is not necessary to disconnect battery.**

7. Remove 2 nuts securing power steering pump reservoir mounting bracket to front, LH inside wing.
8. Move steering pump reservoir aside to gain access to alarm sounder.
9. Disconnect harness multi-plug from rear of alarm sounder.
10. Unscrew 2 bolts and remove alarm sounder from inside wing.
   Top illustration - alarm sounder **with** battery back-up.
   Lower illustration - alarm sounder **without** battery back-up.

J6075

 **NOTE: A new battery backed-up alarm sounder will not operate until charged by vehicle generator for approximately three hours.**

**Refit**

11. Secure alarm sounder to inside wing, tightening bolts to *10 Nm (7 lbf/ft).*
12. Reconnect multi-plug to alarm sounder.
13. Secure power steering pump reservoir to inside wing, tightening nuts to *10 Nm (7 lbf/ft).*
14. Reconnect battery negative lead.
15. Fit battery access cover.
16. Fit LH seat cushion.

## ALARM SOUNDER RELAY

**Service repair no - 86.77.09**

**Remove**

1. Remove screw and lift off LH door check strap cover.
2. Remove 3 screws and lower wiper motor cover from fascia bulkhead, (on RH drive models first remove grab handle).

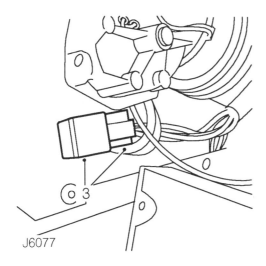

J6077

3. Slide relay multi-plug from retaining bracket and remove relay.

**Refit**

4. Secure multi-plug to mounting bracket and fit new relay.
5. Position wiper motor cover and secure with 3 screws.
6. On RH drive models fit grab handle.
7. Fit door check strap and secure with screw.

## ANTI-THEFT ALARM INDICATOR LIGHT

**Service repair no - 86.45.61**

**Remove**

1. Remove LH front seat cushion.
2. Release retaing clip and remove battery access cover.
3. Slacken battery negative lead clamp bolt.
4. Turn starter switch 'on'.
5. Turn starter switch 'off' and remove key.
6. Disconnect battery negative lead.

> **NOTE: Operation 6 needs to be carried out within 15 seconds to avoid activating battery backed-up alarm sounder, if fitted.**

> **NOTE: If an alarm sounder without battery back-up is fitted, it is not necessary to disconnect battery.**

7. Remove steering wheel *See STEERING, Repair, Steering wheel.*
8. Remove 4 screws securing instrument panel to fascia cowl.
9. Pull instrument panel away from fascia and disconnect speedometer cable, if necessary.

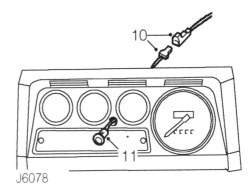

J6078

10. Disconnect alarm indicator light plug lead.
11. Press in retaining lugs and withdraw indicator light from fascia panel.

## Refit

12. Fit alarm indicator light into fascia panel and reconnect plug lead.
13. Reconnect speedometer cable and fit instrument panel to fascia cowl.
14. Fit steering wheel *See STEERING, Repair, Steering wheel.*
15. Reconnect battery negative lead.
16. Fit battery access cover.
17. Fit LH seat cushion.

## ALARM SYSTEM FUSE

**Service repair no - 86.77.04**

**Remove**

1. Remove LH front seat cushion.
2. Release retaining clip and remove battery access cover.
3. Slacken battery negative lead clamp bolt.
4. Turn starter switch 'on'.
5. Turn starter switch 'off' and remove key.
6. Disconnect battery negative lead.

 **NOTE: Operation 6 needs to be carried out within 15 seconds to avoid activating battery backed-up alarm sounder, if fitted.**

 **NOTE: If an alarm sounder without battery back-up is fitted, it is not necessary to disconnect battery.**

7. Remove steering wheel *See STEERING, Repair, Steering wheel.*
8. Remove 4 screws securing instrument panel to fascia cowl *See INSTRUMENTS, Repair, Instrument panel.*
9. Pull instrument panel away from fascia and disconnect speedometer cable, main harness multi-plugs, alarm LED plug lead, heated rear screen leads, gearbox oil temperature lead and immobiliser warning light lead.
10. Remove instrument panel.

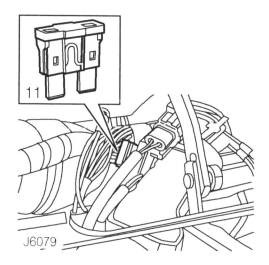

J6079

11. Remove alarm system 15 amp (blue) fuse from holder located behind starter switch.

**Refit**

**12.** Fit new fuse.
**13.** Position instrument panel to fascia cowl area and reconnect immobiliser warning light leads, gearbox oil temperature lead, heated rear screen leads, alarm LED plug lead, main harness multi-plugs and speedometer cable,
**14.** Secure instrument panel to fascia cowl with 4 screws *See INSTRUMENTS, Repair, Instrument panel.*
**15.** Fit steering wheel *See STEERING, Repair, Steering wheel.*
**16.** Reconnect battery negative lead.
**17.** Fit battery access cover.
**18.** Fit LH front seat cushion.

**GENERATOR**

**Service repair no - 86.10.02**

**Remove**

**1.** Disconnect battery.
**2.** Remove drive belt *See Auxiliary drive belt*.

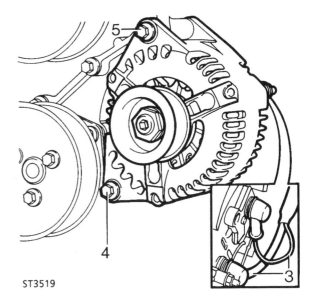

ST3519

**3.** Unscrew 3 fixings, remove heat shield from rear of generator, and disconnect electrical leads from generator.
**4.** Remove generator bottom fixing bolt.
**5.** Remove long through bolt from top fixing and lift generator from engine.

**Refit**

**6.** Fit generator to engine mounting bracket and secure with top and bottom fixing bolts.
**7.** Connect electrical leads.
**8.** Fit heat shield.
**9.** Fit drive belt *See Auxiliary drive belt; Refit*.
**10.** Reconnect battery.

## AUXILIARY DRIVE BELT

**Service repair no - 86.10.03**

⚠ NOTE: If cast lines on tensioner arm and tensioner spring case are aligned, a new drive belt must be fitted.

**Remove**

1. Disconnect battery.
2. Remove fan cowl *See COOLING SYSTEM, Repair, Fan cowl.*

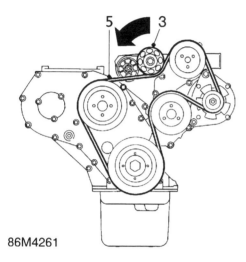

86M4261

3. Apply ring spanner to tensioner pulley retaining bolt.
4. Turn spanner to release pulley tension from belt.
5. Detach belt from pulley.
6. Release tensioner.
7. Complete removal of belt. Mark direction on belt if refitting.

**Refit**

8. Using ring spanner, release pulley tensioner and fit new drive belt.
9. Remove ring spanner, drive belt will automatically tension.
10. Fit fan cowl *See COOLING SYSTEM, Repair, Fan cowl.*

## STARTER MOTOR

**Service repair no - 86.60.01**

**Remove**

1. Disconnect battery.

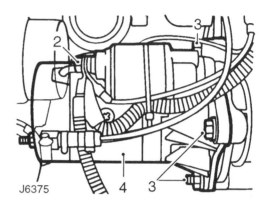

J6375

2. Disconnect electrical leads from starter solenoid.
3. Remove 3 fixings securing starter motor to flywheel housing.
4. Withdraw starter motor.

**Refit**

5. Locate starter motor and secure to flywheel housing.
6. Reconnect electrical leads to starter solenoid.
7. Reconnect battery.

## HEADLAMP

**Service repair no - 86.40.02**

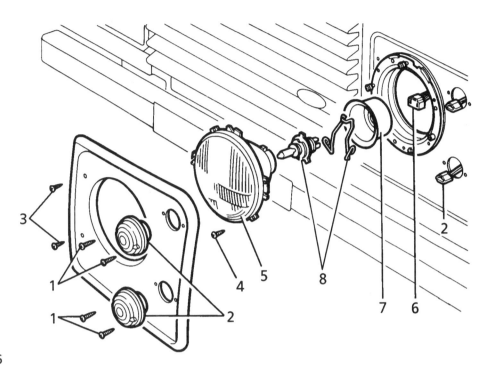

J6376

### Remove

1. Remove screws retaining side and direction indicator lamps.
2. Withdraw lamp units and disconnect plugs.
3. Remove 2 screws and withdraw headlamp finisher.
4. Remove 2 headlamp retaining screws.
5. Rotate headlamp clockwise, disengage from body, and lift out headlamp.
6. Disconnect multi-plug to release headlamp. On vehicles fitted with headlamp levelling unit, also release unit harness plug *See Headlamp levelling unit.*
7. Remove rubber cover.
8. Release spring clip and withdraw headlamp bulb.

 **NOTE: Do not touch bulb glass with fingers. If necessary, clean bulb with methylated spirits.**

### Refit

9. Fit bulb to headlamp and retain with spring clip.
10. Fit rubber cover and reconnect multi-plug. If applicable, fit headlamp levelling unit plug *See Headlamp levelling unit .*
11. Locate headlamp in body and rotate anti-clockwise to engage.
12. Fit headlamp retaining screws.
13. Fit headlamp finisher, side and direction indicator lamps.
14. Check main beam alignment *See Headlamp beam alignment.*

## SIDE, TAIL AND DIRECTION INDICATOR LAMPS

**Service repair no - 86.40.34 - Front side lamp**
**Service repair no - 86.40.45 - Tail lamp**
**Service repair no - 86.40.42 - Front direction indicator lamp**
**Service repair no - 86.40.43 - Rear direction indicator lamp**

**Remove**

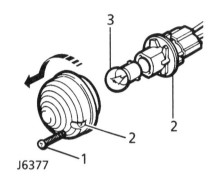

J6377

1. Remove 2 screws and withdraw lamp unit.
2. Hold bulb holder and twist lens to release.
3. Push and twist bulb to remove from holder.

**Refit**

4. Fit new bulb, if necessary.
5. Fit bulb holder to lamp lens.
6. Secure lamp to vehicle.

## SIDE REPEATER LAMP

**Service repair no - 86.40.53.**

**Remove**

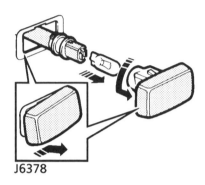

J6378

1. Push lens firmly to the right.
2. Lift left edge and withdraw lamp unit from wing.
3. Twist bulb holder and release from lens.
4. Pull bulb from holder.

**Refit**

5. Fit new bulb, if necessary.
6. Fit bulb holder to lens.
7. Locate lamp unit in wing and push firmly to the left to secure.

## REAR NUMBER PLATE LAMP - BULB RENEWAL

**Service repair no - 86.40.85**

**Remove**

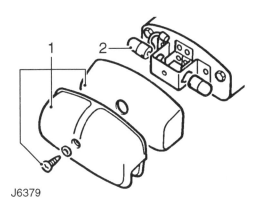

J6379

1. Remove single screw securing lamp cover and lens to bulb holder.
2. Remove bulb/s from holder.

**Refit**

3. Fit new bulb/s.
4. Fit lamp lens and cover.

## REAR NUMBER PLATE LAMP

**Service repair no - 86.40.86**

**Remove**

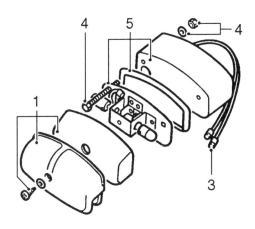

J6380

1. Remove single screw and remove lamp cover and lens.
2. Uncsrew 2 fixings and remove metal cover to gain access to lamp fixings and harness leads inside vehicle.
3. Disconnect lamp leads from harness.
4. Remove 2 bolts, nuts and washers securing lamp to vehicle body.
5. Remove bulb holder, complete with rubber seal and mounting plinth.

**Refit**

6. Feed lamp unit leads through vehicle body and secure bulb holder, seal and plinth.
7. Fit lamp leads to harness connectors.
8. Fit cover to conceal lamp fixings.
9. Fit lens and lamp cover.

## REVERSE AND FOG GUARD LAMP - BULB RENEWAL

**Service repair no - 86.40.90**

**Remove**

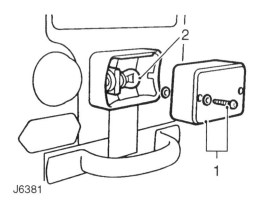

J6381

1. Remove two screws with sealing washers and remove lens from lamp body.
2. Push and twist bulb to release from holder.
3. Clean interior of lamp and lens.

**Refit**

4. Fit new bulb.
5. Fit lens to lamp body.

## REVERSE AND FOG GUARD LAMP

**Service repair no - 86.40.91 - Reverse lamp**
**Service repair no - 86.40.99 - Fog guard lamp**

**Remove**

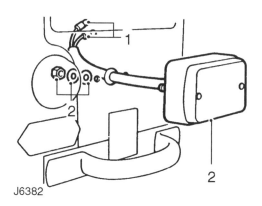

J6382

1. From underneath the vehicle, lift protective flap and disconnect lamp leads at harness connectors.
2. Unscrew 2 nuts and washers and withdraw lamp unit from vehicle.

**Refit**

3. Feed lamp leads through grommet and locate lamp studs in vehicle body.
4. Fit retaining nuts and reconnect lamp leads to vehicle harness.

## INTERIOR LAMP - BULB REMOVAL

**Service repair no - 86.45.01**

**Remove**

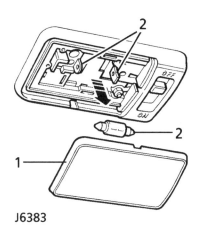

J6383

1. Prise lens from lamp unit.
2. Spread bulb holder contacts and release bulb.

**Refit**

3. Spread bulb holder contacts and fit new bulb.
4. Fit lamp lens.

## INTERIOR LAMP

**Service repair no - 86.45.02**

**Remove**

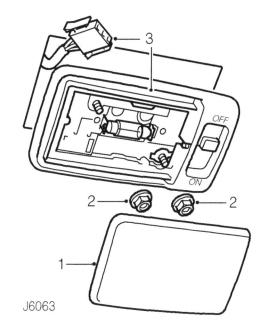

J6063

1. Prise lens cover from lamp unit.
2. Remove 2 nuts securing lamp unit to headlining and roof mounting bracket.
3. Remove lamp unit from mounting bracket studs and disconnect harness plug.
4. Remove interior lamp.

**Refit**

5. Reconnect harness plug and locate lamp unit on mounting bracket studs. Ensure lamp switch eyelet is correctly seated on lamp unit base.
6. Secure lamp unit to mounting bracket and fit lamp lens.

## REVERSE LAMP SWITCH

**Service repair no - 37.27.01**

### Remove

The reverse lamp switch is located on the LH side of the gearbox extension housing and is accessible from underneath the vehicle.

1. Place vehicle on suitable ramp.

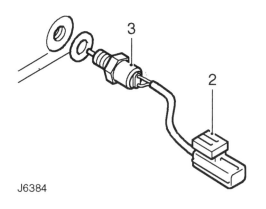

J6384

2. Disconnect reverse lamp switch lead multi-plug from harness connector.
3. Unscrew switch from extension housing.

### Refit

4. Fit new switch to gearbox extension housing. Tighten to **25 Nm (18 lbf/ft).**
5. Fit lamp switch lead multi-plug to harness connector.
6. Check operation of lamp switch.

## WARNING LAMP ASSEMBLY

**Service repair no - 86.45.60 - Warning lamp assembly**
**Service repair no - 86.45.61 - Warning lamp bulb renewal**

### Remove

1. Disconnect battery.

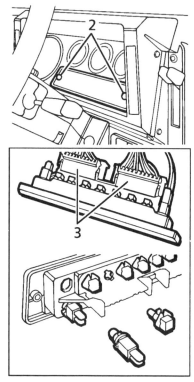

J6385

2. Remove 2 screws and withdraw warning light assembly from instrument panel.
3. Remove multi-plug to give access to warning lamp bulbs.
4. Twist bulb holder and pull it from its socket.
5. Pull bulb from holder.

### Refit

6. Fit new bulb and refit holder.
7. Fit multi-plug.
8. Fit warning lamp assembly to instrument panel
9. Reconnect battery.

## INSTRUMENT ILLUMINATION - BULB RENEWAL

**Service repair no - 86.45.49 - Speedometer**
**Service repair no - 86.45.51 - Temperature gauge**
**Service repair no - 86.45.52 - Fuel gauge**

### Remove

1. Disconnect battery.

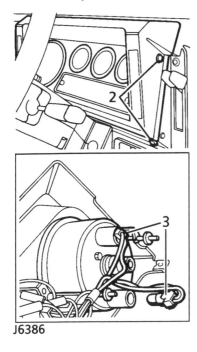

J6386

2. Remove 4 screws retaining instrument panel.
3. Ease panel forward and disconnect speedometer cable to improve access to illumination bulbs.
4. Twist bulb holder and pull from socket.
5. Pull bulb from holder.

### Refit

6. Fit new bulb and refit holder.
7. Reconnect speedometer cable and fit instrument panel.
8. Reconnect battery.

## STARTER SWITCH

**Service repair no - 86.65.03**

### Remove

1. Remove instrument panel *See INSTRUMENTS, Repair, Instrument panel.*
2. Remove steering column nacelle *See STEERING, Repair, Steering column nacelle.*

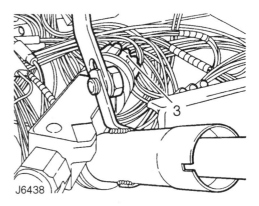

J6438

3. Note position of harness leads on back of starter switch and disconnect lukars. If fitted, remove alarm system passive coil from switch *See Passive coil.*
4. Remove single screw and withdraw starter switch from steering column lock.

### Refit

5. Fit new switch in steering column lock.
6. Connect harness leads to starter switch.
7. If applicable, fit alarm system passive coil *See Passive coil.*
8. Fit steering column nacelle *See STEERING, Repair, Steering column nacelle .*
9. Fit instrument panel *See INSTRUMENTS, Repair, Instrument panel.*

**WINDSCREEN WIPER/WASHER SWITCH**

**Service repair no - 84.15.34**

**Remove**

1. Remove steering column nacelle *See STEERING, Repair, Steering column nacelle.*

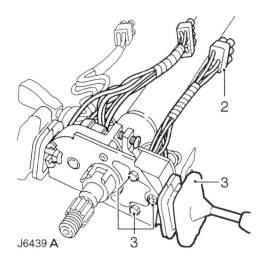

J6439 **A**

2. Disconnect switch multi-plug from main harness.
3. Remove 2 screws and star washer securing switch to mounting bracket.
4. Remove switch complete with harness.

**Refit**

5. Fit new switch to mounting bracket.
6. Reconnect switch multi-plug.
7. Fit steering column nacelle *See STEERING, Repair, Steering column nacelle.*

**DIRECTION INDICATOR/HEADLAMP/HORN SWITCH**

**Service repair no - 86.65.55**

**Remove**

1. Remove steering column nacelle *See STEERING, Repair, Steering column nacelle.*

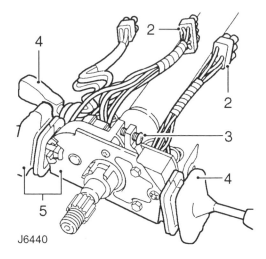

J6440

2. Disconnect 3 steering column switch multi-plugs from main harness.
3. Slacken clamp screw and withdraw switch assembly from steering column.
4. Remove fixings and detach windscreen wiper/washer and main lighting switches from mounting bracket.
5. Renew complete direction indicator/headlamp/horn switch and switch bracket assembly.

**Refit**

6. Fit main lighting and windscreen wiper/washer switches to mounting bracket.
7. Position switch assembly on steering column and fully tighten clamp.
8. Reconnect switch multi-plugs.
9. Fit steering column nacelle *See STEERING, Repair, Steering column nacelle.*

## MAIN LIGHT SWITCH

**Service repair no - 86.65.10**

**Remove**

1. Remove steering column nacelle *See STEERING, Repair, Steering column nacelle.*

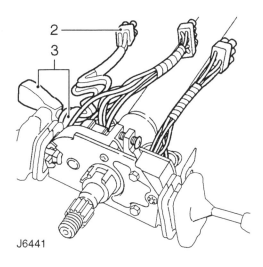

J6441

2. Disconnect main light switch multi-plug from main harness.
3. Slacken locknut and release light switch from slot in mounting bracket.

**Refit**

4. Fit light switch in mounting bracket.
5. Reconnect switch multi-plug.
6. Fit steering column nacelle *See STEERING, Repair, Steering column nacelle.*

## HEATED REAR SCREEN, REAR FOG LAMP AND HAZARD WARNING SWITCHES

**Service repair no - 86.65.36 - Heated rear screen**
**Service repair no - 86.65.65 - Rear fog lamp**
**Service repair no - 86.65.50 - Hazard warning**

**Remove**

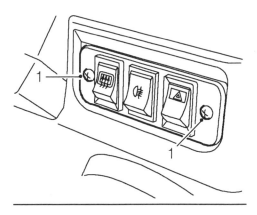

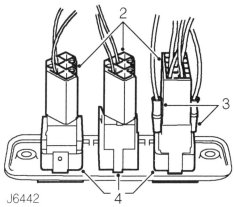

J6442

1. Remove 2 screws and withdraw switch panel from lower fascia.
2. Disconnect multi-plug from rear of switch.
3. On hazard warning switch only, remove 2 separate leads.
4. Press in spring retainers and withdraw switch from switch panel.

**Refit**

5. Fit new switch into switch panel.
6. Reconnect switch multi-plug, and leads if applicable.
7. Fit switch panel to lower fascia.

## CIGAR LIGHTER

**Service repair no - 86.65.60**

**Remove**

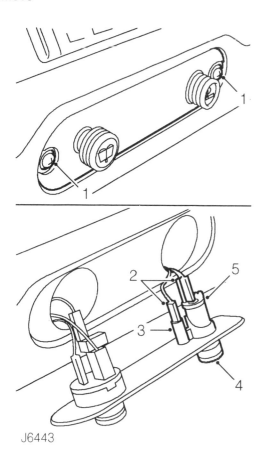

J6443

1. Remove 2 screws and withdraw switch panel from lower fascia.
2. Disconnect electrical leads from switch housing, including illumination bulb.
3. Release 2 retaining tags and remove bulb holder from switch housing.
4. Remove cigar lighter from switch housing.
5. Press in retaining tags and withdraw housing from switch panel.

**Refit**

6. Fit housing to switch panel.
7. Fit bulb holder to switch housing.
8. Connect electrical leads and illumination bulb.
9. Insert cigar lighter into switch housing.
10. Fit switch panel to lower fascia.

## REAR SCREEN WIPER/WASHER SWITCH

**Service repair no - 84.35.34**

**Remove**

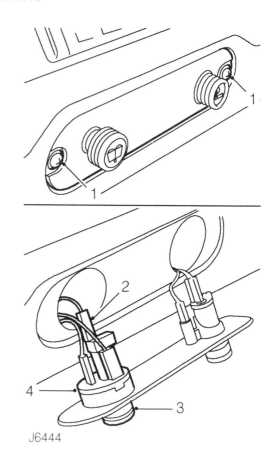

J6444

1. Remove 2 screws and withdraw switch panel from lower fascia.
2. Disconnect electrical leads from rear screen wiper/washer switch.
3. Insert a small screwdriver in base of switch knob, press in retaining lug, and remove knob from switch spindle.
4. Unscrew locking ring, with wavy washer, and withdraw wiper/washer switch from panel.

**Refit**

5. Fit switch to switch panel.
6. Press in retaining lug and fit knob onto switch spindle.
7. Connect electrical leads to switch.
8. Fit switch panel.

## HEADLAMP LEVELLING SWITCH

**Service repair no - 86.65.16**

**Remove**

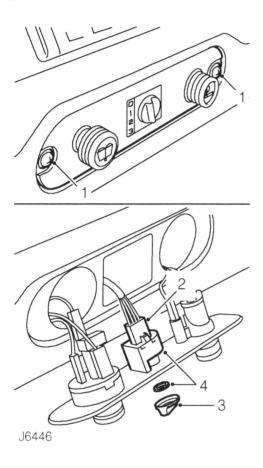

J6446

1. Remove 2 screws and withdraw switch panel from lower fascia.
2. Disconnect multi-plug from rear of headlamp levelling switch.
3. Remove knob from switch spindle.
4. Unscrew retaining nut and withdraw switch from switch panel.

**Refit**

5. Fit switch into switch panel and secure with retaining nut.
6. Fit switch knob.
7. Connect switch multi-plug.
8. Fit switch panel.

## HEADLAMP LEVELLING UNIT

**Service repair no - 86.41.16**

**Remove**

1. Remove headlamp *See Headlamp.*

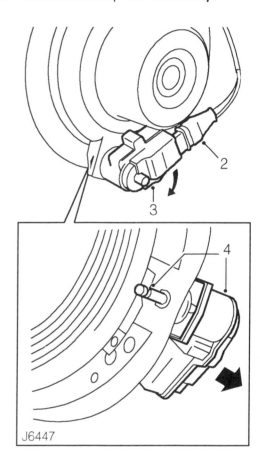

J6447

2. Disconnect headlamp levelling unit harness plug.
3. Rotate levelling unit anti-clockwise to release retaining lugs from mounting bracket on headlamp body.
4. Release levelling unit spindle from retaining slot on headlamp bezel and withdraw unit from mounting bracket.

**Refit**

5. Fit levelling unit into mounting bracket and locate unit spindle into slot in headlamp bezel.
6. Press in unit and rotate clockwise to engage retaining lugs behind mounting bracket.
7. Connect levelling unit harness plug.
8. Fit headlamp *See Headlamp.*

## HEADLAMP BEAM ALIGNMENT

**Service repair no - 86.40.17**

**Check**

Check main beam alignment using beam setting equipment. Should this not be available the beam can be temporarily checked and adjusted as follows:-

1. Position vehicle, unladen, on level ground with tyres correctly inflated, approximately 4 metres from a wall or screen, marked as illustrated below.

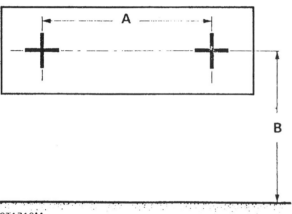

ST1719M

2. The beam centres 'A' are measured horizontally on the vehicle and dimension 'B' vertically from the ground.

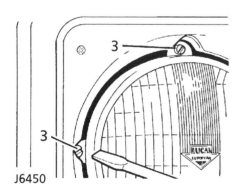

J6450

3. Switch on main beam and adjust setting, as necessary, with trimmer screws.

On vehicles fitted with headlamp levelling units, check and adjust headlamp beam alignment as previously described, with fascia mounted levelling switch at position '0'. The headlamps can then be adjusted, according to load conditions, as follows:-

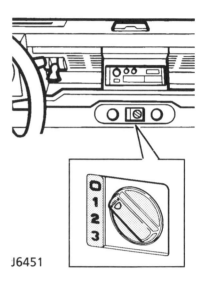

J6451

Position '0' - Driver only, or driver and all front seats occupied (loadspace empty).

Position '1' - All seats occupied (loadspace empty).

Position '2' - All seats occupied by adults and loadspace loaded to maximum rear axle weight.

Position '3' - Driver only with loadspace loaded to maximum rear axle weight.

## DIGITAL DIESEL SHUT-OFF VALVE (DDS)

**Service repair no - 86.77.00**

### Remove

1. Remove fuel injection pump *See FUEL SYSTEM, Repair, Fuel injection pump* .

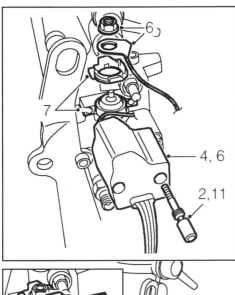

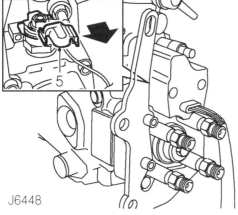

J6448

2. Drill out 2 shear bolts securing DDS valve and clamp, using a 3.2 mm drill, to a depth of approximately 5 mm.

 **CAUTION: Use a drill bushing to guide the drill.**

3. Using an extractor, remove the 2 DDS valve retaining bolts and discard.
4. Release DDS valve from fuel shut-off solenoid.
5. Remove protective cap from shut-off solenoid.
6. Unscrew terminal nut, release terminal lead eyelet and remove DDS valve.

7. Remove protective cap retainer and release DDS valve clamp from behind fuel shut-off solenoid.

### Refit

8. Position DDS valve clamp behind fuel shut-off solenoid and fit protective cap retainer.
9. Fit DDS terminal lead to fuel shut-off solenoid. Tighten nut to *2 Nm (1.5 lbf/ft).*
10. Fit protective cap to fuel shut-off solenoid, ensuring terminal lead is correcly routed on RH side of cap.
11. Secure DDS valve to fuel cut-off solenoid and clamp. Tighten new shear bolts progressively until heads shear.
12. Fit fuel injection pump *See FUEL SYSTEM, Repair, Fuel injection pump.*

# Notes

# 88 - INSTRUMENTS

## CONTENTS

Page

**REPAIR**

# Notes

## INSTRUMENT PANEL

**Service repair no - 88.20.02**

**Remove**

1. Disconnect battery.

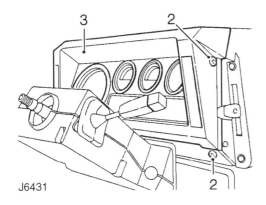

J6431

2. Remove 4 screws securing instrument panel to fascia cowl.
3. Pull instrument panel away from fascia sufficent to disconnect speedometer cable.
4. Disconnect multi-plugs, electrical leads and connections to vehicle alarm system, if fitted *See ELECTRICAL, Repair, Vehicle immobilisation and alarm system.*
5. Withdraw panel, complete with instruments.

**Refit**

6. Offer up instrument panel, connect multi-plugs, electrical leads and connections to vehicle alarm system, if fitted *See ELECTRICAL, Repair, Vehicle immobilisation and alarm system.*
7. Connect speedometer cable.
8. Secure instrument panel.
9. Reconnect battery.

## SPEEDOMETER

**Service repair no - 88.30.01**

**Remove**

1. Remove 4 screws securing instrument panel to fascia cowl.
2. Pull instrument panel away from fascia sufficent to disconnect speedometer cable.

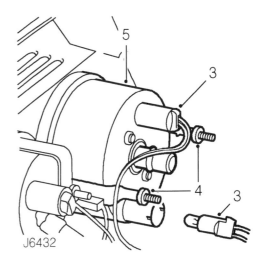

J6432

3. Release both bulb holders from speedometer.
4. Unscrew 2 knurled nuts and remove clamps securing speedometer.
5. Wihdraw speedometer from instrument panel.

**Refit**

6. Fit speedometer into instrument panel and secure with clamps.
7. Fit bulb holders to speedometer.
8. Connect speedometer cable.
9. Secure instrument panel to fascia cowl.

## FUEL AND TEMPERATURE GAUGE

**Service repair no - 88.25.26 - Fuel gauge**
**Service repair no - 88.25.14 - Temperature gauge**

**Remove**

1. Remove instrument panel *See  Instrument panel.*

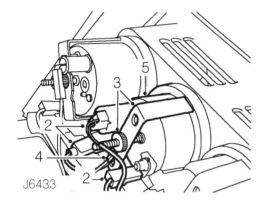

J6433

2. Release illumination bulb holder and disconnect electrical leads from gauge.
3. Unscrew knurled nut and remove clamp securing gauge.
4. Remove earth lead eylet from gauge stud.
5. Withdraw gauge from instrument panel

**Refit**

6. Fit gauge into instrument panel, locate earth lead, and secure with clamp.
7. Fit bulb holder and electrical leads.
8. Fit instrument panel *See  Instrument panel.*

## CLOCK - FASCIA PANEL

**Service repair no - 88.15.07**

**Remove**

1. Remove 4 screws securing instrument panel to fascia cowl.
2. Pull panel away fom fascia sufficient to disconnect speedometer cable.

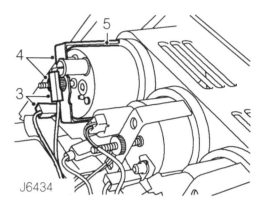

J6434

3. Disconnect electrical leads and bulb holder from clock.
4. Unscrew knurled nut and remove clamp securing clock.
5. Remove clock from instrument panel.

**Refit**

6. Fit clock into instrument panel and secure with clamp.
7. Fit bulb holder and electrical leads.
8. Connect speedometer cable.
9. Secure instrument panel to fascia cowl.

## CLOCK - CENTRE DASH PANEL

**Service repair no - 88.15.07**

**Remove**

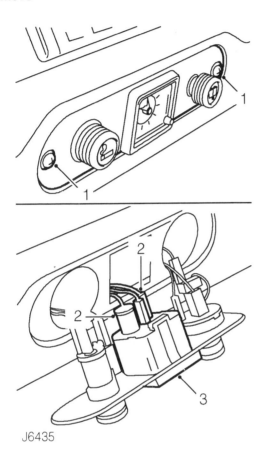

J6435

1. Remove 2 screws and withdraw switch panel from centre dash.
2. Release illumination bulb holder and disconnect electrical leads from clock.
3. Press in spring retainers and remove clock from panel.

**Refit**

4. Fit clock into dash panel.
5. Fit electrical leads and bulb holder.
6. Secure switch panel to centre dash.

## WARNING LIGHT PANEL

**Service repair no - 88.20.18**

**Remove**

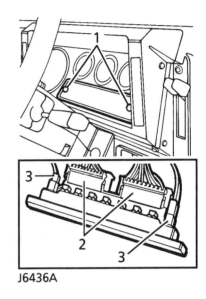

J6436A

1. Remove 2 screws and withdraw warning light panel.
2. Disconect both multi-plugs.
3. Disconnect illumination bulb leads.
4. Remove warning light panel.

**Refit**

5. Fit illumination bulb leads and multi-plugs to warning light panel.
6. Secure warning light panel to instrument panel.

## PRINTED CIRCUIT - WARNING LIGHT PANEL

Service repair no - 88.20.20

### Remove

1. Remove warning light panel *See  Warning light panel.*

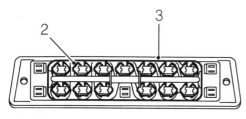

J6437

2. Remove 13 illumination bulb holders from light panel.
3. Release printed circuit from locating pins and remove from panel seatings.

### Refit

4. Fit new printed circuit over panel seatings and position on locating pins.
5. Fit illumination bulbs to secure circuit.
6. Fit warning light panel *See  Warning light panel.*

## FUEL GAUGE TANK UNIT - REAR FUELTANK, 110/130

Service repair no - 88.25.30

 **WARNING: Ensure that fuel handling precautions given in Section 01 - Introduction are strictly adhered to when carrying out the following instructions.**

### Remove

1. Disconnect battery.
2. Remove fuel filler cap.
3. Remove tank drain plug, allow fuel to drain into a clean container, and refit plug.

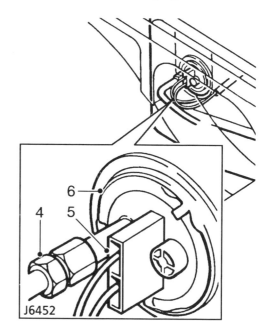

J6452

4. On LH side of tank, disconnect fuel supply pipe from outlet pipe on fuel gauge unit.
5. Disconnect electrical plug from fuel gauge unit.
6. Release locking ring and withdraw fuel gauge unit from tank, complete with sealing ring.

### Refit

7. Insert gauge unit into tank with float positioned to base of tank. Fit new sealing washer, if necessary.
8. Secure gauge unit with locking ring.
9. Fit electrical plug and reconnect fuel supply pipe.
10. Refill fuel tank.
11. Reconnect battery.

## FUEL GAUGE TANK UNIT - SIDE FUEL TANK

**Service repair no - 88.25.31**

⚠️ **WARNING: Ensure that fuel handling precautions given in Section 01 - Introduction are strictly adhered to when carrying out the following instructions.**

### Remove

1. Disconnect battery.
2. Remove RH front seat cushion.
3. Release retaining catch and remove seat base cover to gain access to fuel tank.

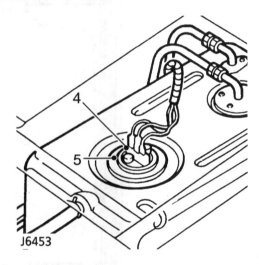

J6453

4. Disconnect electrical plug from fuel gauge unit.
5. Release locking ring and withdraw fuel gauge unit from tank, complete with sealing ring.

### Refit

6. Insert gauge unit into tank with float positioned towards front of tank. Fit new sealing washer, if necessary.
7. Secure gauge unit with locking ring.
8. Fit electrical plug.
9. Fit seat base cover and seat cushion.
10. Reconnect battery.

Distributed by Brooklands Books Ltd., PO Box 146, Cobham,
Surrey KT11 1LG, England  Phone: 01932 865051 Fax: 01932 868803
E-mail: sales@brooklands-books.com

ISBN 1 85520 5041  Part Nos. LRL 0097 ENG (3rd Edition)          15/3Z0

Printed in England                              Ref: B-LRDTWH